The English Face

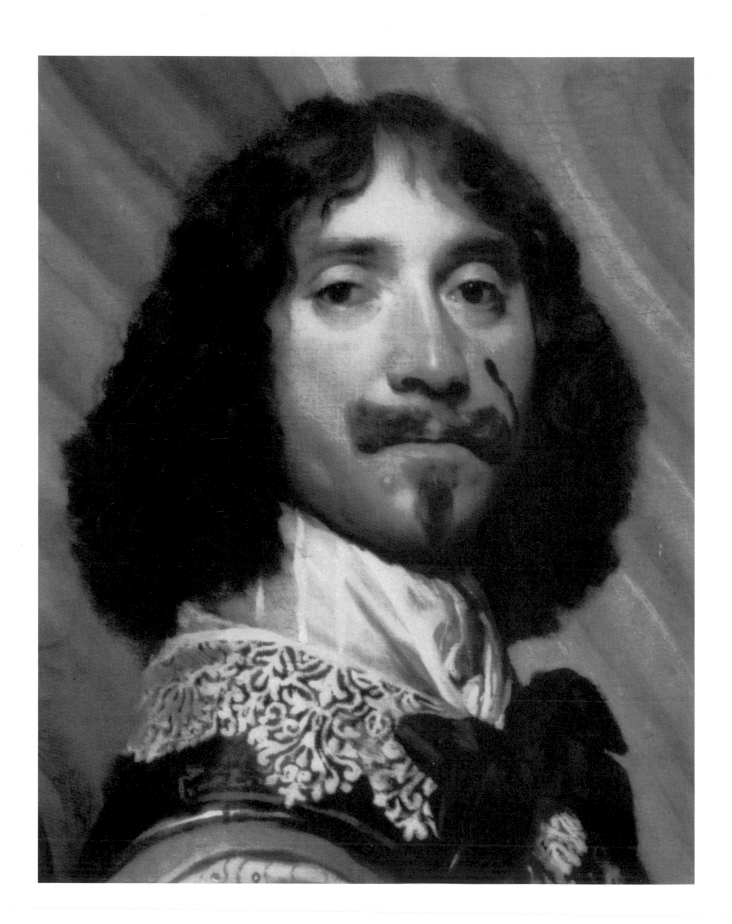

The English Face

David Piper

Edited by Malcolm Rogers

National Portrait Gallery

Published by National Portrait Gallery Publications,
National Portrait Gallery, 2 St Martin's Place, London
WC2H OHE, England, 1992

Copyright © David Piper 1978

ISBN 1 85514 008 X (cloth)
ISBN 1 85514 009 8 (paperback)

A catalogue record for this book is available from the
British Library

House editor: Gillian Forrester

Assistant editor: Katie Bent

Designer: James Shurmer FCSD

Phototypeset in Monophoto Baskerville by Servis
Filmsetting Limited, Longsight, Manchester, England

Printed in England by BAS Printers, Over Wallop,
Hampshire on Fineblade Smooth 150gsm

Cloth edition bound by Green Street Bindery, Oxford

Paperback edition bound by W. H. Ware & Sons Limited

Photographic acknowledgements
The National Portrait Gallery would like to thank the
following for making copyright photographs available in
the following plates. All other photographs are copyright
and were provided by the sources given in the catalogue:
By gracious permission of Her Majesty The Queen: 22, 23,
29, 32, 37, 55, 63, 77, 78, 93, 122, 149, 160, 167, 180, 183, 215;
Windsor Castle, Royal Library © 1992 Her Majesty The
Queen 30, 90; Bildarchiv Foto Marburg 1; Bridgeman Art
Library 243; Conway Library, Courtauld Institute of Art
12 (copyright Canon M. H. Ridgway), 76, 125, 236, 240,
241; *Country Life* 113; Courtauld Institute of Art
102, 146, 155, 165; Copyright National Trust, 1992 59, 70;
Royal Academy of Arts, London 21; Royal Commission on
the Historical Monuments of England 7, 10, 18; Courtesy of
the Board of Trustees of the Science Museum 223; Professor
Lawrence Stone 11; Victoria & Albert Museum 185, 197
(Courtesy of the Dean and Chapter of Westminster);
Courtesy of the Dean and Chapter of Westminster 5, 8;
Vivien White 255; Wilton Trust 82.

(*Front cover*): Nell Gwyn by the studio of Sir Peter Lely,
c.1675 (reproduced p. 99)

(*Back cover*): Emma Hart, Lady Hamilton by George
Romney, *c*.1785 (reproduced p. 191)

(*Frontispiece*): *John, 1st Baron Byron of Rochdale* by William
Dobson, *c*.1643 (detail). Reproduced in colour p. 87

Editorial note: Sizes are given in centimetres with inches in
parentheses, height before width.

Contents

FOR ANNE HORATIA

'Be careful of your face, my dear.'

John Evelyn to his wife,
22 February 1652

Author's Preface

The generous offer by the National Portrait Gallery to publish a new edition of this book, thirty years after it first saw the light of day, and to include colour in its illustration, was naturally very pleasurable to me. The re-setting of the text has allowed me both to correct errors and to update quite a lot of information about locations, attributions and identifications of a number of the portraits discussed. The quantity and quality of illustrations has been greatly increased, and some modest additions have been made to the original text.

The English Face has given much pleasure over the years, to judge from the many friendly comments that have reached me, and I hope that in this new format, any virtues that the old wine may have had will respond to the enhancement of the new bottle.

David Piper

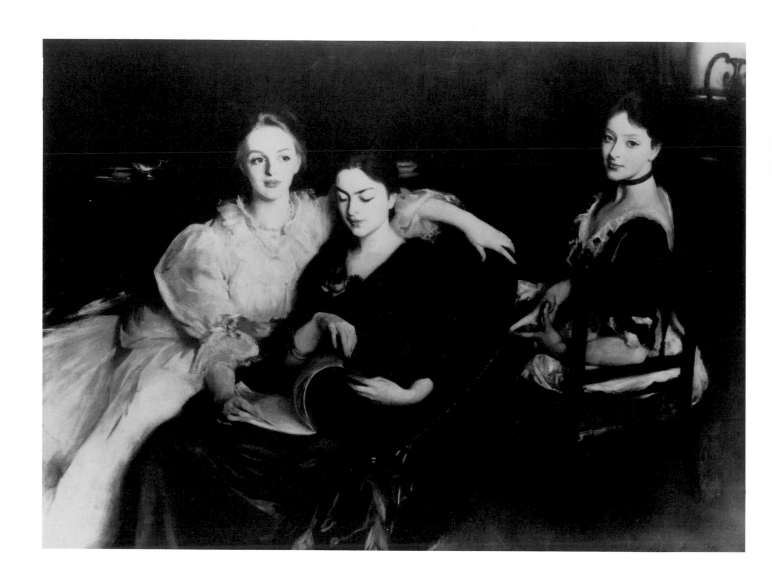

The Misses Vickers by John Singer Sargent, 1884. Oil on canvas, 137.8 × 182.9 ($54\frac{1}{4}$ × 72). Graves Art Gallery, Sheffield

Editor's Preface

Sir David Piper, museum director, art historian and novelist, died in December 1990, whilst his revised and enlarged edition of *The English Face* was still being planned. As writer and critic he had a perceptive and highly original eye for works of art and for the idiosyncrasies of human character, and in this book these gifts are combined in English prose of great distinction and beauty. It would have been impertinent for an editor to interfere with the text in wholesale fashion (and, indeed, unnecessary), and I have restricted myself in the main to those small corrections and adjustments which are inevitable in so wide-ranging a study. At the same time I have taken advantage of the opportunity to reproduce in colour very many of Piper's original black and white illustrations, and to add to their number in a way which I believe illuminates his text.

Colour is an essential aspect of the English face and the English complexion – whether it originates in nature or the cosmetics box – and I have tried to do it justice. Here you will find, among many, the sallow Henry VII with penetrating dark grey eyes and greying hair in a portrait sent to woo an emperor's daughter (he did not succeed); the ageing Elizabeth I with 'face oblong, fair but wrinkled; her eyes small yet black and pleasant; her nose a little forked, her lips narrow, her hair an auburn colour, but false'; the proud Duke of Lauderdale's 'Saracen and fiery face', and Hogarth's anonymous *Shrimp Girl*, with coral lips and rosy cheeks, a picture of unselfconscious natural beauty, 'vibrating still', in David Piper's words, 'with the silent echo of her cry'.

In my work I have been helped by my patient editor Gillian Forrester and her assistant Katie Bent. Karen Hearn undertook the preliminary picture research, and Jill Springall at the National Portrait Gallery Archive answered many queries. James Shurmer devoted his customary care and energy to the book's design. I would also like to thank the staffs of the London Library and the Conway Library at the Courtauld Institute of Art.

Malcolm Rogers

Stone Effigy to Renaissance Portrait

THE BRITISH people were slow to show their faces. Towards the end of the twelfth century their bodies begin to take substance, uniformed in the costume of their calling, robe or armour, knights or priests, but each effigy on the tomb-slab nevertheless a tough memorial of the individual who lies dissolved in dust beneath it. The vast majority of them have no faces; they have been rubbed out by time, by image-breakers or by those who sign desecration by their initials. The faces were probably never very individual to begin with; perhaps contemporaries could read them as individual likenesses, but to us, even when they are in good condition, they are but a general indication of human features.

During the thirteenth and fourteenth centuries the rendering becomes more subtle, and more examples are in fair condition; very often they are individual faces in as much as they are distinguishable one from another. But they are difficult to judge as portraits of living people: half-submerged in the dark aisles and chapels of their churches, they are so intimately involved with death. The monuments of which they are part, tombs sometimes canopied, fretted, carved, into virtual chapels, are not attempts to preserve the joys of life, to catch and picture the individual soul in an open eye; they are statements of what has been, the accomplishment in rank and wealth and piety. For all the hands in prayer, meekly joined upon their breasts, the effigies are also symbols of earthly pride, and official; they proclaim that their originals have upheld an inherited name or estate, or have founded them. A tomb with effigy was a luxury of the great, and generally it demonstrated greatness, one's place in the hierarchy of the world. The king wears his crown, the bishop his mitre and his robes, the knight his armour, a glimpse of his face only in the opening of his helm, the long moustaches escaping over the chain-mail bib. The faces are less eloquent than the clothes; very few of these effigies are likely to make you catch your breath, as you stoop over them, in a sudden premonition that they will blink their eyes; yet gradually they are becoming livelier, not only on the tombs, but on the roof-bosses and the corbels. Soon the faces will wake.

Interest in the description of the human being is an essential characteristic of the Renaissance. The word 'Renaissance' has become suspect, and many scholars are now more concerned to trace the continuity, the gradual evolution of style, and perhaps tend to underplay the revolutionary side of the fourteenth and fifteenth centuries. The movement was not of course a volte-face overnight; it spread over centuries; nevertheless there was a change, a radical one. In art, one aspect of this change was that the individual, temporal history of the human being becomes a major theme. For the artists of the Middle Ages the body was but the ephemeral

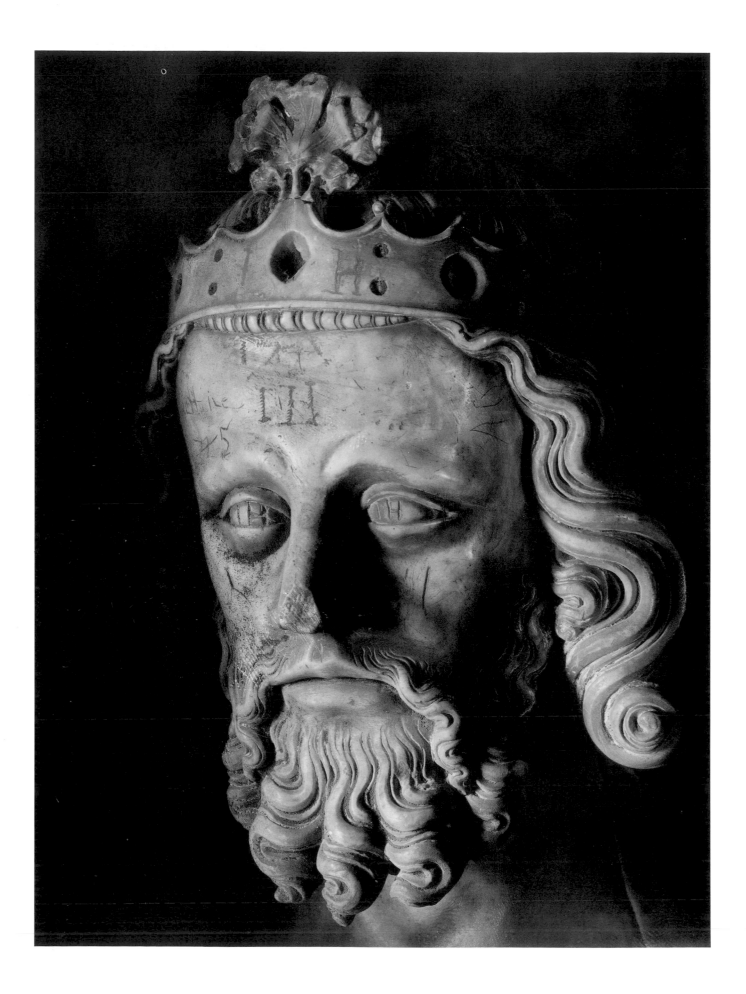

lineament that the soul takes on for a second of eternity; its quirks and characteristics, its displacement of time and space, its differences from other human bodies, were of no interest. Like Plato's prisoners, they saw the bodies of the passers-by as frail coloured shadows of a hidden reality cast upon a wall. The reversal of this process is clear already in Dante; the vivid and subtly differentiated characters that people Hell, Purgatory and Paradise are essentially projections upon infinity of earthly originals. Dante himself is one of the first men of the late Middle Ages of whom a reasonably individual likeness has come down to us.[1]

In England it comes later; only in Chaucer does the anonymous crowd of pilgrims fully resolve into its component individuals. Chaucer's own portrait, in Occleve's manuscript in the British Library (Plate 2), is the earliest portrait, in the modern sense, of an English poet: his face would not surprise you on top of a shooting jacket in the 1880s. You might even glimpse it today, beard and all, at a Royal Academy private view. It is a posthumous portrait, but Occleve makes his intentions in including it plain: 'that in order to remind other men of his personal appearance I have had his likeness made here to the end, in truth, that those who have least thought and memory of him may recall him by this painting'.[2] But individual faces are distinguishable rather earlier perhaps than Chaucer's, and it is easiest to trace their emergence in the funeral effigies at Westminster Abbey.

Plate 1 (*facing page*)
Edward II (1284–1327) by an unknown artist, 14th century (detail)
Alabaster effigy, life-size
Gloucester Cathedral

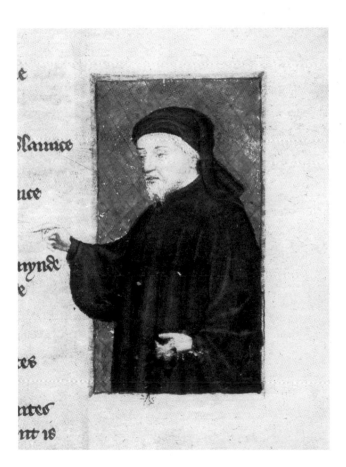

Plate 2
Geoffrey Chaucer (1340?–1400) by an unknown artist, *c.*1412
Detail from an early manuscript of *De Regimine Principium* by Thomas Occleve
Vellum, 26.5 × 18.5 (10½ × 7¼)
The British Library, London

The first detailed account of a king's burial that is relevant is probably that of Henry II, who died on 6 July 1189, at Chinon in France. The following day he was carried to be buried 'clothed in royal apparel, wearing a golden crown on his head, and having gloves on his hands and a golden ring on his finger, a sceptre in his hand, footgear woven with gold, and spurs on his feet, girt with a sword, he lay *having his face uncovered*'.

Almost exactly thus Henry's tomb effigy still lies, in that strange English shrine at Fontevrault (Plate 3), in the vaulted and empty silence of the abbey church. Close by him lies Richard I, or Cœur de Lion, who died ten years later of wounds at Chaluz (Plate 4). Their faces, though doubtless originally idealized and now restored, are clearly differentiated, at least in as much as Henry, who is recorded as a very stout man, is much fatter in the face than Richard. The habit seems to have been to expose the dead king, vested with all the regalia of kingship, with his face uncovered. This last would be of grave political importance (as it was more recently in Stalin's case), in order to demonstrate that the king really was dead, and his successor justly entitled to his place. The face of the dead man was shown that it might be recognized.

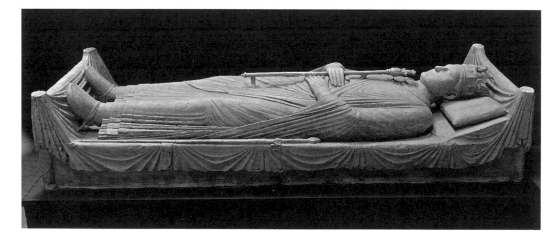

Plate 3
Henry II (1133–1189)
by an unknown artist,
13th century
Stone effigy, life-size
Abbey of Fontevrault,
Maine-et-Loire,
France

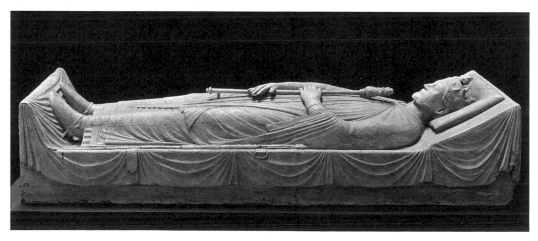

Plate 4
Richard I (1157–1199)
by an unknown artist,
13th century
Stone effigy, life-size
Abbey of Fontevrault,
Maine-et-Loire,
France

Plate 5
Edward III
(1312–1377) by an
unknown artist, 1377?
(detail)
Wooden funeral
image, life-size
Westminster Abbey,
London

Plate 6 (*right*)
Edward III
(1312–1377) by John
Orchard (?),
*c.*1377–1380 (detail)
Gilt-bronze effigy,
life-size
Westminster Abbey,
London

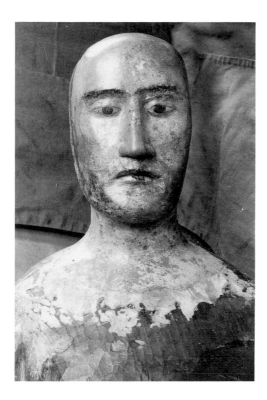
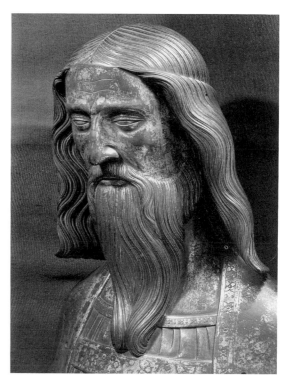

The relation of the tomb-effigy to the burial is probably simply explained; the box-like tomb represents the coffin, the effigy the dead man displayed on top of it. The function of the funeral effigy, not to be confused with the tomb-effigy, was, as it were, transitional between the king's body and his enduring image, the tomb-effigy. As funeral ceremonial became more elaborate and so more protracted, it became impracticable, for reasons of putrefaction (in spite of embalming), to display the king's body. A facsimile became necessary. Documentary evidence suggests that such a facsimile may have been used for Henry III's funeral in 1272, but the first royal funeral in which beyond doubt one was used was that of Edward II, in 1327, when 40 shillings was paid for a wooden image of him to set on the coffin: a likeness — *ymaginem de ligno ad similitudinem dicti domini E[dvardi] deffuncti*. Significantly, three months elapsed between the king's death and his burial at Gloucester Cathedral. It would be natural for the sculptor of the alabaster effigy at Gloucester to work from the temporary wooden funeral effigy, but though there is probably some element of portraiture in that serene and saint-like face, it is much idealized. Its function is no longer the same; it is primarily memorial, hagiographical (Plate 1).

The wooden funeral image used in 1377 for his successor, Edward III, survives still in Westminster Abbey (Plate 5). Though it has long since lost its beard and wig, and most of the coloured gesso which built up the features, it agrees well enough in shape with what little is visible of Edward's face behind the venerable whiskers of the gilt-bronze effigy in Westminster Abbey (Plate 6). A considered (but not unanimously accepted) opinion has suggested that the face of the funeral image is based closely on a death-mask, and that it shows, on its left cheek, the physical effect of the stroke from which the king died.[3] Richard II renounced the throne before he died, and so a king's funeral was not to be his lot. He died in obscure circumstances in 1400; as his renunciation might be held by his partisans to have been made under duress, and the finality of his extinction was extremely desirable to his usurper, his body was 'embalmed and seared and covered with lead all save his face (to the extent that all men might perceive that he was departed out of this mortal lyfe)', and so accoutred, Richard was borne openly from Pontefract to London.[4]

It seems likely that the funeral effigies of the fourteenth century were made as likenesses, with the deliberate intention that they should be recognizable. It is not impossible, indeed, that they were almost facsimiles, modelled upon masks taken from the face of the dead. Their function, however, was probably in the first place a political one, and they do not necessarily indicate a wider interest in realistic portraiture; their purpose was to show that their subject was dead. With Richard II, although no funeral image was made for him, the case alters, for he is

Plate 9 (*facing page*)
The Wilton Diptych (left panel) by an unknown artist, French School (?), *c.*1395 (detail) Egg tempera on oak panel, 53 × 37 (20⅞ × 14½) National Gallery, London

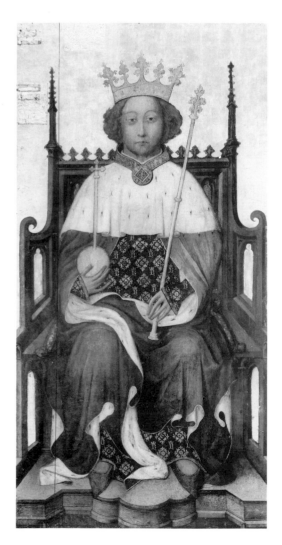

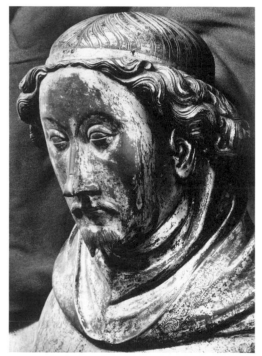

Plate 7 (*above*)
Richard II (1367–1400) by Nicholas Broker and Godfrey Prest, 1395–1397 (detail). Gilt-bronze effigy, life-size. Westminster Abbey, London

Plate 8 (*left*)
Richard II (1367–1400) by an unknown artist, *c.*1395. Oil on panel, 213.5 × 110 (84 × 43¼). Westminster Abbey, London

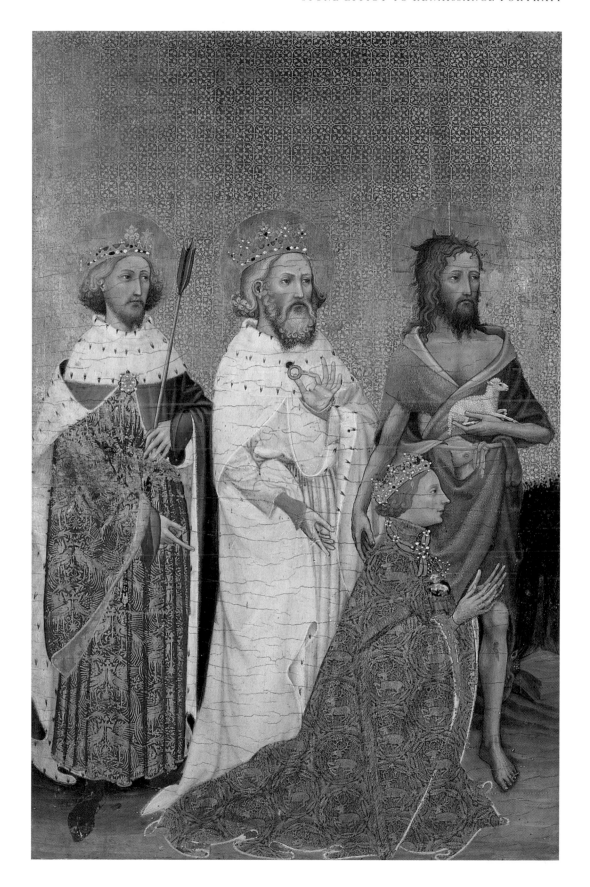

the classic point of demonstration that the English portrait has, at last, arrived, at the turn of the fourteenth to the fifteenth century. There are three major portraits of Richard. The gilt-bronze tomb-effigy in Westminster Abbey was ordered from Nicholas Broker and Godfrey Prest, citizens and coppersmiths of London, in 1395, that is, five years *before* Richard died (Plate 7). The contract allowed Broker and Prest two years for their work, and the suspicion seems legitimate that Richard took a personal interest in his own image; one would expect a portrait. The resulting face is stylized to a degree but seems recognizably individual with a most unusual nose, tipped like an arrow-head.[5]

The date of the other two portraits is more problematic. They are both paintings, the colossal throned whole-length 'in majesty', in Westminster Abbey (Plate 8), and the famous Wilton Diptych in the National Gallery (Plate 9). The Abbey painting, it has been suggested, was painted to commemorate Richard's visit to Westminster on the translation of Edward the Confessor, 15 October 1390, but there is nothing much either for or against this suggestion. From the stylistic evidence, one might expect the painting to be rather later. The Wilton Diptych, as to date and authorship, French or English, remains a field for unresolved scholarly tilting.[6] But all authorities agree in placing these two paintings, if not within Richard's lifetime at least within living memory of him; in both of them the king has a more youthful appearance than in the effigy.

The full-face view of the Westminster picture confirms the full-face view of the effigy, and the profile in the Wilton Diptych, as Richard, sponsored by his patron saints, kneels in adoration to the Virgin and Child, is even more decisive, with precisely that sharp point of nose. Here are three portraits clearly representing the same man, but each one leaving the impression of a distinct and individual view of him. They approach very closely to realistic portraiture, detailing and perhaps even dwelling on the physical characteristics by which his contemporaries recognized him.

The portraits of Richard do not however mean that realistic portraiture is becoming commonplace, an everyday occurrence. What is known of his character suggests that his tastes were sophisticated and in advance of his time, and his portraits may be a reflection of his taste rather than that of his contemporaries. Art certainly was becoming more realistic in the way it strove to present an imitation, an illusion, of the surface of the world. The representation of a tree must look like a tree that has grown from the earth, with boughs in which the wind moves and on which birds sit, but not a particular tree; so too a man's face must be credible, have the tincture of flesh and blood and show the wearing of time and of experience. But the number of cases in which the lively and individual faces of the fifteenth century can be said with confidence to be the faithful portrait of this or that man or woman are remarkably few in comparison with the wealth of portraiture that the Italians and the followers of Jan van Eyck in the Netherlands were dispensing on the Continent.

Plate 10 (right)
William (1399?–1474) *and Joan Canynge*
by an unknown artist, 1475–1490
Stone effigy, life-size
St Mary Redcliffe, Bristol

Plate 12 (below right)
Richard Beauchamp, Earl of Warwick (1382–1439)
by William Austin, 1453–1456 (detail)
Gilt-bronze effigy, life-size
St Mary, Warwick

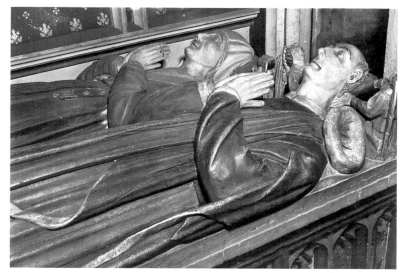

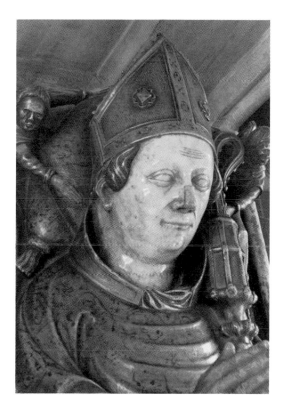

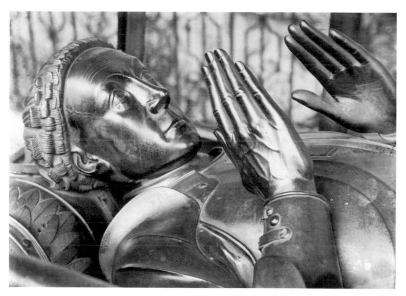

Plate 11 (above)
William of Wykeham,
Bishop of Winchester
(1324–1404) by an
unknown artist,
(detail)
Alabaster effigy,
life-size
Winchester Cathedral

In 1442 Henry VI was wondering whether to marry one of the daughters of the Count of Armagnac, and if so, which; he gave his envoys very specific instructions, to 'portraie the iii daughters in their kertelles simple and their visages like as ye see their stature and their beaulte and color of skynne and their countenances with al maner of fetures'.[7] But here there was a specific function for the portraits, though a warmer one than in the case of the funeral effigies. Many of the late thirteenth-century and fourteenth-century tomb-effigies are vivid in their realism; faces like those of the Canynges in St Mary Redcliffe, Bristol (Plate 10), of many of the knights, their heads now no longer boxed in their helms, and clean-shaven.

Surely the astute, authoritative face of William of Wykeham (died 1404) in Winchester Cathedral (Plate 11), the intent aspiration of Sir Robert Harcourt (1471) at Stanton Harcourt, the wholesome features of 'Mrs Oteswich' in

St Helen's, London – surely these are portraits? Sometimes, as in fact with William of Wykeham, it is possible to check them against other representations of the same person; but more often it is impossible to confirm that they are portraits.

A well-known example, and one of the finest, most striking, of English fifteenth-century effigy-heads, is that of Richard Beauchamp, Earl of Warwick, in St Mary, Warwick (Plate 12). He wears his hair trimmed, like a fitted cap, his mouth is drawn down towards the corners, his eyes are wide open under the raised eyebrows, looking up in perhaps not entirely confident anticipation; his hands are raised on his breast, not together, but apart, as if caught in an involuntary exclamation of incredulous amazement. It is, it would seem, a portrait modelled with the most remarkable humanity. But Warwick died in 1437, and his tomb was not started till 1453 and completed in 1456, almost twenty years after his death; the contract, which was drawn up in 1453 and which survives, gives no hint that this is a portrait, rather the contrary:

the said Will Austin doth covenant to cast and make *an image of a man armed*, of fine latten garnished with certain ornaments, viz. – with sword and dagger; with a garter; with a helme and crest under his head, and at his feet a bear musled, and a griffon, perfectly made of the finest latten, according to patterns, and to be layd on the tombe, at the perill of the said Austin, for the sum of xl/[li].[8]

Did the 'patterns' include a portrait of Warwick, or were they only for the perhaps more important detail of armour and of heraldry, the labels of rank and of blood? Was the image intended to be more than merely that 'of a man armed'? It was noted by the antiquary Leland in the sixteenth century – 'entombed right *princely* and porturyd with an image of copper' – but exactly what Leland meant by 'porturyd' is as uncertain as the nature of the 'patterns' used by Will Austin.

The fifteenth century was an age of uncertainty. The humanistic conception of portraiture was slowly filtering in from the Continent, together with the technique of the Van Eycks, the science of perspective, the desire to leave a more permanent, unfading facsimile of one's flesh and blood behind. But England was not yet a prepared soil in which such refinements would flourish. The internal disturbances, the Wars of the Roses, have, as direct causes of the meagreness of English fifteenth-century art, been exaggerated. The major causes were probably the immaturity of the country and its relative poverty, as compared, for example, with Italy; the poverty was intensified by war, but Italy too at this time was not precisely a peaceful country. In England the minds of great men seem to have concentrated on the struggle for power to the exclusion of most considerations of art; when they were dead, their family might consolidate their pride and achievement in an expensive tomb, but while they were alive they had little time for the refinements of painting and sculpture.

For posterity such negligence is sad; one has only to see what we lack, to think of the Van Eycks, of Van der Weyden, of Memlinc in the Netherlands; of Fouquet in France; and of the astonishing profusion in Italy: the medals of Pisanello, and the portraits of the Venetian and Florentine schools. A very few Englishmen of the time were painted abroad, and have their resulting monuments in the canon of European art, from the huge posthumous equestrian portrait of Sir John Hawkwood – *Ioannes Acutus Eques Britannicus* – painted by Uccello in the Duomo at Florence in 1436, to the minutely particular Edward Grimston, painted by Petrus Christus (Plate 13). Hawkwood is indistinguishable in general appearance from any other Italian *condottiere*,[9] Grimston from any equally well-to-do Fleming.

Between 1471 and 1483, under Edward IV, the country began to prosper, and the king himself died a very rich man; this prosperity was not gravely shaken by Richard III; and Henry VII, from the field of Bosworth in 1485, was able to proceed upon a consolidation of the Tudor dynasty and of England, a combination that was to survive through fair weather and foul, for the next century. It is the century of the first full flowering of the English face, and the faces of the Tudors themselves are amongst the most rare and curious specimens.

Plate 13
Edward Grimston by
Petrus Christus, 1446
Oil on panel,
33.6 × 24.7 (13¼ × 9¾)
The Earl of Verulam,
on loan to the National
Gallery, London

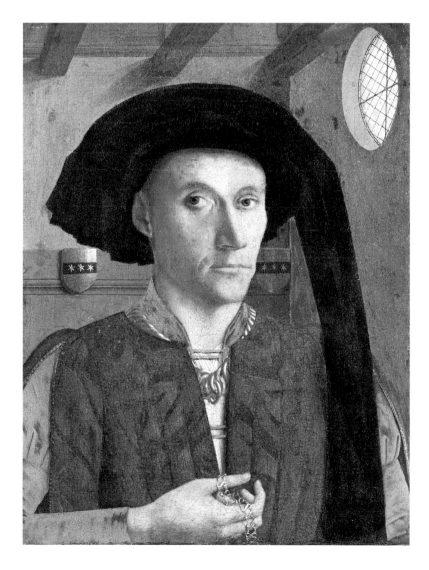

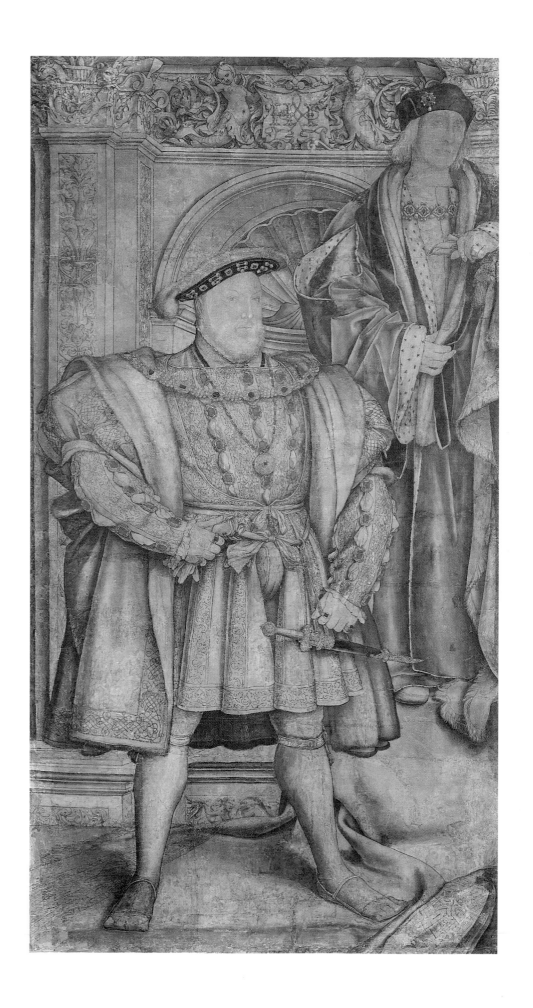

Holbein - Painter at Court

HENRY VII, first of the Tudors, was not a very lavish patron of the arts; that role he left to his son. He himself is in fact the only person of his reign whom one can assess from a variety of surviving images, none of them probably (and certainly not the most revealing ones) commissioned by himself. They are of great interest.

Henry was the first king of England since the Norman Conquest to have predominantly British blood – specifically, Welsh blood (the Tudors were succeeded in England by Scottish kings, and the Scottish by Hanoverians). His family was of obscure but certainly Welsh origin; his great-grandfather was steward to the Bishop of Bangor; his grandfather was a clerk of the wardrobe to Henry V's queen, Catherine of France, but, astonishingly (probably) married her after Henry's death; their son, Henry's father, married Lady Margaret Beaufort. In Henry's veins there ran then the royal blood of France, and, through the rich and various strain of the Beauforts, the royal blood of England. He might be claimed, in

Plate 15 *(right)*
Margaret Pole, Countess of
Salisbury (?) (1473–1541)
by an unknown artist, *c.*1535
Oil on panel,
62.9 × 48.9 (24¾ × 19¼)
National Portrait Gallery,
London

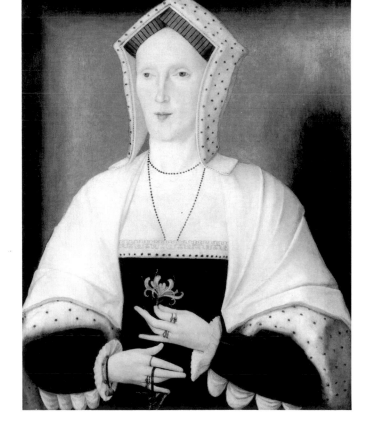

Plate 14 *(facing page)*
Henry VIII (1491–1547) (left) *and*
Henry VII (1457–1509) by Hans
Holbein the Younger, 1536–1537
Cartoon for the left-hand section
of the wall-painting formerly
at Whitehall Palace.
Ink and watercolour on paper,
257.8 × 137.2 (101½ × 54)
National Portrait Gallery,
London

mixture, as a typical Britisher of the ruling classes of the period, though with a pronounced Welsh and unusually royal flavour.

What did he look like? There seems to have been a standard portrait of him that was, with variations, in circulation during his reign; a pale and impersonal image, somewhat, I would guess, of a token image (painted in what was probably the current native style, of which the Countess of Salisbury is a fine example (Plate 15). Several examples still exist, notably two belonging to the Society of Antiquaries, but they are not impressive when compared with the three that I have to discuss.

In 1505 there came to England, upon an embassy of marriage, one Hermann Rinck; with him came a painter who has been plausibly identified as Michiel Sittow, a court-painter who worked for Isabella the Catholic and Margaret of Austria. The portrait that Sittow painted of Henry VII for Rinck on that occasion is now in the National Portrait Gallery (Plate 16). It is a very popular portrait, and its popularity must rest on the trenchant vividness, hitherto unparalleled in painting in this country, with which it conveys the impression of a living character; it is completely *vraisemblable*. Conceived in the Northern tradition that derives from the Van Eycks, it is less than life-size, but surely studied from the life. The design, with one hand as though resting on the frame, was already a stock one, used by painters such as Memlinc, and the portrait was also conditioned to an extent by political

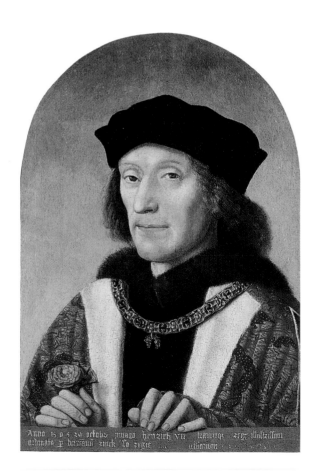

Plate 16
Henry VII (1457–1509) by Michiel
Sittow, 1505
Oil on panel, 42.5 × 30.5 (16¾ × 12)
National Portrait Gallery, London

considerations; it was destined to delect a woman whom he might wish to marry, a woman moreover who was a daughter of Maximilian I, King of the Romans and in line for the Emperorship of the Holy Roman Empire. Hence no doubt the red rose in his hand, for love and friendship (and also for Lancaster), and hence the Order of the Golden Fleece about his neck rather than the insignia of the Order of the Garter, for the Fleece would carry greater weight abroad than the Garter.

But the face is naked, and it is not a face that most people now would care to send as a bid for marriage, although, for Maximilian, if not for the daughter, the flesh would be the least part of the bargain. It is the face of an elderly man, though sprightly, though very much alive. It is a fascinating face but not a sympathetic one; most people find it sly; the thin lips in a line that borders on the smirk, the almost sharp nose and the bead-bright eyes calculating under the utterly untrustworthy angle of the eyelids. He has the air, in his little niche, with the Golden Fleece round his neck, of a far too worldly saint, a mean St Money-Bags.

It is perhaps unfortunate for Henry's reputation that this portrait should hang, in the Portrait Gallery, close to that of Richard III (Plate 17), in which Richard's admirers (oblivious of the fact that the portrait is not contemporary, but a later copy, and of extremely doubtful value as evidence) are inclined to find a frank, manly and open countenance, so unlike that of his usurper. A more favourable

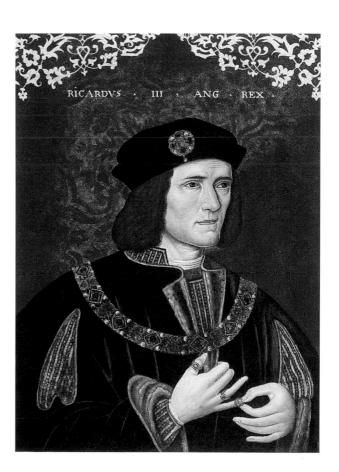

Plate 17
Richard III (1452–1485) by an
unknown artist
Oil on panel, 63.8 × 47 (25⅛ × 18½)
National Portrait Gallery, London

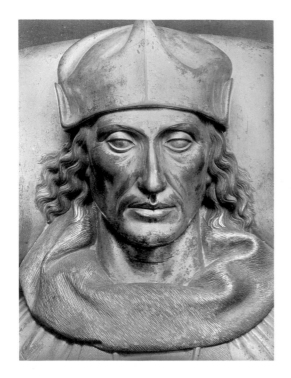 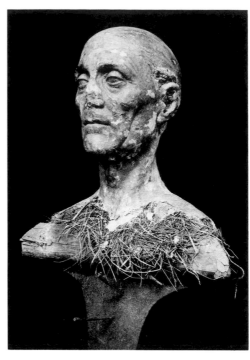

Plate 18 (*far left*)
Henry VII
(1457–1509) by
Pietro Torrigiani,
c.1512–1518 (detail)
Gilt-bronze effigy,
life-size
Westminster Abbey,
London

Plate 19 (*left*)
Henry VII
(1457–1509) by an
unknown artist, 1509
(detail)
Coloured plaster
effigy, life-size,
probably based on a
death-mask
Westminster Abbey,
London

advocate for Henry is the tomb-effigy in Westminster Abbey (Plate 18), modelled by an Italian sculptor of the High Renaissance, Pietro Torrigiani, who was also responsible for the admirable coloured bust of Henry in the Victoria & Albert Museum (Plate 20). The bronze is a posthumous portrait, contracted for in 1512, over three years after Henry's death, and the features have been idealized, the expression deleted from lips and eyes. It is the image of a Renaissance prince, of immense dignity, but as a factual account of Henry's face, most people, I think, would guess it to be further away than is Michiel Sittow's painting.

This is not borne out by the fourth portrait of Henry; we turn again to the funeral effigies in Westminster Abbey, where the head of Henry's image survives (Plate 19). It is the most remarkable of the early funeral effigies, and attention has been drawn to very plausible technical evidence that the face is a death-mask, a cast, that is, taken from a mould on the king's face after his death, and then worked up in some degree, notably in the eyes. Here, then, must be the actual lineaments and proportions of Henry's face, and Torrigiani's idealized portrait approaches them more accurately than does the apparently extremely naturalistic rendering by Sittow. (Torrigiani almost certainly knew the funeral effigy and no doubt based the face of his tomb-effigy largely on it.) The face of the funeral effigy, stripped of its datable frame of hair, and clothes, has a timeless quality in spite of the mutilation of his nose; it might be the face of a Roman, it might be the face of an outstandingly capable business magnate of today.[10]

I have dwelt on the face of Henry VII in greater detail than I shall be able to allow for most, because in it are clear already several of the fundamental problems that concern the relationship of the face to its portrait. All portraits can be related to two extremes: on the one hand, the accurate facsimile of the individual, and, on the other, the contemporary conception of what the individual ought to look like. One extreme is represented by the death- or life-mask, actually moulded on the person; the other, on its highest level, by the ideal portrait, on its lowest by the fashion-plate. One tendency is to particularize the subject, to distinguish him from all other men; the other is to merge him in the type.

To see how difficult it is to achieve the facsimile, one need only look at the funeral effigy of Henry; the mask itself is timeless, I have suggested. Yet is it? Is a face of flesh and blood, even though dead, ever so final in its modelling? Nor can one ignore the extensions of the face, which are not cast, but modelled; the hair has gone, but the neck remains. When the effigy was seriously investigated for the first time, in 1907, the experts, not yet claiming the face as a death-mask, came to the conclusion that it was probably Italian work; apart from technical considerations, the superb, princely carriage of the head on the elongated neck may have influenced this conclusion. If the hair were shown, the face would of course be set more firmly in its time; few things place a man – and even more, a woman – in time than the way they wear their hair. Few things, as any designer of costume for stage or film knows, are harder to imitate. In theory, the face is naked; in practice it is subject to innumerable ephemeral whims of fashion; it may even be covered with paint (a consideration that we shall have to take into account at a later stage), but even if untouched by cosmetic, its whole character and expression is acutely sensitive to the

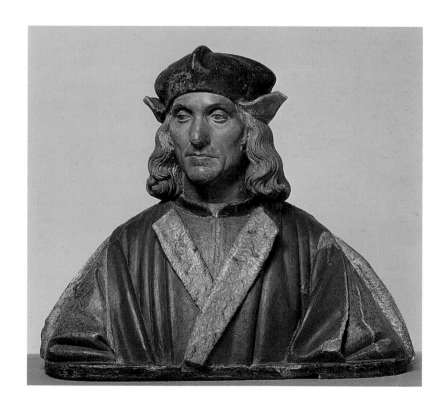

Plate 20
Henry VII
(1457–1509) by
Pietro Torrigiani
Terracotta, painted
and gilded,
height 60.6 (23$\frac{7}{8}$)
Victoria & Albert
Museum, London

slightest change in the variable frame of hair and whiskers, of hat and neckwear. It is even more subject to the artist who paints or sculpts it, and to his style.

And here the curious fact must be stressed, that from the time of Henry VII onwards, for two and a quarter centuries till about 1735, the most influential portrait-painters who shape the British face will be foreigners: Holbein, Eworth, the Dutch and Flemish immigrants at the end of the sixteenth century, Mytens, Van Dyck, Lely, Kneller. Even for those little interested in the arts, the names of Holbein, Van Dyck, Lely and Kneller may summon up each one an aspect of English history.

There are, of course, English portrait-painters of great ability, perhaps of genius, but even with due acknowledgement granted to William Dobson and Samuel Cooper, the only true exception to this foreign predominance, the only English painter who was the most important, the most characteristic of his age in this country, was Nicholas Hilliard. On the whole (and this is true, though to a lesser degree, of the sculptors) for over two hundred years we see the British face through the eyes of foreigners, or through the eyes of British painters who are, in more or less degree, imitating the foreigners.

In the perennial contest between artist and sitter, this, though it is a factor which must always be borne in mind, does not mean, of course, that the artist had it all his own way. Given the time and the sensibility to acclimatize himself, the artist will adapt himself and modulate his style, but when he comes on a short visit, as did Sittow and Torrigiani, he will tend to express his new sitters in terms of his accustomed style, to turn Henry VII into an intriguing Burgundian royalty or into an Italian magnifico of the Renaissance. Henry VII himself would probably have been more sympathetic to the former view (Sittow's). But Henry VIII, who commissioned Torrigiani's effigy after his father was dead, was more interested in the Italian way of life.

From Henry VII's portraits also it is clear how the purpose for which a portrait is made may affect it; the overture of wooing in the Sittow portrait, the funeral tradition of an exact likeness in the death-mask, the idealized formality of the tomb-effigy. Every portrait arose out of a specific occasion; there was no idea yet in England that they might be simply desirable house furniture; that was only to begin in the reign of Henry VIII.

Henry VIII came to the throne young and handsome, in many ways the exact opposite of his father – extravagant, cultured, a good scholar, a wily theologian, a musician – above all, from our point of view, a generous patron of the arts. To begin with, his delight in visual splendour took a more extrovert form than the reduplication of his own person in the mirror of portraits; his coronation was of considerable splendour, and he took great delight in less formal revels, in masques newly introduced from Italy, in pageantry that was to reach its peak at the Field of Cloth of Gold in 1520. His court rapidly began to rank as one of the foremost in Europe, and to it came the artists from abroad: Torrigiani already by 1511; a

Neapolitan, Volpe, by 1512. Some stayed only a short time; others, like Toto del Nonziata, the future Serjeant-Painter who came about 1519, settled for life. With these foreigners came a new conception of the human form.

Henry's form, in the early part of his reign, was the subject of universal admiration:

the handsomest potentate I ever set eyes on; above the usual height, with an extremely fine calf to his leg; his complexion fair and bright, with auburn hair combed straight and short in the French fashion, and a round face so very beautiful that it would become a pretty woman, his throat being rather long and thick.[11]

This was not a biased report, but from a foreigner reporting home; so too, a little later, in 1519, another wrote that he was the handsomest sovereign in Europe: 'a great deal handsomer than the King of France'. Henry would have liked that, for Francis I was his great rival, and Henry had just grown a red-gold beard to rival Francis's. 'He is', goes on the writer, 'extremely fond of tennis, at which game it is the prettiest thing in the world to see him play, his fair skin glowing through a shirt of the finest texture'.[12] In fact, he enchanted and attracted his contemporaries, and in 1520, face to face with Francis I at the Field of Cloth of Gold, he emerged well from the comparison. One witness said that though Francis was taller, Henry had the more handsome and feminine face.[13]

This last comment will surprise those whose image of Henry is that supplied by Holbein. But apart from some pale and conventional icon-like images that reveal little and are almost interchangeable with similar paintings of earlier kings, there is no portrait of Henry VIII as he was during the first fifteen years of his reign, until 1525. Then there came two very competent and unjustly neglected miniatures, both dating, according to inscriptions on them, from his thirty-fifth year, though one shows him beardless and the other bearded (Plates 22 and 23). The plumpness that had been commented on at the Field of Cloth of Gold is notable, especially in the shaven jowl, but neither of them are yet aweful images. Their attribution to Lucas Hornebolte is now thought likely to be correct; they are wholly in a tradition first fully manifested about 1520 in some miniatures attributed to Clouet in a manuscript in France, full-bodied and remarkably realistic. The miniature work of Holbein grows naturally out of this tradition.

There follow in time a number of portraits, life-size, of Henry VIII, in which we see him thickening, the jowl growing weightier, until at last, about 1536, he is ripe for Holbein: he had divorced Catherine of Aragon, challenged the Pope and the whole of Catholic Europe, and had set up his own Church with himself as its Supreme Head; he had begotten Queen Elizabeth and executed her mother; he was marrying for the third time and to achieve the security of an heir.

So it was that Holbein saw him for the first time in paint, and he painted him half-length, less than life-size (Plate 21). It was apparently in celebration of his marriage, and there was a companion portrait of Jane Seymour (Plate 24): they are

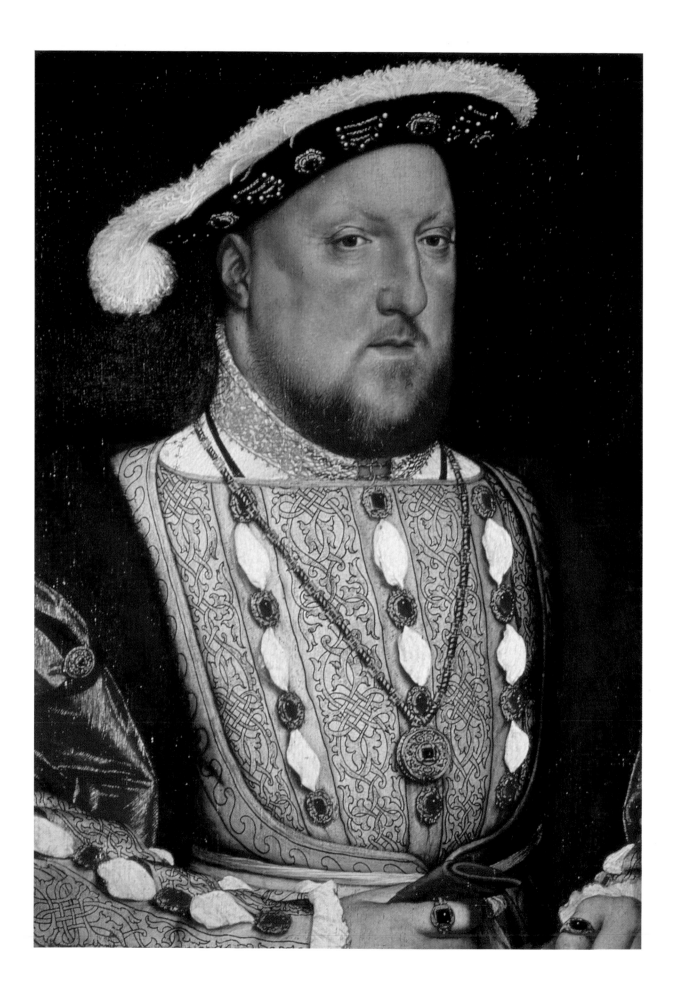

Plate 21 *(facing page)*
Henry VIII
(1491–1547) by Hans
Holbein the Younger,
1536
Oil and tempera on
panel,
27.5 × 19.5 (10¾ × 7¾)
Thyssen-Bornemisza
Collection, Lugano,
Switzerland

now split, but in 1547 were still together. 'Item a table like a book with the picture of kynge Henry theight and Quene Jane.' But, even though they once folded on a hinge face to face in darkness, neither are friendly faces. Earlier in his career, Holbein, as in his painting of his wife and children, had been capable of imaginative masterpieces of the greatest tenderness, intimacy and compassion; by 1536, however, he had become Court-Painter, and it was no longer his business to woo the subtler, spiritual undertones from the visible surface, though he could still do so. His business was to paint the surface with accuracy, losing none of the splendour of fur and brocade and jewel; his enduring success arises not merely from his technique in doing this, but in the artistry with which he could preserve the physical weight of personality of his sitters, and in the case of Henry VIII, his power, his magnificence, his ruthlessness.

Soon after the marriage portrait, Holbein painted Henry VIII as he faced him, four-square; one hand on hip, one hand on the dagger, the shoulders wide, the legs straddled like those of Atlas, but to bear his own weight, his own Church, his own kingdom. So Holbein painted him in the Privy Chamber at Whitehall; at the end of the century people still shivered when they saw that picture, and it is difficult to conceive any other image that Sir Walter Raleigh could have had in mind when he

Plate 22 *(right)*
Henry VIII
(1491–1547)
attributed to Lucas
Hornebolt,
c.1525–1526
Vellum,
4.1 (1⅝) diameter
Royal Collection (by
gracious permission of
Her Majesty The
Queen)

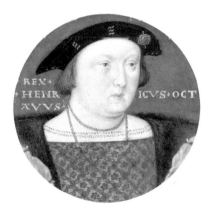

Plate 23 *(below right)*
Henry VIII
(1491–1547)
attributed to Lucas
Hornebolt,
c.1525–1526
Vellum,
4.1 (1⅝) diameter
Royal Collection (by
gracious permission of
Her Majesty The
Queen)

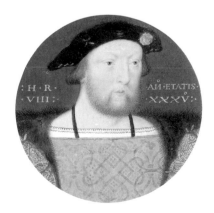

Plate 24 *(far right)*
Jane Seymour
(1509?–1537) by
Hans Holbein the
Younger, 1536
Oil on oak panel,
65.4 × 40.7 (25¾ × 16)
Kunsthistorisches
Museum, Vienna,
Gemäldegalerie

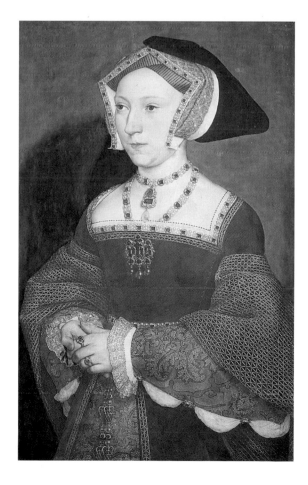

wrote, about 1614: 'for King Henry the Eighth, if all the Pictures and Patterns of a merciless Prince were lost in the World, they might all again be painted to the Life, out of the Story of this King'.[14]

The Whitehall painting, lost in a fire at the Palace in 1698 was more than a portrait of Henry VIII (Plate 14); it was one of those dynastic visual decrees in which the Tudors, from Henry VII's planning of his chapel in Westminster Abbey onwards, took such delight. It showed Henry and Jane Seymour (mother of his male heir), and, behind them, Henry VII and Queen Elizabeth of York. Of Henry VIII's own portrait, the face is but a small proportion of the whole, the Tudor majesty of which Henry is but the tenant. The life-size standing whole-length, as a pictorial formula, had been used already by lesser painters in Germany and Austria, and, most superbly, by Titian for his Charles V (now in the Prado) in 1533. It was a formula reserved by both Titian and Holbein for their most important clients; only one whole-length of a subject Englishman by Holbein is recorded.

In Holbein's state-portraits the full conception of the Renaissance theory of portraiture is first realized in practice in England. Holbein, of course, was a German-Swiss, but no narrow provincial; he had travelled in Northern Italy and in France; he knew the work of Raphael and Leonardo da Vinci, and he came to England bearing a passport from his intimate friend, perhaps the greatest and most articulate of the northern humanists, Erasmus, to Thomas More.

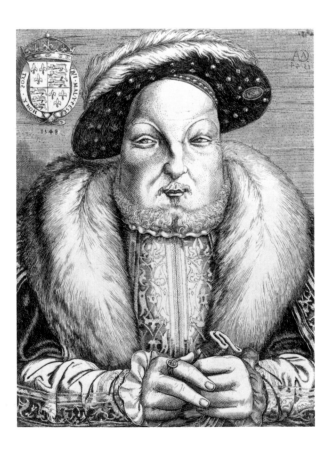

Plate 25
Henry VIII (1491–1547) by
Cornelis Matsys, 1548
Engraving, 17.5 × 13.1 (6⅞ × 5⅛)
British Museum, London
(Department of Prints and
Drawings)

Holbein knew the artistic theory of his time. This theory, particularly in as much as it concerned portraiture, was codified in explicit detail by Giovanni Paolo Lomazzo later in the century. Italian critics were agreed that a literal copy of nature was not the be-all and end-all of painting: behind the superficial phenomenon lay, as for Plato, the Idea. The artist's concern was with both. Lomazzo therefore praises 'i ritratti intellettuali' – intellectual portraits, expounded by the artist 'in natural form expressing the concept of his mind or idea'. This ideal approach cannot but condition portraiture. Lomazzo recommended, amongst other things, that only those people should be portrayed who were worthy of recording. They must be shown in suitable apparel, and their rank and splendour might decorously be stressed by attributes such as armour, regalia, laurels and batons.

Emperors above all other Kings and Princes should be endowed with majesty, and have a noble and grave air which conforms to their station in life . . . *even though they be not naturally so in life.*[15]

In Holbein's state-portrait of Henry, without the assistance even of permissible attributes such as crowns and robes, the painter has confirmed the king surely in imperial rank. Majesty in his port, sheer omnipotence in his bulk, and in his face power, pride and gravity, and some, at least, of the qualities that might be admitted as pertaining to nobility. Yet it is far from obvious that, to achieve this, Holbein has flattered Henry or departed from the truth. Something of the king's titanic width may be padding, but that was doubtless there already, in the clothes; the face, feature by feature, though it be not lovely, as in those small eyes whose very existence is threatened by the encroaching flesh, seems scrupulously recorded. This is the account that posterity has accepted as Henry.

Other views however are legitimate. The engraving by Cornelis Matsys of 1548 is taken from another angle (Plate 25). The artist might easily now be accused of a satirical or at least ironic intention, but probably unjustly. This is an essay in that tradition of portraiture of which Sittow's Henry VII is one example: a tradition already old-fashioned when this plate was engraved. Matsys worked in Antwerp, and there is no record of his being in England; yet, however this portrait came into being, whether from the life or at second-hand, it suggests very vividly an aspect of Henry's closing years that would not be guessed either from Holbein's account or (for Holbein's is perhaps seven years earlier than Matsys') from the Holbeinesque portraits of about 1544 as at St Bartholomew's Hospital. Towards the end, Henry's legs could no longer sustain their unwieldy burden, and he had to be moved by some form of conveyance, even from one room to the next.

People of slightly less exalted rank also began to be interested in the perpetuation of their own faces. The first group of private citizens whom we find acting as patron of a portrait-painter is the group that centres round Thomas More (Plate 26); from them Holbein probably received most of such encouragement as he did get on his

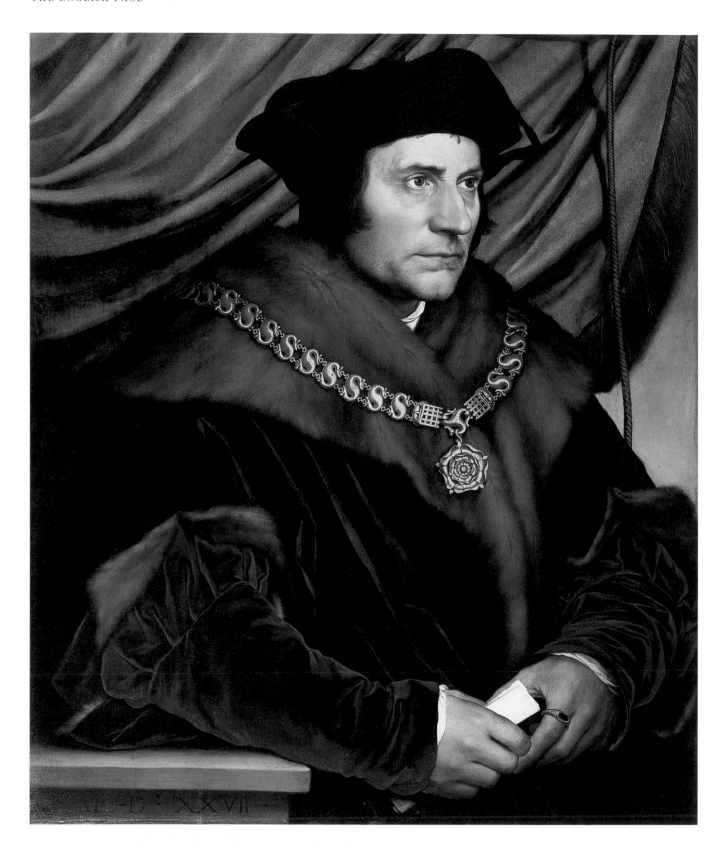

Plate 27 *(right)*
The Withypol Triptych
(centre panel) by
Antonio da Solario,
1514
Oil on panel,
77.4 × 63.5 (30½ × 25)
Bristol Museums and
Art Gallery

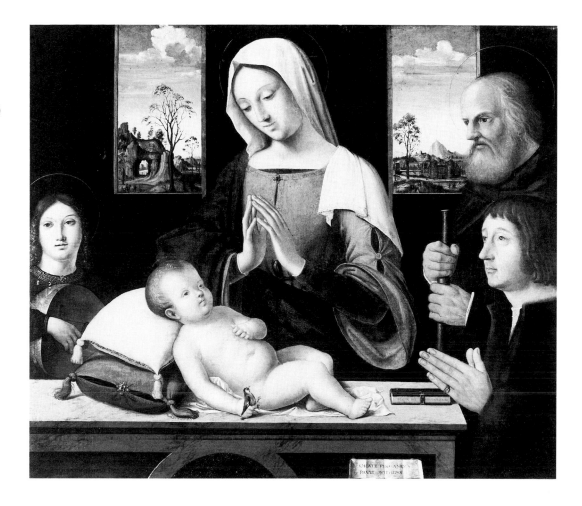

Plate 26 *(facing page)*
Thomas More
(1478–1535) by Hans
Holbein the Younger,
1527
Oil on panel,
74.9 × 60.3
(29½ × 23¾)
The Frick Collection,
New York

first visit to England in 1526: the Mores, the Ropers, William Warham, Brian Tuke. On his second visit, when More had already fallen, Holbein was patronized mainly by German steelyard merchants, and only in 1537 or 1538 did he become king's painter; thereafter he seems to have painted mainly courtiers.

Outside the limited circles that patronized Holbein there were a few prosperous merchants, whose interests straddled the Channel and whose portraits have an international flavour: the Withypols (painted by Antonio da Solario, who may have been in England in the second decade of the century; Plate 27),[16] the Kytsons, the Greshams. But the majority, perhaps, of the faces that we know now of Henry VIII's reign were recorded for us by Holbein.

In the whole history of art there is perhaps no painter through whom one could hope to know a sitter's face better. 'Holbein', wrote Evelyn to Pepys in 1689, 'really painted to the life beyond any man this day living': the same might have been said at any time since. *To the life:* Holbein's style is not merely as crystal, through which his sitters' faces are seen naked, but it carries for many people a feeling of revelation, a sensation like seeing someone you know stripped of their habitual spectacles. In almost all later portraits, fashion, whether artistic or sartorial, obscures the face, shaping the features and affecting the glance. Holbein's people, massive, unquestioning and unquestionable in the illusion of their flesh, still stand after four centuries from their dust.

It has been suggested, very plausibly, that he used some mechanical contrivance to take the initial drawings from the life; but, if so, it was an aid entirely subservient to his genius. Though it might be thought to account in part for a certain rigidity in some of his later work, that at times verges upon the uncanny and improper silence of wax-works, it is nevertheless precisely in his preparatory drawings, as in the great series at Windsor Castle, that the individual genius of his style is most easily grasped. Almost all are but ghosts of what they once were – rubbed, retouched by the hands of succeeding centuries – but through almost all of them the quality of Holbein's line still tells in its acute, selective economy, and his sitters live as creatures of his own imagination. By his drawing of Anne Boleyn alone (Plate 28) he makes Henry's passion comprehensible, rebuking with his entranced eye the cold conclusions of the Venetian envoy –

not one of the handsomest women in the world . . . Of middling stature, swarthy complexion, long neck, wide mouth, bosom not much raised, and in fact has nothing but the King's great appetite, and her eyes, which are black and beautiful.[17]

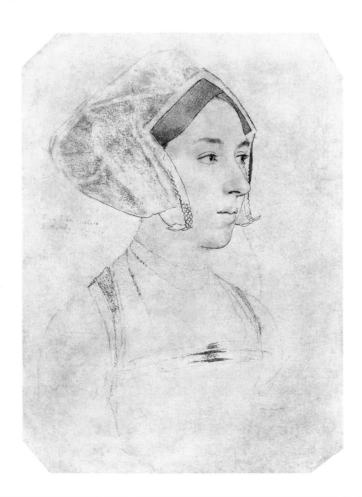

Plate 28
Anne Boleyn(?) (1507–1536) by
Hans Holbein the Younger,
*c.*1536 (?)
Black and red chalk and ink on
paper, 31.7 × 24.1 (12½ × 9½)
British Museum, London
(Department of Prints and
Drawings)

Plate 29 (*right*)
Sir Henry Guildford (1489–1532) by Hans Holbein
the Younger, 1527
Oil on panel, 82.6 × 66.4 (32½ × 26⅛)
Royal Collection (by gracious permission of Her
Majesty The Queen)

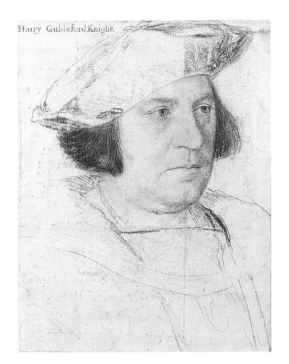

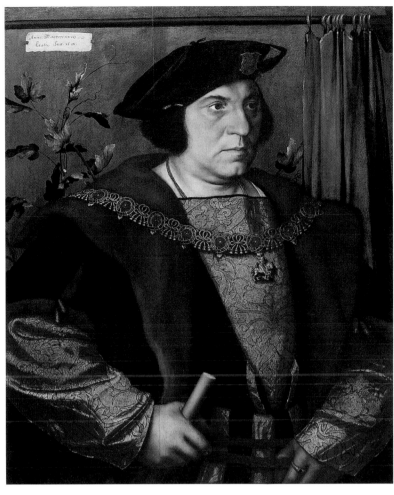

Plate 30 (*above*)
Sir Henry Guildford
(1489–1532) by Hans
Holbein the Younger,
1527
Black and coloured
chalks and
watercolour on paper,
38.4 × 29.4
(15¼ × 11½)
Royal Library,
Windsor Castle (by
gracious permission of
Her Majesty The
Queen)

Although the identification as Anne has been queried, it goes back to the seventeenth century, and I am content to accept that tradition.

In the drawings, Holbein seems often to catch and hold, on a rectangle of rose-tinted paper, the evanescence of life, to indicate the imponderables and the infinite possibilities of movement. When, from a drawing, he built up a painting, these tangential extensions, into other dimensions, of time and of human society, almost vanish; against a flat and static background, perhaps of an empyrean blue, the sitter bulks in a definition that is final and monumental (Plates 29 and 30). He is assessed, as though in an inventory for posterity, item by item; that this sum total is more than an inventory he owes to the skill, never surpassed, by which Holbein held the compromise between his love of detail and his power of modulating the broad movement of volume, and of contour upon contour.

His sitters do add up; one might almost invent an instrument by which their displacement or their specific gravity could be measured. That this apparent naturalism is in fact achieved by the most sophisticated artifice, needs stressing, and yet it is true that in Holbein's paintings, in the best of them, the claims of sitter and artist are balanced as perhaps they have never been balanced since. Charles V has succumbed to Titian, Philip IV to Velazquez, even Charles I to Van Dyck; between Holbein and Henry VIII (unless this be an illusion natural to English eyes) the match is drawn.

In comparison with Holbein, every taker of portraits who has worked in Britain seems mannered, and only Holbein seems to have that purity of style through which a sitter appears to tell his own story, with a clarity that is a distillation of the truth. He worked for not more than twelve years in England, and he has left us at the most a few dozen faces of Henry VIII's subjects. Quantitatively, in the vast flood of portraits that gradually spreads after him, it is nothing; his importance for this book is overriding, for no one ever surpassed him in reconciling the obstinate individuality of a given face with the claims of a great work of art.

He was aided by a variety of chances, of which not the least was that he was the first major artist in the English field. He was helped, as far as the face is concerned, by the costume of his time; rarely have neck and hair been so little fussed. With the women, indeed, the hair was almost invisible, rolled under the hood, or glimpsed, smooth, centrally parted, and flat, under its gable or curve, so that the face appears as though in naked high relief from its frame. In his time the clean-shaven page-boy-bobbed faces of the men gave way to the close-cropped hair and the beard of the last years of Henry's reign, from 1536 onwards. The beard seems to have been worn relatively straight, at least in comparison with the Elizabethan extravagances which were to come. Although one finds writers like Horman in his *Vulgaria* stating as early as 1519 that women 'whyte theyr face, necke and pappis with ceruse', cosmetics had clearly not yet the importance that they were to have at the close of the century; there is no evidence either of eyebrow or hair plucking in Holbein's portraits. His sitters, moreover, had in artistic matters no doubt a certain uninhibited naïveté, that left their faces wide open to the painter. After Holbein, both painters and sitters became more and more subject to precedent and to fashion.

III

The Elizabethans – A Rock Against Time

HOLBEIN, dying of the plague in 1543, left no school of painters developing directly out of his own style. He had, however, helped largely to condition the English to certain habits, one of which was the desirability of perpetuating in paint an accurate reflection of one's face. Indications of the two trends that were to run parallel through later Tudor portraiture are distinguishable in his work: on the one hand, the more naturalistic tendency, often German or Dutch in flavour, and on the other, notably in his use of flat arabesque design, that delight in more abstract formal values which was to be characteristic of the Mannerists.

Although the painters who succeeded him immediately show at least an awareness of his work, and occasionally almost quote from him, they nearly all have their roots in Northern European movements which had developed parallel to Holbein rather than out of him. Edward VI employed William Scrots (or Streetes), a Netherlander who came to England about 1545 from service with Queen Mary of Hungary, the Regent of the Netherlands, and who was well aware of fashionable court portraiture as practised on the Continent. Edward also employed Hans Eworth, an Antwerp painter, who was established here by 1549, and who was to paint also Mary I and Elizabeth.[18] There was also the Westphalian painter, Gerlach Flicke, active in England between 1547, or earlier, and his death in 1558.

Of these Scrots is notable for his whole-length portraits of Edward VI in a pose adapted, probably partly for political reasons, from Holbein's Henry VIII (Plate 32). They are very similar to Clouet in feeling, but the rendering of the face is both less sensitive in detail, and weaker in grasp of structure, than with Holbein, though still very naturalistic.

Flicke, the German, a painter of the most accomplished though somewhat strident ability, is closer in sentiment to Holbein, yet how inferior in subtlety is evident from his Cranmer (Plate 33). Remarkable a portrait though it is, it is not remarkable enough to convey that complex character, timid and subtle and ultimately more stubborn than the fire into which he thrust the right hand that had offended by recanting; it seems rather to me the face of ecclesiastical power politics.

But the artist in whose work the effect of the movement of style upon the face can be traced, during the transitional phase between Holbein's death in 1543 up to about 1570, is Hans Eworth. He was a Flemish painter from Antwerp, of great technical skill, but not an artist of the first rank: not an original genius, like Holbein, able to create a style, but one very sensitive to fashion and adapting himself to it, sensitive to his patron's wishes, and sensitive, too, to their faces. A most able portrait painter, he was trained in the Antwerp school; that is, not as a court-painter, but as

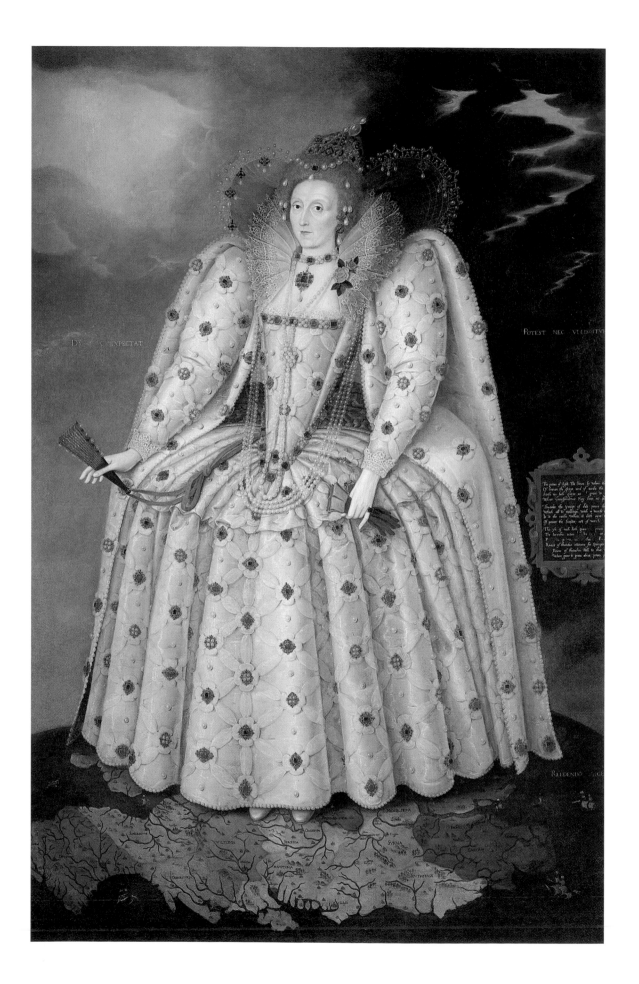

one who had to provide likenesses that had no nonsense, and at the same time a certain fashionable trimming of nonsense, sometimes an allegorical scene in the Mannerist style, an intrusion of naked smooth-limbed deities, labelled here and there with explanatory verses:

More than the rock amidst the raging sea, the constant heart no danger dread nor fears.

Such is Eworth's portrait of Sir John Luttrell (Plate 34) of 1550, his realistic bearded head consorting strangely with his pale body waist-deep in a tempestuous sea, and, more strangely, with the elegant figure of Peace, who, from a crowded Heaven of uncertain stability, takes him by the arm. But also, in the composition of some of his portraits, he draws heavily on Holbein, and later on Antonis Mor who was in England in 1554 long enough at least to paint Queen Mary Tudor. Eworth worked on most scales, except perhaps that of the smallest miniature. He painted portraits not unlike the little pieces of Corneille de Lyon; he painted them on all scales upwards to life-size. But constant among his variations is his concern for the individual character of the face. (If he had not had the forethought to sign many of his works, we might well have made at least three separate masters out of him on

Plate 32 (*right*)
Edward VI (1537–1553) attributed to William Scrots, *c*.1550
Oil on panel, 167 × 90.8 (65¾ × 35¾)
Royal Collection (by gracious permission of Her Majesty The Queen)

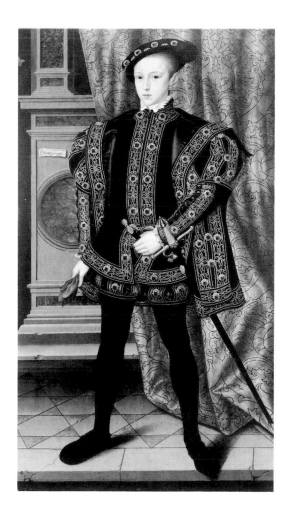

Plate 31 (*facing page*)
Elizabeth I (The Ditchley Portrait) (1533–1603) by Marcus Gheeraerts the Younger, *c*.1592
Oil on canvas, 241.3 × 152.4 (95 × 60)
National Portrait Gallery, London

stylistic grounds.) From about 1554 onwards (when he was established as a court-painter) there is traceable in his faces a more schematized rendering of the features, in line with an increasing insistence on a flatter pattern of background and on the detail of dress; he is developing towards what is generally known, though unjustly, as the late Elizabethan costume piece.

But throughout all his work his interest in the individuality of his sitters' faces remains; as in his double portrait, small in scale but superbly incisive in character, of Mary Neville, Lady Dacre, and her son Gregory, the 10th Baron Dacre (Plate 35). The modelling, though softer than Holbein's, is scrupulous; the flesh has a curious transparency, plumply taut, sometimes almost ballooned.

Eworth's work can be considered as a sort of microcosm, in which almost all the trends that will develop in painted portraiture to the end of the sixteenth century are visible, with the chief exception of the miniature in which Hilliard was to develop his own original genre. The characteristic composition of the portrait between 1550 and 1580 shows the subject three-quarter length, the body cut off at mid-thigh, standing, turned three-quarters to left or right, the hands tranquil, one of them perhaps resting on the sword-hilt or holding a pair of gloves. The general impression is cold, of a proud and aloof dignity; one seems to see them from below their own level.

Magnificent exemplars of this design were supplied by Titian, and in the North, most successfully, Mor drew heavily upon them, chilling and glazing Titian's rich

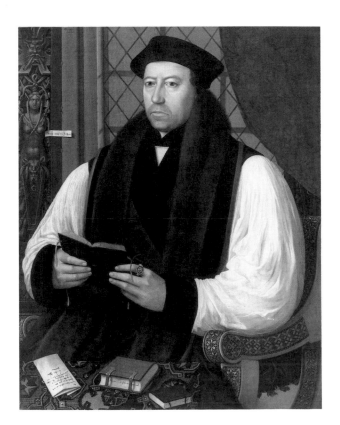

Plate 33
Thomas Cranmer, Archbishop of Canterbury (1489–1556) by Gerlach Flicke, 1546
Oil on panel, 98.4 × 76.2 (38¾ × 30)
National Portrait Gallery, London

Plate 34 (right)
Sir John Luttrell (1518?–1551)
by Hans Eworth, 1550
Oil on panel,
109.3 × 83.8 (43½ × 33)
Courtauld Institute Galleries,
London

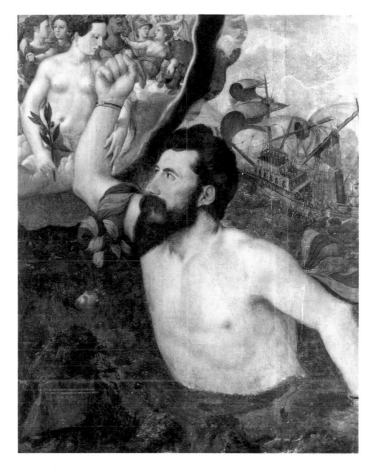

Plate 35 (below)
Mary Neville, Lady Dacre
(1524–1576?) *and her son*
Gregory, 10th Baron Dacre
(1539–1594) by Hans Eworth,
1559
Oil on panel,
50 × 71.4 (19¾ × 28)
Private collection, on loan to
the National Portrait Gallery,
London

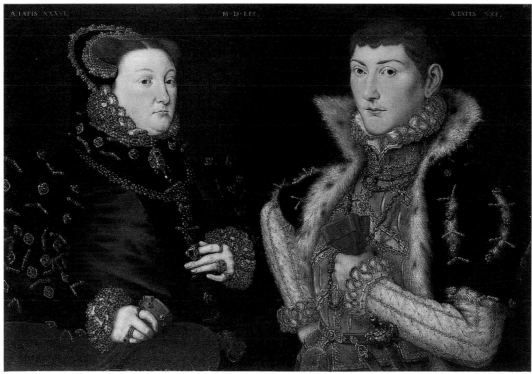

and broken colour, stiffening the pose (Plate 36). This same coldness and surface glaze, combined with a careful imitation of minute detail, from the wiry curl of the individual hair to the tiniest facets of complex jewellery, is common to all North European portraiture of the period. It occurs in England, sometimes on a life-size scale, sometimes on a smaller scale; sometimes Flemish or Dutch in atmosphere, sometimes approximating to the German harshness of Tom Ring. Even most of the head-and-shoulders portraits might be, as it were, truncated three-quarter lengths.

A little before 1580, whole-lengths – rare since about 1555 – come into fashion again; the three-quarter lengths are extended, though the desired impression of detached magnificence is not necessarily thereby increased, for once the feet appear they have to be harnessed to the common ground. Paradoxically, it is the whole-lengths on a miniature scale that are most impressive.

To some degree, all these portraits are state portraits, even when their sitters had but the most tenuous connections with the court, if any at all. They are visual demonstrations of a code of manners, corresponding very closely with that laid down in Castiglione's *Book of the Courtier*, known in England soon after its first appearance in 1528, and very widely known after the translation by Sir Thomas Hobie of 1561. An emphasis on sobriety of clothes and bearing, and a certain calm magnificence of spirit, best indicated by Castiglione's account of Francis I: 'and it seemed to me that besides the grace of his person and the beauty of his face, he had in

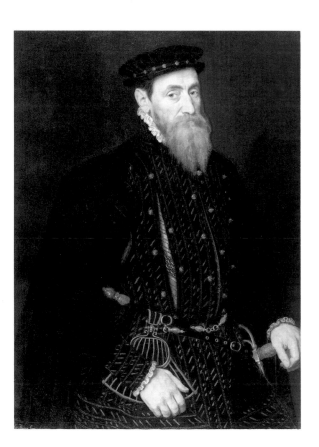

Plate 36
Sir Thomas Gresham (1519?–1579)
attributed to Antonis Mor, c.1565
Oil on panel, 100.3 × 72.4 (39½ × 28½)
National Portrait Gallery, London

his aspect such loftiness, joined however with a certain gracious humanity, that the realm of France must always seem too small for him'. It is vain therefore to hope for much intimacy with these portraits: intimacy was not their object, indeed it was contrary to their object. The idea of a portrait is still closely linked with that of the tomb-effigy. After an inconclusive flirtation with the purely Italian Renaissance style in the first half of the century, the Gothic tradition, in the effigies themselves if not so firmly in their settings, prevailed. Stiff, flat on their backs, hands together, they lie, formally clothed according to their degree in life.

The painted portrait may often seem to be but a domesticated tomb-effigy; its object to fix and perpetuate the mortal achievements, the rank, wealth and lineage of its subject; to demonstrate him in his own long gallery, by his own hearth, perhaps as the founder of his line, as Sir William Petre at Ingatestone, or to set him in context with the other great men of his time and of the past, as in the enormous portrait galleries of the Earl of Leicester, of the Fitzalans, Earls of Arundel (later Lord Lumley's) and of the Archbishop of Canterbury, which began to build up in the 1560s. Sometimes, portraits were re-duplicated almost in mass, and distributed perhaps almost as political propaganda. There are many portraits of Leicester, while Burghley seems to have been represented, to judge by our scanty knowledge of contemporary inventories, in almost every house that boasted a collection of pictures.

There may be complaints that I am neglecting the face, but the neglect is inevitable. For this sort of portraiture the face was far from enough. Apart from the fact that the face of flesh grows, shrivels over the toothless mouth, decays, betraying the splendid face of paint, there is the intolerable fact that other people have faces as good, perhaps better, than yours, whatever their standing. The face is naked, and nakedness is a great leveller, as the numerous though apparently ignored sumptuary laws tacitly admitted. How might a king be known from a lord, a lord from a knight, a gentleman from a serf, but by their clothes? Therefore it was laid down, who might wear ermine and who sackcloth.

In their portraits the Elizabethans insist on their rank through their clothes. Size was soon proved vain; Holbein might seem to reserve whole-lengths for royalty, but in the year after his death the rich young Mercer, Thomas Gresham, had a magnificent whole-length painted when he got married. A precise indication by clothes proved to have its drawbacks. Castiglione had observed that the 'principle and true profession' of a man of rank was that 'of arms'; hence the tendency of everyone entitled to armour to appear in it. Sir Philip Sidney – courtier, poet, patron and all other talents, chose to be painted wearing a soldier's gorget (see Plate 52) but so too Sir William Petre on his tomb lies encased in steel, though if ever a man was a Secretary by nature and by calling, it was he. Something still more precise was needed.

At this point, in order to learn to read the painted images of themselves that the Elizabethans have left us, it is necessary to consider the crucial case of the Queen herself.[19] The first sight we have of Elizabeth is in her twelfth or thirteenth year, about 1546: a three-quarter length painting (Plate 37). It is near enough to Holbein to have attracted his name within a century (it is listed as by him in Charles I's catalogue); it was however painted after his death, is at once softer and more elegantly mannered than his work, subscribing already to the standard inter-national three-quarter length design. It is evoked adequately by the entry in the Royal Inventory of 1546/47: 'item a table with the picture of the ladye Elizabeth her grace with a booke in her hande her gowne like crimson cloth of golde withe workes'. A portrait of an extraordinary adolescent sobriety, her face of a delicate clarity in which only the shadowy depths of the eyes have refused definition. It is in harmony, except for the mystery of the eyes, with Roger Ascham's schoolmasterish report of her made not long afterwards: 'in adornment she is elegant rather than showy'; a scholar already fluent in French, Italian and Latin and perhaps grounded well enough in Greek. He goes on to describe her literary style which she liked

to grow out of the subject, chaste in its appropriateness, beautiful in clarity. She admires above all, modest metaphors and comparisons of contraries well put together and contrasting felicitously with one another.

Here are already the seeds of her later style and her later appearance, though they were to grow away from modesty and restraint into a fantastic complexity of profusion. But it is Elizabeth herself who discloses the plot of her future portraiture. Writing to her brother Edward VI in her late teens, when sending a portrait (now lost) of herself to him, she said: 'for the face, I grant, I may well blush to offer, but the mind I shall never be ashamed to present.'

Nothing satisfactory or relevant to our purposes has yet come to light of Elizabeth in her twenties. She succeeded to the throne in 1558, and seems almost at once to have had trouble with her portraits, for in 1563 William Cecil, that supreme Elizabethan public relations officer, was drafting a decree to attempt some sort of control over the publishing of her image. The draft complains of the daily proliferation of unsatisfactory likenesses of the queen ('errors and deformities'), and records a demand that she

be content that some special cunning painter might be permitted by access to her Majesty to take the natural representation of her Majesty whereof she hath always been of her own will and disposition very unwilling, but also to prohibit all manner of other persons to draw paint grave or portrait her Majesty's personage or visage for a time until by some perfect pattern and example the same may be by others followed.

Whether this draft was put into execution is unknown, although at the end of her reign there was certainly an official holocaust of portraits of her judged unseemly and improper 'to the great offence of that beautiful and magnanimous Majesty wherewith God hath blessed her'. But it is clear that Elizabeth disliked sitting for her portrait and at the same time had strong views about the way in which she should be portrayed. These views she elaborated in a famous interview recorded by

Plate 37
Elizabeth I when Princess (1533–1603) by an unknown artist, *c.*1546
Oil on panel, 108.9 × 81.6 (42⅞ × 32⅛)
Royal Collection (by gracious permission of Her Majesty The Queen)

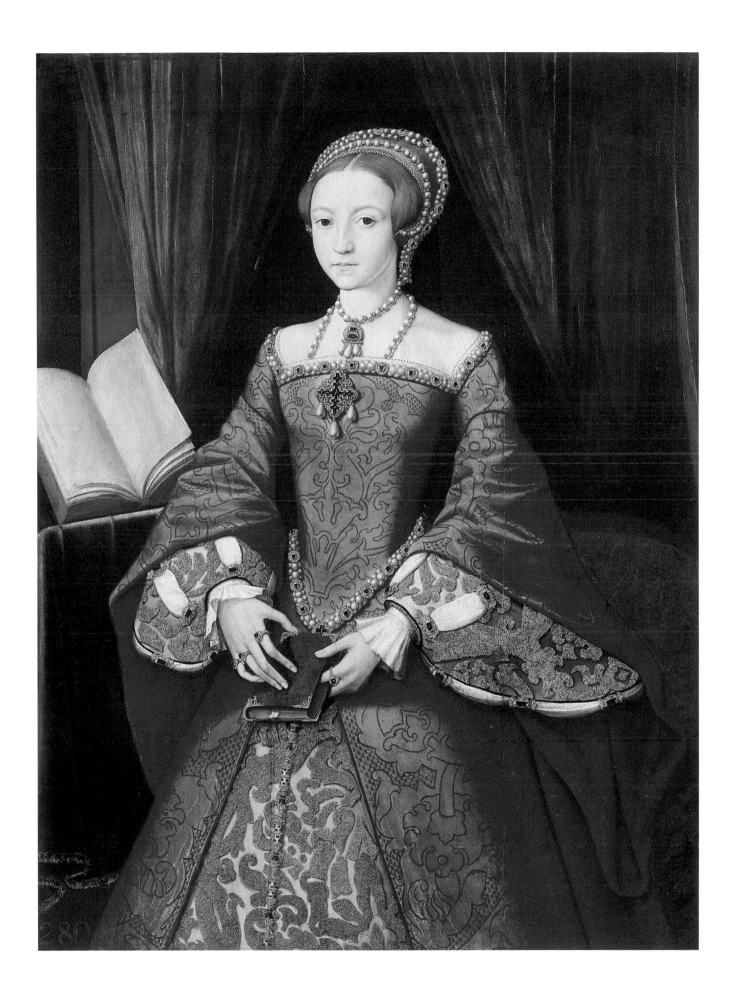

Hilliard 'when first I came in her Highnes presence to drawe'. That is presumably in or before 1572, the date of his earliest extant miniature of her, in the National Portrait Gallery, that seems to be a likeness drawn from the life (Plate 39). This is Hilliard's report:

This makes me to remember the wourds also and reasoning of her Majestie when first I came in her Highnes presence to drawe, who after showing me howe shee noted great difference of shadowing in the works and diversity of drawers of sundry nations, and that the Italians, who had the name to be cunningest and to drawe best, shadowed not, requiring of me the reason of it, seeing that best to showe oneself nedeth no shadow of place but rather the oppen light; to which I graunted, and afirmed that shadowes in pictures were indeed caused by the shadow of the place or coming in of the light as only one waye into the place at some small or high windowe, which many workmen covet to worke in for ease to their sight, and to give unto them a grosser lyne and a more aparant lyne to be deserned, and maketh the worke imborse well, and shewe very wel afar off, which to liming work nedeth not, because it is to be viewed of necessity in hand neare unto the eye. Here her Majestie conceived the reason, and therfore chose her place to sit in for that purpose in the open alley of a goodly garden, where no tree was neere, nor any shadow at all, save that as the heaven is lighter than the earthe so must that little shadow that was from the earthe. This Her Majestie's curious demaund hath greatly bettered my judgment, besides divers other like questions in art by her most excellent Majestie, which to speak or write of were fitter for some better clerk. . . .[20]

The close similarity between the Queen's views on painting and those of the Italian mannerists has been clearly demonstrated by John Pope-Hennessy: the insistence on the avoidance of shadow, and on 'the depiction of form through the scarcely perceptible gradations of tone, which Zuccari likens to the receding surface of a column'.[21] The Queen herself hints that chiaroscuro, the use of light-and-shade in the modelling, might serve to conceal imperfections in the sitter, but that it was too gross a method for a portrayal of flawless beauty. She might have been asking for a crystalline naturalism in the rendering of her own features, and although Hilliard's own miniature of 1572 is an admirable and credibly unflattering likeness of a woman of thirty-nine, it is one of the last portraits of her to suggest such candour. In the painting known as the Cobham Portrait (Plate 38), of around 1575, we have probably in fact the last authorized approach to a naturalistic rendering of the Queen; an admirable and inexpressive face, yet a little haggard and worn, the face of a much-tried woman in her early forties. And by then the dilemma was already upon her.

Elizabeth was of course far more than a mere woman. She was Queen, she was the Virgin Queen; she was the figurehead not only of State but of Church, so that a poet might exhort his readers to sing 'Vivat Eliza for an Ave Maria'; she was the centre of an extraordinary court cult, constantly re-defined from an inexhaustible symbolism – she was the rose, the Rosa Electa, at once that esoteric rose that burns at the heart of Jean de Meung's *Roman de la Rose* and the rose that is the Virgin Mary; she was Pandora, Astraea; she was the pearl, the phoenix, the pelican in its piety suckling her country on her own blood. Yet she remained, in spite of all, a mere woman, ageing.

But a decaying face was incompatible with a votive deity, and so, from about 1580 onwards, she, no longer blushing, offers her face, but substitutes an exposition of some aspect of her mind. Her face, in the portraits, is rendered by an opaque and unblemished mask; her identity is portrayed by the regal splendour of costume, by a richer cloth, by more jewels than any subject could display, and, more specifically, by crown, sceptre and orb. Particular qualities of her identity are displayed emblematically, by such symbols as the sheathed sword, the pelican, the phoenix, the olive branch; by a rainbow held bodily in the hand, or, as in the Ditchley Portrait (Plate 31), by a whole sonnet let into the picture, and by her passage through storm and sunshine, recalling Sir John Harington's account:

when she smiled it was a pure sunshine, that everyone did chuse to baske in, if they could: but anon came a storm from a sudden gathering of clouds, and the thunder fell in wondrous manner on all alike.[22]

In painting, this method answered at least one temper of the Elizabethan imagination: the piling together of images, the heaping of inflated unanatomical limbs, regalia, gems, the entire disdain of naturalistic illusion. Eventually it escapes altogether from the orthodox canons of European art: it is vain to judge it by its plastic values, for it is a hybrid of costume, of calligraphy, of flat repetitive design; of literature and of emblematic love.

It is perhaps easiest read if considered almost as heraldry. Each part has its significance; pose, costume and attributes establish the subject precisely in its rank, in its lineage, and in the centre its final individuality is differenced, as by a heraldic label, by the pale mask of the face. A later French theorist, Henri Estienne, though speaking specifically of emblematic devices, indicates the claim that can be made for emblematic portraiture, surpassing

not only all other Arts, but also Painting, since this only representeth the body and exquisite features of the face, where as a Device exposeth the rare conceits and gallant resolutions of its author far more perspicuously, and with more certainty than Physiognomy can by the proportions and lineaments of the face.[23]

When she was sixty, Elizabeth on one of her progresses stayed with Cecil at Theobald's, his house in Hertfordshire; the usual pageant opened with a Hermit. 'I behold you,' said the Hermit,

the self-same Queene, in the same esteate of person, strength and beautie, in which so many yeares past I beheld you, finding no alteration but in admiration, in so much as I am persuaded that Time, which catcheth everyebody, leeves only you untouched.

Time, in fact, as in the poet's imagination, has stopped. Age cannot wither her. Hilliard used one unwrinkled mask for her in all his miniatures of her last fifteen years. But, alas, age of course had caught her, at least in the unblinkered eyes of

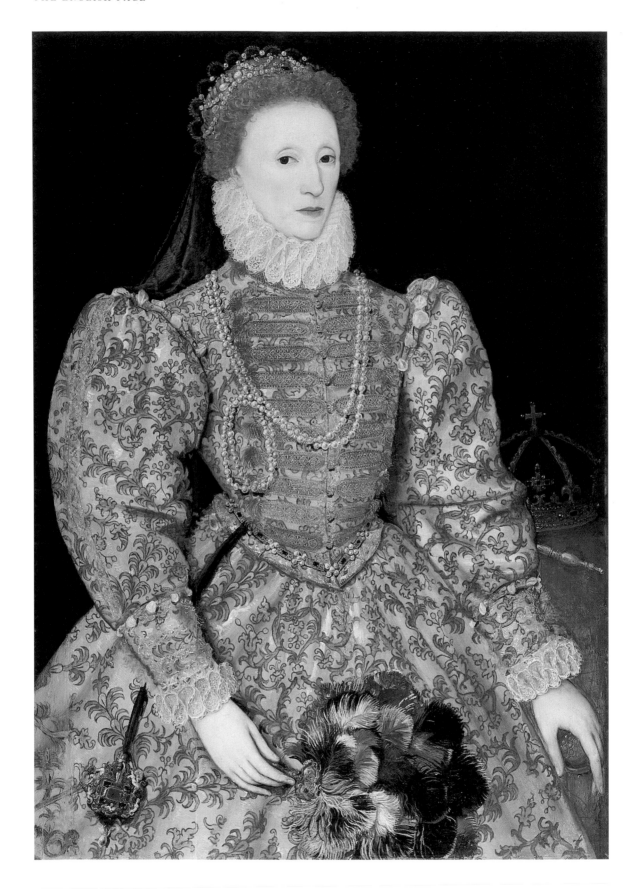

Plate 38 (*facing page*)
Elizabeth I (The Cobham Portrait)
(1533–1603) by an unknown artist,
*c.*1575
Oil on panel,
113 × 78.7 (44½ × 31)
National Portrait Gallery, London

unprejudiced observers like the French ambassador, who describes the great reddish wig, and then:

as for her face, it is and appears to be very aged, and her teeth are very yellow and unequal compared with what they were formerly, and on the left side less than the right.[24]

Elizabeth herself no doubt clung to the abstract notion of her feminine charm, consolidating the abstract by paint as much on her person as in the images of it, but the tragedy of Essex must have brought home to her, as perhaps no other defection could have done, the vulnerability of her myth of agelessness. 'Her delight', wrote an observer, 'is to sit in the dark and sometimes with shedding tears to bewail Essex.' Her reluctance to see herself truly mirrored is rumoured by several sources, most graphically – with almost a touch of King Lear – by Ben Jonson to William Drummond of Hawthornden: she 'never saw herself after she became old in a true glass; they painted her, and sometymes would vermilion her nose.'[25]

Hilliard's mask of the Queen has the effect of broadening her brow – 'her forehead large and faire, a seemly seat for Princely grace' – of plumping the cavities of the cheeks and shortening the face (Plate 40). It is repeated in certain life-size portraits in the Hilliard style, such as the Armada portrait at Woburn and the Rainbow portrait of Hatfield. Not all her late portraits of course are quite so idealized; the face in paintings generally associated with the Anglo-Flemish manner of Gheeraerts, like the Ditchley whole-length and that at Hardwick Hall, is long

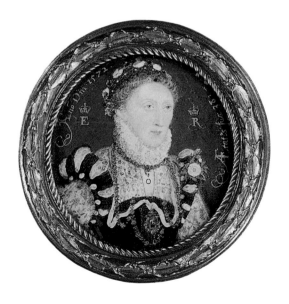

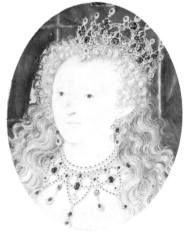

Plate 39 (*right*)
Elizabeth I (1533–1603) by Nicholas Hilliard, 1572
Vellum, 5.1 × 4.8 (2 × 1⅞)
National Portrait Gallery, London

Plate 40 (*above far right*)
Elizabeth I (1533–1603) by Nicholas Hilliard, *c.*1600
Vellum, 6.2 × 4.8 (2 7⁄16 × 1⅞).
Victoria & Albert Museum, London

Plate 41 (*below far right*)
Elizabeth I (1533–1603) by Isaac Oliver, *c.*1592
Vellum, 8.2 × 5.2 (2 7⁄16 × 2⅛)
Victoria & Albert Museum, London

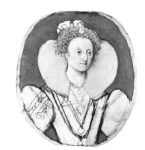

and gaunt with indubitable age, although smoothed out no doubt by the painter's brush. The most vivid witness to her age is Isaac Oliver's unfinished miniature (Plate 41).

The Hilliard mask is probably the best exemplar of the ideal Elizabethan female beauty, and it corresponds to the descriptions of the poets. The colour scheme was red and white, 'roses in a bed of lilies shed', as Spenser described Belphoebe in *The Faerie Queene*, with hair 'like golden wires'; the face should be round with ruddy cheeks and a broad brow; delicate, very slight 'pensild' eyebrows; grey eyes set wide, lips like the inevitable cherry, and the neck like an ivory column. Thus Elizabeth herself, without too gross a departure from fact, might be rendered by her painters, and all ladies of rank modelled themselves upon it, though not all were blessed with golden hair. Hence, in part, the reason that so many portraits of unknown Elizabethan women have been wrongly re-baptised with the Queen's name. Not even the greatest of couturiers have dictated fashion and beauty culture to the extent that Elizabeth did. From portrait after portrait the smooth pale unshadowed faces gleam out, the contrasting red of their cheeks generally now faded by time or dimmed by old varnish.

The perfection of these 'masks' was contrived with perhaps even more trouble than is the case today; they were guarded, outdoors, by real masks from the grave threat of roughening or of tan and particularly from the ultimate hideousness of freckling. Lotions were brewed from roses and cherries; ass's milk was commended as a cleansing agent. For blemishes, extraordinary concoctions, like that of turpentine, rosin, beeswax, hog lard and honey, were made up. These were mainly prophylactic; for accenting beauty there were cosmetics. Painting the feminine face was now an established habit, not confined to the court, and there is a considerable contemporary literature on the subject, for the most part abusive. The agonized search for new cosmetics already foreshadows the beauty pages of modern women's magazines; eyes were sharpened with kohl, and no doubt, in the words of the fashion editress, if 'made up with discretion would last their owners all evening and dominate their face'.

There was already trouble with non-permanent red for the lips, and numerous recipes for mouth-washes suggest difficulty over one aspect of personal hygiene. Sir Walter Raleigh, opening up the distant wonders of Guiana, was interested enough to note

divers berries, that die a most perfect crimson and Carnation; And for painting, all France, Italy, or the east Indies, yeild none such: For the more the skyn is washed, the fayrer the cullour appeareth . . .[26]

Egg-white seems to have been a popular base, in extremes, for 'renewing old riueld faces', but primarily for a glaze, a fine shine and polish to the skin, which then, unlike now, was fashionable.

This votive mask was poised generally upon a stiff froth of lace and canopied by an artifice of hair. The lace is the ruff, which appears in the forties and fifties as a simple frill on the collar, but which by 1560 envelops the throat, clustering like an elaborate cake-frill, tight to the ears. It was to remain, in various shapes and sizes, more or less in fashion for the next seventy years. About 1580 it expands into the cartwheel ruff, on which the head sits like John the Baptist's on a platter, but by 1590 it has opened in front to show the throat, and from 1600 it is decadent, in an extreme diversity of forms. Above it the hair, which until about 1575 is contained generally modestly under a hood with a falling veil, tends to puff in a matching profusion of tight curls 'and least it should fall down, it is under propped with forks, wyers & I cannot tel what, rather like grim sterne monsters, than chaste christian matrones'. Curled with irons, anointed with pomades and perfume, the hair had often been dyed to the fashionable blonde – 'to make haire as yellowe as gold. Take the rine or scrapings of Rubarbe, and stiepe it in white wine or in cleare lie . . .' If there was not enough hair, it was supplemented by false; on top, and amidst and amongst, was the display-ground for lavish jewellery, while from one ear, but rarely both, would dangle a large pearl.[27]

The men, in their outward appearance, were not of course so regimented as the women – rather, the reverse. In 1559 the Lower House had urged upon the Queen the wisdom of marriage, and in reply she drew off her coronation ring:

yea, to satisfie you, I have already ioyned myselfe in marriage to an husbande, namely, the Kingdome of *England*. And beholde the pledge of this my wedlocke and marriage with my Kingdome.

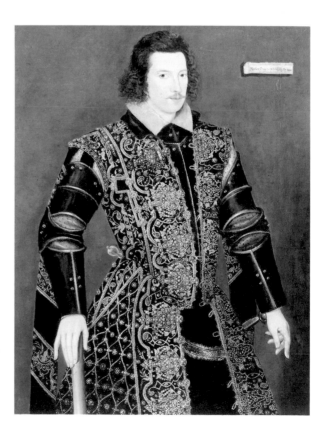

Plate 42
Robert Devereux, 2nd Earl of Essex
(1566–1601) by William Segar, 1590
Oil on panel, 113.1 × 87.7 (44½ × 34½)
National Gallery of Ireland, Dublin

That this pledge was to be fulfilled became apparent only in the seventies, after many alarms and excursions, and it was sealed by the final breakdown of negotiations with the Duke of Anjou in the eighties.

With the abstraction of Elizabeth from the practical marriage market (she was fifty when it happened) her court became even more like a male, but platonic, harem; now that the wooing of her was but play, her courtiers had to play with all the greater concentration to maintain the suspension of disbelief. Sartorially, they reacted with frantic splendour and unparalleled variety, each a bird of different species sprouting its mating plumage before a common queen. And it is as birds of display that their portraitists delineate them, with something of the meticulous and stiff precision that John Gould was later to exercise on the plates for his ornithological books: peacocks, popinjays and birds of paradise. Only the older men, like Burghley, Heneage and Walsingham, retain the official sobriety of bureaucracy, but even against their sombre gowns may dangle a gleaming token of their devotion, a cameo of Elizabeth's head.

The details of the variations of dress, huge Spanish slops or Danish codpiece, peascod belly and mandilion capes, that lace surcoat knit of pearls worn by Essex (Plate 42) over his black armour – these do not concern us, except where they are the immediate frame for the face. The fashion for ruffs applied to men exactly as to women, reaching its full bloom in the cartwheels of the eighties; but simultaneously with that monstrous flower there was a more informal neck-wear which consisted of a simple, though generally lace-edged, turn-down shirt collar.

Hats appear relatively rarely in the portraits, but range from the tall black sugar-loaf with curly brim – the copintank, as it were a cross between a top-hat and a bowler – and the flat velvet cap; on these, generally, jewellery was worn or at least a feather, while the Earl of Cumberland displayed in his a jewelled glove of Elizabeth's (Plate 43). The hair, since Henry VIII had his own head 'polled' in 1536, continued short, usually cropped very close, but from the seventies was subjected by most courtiers to a carefully calculated dishevelment, combed forward on brow and temples in obligatory curls, with an effect that looks forward to the dandies of the Regency.

In the middle of the century most men wore beards – elderly men apparently always – a curious two-pronged form remaining fashionable until about 1580, although what is thought of as the characteristic Elizabethan beard, short and pointed, is found throughout the reign. Hilliard's own self-portrait of 1577 is a perfect exemplar of the presentation of a man about court, although he lacks the single ear-ring that some of them wore (Plate 44). In the eighties beards went out of fashion with some for a brief spell, until Essex grew a fine reddish spade-shaped specimen during his excursion to Cadiz, and with it set a fashion on his return.

But this variety was controlled by the painters, the same painters who were transubstantiating Elizabeth into icon. They produced, with two exceptions, no major innovations in their pictorial designs, which remained basically variations on

Plate 43 (*right*)
*George Clifford, 3rd Earl
of Cumberland*
(1558–1605) by
Nicholas Hilliard,
*c.*1590
Vellum,
25.8 × 17.6 (10⅛ × 6⅞)
National Maritime
Museum, Greenwich

Plate 44 (*above far
right*)
Nicholas Hilliard
(1537–1619),
self-portrait, 1577
Vellum,
4.1 (1⅝) diameter
Victoria & Albert
Museum, London

Plate 45 (*below far
right*)
Sir Walter Raleigh
(1552–1618) by
Nicholas Hilliard,
*c.*1585
Vellum, oval
4.8 × 4.1 (1⅞ × 1⅝)
National Portrait
Gallery, London

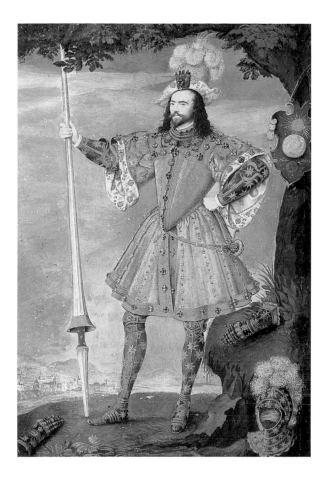

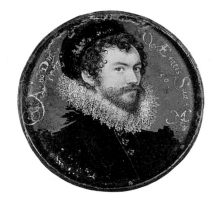

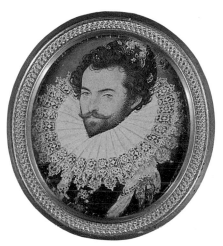

the static three-quarter length court-portrait theme: polite, aloof, polished and rigid, still the two-dimensional counterpart of the tomb-effigy. Beneath the jewelled doublets and the ruffs, the bodies are but lay-figures, posed; on top of them, expressionless, the mask, hirsute or clean-shaven. They are more individualized than the Queen's, but the same heraldic quality of the whole is rarely absent. The technique, at its extreme, gives the impression of flesh like translucent wax stretched on the skull; usually the paint is thin, and sometimes even the 'bones' of the underlying pencil drawing on the ground can be discerned through it. On a life-size scale, the result, in the hands of those who worked in the manner of Hilliard, like William Segar, and to a less extent George Gower, is often vacant and dead; in Hilliard's own hands, in the compression of the miniature, its justification can be breathtaking.

The majority of Hilliard's miniatures show little more than the head. He was one of the exceptions to the rule, a great formal innovator, the master of the oval miniature in locket-shape. Trained as a goldsmith, his portraits are also jewellery; whereas the life-size portrait was house-furniture, his were furniture for the person, and a new intimacy is endemic if only in their size and purpose – small enough to be held in the palm of the hand, they could be private; they might be displayed publicly, worn on a long chain, or even, as Elizabeth wore Cecil, on a shoe; but they might also be worn under the dress, over the heart or kept close in a lidded locket. Sometimes they are inscribed with a motto or tag, haunting and now inexplicably relevant as a refrain; or some symbolic allusion may be incorporated in the design.

But here at last it is the face that is the thing, and much of Hilliard's fascination lies in the tension between his masterly sense for design and his respect for the individuality of his sitter. In a passage, for the requotation of which no apology is necessary, he wrote:

so hard a matter the artist hath in hand, calling these graces one by one to their due place, noting how in smiling the eye changeth and narroweth, how the mouth a little extendeth both ends of the line upwards, the cheeks raise themselves to the eyewards, the nostrils play and are more open, the neck commonly erecteth itself and the forehead casteth itself into a plane as it were for peace and love to walk upon.[28]

At one extreme of his work are the stylized portraits of Elizabeth, and much of his stylization appears also in his court-portraits, where the formal interest is perhaps not entirely fused with the human one. So with his Raleigh (Plate 45) – the dark pointed head set on the dazzling lace-dish of the ruff; it is admirable, Raleigh the wit, the dandy, but it does not imply the whole man as we know him. John Aubrey (although, writing long afterwards, about 1680, in *Brief Lives*, he is suspect) adds with words almost another visual dimension:

He was a tall, handsome, and bold man. . . . His beard turnd up naturally. . . . He had a most remarkable aspect, an exceedingly high forehead, long-faced, and sour eie-lidded, a kind of pigge-eie.[29]

Hilliard is perhaps most exciting to the modern eye in those portraits that have lost their identity or bear an obscure name that has left no reverberations in history, faces which can be confronted with no previously-conceived image of what they ought to look like, and each of which is as fraught with mystery and as unanswerable and still demanding as the tomb of the Unknown Warrior.

Such are the portraits of Mr and Mrs Mole (Plates 47 and 48); he was an obscure official and tutor who is said to have been made against his will (he was a devout Protestant) to travel in Italy, where he was trapped by the Inquisition and imprisoned for life. The miniature of his wife was with him, and returned to his family by a visitor who was allowed to see him. The accretion of some such legend, if the story be not truth, seems almost inevitable about these two faces, while one of our most austere and restrained scholars has been moved to divine *angst* in them.

Hilliard, as we have seen earlier, subscribed to the Queen's artistic views, and so in practice did almost all the painters who portrayed the court. It would, however, be wrong to suggest that all Elizabethan portraits are so dominated by extreme artistic theory that there was no concern for naturalism. There seems to have been always a demand for a lively and likely likeness, but the artists who could have supplied them were mainly subordinate to the court fashion. In 1569 the Mercers rejected a statue of Sir Thomas Gresham because it differed 'from his trewe image and picture'.[30] At the close of the century the tide began to turn; about 1596, Essex, with his fresh red Cadiz beard, sat to Isaac Oliver, and not to Hilliard, who had previously painted him.

Oliver, Hilliard's former pupil, retained his master's love of delicate and rich detail, but his approach was basically different, and his art more naturalistic; unlike Hilliard, he built his people up by light out of shadow, and the results are fleshier, more palpable. In his work, English portraiture begins to come back into line with the main North European tradition; although it was not to fall fully into line until more than thirty years later, the Elizabethan experiment gradually gives way from this date onwards.

It must be confessed that the Elizabethan face that survives is inadequate; inadequate as image or mirror of the age. Hilliard might have left us a Benedick, even perhaps a Mercutio; he could scarcely hint at Hamlet, and Lear is beyond his horizon. His miniature of Drake (Plate 46), though agreeing admirably with Stow's description – 'round headed, browne hayre, full bearded, his eyes round, large and clear, well favoured, fayre and of a cheerefull countenance' – is simply too small. There is hardly a hint in Elizabethan portraiture at the largeness so characteristic of the age, at its incredible intellectual variety and curiosity; there is a positive contradiction of its essential movement, of that swift, robust and dangerous vitality that circled the world and explored the heaven and hell of Shakespearian tragedy.

Yet the main reason for this inadequacy is itself part of the Elizabethan character; they were not interested in the visual arts as such. Nowhere, apart from Hilliard and a handful of artists, is there evidence of any awareness of the nature and importance

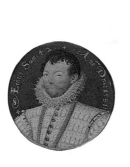 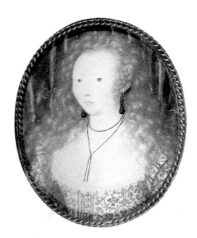 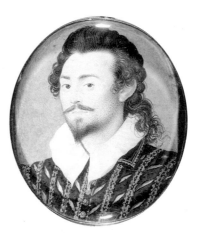

Plate 46 (above left)
Sir Francis Drake (1540?–1596) by (?) studio of Nicholas Hilliard, 1581. Vellum, 2.8 ($1\frac{1}{8}$) diameter. National Portrait Gallery, London

Plate 47 (above centre) *Mrs Mole* by Nicholas Hilliard, c.1605. Vellum, 5.1 × 4.2 ($2 \times 1\frac{5}{8}$). The Pennington Mellor Charity Trust

Plate 48 (above right) *Mr Mole* by Nicholas Hilliard, c.1605. Vellum, 4.8 × 3.8 ($1\frac{7}{8} \times 1\frac{1}{2}$). The Pennington Mellor Charity Trust

of, for example, the Venetian painting of the time, which was that of Titian, Tintoretto and Veronese. Sidney, in Venice, sat to Veronese, at someone else's behest, but shows in his letters no comprehension of, and little interest in, the prodigies of genius unfolding about him in that city. It is probably not unfair to cite Robert Dallington's opinion of the Italians as characteristic of that of the English to the visual arts: conceding that Italy excelled in architecture (the reason being obvious, that marble was to hand), and in painting and poetry 'and no marvaile, when all their time is spent in Amours and all their churches deckt with colours'.[31] The English had other things to do.

Although the habit of portraiture had spread, the clientele was still limited. It seems to have been practised hardly at all in Ireland and Wales, and relatively very little in Scotland. It was popular in court circles, and is reasonably inclusive. We know, for example, what almost all the Knights of the Garter about 1580 looked like. Outside the court, the habit was still restricted. Bishops showed a worldly interest in perpetuating their mortal images, leaving behind them a series of gaunt wooden and unfriendly faces; to a lesser extent aldermen, mayors and merchants were interested, but they usually employed inferior artists, and were anyway perhaps more inclined, like country squires, to entrust memory of themselves to robed stone effigies on their tombs. The College of Physicians allowed their fellows a

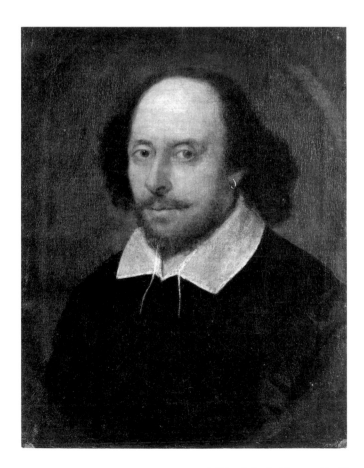

Plate 49
William Shakespeare (The Chandos Portrait) (1564–1616) attributed to John Taylor, *c.*1610
Oil on canvas,
55.2 × 43.8 (21¾ × 17¼)
National Portrait Gallery, London

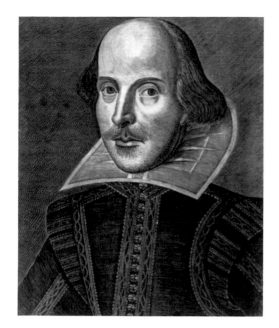

Plate 50 (*above*)
William Shakespeare (1564–1616) by Martin
Droeshout
Engraving, 19.1 × 15.9 (7½ × 6¼)
National Portrait Gallery, London

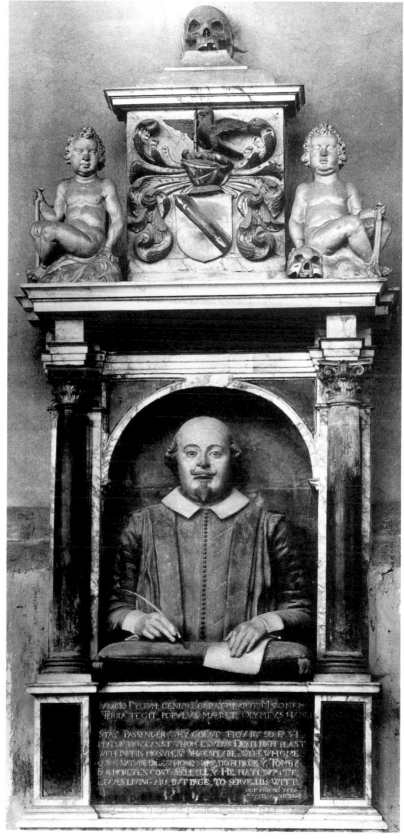

Plate 51 (*right*)
Monument to William Shakespeare (1564–1616)
by Gerard Johnson, *c.*1620
Alabaster, 129.5 × 54.6 (51 × 21½)
Holy Trinity Church, Stratford-upon-Avon

curious privilege on payment of a small fee: that of displaying their own portraits in the College, presumably as memorial but apparently also possibly as advertisement.[32] An exception was the great family of the Greshams, who employed, amongst others, Mor and Cornelius Ketel (see Plate 36). But apart from the lower ranks of society, whole professions remain almost unrepresented; the most aggravating gap is amongst the poets, Peel, Kyd, Greene, Marlowe, Webster, even Spenser: nothing remains of them. For Shakespeare himself we are perhaps lucky; on the evidence of his social standing, there is no valid reason for expecting anything. We have in fact three portraits which must have some tenuous connection with living memories of his person, though two are posthumous: the sad scratch that Droeshout engraved for the First Folio, 1623 (Plate 50), and Gerard Johnson's bust at Stratford, memento of a sober citizen of some standing (Plate 51). The irrelevance, the impertinence of both, is painful, but historically we have no right to expect more.

The case for a much-disputed portrait, however, the so-called 'Chandos' in the National Portrait Gallery, being a representation of Shakespeare taken from the life, seems to be strengthening rather than weakening (Plate 49). From early on, it was said to have been painted by John Taylor, both a player and a painter, who left it to Sir William Davenant, from whom it was acquired by Thomas Betterton. There was an actor called Joseph Taylor (listed in the First Folio of 1623) but he is unknown as a painter. Recent investigation into John Taylor has revealed him as a member of the Painter-Stainers' Company, and documented work by him seems very consistent with the handling of the Chandos painting, conventional but certainly modestly efficient, surely professional. The sitter wears a rather clerkly dark doublet; owns a beard; has a high domed forehead (as in the other two images of Shakespeare, if less markedly so). The presentation of the sitter and the costume are very similar to that of the portrait of Ben Jonson (to which I shall come later; see Plate 61), though the painter of the latter conveys an intensity of presence and personality to which the artist of the Chandos does not aspire. The sitter in the Chandos has however a glint of gold about him that might be read as indication of latent riches beneath that modest exterior: an ear-ring. That is an adornment not all that uncommon in late Elizabethan male portraits (though generally for younger men, as was the case when the fashion recently revived). The features are not striking in individuality, dark in complexion (though the paint surface has suffered somewhat in the course of the centuries), but most people nevertheless do agree that it carries conviction as having been painted from the life. By the late seventeenth century, when it belonged to Betterton, it seems to have been accepted unquestioningly as Shakespeare, and from it, from then until today, innumerable copies, derivations, variations – painted, engraved, sculpted – have been produced. As votive image, for the 'bardolators', as 'Presider' for the poets, for Dryden as for Keats, it served a purpose, even if, as the face of a man often described as the greatest Englishman ever born, it is sadly inadequate.[33]

Sir Philip Sidney, paragon of Elizabethan virtues, is a disappointment of almost the same order. There are two portraits only, of each of which several versions exist: both are well authenticated, but they might well represent two different people (the Veronese is lost). One, probably painted in the Low Countries around 1576, shows him posed according to etiquette as a conventional soldier, wearing a gorget (Plate 52); the other, of about 1585, with his head on a circular ruff, as a conventional courtier. Neither sheds any light on the discrepancy between Ben Jonson's account – 'no pleasant man in countenance, his face being spoiled with pimples and of high blood and long' – result of measles and small pox, as confirmed by Moffet's contemporary *Life*, and the passionate eulogies poured forth at the time of his death, of which this is but one sample:

> When he descended downe the mount
> His personage seemed most divine,
> A thousand graces one might count,
> Upon his lovely cheereful eine . . .

If, in some catastrophe, all vestiges of Elizabethan civilisation had been swept away, save only their life-size painted images, we should scarcely be able even to guess at its unparalleled richness and variety. It would seem, rather, like some era of

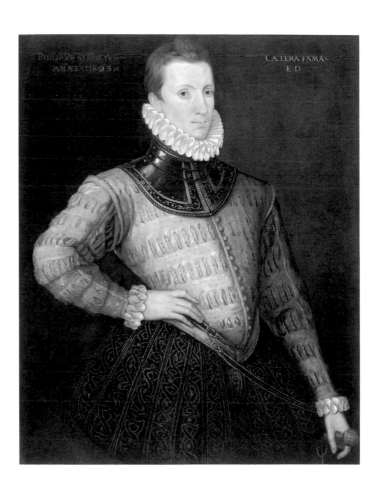

Plate 52
Sir Philip Sidney (1554–1586)
by an unknown artist, *c.*1576
Oil on panel,
113.9 × 84 (44⅞ × 33⅛)
National Portrait Gallery,
London

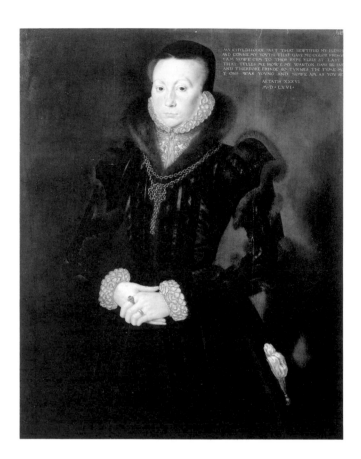

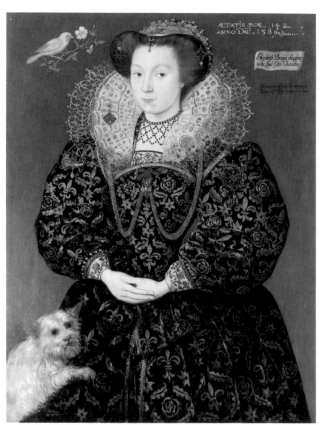

decadence, inhabited by a remote race of beings, gaudy in their vanity yet veiled with their pride; men and women of stiff bodies, stiff habits, stiff minds, their imaginations blinkered and confined like mill-horses within the well-worn orbit of a dead mythology – an illusion that many of them, presenting faces like rocks against time, seem to have wished to perpetuate even in their features, the 'windows of their souls'.

A curious comment sometimes offered, as if in explanation of one aspect of the Elizabethan character, is that it was young. It is too often forgotten that England was already old, and it is on the age and pedigree of race that so many portraits insist. Certainly this was an uneasy period of social resettlement and expansion, and the insistence on antiquity reflects men's unease when values were shifting so rapidly and incalculably. They liked, those who could, to dwell for their own comfort and peace of mind on at least the legitimacy of their blood and state.

So their portraits have a heraldic quality, often made more precise by the presence of a many-quartered coat of arms, and so their faces are set in rigid moulds that will give as little as possible away. This pride is expressed vividly in an explosion of Richard Bertie to Burghley, after a Fitzalan had impugned his ancestry:

Plate 53 (*above left*)
Mrs Joan Wakeman
(1530–1598) by Hans
Eworth, 1566
Oil on panel,
91.4 × 71.1 (36 × 28)
Private Collection

Plate 54 (*above right*)
Elizabeth Brydges,
Lady Kennedy by
Hieronimo Custodis,
1589
Oil on canvas,
92 × 69.8 (36¼ × 27½)
The Marquess of
Tavistock, and the
Trustees of the
Bedford Settled
Estates, Woburn
Abbey

my lord of A[rundel] (as I am informed, more of his accustomed good nature than of my desert) told the Queen I was no gentleman, which perhaps being otherwise unwilling, somewhat stayeth, but if that respect had stayed her ancestors in the time of Fitzalan, bailiff of London, my lord should have lacked his lordship thus to embroil others. As I have no cause, so I am no whit ashamed of my parents, being free English, neither villeins nor traitors. And if I would after the manner of the world bring forth old abbey scrolls for matter of record, I am sure I can reach as far backward as a Fitzalan.[34]

But they had too a well-developed corporate arrogance; already in 1497 Trevisano had noted that the 'English are great lovers of themselves . . . and whenever they see a handsome foreigner, they say that "he looks like an Englishman", and that "it is a great pity that he should not be an Englishman"'. (Trevisano commented that Scotsmen, however, were said to be handsomer.)[35] This trait was remarked by others in the sixteenth century, and it is still sometimes sensible in the tone of voice with which, say, a Frenchman from Normandy may be appraised: 'you'd think he was an Englishman.'

Yet against this arrogance is often to be set a religious humility; each portrait is but another vain attempt to fix a moment, an ephemeral phenomenon, on the retina of time; and the vanity is often openly admitted by a motto or by a skull. Mrs Joan Wakeman stands (Plate 53), composed and resigned, in black, her hands folded, in the year 1566:

> My chyldhodde past that bewtifiied my flesshe
> And gonne my youth that gave me color fresshe
> Y am now cum to thus rype yeris at last
> That telles me howe my wanton days be past
> And therfore frinde so turnes the tyme me
> Y ons was young and nowe am as you see.

It is a resignation that few women of her age would submit to today; she was only thirty-six, and still very much alive, with thirty-two more years of old age to endure.

Many of the Elizabethan faces of course still come alive through no virtue of their painters. Give them a name – and what names: Elizabeth herself; Cecil, Walsingham; Frobisher, Grenville, Raleigh or Drake; Sidney; Leicester or Essex – and their stiff faces light up like transparent masks lit by a brilliant candle within. And sometimes the cool, clear-cut technique of the painters succeeds in detaching an image of the most pristine quality like a spring flower against a clear blue sky. Such are not only the best of Hilliard's miniatures, but even occasionally the life-size portraits, as Hieronimo Custodis' exquisite rendering of the young Elizabeth Brydges at Woburn Abbey (Plate 54).

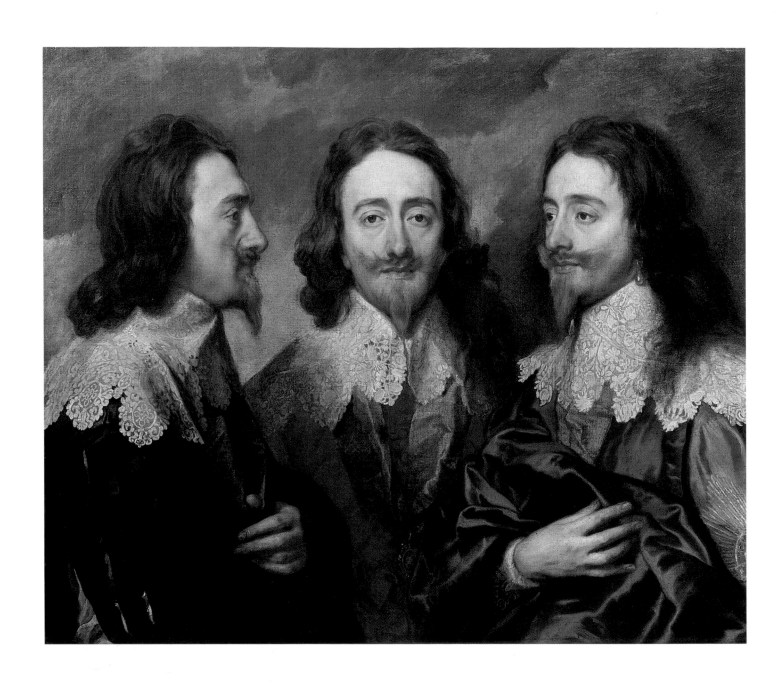

Plate 55
Triple Portrait of Charles I (1600–1649) by Sir Anthony van Dyck, 1635. Oil on canvas, 84.5 × 99.7 (33¼ × 39¼)
Royal Collection (by gracious permission of Her Majesty The Queen)

IV

Jacobean Melancholy

THE COINAGE 'Jacobethan' can be applied with equal aptness to the human frontispieces of the period as to those of architecture. The mixture of style continues; in some portraits, till as late as 1620, the Elizabethan court-manner persists, by now distilled into true fashion plates, inflated whole-length costumes standing in a display-niche draped with metallic curtains the texture of which prophesies plastic. Amongst the spectacular group of paintings in this style at Ranger's House, Blackheath, two ladies are represented by identical portraits, only the heads being different (Plates 56 and 57).

But simultaneously the naturalistic tendency announced by Oliver's miniatures is gathering strength; by 1620 three painters of considerable ability from the Netherlands were working in London: Paul van Somer, Abraham van Blyenberch and Daniel Mytens, and though they brought no radical originality, their sitters emerge in a more human probability. Oliver himself was working until his death in

Plate 56 (*right*)
Diana Cecil, Countess of Oxford (died 1654) by William Larkin, *c*.1614
Oil on canvas, 205.8 × 120 (81 × 47¼)
Ranger's House, Blackheath (English Heritage)

Plate 57 (*far right*)
Anne Cecil, Countess of Stamford (1603?–1676) by William Larkin, *c*.1614
Oil on canvas, 205 × 119 (81 × 46⅞)
Ranger's House, Blackheath (English Heritage)

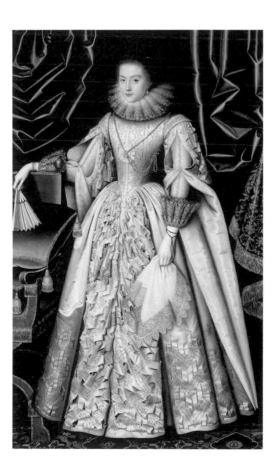
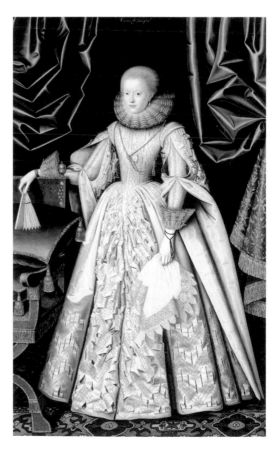

1617 (and Hilliard to 1619, a paling and ageing shadow of his former self), and before he died one Cornelius Johnson had begun a career that was to outlast the as yet unheralded Van Dyck, painting, to begin with, close in manner to Oliver's miniatures, but on a life-size scale.

But on the whole, at the court, the faces read as a prolongation of the Elizabethan masks. James' large and 'rowling' eyes, his thin beard, are composed near enough to dignity not to disgrace majesty, and his tongue, 'too large for his mouth', constrained behind his lips (Plate 58); Queen Anne's high nose is in the true Elizabethan tradition, and about them are ranged the courtiers, more densely bearded now, shapeless and perhaps even often stodgy in bolstered breeches.

A few of them emerge with startling clarity; Lord Herbert of Cherbury, whose vanity, elsewhere so pyrotechnically displayed in his autobiography, laid itself out in an iconography of astonishing variety. We see him solemn in robes of the Bath; melancholic, prostrate in a landscape by a stream (Plate 59), while his charger stands by; lovelorn in his lacy shirt or in medallic profile like a new emperor, and, finally, his bodiless and staring head, floating amongst clouds.[36] Francis Bacon, in his formal painted portraits, is muted by a top-hat and chancellor's gown, but in his seated effigy head on hand, in the church at Verulam (St Albans) (Plate 60) the tireless mind may seem to have but dozed off, the better to take up, after a few seconds or millennia, its train of thought; death is no reason to lie down. In

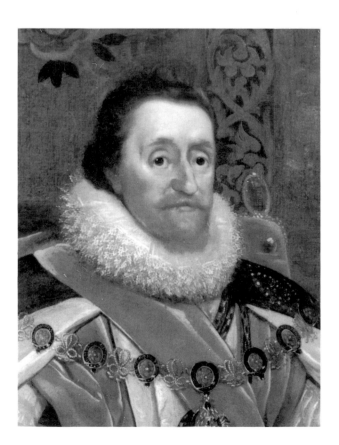

Plate 58
James I (1566–1625) by Daniel
Mytens, 1621 (detail)
Oil on canvas,
148.6 × 100.6 (58½ × 39⅝)
National Portrait Gallery, London

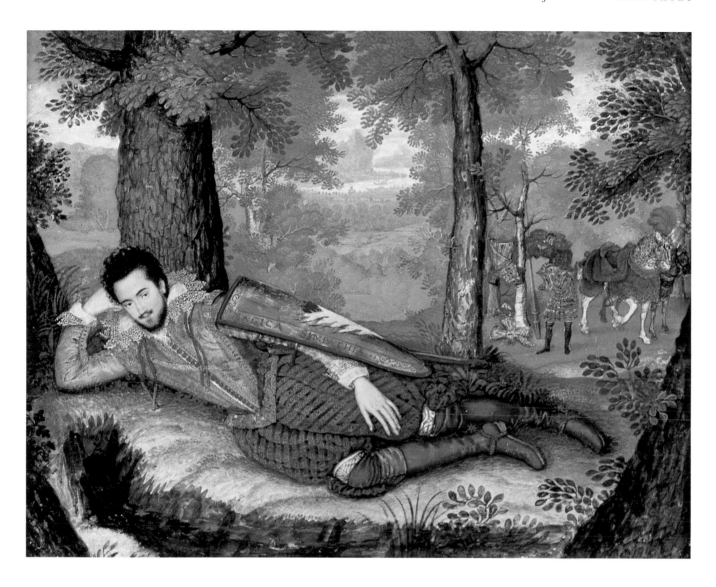

Plate 59
*Edward, 1st Baron
Herbert of Cherbury*
(1583–1648) by Isaac
Oliver, *c*.1610–1613
Vellum,
18 × 23 (7⅛ × 9)
National Trust, Powis
Castle

Oliver's profile of that meteor, Henry, Prince of Wales, there is comprehensible something of the ardour, tough and sensitive as a ship's prow, that so struck his contemporaries (Plate 62). Although, in the same artist's miniature of Donne (Plate 63), the poet's personality seems trimmed with his beard to an almost suburban spruce, it escapes still in that fantastic gesture to death and to posterity, his monument in St Paul's (Plate 64); of the 'sitting' for this Walton has left his unforgettable account:

Several charcoal fires being first made in his large study, he brought with him into that place his winding-sheet in his hand, and having put off all his clothes, had this sheet put on him, and so tied with knots at his head and feet, and his hands so placed as dead bodies are usually fitted, to be shrowded and put into their coffin, or grave. Upon [an urn] he thus stood with his eyes shut, and with so much of the sheet turned aside as might shew his lean, pale and death-like face, which was purposely turned towards the East, from whence he expected the second coming of his and our Saviour Jesus . . .[37]

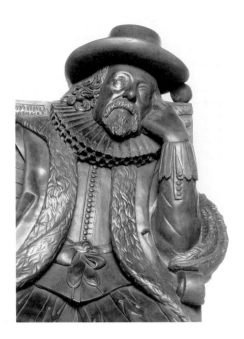

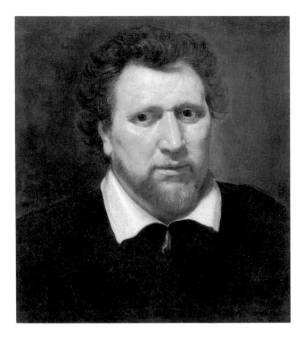

Plate 60 (*far left*)
Francis Bacon, Baron Verulam and Viscount St Alban (1561–1626) by an unknown artist (detail)
Electrotype of effigy in St Michael, St Albans, height 152.4 (60)
National Portrait Gallery, London

Plate 61 (*left*)
Ben Jonson (1573?–1637) by Abraham van Blyenberch
Oil on canvas, 47 × 41.9 (18½ × 16½)
National Portrait Gallery, London

Yet in its more prosaic way, the massive belligerent head of Ben Jonson, painted probably by van Blyenberch about 1617–1620, has a more immediate, because less contrived, impact (Plate 61). A face at once brutal and subtle, burning and melancholic, the face of

a great lover and praiser of himself, a contemner and scorner of others, given rather to losse a friend, than a Jest, jealous of every word and action of those about him (especiallie after drink which is one of the Elements in which he liveth) a dissembler of ill parts which raigne in him, a bragger of some good that he wanteth, thinketh nothing well bot he himself, or some of his friends and Countrymen hath said or done . . . passionately kynde and angry, careless either to gaine or keep, Vindicative, but if he be well answered, at himself.[38]

It is the face of the author of *Volpone*, as of *The Alchemist*, as of 'Drink to me only with thine eyes'; the face of a man who 'heth consumed a whole night in lying looking to his great toe, about which hath seen tartars & turks Romans and Carthaginians fight in his imagination'.[39] Even the bruising suffered over three centuries by the paint that records his image seems not inappropriate.

In these cases, all men outstanding, not only in their generation, for the quality of their imagination, the sitter seems to burst the conventions of the art of the day. Van Blyenberch's head-and-shoulders of Jonson is an orthodox composition from which Jonson insists like a momentarily mild bull from too small a cattle-van. But gradually the technique and the scope of the painter's art develops. Daniel Mytens, precursor and to some extent the herald of Van Dyck, softens up the tight conventions of society portraiture, though his effects are gained by his skill and dignity in the handling of the whole composition, rather than by a noticeably much freer handling of the face.

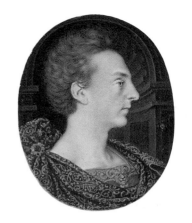

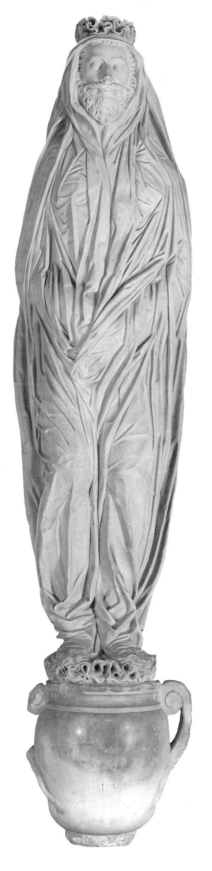

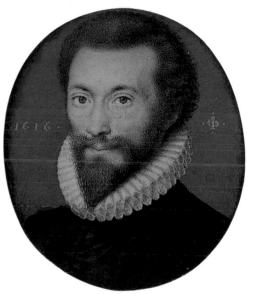

Plate 62
Henry, Prince of Wales (1594–1612) by Isaac
Oliver, *c*.1610–1611
Vellum, 5 × 4.1 ($2 × 1\frac{5}{8}$)
Fitzwilliam Museum, Cambridge

Plate 63
John Donne (1573–1631) by Isaac Oliver,
1616
Vellum, 4.4 × 3.6 ($1\frac{3}{4} × 1\frac{7}{8}$)
Royal Collection (by gracious permission of
Her Majesty The Queen)

Plate 64 *(left)*
Monument to John Donne (1573–1631) by
Nicholas Stone, 1631
Alabaster effigy, life-size
St Paul's Cathedral, London

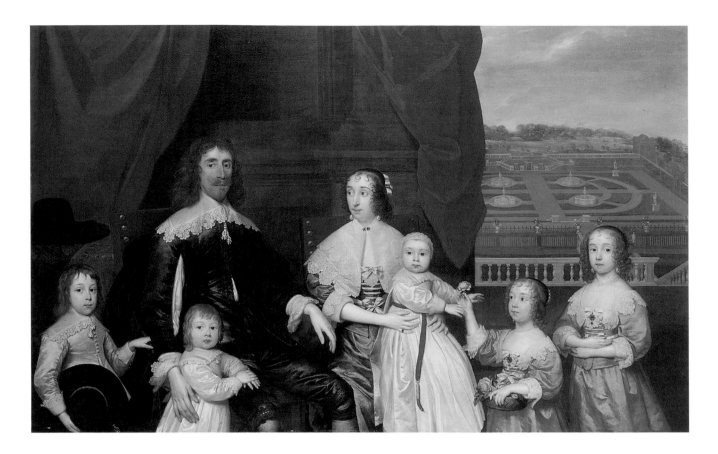

More significant is the work of Cornelius Johnson, who, after the rather wooden portraits of his earlier years, began in the late 1620s to harvest a rich crop of sitters in which all critics agree in finding a specifically English atmosphere of character (Plate 65). Johnson was not a great painter; he steered a demure course through the various distractions that beset the taker of portraits. His modesty was such that stronger personalities could invade and possess his own, and his paintings are sometimes all but indistinguishable from those by the purely Dutch Michiel van Miereveldt, and at other times from those by Mytens, while in his final English period, between 1632 and 1643, he can be no more than a muted echo of Van Dyck. Yet his work as a whole is quite distinctive. Most of his sitters give the impression of belonging to a well-to-do, well-mannered and unostentatious level of society.

Johnson worked for the court, but his clientele extended far wider than that, to the country squires; and, with rare exceptions, it is not as courtiers that his sitters appear. His characteristic design is a half-length, to the waist, the hands not showing, set against a plain background, the costume sober for the time, uncomplicated by draperies. The rhetoric in which both Mytens and Van Dyck, in their different ways, were masters, was foreign to him; he might ape it, but he could produce no original development of it. Glancing round his sitters, it is rather as

Plate 65
Arthur Capel, 1st Baron Capel of Hadham (1610?–1649) *and his family* by Cornelius Johnson, *c*.1641
Oil on canvas, 160 × 259.1 (63 × 102)
National Portrait Gallery, London

though one were at a luncheon-party of local gentry that Dorothy Osborne might have later written up. They are polite, their hands are underneath the table; they are reserved, sitting a little back behind the picture-surface, yet at ease, unself-conscious, inhabitants of a common culture in which decorum, the facts of life and also poetry all have their importance. They are formal, and yet they have that warm elusive intimacy that can be distilled from the felicitous interplay, by masters, of social conventions. This effect is that of the whole portrait; to the painting of the faces in particular he brought no new technique, but a sympathy for the individuality of the sitter perhaps more sensitive, on a life-size scale, than that of Isaac and Peter Oliver in the miniature.

Johnson is, from the point of view of the social historian, of great importance, for he records a new level of life. But for the ostentatious world of high fashion he was simply not enough. By 1620, a small but outstanding group at court had become conscious that England was backward in her design for living. The movement to leaven this provincialism was headed by the great connoisseur, patron and collector, Thomas Howard, Earl of Arundel (Plates 66 and 67); hard on his heels came first Henry, Prince of Wales, then his brother, later Charles I, and the Duke of Buckingham. All these men – apart perhaps from Buckingham – seem to have been extremely sensitive in their purely aesthetic reactions, but for all of them, though probably least in the cases of the two princes, the works of art that they collected with such far-ranging energy were also very much furniture for their own personal grandeur.

Arundel himself was one of the greatest and in some ways most unsympathetic snobs (as in his behaviour to Strafford) in British history, yet one who might seem almost to justify it, apart from his great learning and his generous patronage, sheerly by his physical projection of his character; 'Here comes', said the Earl of Carlisle, 'the Earl of Arundel in his plain stuff and trunk hose, and his beard in his teeth, that looks more like a Noble Man than any of us'. While reactionary in his attitude to costume (maintaining that the looser French fashions 'would bring Majesty into contempt') he was very progressive in his choice of the painters who portrayed him. One of Mytens' earliest portraits, about 1618, shows him with his statuary deployed behind him (Plate 67); he may have had a hand in Van Dyck's first, though largely unprofitable, visit to England in 1620 and was then painted by him; in the twenties he sat at least twice to Rubens (Plate 66), in the thirties at least twice to Van Dyck again.

By 1620 the Baroque movement was well established throughout the main continent of Europe, liquidating the entangled conventions of Mannerism with a rush of movement, melting the artificiality with a new naturalism. With Rubens' return to Antwerp from Italy in 1608, the portraiture of at least the Catholic Northern Courts had succumbed to the Baroque vision, which managed to convey, as no portraits had yet done, a sense of naturalistic illusion, of the breathing and lively presence, and at the same time still to exalt the person, superhuman, to

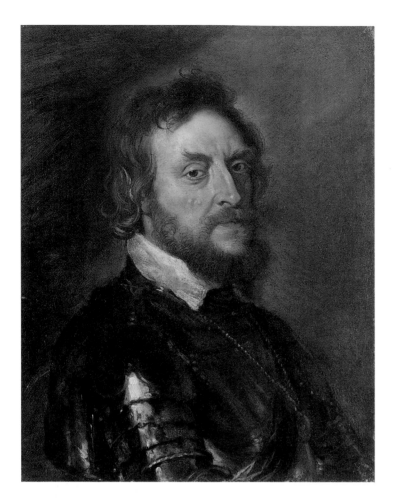

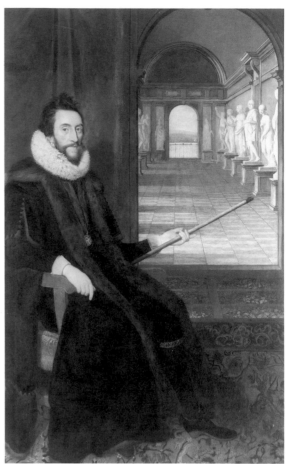

convey through him an ideal majesty no whit less impressive than that of the rigid effigies of Clouet or Sustermans.

It was to Rubens that Buckingham went in Paris in 1625: Rubens did not come to him. Although of course he did not travel specifically to sit to Rubens, he took good care not to miss the opportunity. Buckingham's earliest portrait, that of about 1616 by one of the most formal of the Jacobethan 'Curtain-Masters', probably William Larkin (Plate 68), a whole-length in which the Garter Robes seem too loud for a smart yet insipid mask, and Rubens' equestrian apotheosis of him (probably posthumous, about 1628) are a world apart. In Rubens' head-and-shoulders portrait, in the Pitti Palace, Florence, and in the drawing in the Albertina (Plate 69), there is at last discernible something of 'one of the handsomest men in Europe', of that 'enigma of the world' who flew, rather than grew, as Clarendon said, almost from gutter to Dukedom. Some may detect a certain brassiness, a vulgarity in the features, that has something of the 'flash boy'. Buckingham, as a collector of works of art, was certainly an accumulator for prestige purposes, in the early American millionaire tradition, rather than a connoisseur with the learning and discrimination that both Charles and Arundel commanded.

Plate 66 (left)
Thomas Howard, 2nd Earl of Arundel and Surrey (1586–1646) by Sir Peter Paul Rubens, 1629 Oil on canvas, 68.6 × 53.3 (27 × 21) National Portrait Gallery, London

Plate 67 (*facing page, right*)
Thomas Howard, 2nd Earl of Arundel and Surrey (1586–1646) by Daniel Mytens, *c.*1618
Oil on canvas, 214.7 × 133.4 (84½ × 52½)
National Portrait Gallery, London, on loan to Arundel Castle

Charles himself did not go to Rubens: Rubens came to Charles in England, in 1629 or 1630, not as a hired painter, but as an ambassador for Spain. Charles knighted him, and he painted Charles as St George (he also painted Arundel). It is symptomatic of an entirely new relationship between sitter and artist in this country; at last the artist is recognized, if only by a small coterie, as an aristocrat – at least of the aristocracy of genius. It is also in its way symptomatic of the unreality of that small coterie to whom the arts meant so much; Charles was not, with a Baroque flourish of sword and of shining armour, to conquer the dragon; of Rubens' other two English patrons, Buckingham was already dead from an assassin's knife, and Arundel was to die in voluntary exile during the Civil Wars, in 1646.

Rubens himself would not be confined in England, and it was only in 1632 that the court managed to attract a satisfactory substitute, an artist also of major stature and former colleague of Rubens, an artist whose hand is often discernible, even after three and a half centuries, in portraiture today: Anthony van Dyck.[40]

Sartorially, it was as though England had been loosening up for the event for years. Men's clothes, especially breeches, had swollen to their elephantine climax under James I, but had been softening since before his death in 1625; the hair worn

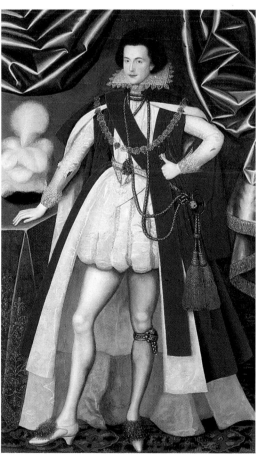

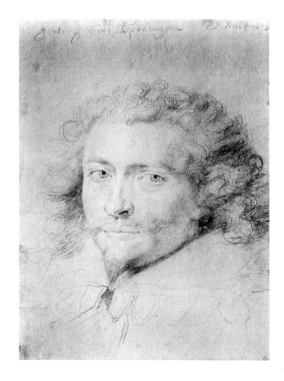

Plate 68
George Villiers, 1st Duke of Buckingham (1592–1628) attributed to William Larkin, *c.*1616
Oil on canvas, 205.7 × 119.4 (81 × 47)
National Portrait Gallery, London

Plate 69
George Villiers, 1st Duke of Buckingham (1592–1628) by Sir Peter Paul Rubens, 1625
Black, red and white chalk, 38.3 × 26.6 (15 × 10½)
Fonds Albertina, Vienna

comparatively close since the end of Elizabeth's reign, or at the most bobbed over the ears, began, with the young courtiers, to grow, long but asymmetric, into the trailing lovelock, sometimes with curls that suggest the agency of tongs, and always falling on the left shoulder, a mode already practised by Henry Wriothesley in the first decade of the century. And about the year Van Dyck arrived, 1632, the lace collar for ever associated with his name was finally adopted by the king in place of the falling ruff, although the so-called Van Dyck beard had been in fashion since 1610 at least. The full beard, however, became unfashionable except for older men, and in the thirties and onwards the *reductio ad absurdum* of the beard, a minute patch of hair immediately under the lower lip, was worn by many, always with a moustache. In women's clothes, the formidable cartwheel-topped skirts began to melt into softer falling lines, but the sleeves swelled into the twenties, until women's arms looked like the bulbous legs of Jacobean furniture; neck-wear varied from broad starched lace edgings cut usually low and square, to many variations of the obstinate ruff. After Buckingham's death in 1628, and Henrietta Maria's subsequent conciliation with Charles, the Queen's French taste began to exert its influence on costume, in a line of dress at once much simpler, much more elegant and surely much more comfortable.

The hair is worn low on the crown, with a fringe, and clustered thickly over the ears, also often with a lovelock (Plate 70); curls appear to have been imperative, and the Elizabethan preference for blondes has yielded considerably, no doubt in compliment to Henrietta Maria, to brunettes. The fantastic jewellery of the Elizabethans vanished almost completely, and a simple string of pearls, with often a pearl in the ear, seems to have been as *de rigueur* as it was on English twin-sets between the wars. Painting of the face with cosmetics appears to have fallen from favour, perhaps already in the reign of James, who, in spite of his own breeches, was harshly outspoken on what he considered immodest excesses in the appearance of his subjects. There is, however, evidence enough that it was still practised, perhaps with discretion at court, with the usual indiscretion amongst the women of professional sex, and not at all by the gentry and the middle-classes. The ideal of feminine beauty is plumper now, more roundly sensual; the colour scheme is no longer pink and white, but, as described by Robert Herrick, more lushly claret and cream:

> Black and rowling is her eye,
> Double chinn'd, and forehead high:
> Lips she has, all Rubie red
> Cheeks like Creame Enclaritèd:
> And a nose that is the grace
> And Proscenium of her face.[41]

('The face', as John Bulwer was to write in 1650, 'must needs be plain that wants a nose.')

Van Dyck arrived in England at the height of his powers, and was greeted as royally as Rubens, with a knighthood, a pension, a golden chain and the lease of a house at Blackfriars. Within a year he was fully established, incorporated even into the language; less than ten years later he was dead, and his activity actually in England was hardly more than eight years, but the impact he made was out of all proportion to the length of his stay. He was already a fully-formed painter, but still chameleon-like, as he had shown himself in Italy, in his sensitivity not only to local colour and atmosphere, but to national character, and it is fascinating to attempt to analyse how one knows that his English portraits are English, that they could have been painted nowhere else in the world.

With him he brought of course the whole panoply of the Continental Baroque style, and, willy-nilly, he swept the rigid upstanding Englishmen into its rhythm; the picture-space, that had been a tight box, or effigy-niche, opens on his strongly-stressed diagonals into infinity, as if burst open by a sudden wind, in which curtains and draperies leap into life. His portraits are conceived as a whole, not as figures with objects. This too he had done in Genoa and in Antwerp, but now his colour is keyed higher, silvery in tone, shimmering with an English light (Plate 73). And there is, too, against the Baroque movement of his paint, a still restraint. The figures themselves do not move, but are caught as it were in an exquisite poise of balance. When he attempted to transfer something of the sweetly-aspiring saintliness of his Genoese religious manner on to his English sitters, the result tends to the ludicrous; he did it rarely, but the spectacle of the stout Rachel, Countess of Southampton, on a cloud upborne with a glistening globe (as Fortune), is curious rather than convincing. But in most of his English portraits there is this certain reticence combined with a certain somehow disdainful elegance of posture (see Plate 70).

Van Dyck's name, like Holbein's, immediately conjures up in the mind a lost society. He is responsible for the visual glamour of the Cavaliers, though his picture answers most obviously to only a part of the truth. His sitters, with very few exceptions, come from the closed circle of the court, and he painted them as it were in masque-ing mood; in their very last, most exaggerated clothes, sometimes hopelessly involved, for practical purposes, with drapery, at other times as shepherds or shepherdesses in an unlikely Arcadia, as warriors in armour already obsolescent.

Yet behind the make-believe, generations now have sensed something more, a melancholy, a bitter-sweet vernal acknowledgement of transience such as that that Herrick sang. It may be that one exaggerates Van Dyck's melancholic temper in foreknowledge of the doom that was soon to overtake the society that he painted, but the strength of the myth that he created remains almost untouched in the popular imagination by the realistic probings of modern scientific historians. The myth focuses of course on one man: Charles I.[42]

Charles' appearance can be plotted almost year by year from when he was eight

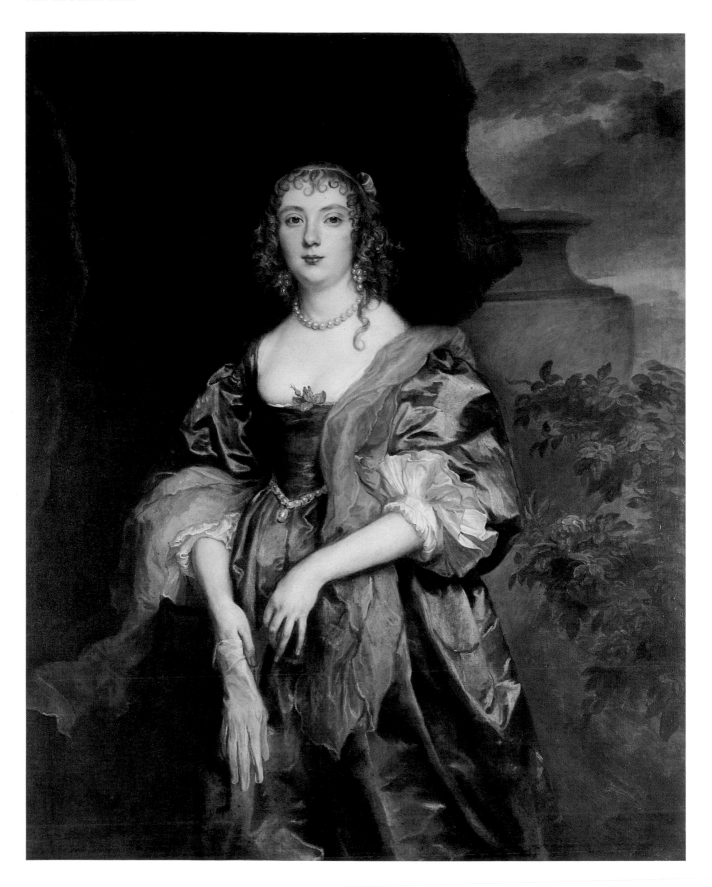

Plate 70 (*facing page*)
*Lady Anne Carr,
Countess of Bedford*
(1615–1684) by Sir
Anthony van Dyck,
*c.*1635
Oil on canvas,
136.2 × 109.9
(53⅜ × 43¼)
National Trust,
Petworth House

until he was forty-two; only four portraits of any significance are known from the last war-harassed seven years of his life. The earliest likeness of him extant is a tiny miniature by Hilliard of about 1608–1609, in the full Elizabethan tradition (Plate 71); it shows an expressionless boy's face, the hair brushed up into a quiff, with a tall, bulging forehead. A medical diagnosis of this image has suggested rickets,[43] and certainly Charles was an awkward boy, weak in the legs and with an impediment in his speech. The Hilliard is rather characterless, and portraits of Charles at this period (Plate 72), and indeed until as late as 1616, tend to be confused with those of his brother Henry, in whose shadow his first twelve years were so palely and obscurely drawn out.

This image gradually takes on a more characteristic shape, most markedly in Isaac Oliver's miniature of 1614, and then in the National Portrait Gallery whole-

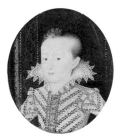

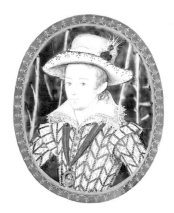

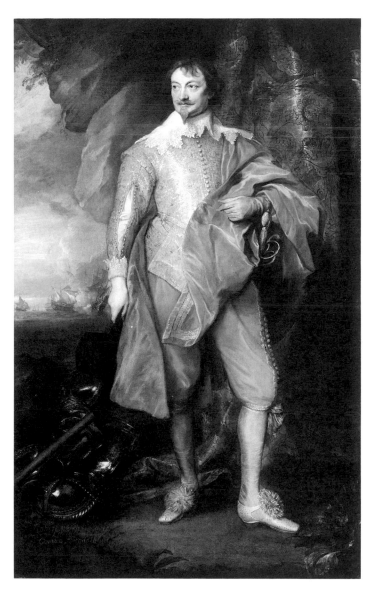

Plate 71
Charles I when Duke of York (1600–1649)
by Nicholas Hilliard, *c.*1608–1609
Vellum, 3.3 × 2.7 (1¼ × 1⅛)
Victoria & Albert Museum, London

Plate 72
Charles I when Duke of York(?) (1600–1649)
by Nicholas Hilliard, *c.*1613
Vellum, 5.1 × 4.1 (2 × 1⅝)
Victoria & Albert Museum, London

Plate 73 (*right*)
Robert Rich, 2nd Earl of Warwick (1587–1658)
by Sir Anthony van Dyck, 1634
Oil on canvas, 213.4 × 128 (84 × 50⅜)
Metropolitan Museum of Art, New York,
The Jules Bache Collection

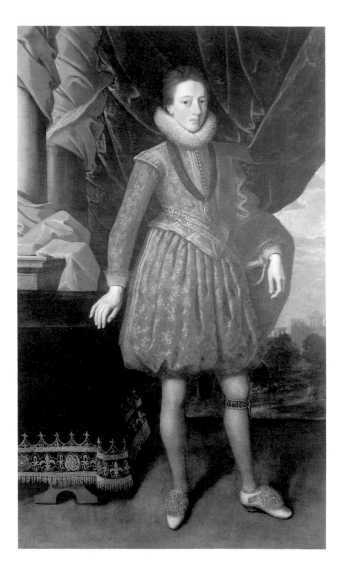

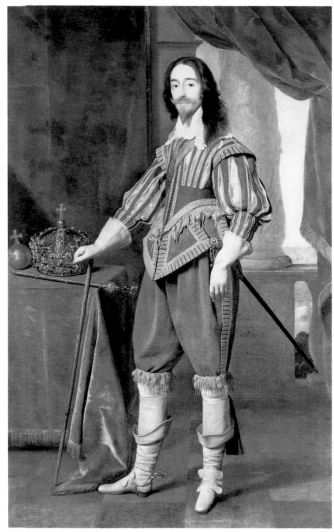

length probably by Van Blyenberch (Plate 74). It is, however, only about 1620 that the face we know from Van Dyck begins to cohere, in a series of portraits by Mytens. First the moustache appears; then, about the time of his accession, the beard, at first wispy, then consolidated into a rather Dutch pointed sobriety. In his face so far there is dignity and decorum, but nothing discernible as melancholy, and it is indeed extremely hard to state wherein lies the melancholy of Van Dyck's interpretation. The face of the man in his thirties has by now shed its puppy fat, and set, a little long, heavy-lidded; the love-lock falls elegantly on to his left shoulder, a little distrait; the beard has its crisp individuality (Plate 75).

The melancholy seems a matter of overtones; and yet was not Bernini, according to a story of very respectable antiquity, profoundly moved by the doom written in those features, though twelve years had yet to run before Charles went to the scaffold? But Bernini's own interpretation (to judge from an engraving believed to

Plate 74 (*facing page, left*)
Charles I (1600–1649) attributed to Abraham van Blyenberch,
*c.*1617–1620. Oil on canvas, 200.7 × 115.6 (79 × 45½)
National Portrait Gallery, London

Plate 75 (*facing page, right*)
Charles I (1600–1649) by Daniel Mytens, 1631. Oil on canvas,
215.9 × 134.6 (85 × 53). National Portrait Gallery, London

Plate 76 (*below*)
Charles I (1600–1649) by Hubert Le Sueur, 1633 (detail)
Bronze, over life-size. Whitehall, London

Plate 77 (*above right*)
Charles I (1600–1649) by John Hoskins, *c.*1642
Vellum, 7.6 × 6.4 (3 × 2½). Royal Collection (by gracious
permission of Her Majesty The Queen)

Plate 78 (*below right*)
Charles I at his Trial (1600–1649) by Edward Bower, 1648
Oil on canvas, 131.1 × 98.7 (51⅜ × 37⅞). Royal Collection (by gracious
permission of Her Majesty The Queen)

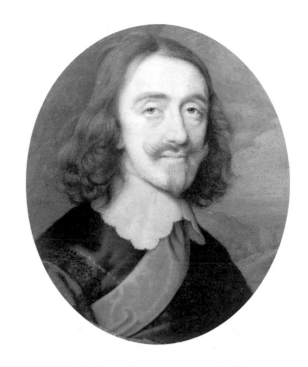

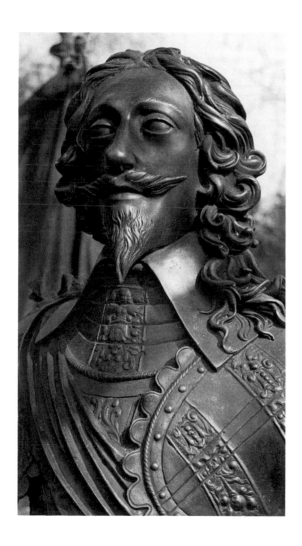

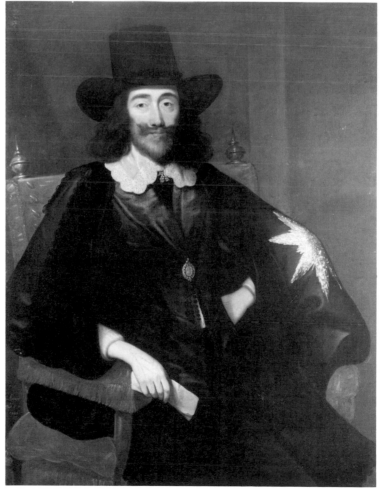

be based on the long-lost marble), carved from Van Dyck's triple portrait (Plate 55) without any firsthand knowledge of the sitter, seems to me to project a typically Bernini robustness, almost swash-buckling, on to Charles. Charles' essential character seems to evade all questions, not only those of the historians who return again and again to it, but also those of his contemporaries, two of them men of genius, who tried to find it in his face. Le Sueur's version of Charles, the famous equestrian portrait at Whitehall (Plate 76), is, as Dame Veronica Wedgwood has pointed out elsewhere, almost jaunty if you consider it with an honest eye; yet it inspired Lionel Johnson to write a poem scarcely less well known than the statue itself: 'Never was face so stern with sweet austerity'.[44] But many people will still agree with Northcote, who early last century admired Van Dyck's head of Charles so much: 'it might', he said, 'almost serve as model to paint the Saviour from.' Van Dyck seems to have painted Charles the Martyr long before the event.

Moreover, it is certainly Van Dyck's view of him that persists in the mind's eye; the interpretations of Mytens in the twenties (even though he sometimes showed Charles with eyes nearer to brown than to light grey) are respectable. So too are those of Hoskins in around 1642 (Plate 77) and of Lely in 1647, showing Charles with a lip-tuft instead of a beard. Finally, at his trial, the beard spread rather roughly over his jawbone and lower cheeks, and so he was painted by Edward Bower (Plate 78). Yet an early eighteenth century engraver, J. Simon, when he reproduced Bower's painting, tidied and trimmed the beard back to the canon sanctified by Van Dyck.

It is, of course, Van Dyck's head that inspires all the nineteenth-century representations of the king; it was also to a Van Dyck of Charles that Madame Dubarry pointed when lecturing Louis XV on the probable consequences of his behaviour whenever he 'seemed inclined to listen to the suggestions of his natural goodness of heart' and act with clemency towards his subjects. Van Dyck succeeded, of course, in concealing the infirmity of the king's legs, and, by introducing no factors that might give a scale of comparison, his small stature. But others did that too; it was not difficult. Charles has been estimated to have been about 5 feet 4 inches in height, but the directions to Le Sueur for his equestrian statue were to make a 'Horsse in Brasse bigger than a greate Horsse by a foot, and the figure of his Maj. King Charles proportionable full six foot'. What then did Van Dyck do for Charles that no other artist could do?

He excelled in the first place by sheer quantity. It is impossible to estimate precisely how many sets of sittings Charles gave him between 1632 and 1641; not more than ten, and perhaps considerably less. But from that meagre contact Van Dyck embroidered the theme, re-duplicating his variations in the shadow-factory of his studio; he painted Charles as the paternal monarch amidst his family, he painted him with his horse in a landscape as the country landowner (Plate 79); in armour in many variants, some heroically equestrian; he painted him in full coronation regalia and as a Knight of the Garter, and for Bernini he painted him three in one.

He excelled again in sheer quality; the construction and design of his portraits are professionally magnificent, even though he had not, particularly in his groups of more than two, the organic surety of composition of his master, Rubens, and this soundness of structure tells even in the countless copies whence the finer subtleties have evaporated. There is an old story that Rubens encouraged Van Dyck in portrait-painting because he feared his abilities in a wider field, but it is more probable that he recognized in Van Dyck what is perhaps the specific quality of a great portrait-painter, the ability to preserve the individuality of a sitter and yet at the same time to enhance it, by absorbing it into a grand pictorial design. It is a quality that generally implies a weakness in its owner, a certain lack of essential urgency, as though the painter needed the extraneous response and opposition of his subject to impel him; in Rubens himself it was drowned in his own strength, to which too the individuality of his sitters succumbs.

In the midst of the parade and pomp of the most grandiloquent portrait by Van Dyck, there remains a hard core, an individual human face, observed and recorded with the most scrupulous and subtle skill. The faces, in the liquid cascades, silks and satins of the women's clothes or above the peacock male foppery of the men, are often outshone, withdrawn behind the fashionable mask, a smooth oval; but, if isolated, almost all the faces that Van Dyck painted are miracles of sensitive apprehension. In skill he had no rival in England, and it was the skill that dazzled the majority of his sitters, unlearned in aesthetics; the same magic, illusionism, that has enchanted the public since Apelles. His sitters found themselves, their spit and living image, but somehow a little larger than life, and more glamorous.

Whether he positively flattered, and if so, how, remains largely open to speculation. In Charles' case there are two portraits that may indicate a hint of the answer; these are not by Van Dyck himself, but by the medallist Nicholas Briot. One medal was struck in 1630, the year before Van Dyck arrived; the other in 1639, when Van Dyck's reign was all but over. The medals are by the same artist (in this case a Frenchman) of the same man; in ten years, between thirty and forty, a man may change, but the difference in this case postulates an impossible change of bone-structure: the physical proportions have altered, the face is longer. No one can say whether Briot, in his second medal, was seeing through Van Dyck's eyes, but the image certainly corresponds very nearly to the Van Dyck image of Charles; it may be that the characteristic effect of his style on the English face was a lengthening, and a long face is proverbially the face of melancholy.

A long face can be found again and again in Van Dyck's male portraits of the Caroline court; his men tend to the indifferent proud in expression, heavy-lidded, with long noses somewhat equine, aloof and perhaps somehow a little blind, if only to the extent of an utter unconcern for defeat (Plate 80). Generalized, it is a cast of feature that is repeated in Lely's and in Kneller's sitters, and right through to Reynolds and Gainsborough. One might suggest that Van Dyck invented the English gentleman, but such generalizations can always be

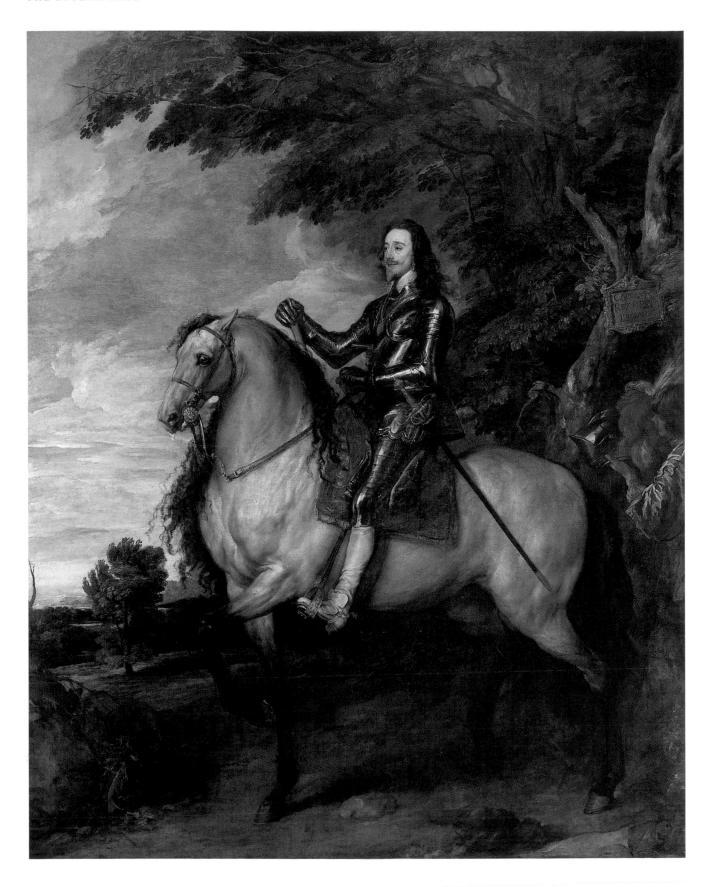

contradicted by the subtle individuality of the faces that he painted, and sometimes, as in his astonishing portraits of Strafford, 'Black Tom', by the eruption of titanic character.

The convention of manners is expressed in the bearing rather than in the face, but it is marvellous how Van Dyck can marry the convention to the most unlikely face without the face being swamped. His Archbishop Laud, for example (Plate 81), the Anglican prelate at his most worldly, a little stout perhaps, but inhabiting his gracious voluminous lawn rochet with an aristocratic poise; and yet, once one's eye has been caught by Simonds d'Ewes' maliciously concise account of Laud – 'a little, low, red-faced man, of mean parentage' – one questions Van Dyck's version, only to

Plate 80 (right)
Lord John Stuart
(1621–1644) *with his brother Lord Bernard Stuart, later Earl of Lichfield*
(1623?–1645) by Sir Anthony van Dyck
Oil on canvas,
237.5 × 146.1 (93½ × 57½)
National Gallery,
London

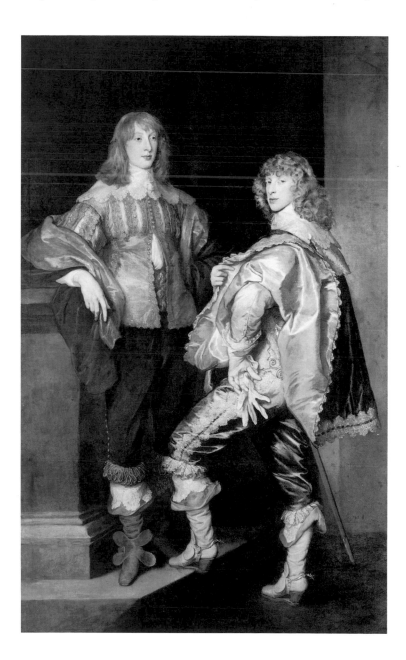

Plate 79 (*facing page*)
Equestrian portrait of Charles I (1600–1649) by Sir Anthony van Dyck, *c.*1637
Oil on canvas,
367 × 292.1 (144½ × 115)
National Gallery,
London

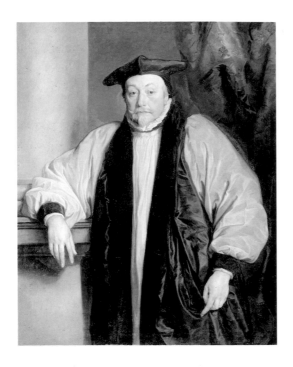

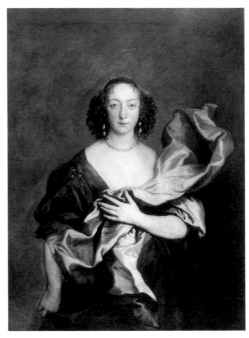

Plate 81 (*far left*)
*William Laud,
Archbishop of
Canterbury*
(1573–1645) by Sir
Anthony van Dyck,
c.1638
Oil on canvas,
120.5 × 96 (47½ × 37⅞)
Fitzwilliam Museum,
Cambridge

Plate 82 (*left*)
*Elizabeth Brydges,
Countess of Castlehaven*
(died 1679) by Sir
Anthony van Dyck,
c.1636–1637
Oil on canvas,
127 × 101.6 (50 × 40)
The Earl of
Pembroke, Wilton

find that there is nothing in the face that contradicts Simonds d'Ewes, though he was a hostile witness.

With women, perhaps, he flattered more blatantly; Mytens' sober version of Henrietta Maria is quite incompatible with Van Dyck's, and the dismay of Henrietta's niece, when she saw her aunt in the flesh for the first time, after knowing her only through Van Dyck's portraits, is well known: she found the teeth stuck out like defence-works. But the evidence is contradictory; here is the Countess of Sussex, very mortified on seeing her own portrait (now, unfortunately, lost) for the first time:

very ill-favourede, makes me quite out of love with myselfe, the face is so bige and so fate that it pleases me not at all. It lokes lyke on[e] of the windes puffinge – but [she adds ruefully] truly I think tis lyke the originale.[45]

The portrait of Lady Castlehaven is probably as good evidence of Van Dyck's integrity as any, her face conforming to the smooth fashionable oval outline, yet distinguished from all other faces with the most troubling skill (Plate 82). She is clearly a woman of rank, fashion and beauty. She is also recorded in history as a woman of passion sometimes amounting to promiscuity, who as a child-bride had committed adultery with her adulterous mother's lover, and later in her career passed a night in 'the Cage' for an unknown misdemeanour. Van Dyck has not labelled her face with these singular achievements, but he has left us the living image of a character vivid enough to contain them, and much more, even the spectator's charity.

Van Dyck's picture, however, is of the Caroline court, and he painted most of the men who, a year after his death, were to form the vanguard of the Royalist cause in action. The opposing faction had no social ceremonial to match the court's; for a courtier, one may guess, to sit to Van Dyck was something that one did, like going to Ascot. Outside the court, to have one's portrait painted was far more haphazard, and the quality of the portraiture far inferior.

Van Dyck had no rival. Few people fundamentally out of sympathy with Charles were painted by Van Dyck: the Earl of Warwick perhaps was one, and also a few of those whose loyalties were later to prove ambivalent, men like George Goring and the Earl of Holland (who began an ardent Royalist, toyed and clinched with the Parliament, but was at last executed as a Royalist) – but none of the great names of the Parliamentary cause were personified by Van Dyck. Of Sir John Eliot there is but a sickly ghost-like reflection, of John Hampden no certain portrait at all survives, and hardly anything even of Essex. John Pym and Sir Thomas Fairfax were painted by a former assistant of Van Dyck's, Edward Bower, but the only considerable portrait Bower ever painted was of Charles I at his trial, and the virtues of that portrait arise from the drama of the occasion, not from the intrinsic merit of a work of art (see Plate 78).

The body of professional painters serving the public at large was of mediocre ability, sometimes thrusting their clients, gawky as rustics, into Van Dyckian postures, sometimes, with a more modest and often charming naïveté, content to record their heads and shoulders frankly and unassumingly, as often did Cornelius Johnson, until he withdrew from the noise of war to Holland in 1643. It is in his portraits that there can be sensed that steady placid continuity of life: they are family-portraits, dining-room portraits, whereas the great set-pieces of Van Dyck demand the setting of the state-room, as, *in excelsis*, in Inigo Jones' great double-cube room at Wilton. Many of Johnson's portraits have now lost their names; most of them were of people not in the centre of the stage, unused to limelight, content with local and domestic virtues; yet some of them no doubt were the 'village Hampdens' of Gray's 'Elegy'. John Milton sat to an unknown painter, working much in the manner of Cornelius Johnson, a portrait containing that immense sonorous genius almost primly within an utterly unremarkable surface presentation (Plate 83).[46] He might have sat to Van Dyck, but it is somehow unthinkable; he might, on the other hand, have sat to Poussin.

To Van Dyck at court succeeded William Dobson, an English painter.[47] His reign lasted only four years until his premature death in 1646, when only thirty-six years old. His beginnings are mysterious, and still to be uncovered; hardly anything certain from his hand is known before 1642, but during the four years that he was active in London and at Oxford he recorded a picture of the Caroline court essentially different from that of Van Dyck. He is the painter not of the peacetime court, but of the embattled Royalists, of the Cavaliers.

It is, to generalize very broadly, as though Van Dyck painted his sitters as members of the Dramatic Society, while Dobson showed them (sometimes the same sitters as Van Dyck's) as members of the Rugby Club. He was a painter of great technical ability, but coarser and often clumsier in his handling than Van Dyck, with a broken richness of texture that is barbaric in comparison. He worked closer to his sitter than Van Dyck, so that his people are more burly, sometimes seeming a little larger than life; yet they are of life in a way that Van Dyck's never are, high in colour, wearing their flesh, at once gross and enjoyable, and, alas, sad, with the same parade as their turbulent satin and lace. Their characteristic weapons are not swords, but firearms (a great rarity in Van Dyck). They will go into battle; it will be no stage-skirmish, and in it they will sweat, and kill or be killed. Yet they are often also men of culture and of breeding, sometimes insisted upon by the introduction of a classical bust or bas-relief. The portrait of John, 1st Lord Byron (Plate 84), a more purely martial portrait, dangerous, even a little Satanic with his scar, the eyes very slightly hooded; a face proclaiming, better than could medals, the man of action, who fought in the Low Countries, and at Powick Bridge, Edgehill, Roundway Down, Newbury and Marston Moor.

Many of the Cavaliers seem to have found time between battles to sit to Dobson; the Parliamentarians seem to have thought, possibly with reason, that they had better things to do. Also they had no painter to hand of the calibre of Dobson. Only when they had consolidated their position, and had become the government, did they have to face the problem of official portraiture.

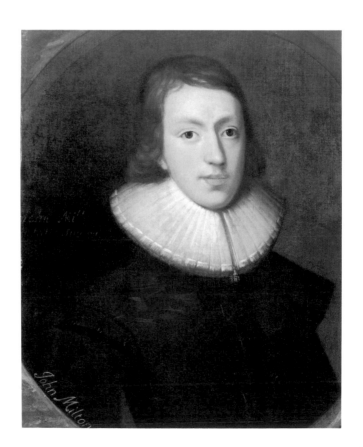

Plate 83
John Milton (The Onslow Portrait)
(1608–1674) by an unknown artist, *c.*1629
Oil on canvas,
59.7 × 48.3 (23½ × 19)
National Portrait Gallery, London

Plate 84
*John, 1st Baron Byron
of Rochdale* (died
1652) by William
Dobson, *c.*1643
Oil on canvas,
142 × 120 (55¾ × 47)
The University of
Manchester (Tabley
House)

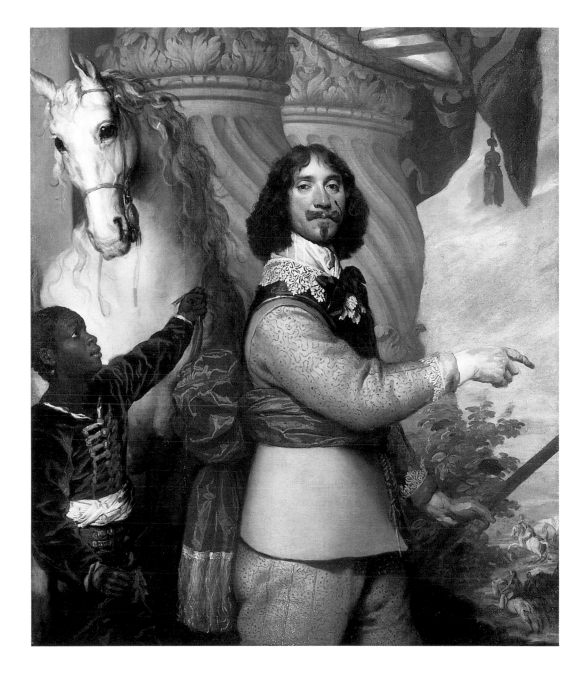

Portraits were wanted, not only by their loyal followers but by foreign potentates. Though it would be disingenuously naïve to expect barbarian portraits of Roundheads, the extent to which the new rulers succumbed to tradition is startling, and its manner macabre. For their appointed painter was Van Dyck, the chosen painter of the apotheosis of autocratic monarchy. They did not, of course, resurrect him from St Paul's, but they employed to take their portraits one Robert Walker, who openly avowed that as far as he could find Van Dyck had been the greatest master of poses, and that if he could find a better one, he would borrow from him.

Walker was not merely influenced by Van Dyck; he painted Van Dyck's portraits all over again, with different heads. On the body of Sir Edmund Verney, who had died heroically at Edgehill defending the royal standard, was set now Oliver Cromwell's head, now Ireton's, now Haselrigg's. On to the body of the Royalist High Admiral, Percy (Plate 85), went the head of the Parliamentary naval commander, Richard Deane (Plate 86). Other artists besides Walker did the same trick. Lombart's engraving of Van Dyck's equestrian portrait of Charles I (Royal Collection) was altered mercilessly and on the decapitated shoulders grew Cromwell's head; while Van Dyck's body of the Duke of Hamilton (beheaded in 1649) also was found suitable for Cromwell.

Walker unfortunately lacked the skill of Van Dyck when it came to recording the

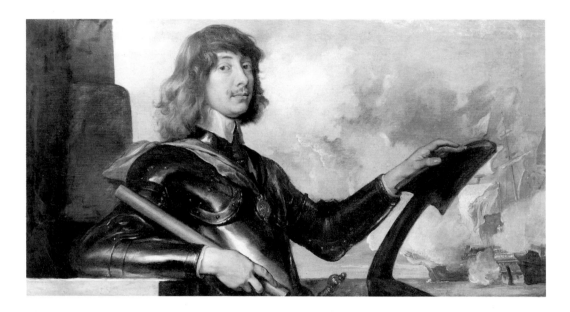

Plate 85 (above)
Algernon Percy, 10th Earl of Northumberland
(1602–1668) by Sir Anthony van Dyck, c.1636
Oil on canvas, 72.7 × 136.5
($23\frac{5}{8} \times 53\frac{3}{4}$)
The Duke of Northumberland

Plate 86 (right)
Richard Deane
(1610–1653) by Robert Walker, 1653
Oil on canvas, 94 × 127 (37 × 50)
National Maritime Museum, Greenwich

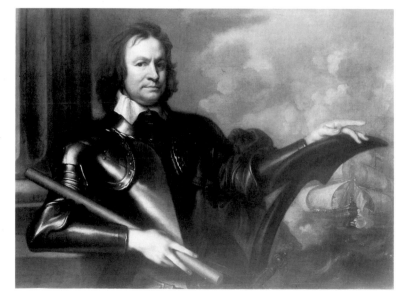

features; he was a smooth and dull painter. I have already lingered at some length on the face of Charles I; it is as well to consider in detail the face of his great antagonist, not only for balance but because here is the face of a man who is of the essence of the English genius.[48] One of the anecdotes let in to enliven most textbooks of English history is that of Cromwell's instructions to his painter:

Mr. Lilly I desire you would use all your skill to paint my picture truly like me & not flatter me at all but [pointing to his own face] remark all these ruffness, pimples, warts & everything as you see me; otherwise I never will pay a farthing for it.

It is a story of compelling antiquity, said to have been told by the second Duke of Buckingham to Captain Wind and by him to George Vertue, who wrote it down about 1720.[49]

It was certainly not said by Cromwell to Walker (as is sometimes wrongly stated), to judge by the warts, which Walker glossed over; but was it said to 'Lilly', Sir Peter Lely? Lely painted Cromwell (Plate 87), and there are many copies of his portrait of him, but there is also a very similar portrait on a miniature scale by Samuel Cooper (Plate 88). Cooper's and Lely's portraits are so close that one must depend on the other; no two painters could arrive at so identical an image from different sittings from the life; that it is Cooper's miniature that is the original is, I think, reasonably proved by a simple count of warts. Lely has left one out, in the corner of Cromwell's right eye by his nose, or, if not left it out, glossed it into a polite bump.

There are of course other images of Cromwell; the idealized profiles by Abraham Simon on the coinage constitute one of the finest achievements in English medallic art, while at the other extreme there are a whole series of death-masks (Plate 89), and one mask, at Chequers Court, said to be modelled on the life. The death-masks are an exact transfer of the flesh, yet personally I find they leave the mind unstirred, as any survey of the locked stable after the horse has fled; even the life-mask will not kindle – it has none of the sensitive magic that certain later life-masks can communicate, such as those of William Blake or John Keats. Practically, on technical grounds, there is no reason to challenge its authenticity, though its very identification as of Cromwell has been challenged; I object to it on psychological grounds – I find it impossible to imagine Cromwell having his face daubed with pomatum, and covered with wet plaster, possibly even with straws stuck up his nostrils. (The process is described by Samuel Pepys and others.)

It is to Cooper's portrait that I return again and again, and it is an image in the light of which all accounts of Cromwell should be read. It ennobles Warwick's account of him speaking in Parliament, in a plain ill-cut cloth suit:

his linen plain and not very clean . . . a speck or two of blood upon his little band . . . his countenance swollen and reddish, his voice sharp and untunable and his eloquence full of fervour.[50]

It cancels the grudgingness in Clarendon's great assessment, and exposes Evelyn's description as peevish partisanship. Evelyn found in 'the Lines of his ambiguous and double Face . . . Characters of the greatest Dissimulation, Boldness, Cruelty, Ambition in every touch and stroak.'[51] And from it most of Carlyle's rhetoric falls away into silence. It is for me one of the most moving, one of the greatest of British portraits.

It should therefore follow, if one is to play that particular game, that Cooper is one of the greatest British portraitists. For me, this is so; indeed as a face-painter I would claim that he has no rival in Europe in the seventeenth century; this is not of course to set him above the great imaginative geniuses of the century, who included Rembrandt and Rubens, Vermeer and Poussin and Hals – and Velazquez. Cooper's masterpieces are not his 'finished' works, brilliant though many of them are, but that handful of studies from the life, painted a little larger than his normal miniature scale, and apparently retained by the painter as patterns from which he could produce replicas as and when required. One of the reasons why he is so under-rated, or perhaps rather so infrequently rated, is the difficulty of writing about him. 'In speaking of portraits', as Thackeray was to remark wryly, 'there is never much to say'.

One can point to the artist's fantastic manual skill, one can even demonstrate his habits of presenting his sitters, his forced lighting, his characteristic treatment of the eyelids, but the artist himself nevertheless remains unrevealed. The style is the man, the style is Rembrandt or Delacroix, Hilliard or Cosway, but with Cooper the style is the man he is portraying, and he annihilates himself in his sitter, in this still, yet almost breathing image. Nothing could be farther from the debased naturalistic illusionism of, for example, certain painters of the late nineteenth century, whose works, as you look at them, disintegrate into an inventory of detail. Behind Cromwell's warts (each casting its own private shadow, a shadow that could belong to no other wart) there lies again, as with Holbein, that sure summary of the essential volume and displacement of the head, though unlike Holbein, Cooper achieved this largely by the contrast of light and shade.

On 10 January 1662, Evelyn saw him setting about it:

being call'd into his Majesties Closet, when Mr Cooper (the rare limner) was crayoning of his face & head, to make the stamps by, for the new mill'd mony, now contriving, I had the honour to hold the Candle whilst it was doing; choosing to do this at night & by candle light, for the better finding out the shadows.[52]

This of course was a special case, a drawing (probably that now in the Royal Collection) (Plate 90) for a low relief, and Cooper may not always have forced the light to that extent when building up his portraits, but Thomas Gainsborough, as we shall see, used much the same technique in his oil portraits.

In the entranced, minute observation of surface phenomena that Cooper reveals in these unfinished studies, he was very much of his time; with just that

Plate 89 *(right)*
Oliver Cromwell (1599–1658) by an
unknown artist
Plaster cast of death-mask,
height 28.6 (11¼)
National Portrait Gallery, London

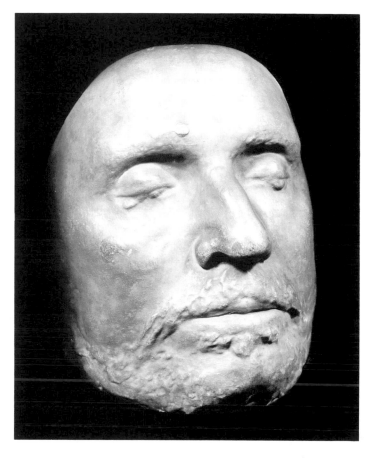

Plate 87 *(below)*
Oliver Cromwell (1599–1658)
by Sir Peter Lely, *c.*1654
Oil on canvas,
77.5 × 62.9 (30½ × 24¾)
Birmingham City Museums and
Art Gallery

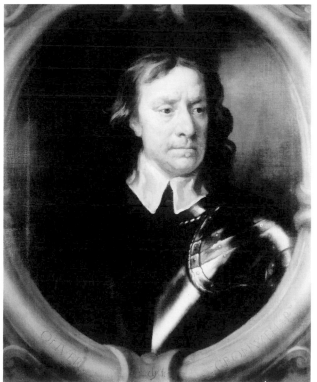

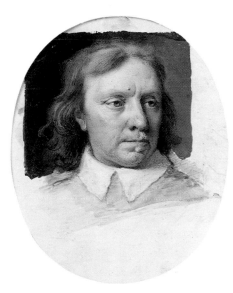

Plate 88
Oliver Cromwell (1599–1658) by Samuel
Cooper, *c.*1650
Vellum, 8 × 6.4 (3⅛ × 2½)
The Duke of Buccleuch and
Queensberry KT

scrupulousness and curiosity did the early fellows of the Royal Society record all strange departures from the norm in the physical world, 'warts and all'. The nearest parallel is John Aubrey,[53] for whom Cooper was 'the Prince of Limners'. Isolated examples of attempts at verbal physical characterization exist before Aubrey, but on nothing like such a scale, and whereas Cooper was restrained by his chosen medium to a study of the head and shoulders, Aubrey often tackled undismayed the whole-length portrait. In 1660 Aubrey persuaded Hobbes to sit to Cooper (Plate 91), and between Aubrey's description and Cooper's portrait one can still see Hobbes almost in the quick. Here is part of Aubrey's account:

In his youth unhealthy; of an ill yellowish complexion . . . he tooke colds, being wett in his feet (then were no hackney coaches to stand in the streetes), and trod both his shoes the same way. . . . From forty, or better, he grew healthier, and then he had a fresh, ruddy, complexion. . . . In his old age he was very bald (which claymed a veneration); yet within dore, he used to study, and sitt, bare-headed, and sayd he never tooke cold in his head, but that the greatest trouble was to keepe-off the flies from pitching on the baldness. His head was in compasse (I have the measure), and of a mallet-forme (approved by the physiologers).

His skin was soft and of that kind which my Lord Chancellor Bacon . . . calles a goose-skin, i.e. of a wide texture. *Face* not very great; ample forehead; whiskers yellowish-redish, which naturally turned up – which is a signe of a brisque witt, e.g. James Howell, Henry Jacob of Merton College. Belowe he was shaved close, except a little tip under his lip. Not but that nature could have afforded a venerable beard, but being normally naturally of a cheerfull and pleasant humour, he affected not at all austerity and gravity and to looke severe. He

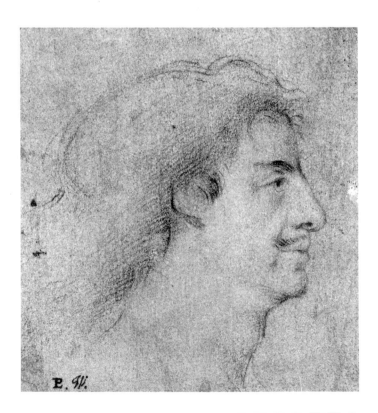

Plate 90
Charles II (1630–1685) by
Samuel Cooper, *c*.1662
Red and black chalk on
brown paper,
17.8 × 14 (6⅞ × 5½)
Royal Library, Windsor
Castle (by gracious
permission of Her Majesty
The Queen)

desired not the reputation of his wisdome to be taken from the cutt of his beard, but from his reason. He had a good eie, and that of a hazell colour, which was full of life and spirit, even to the last. When he was earnest in discourse, there shone (as it were) a bright live-coale within it. He had two kind of looks; when he laugh't, was witty, and in a merry humour, one could scarce see his eies; by and by, when he was serious and positive, he open'd his eies round (i.e. his eie-lids). He had midling eies, not very big, nor very little. He was six foote high, and something better, and went indifferently erect, or rather, considering his great age, very erect. .·. .[54]

Aubrey tends of course to get lost in recording the warts and to forget the all; in his accumulated accounts, such as that of Hobbes, he carries a confused but vivid impression as of a number of film-shots, uncdited. On other occasions, plumping his shots about his objective in a short salvo, he achieves extraordinary definition. Sir John Birkenhead of Cheshire:

He was exceedingly confident and witty, not very grateful to his benefactors, would lie damnably. He was of middling stature, great goggli eies, not of a sweet aspect.[55]

Or, simply, of Isaac Barrow:

He was a strong man but pale as the candle he studied by.[56]

For neither Aubrey nor Cooper were their studies from the life objects of art. Aubrey's notes served as raw material for Anthony Wood's biographical dictionary of Oxford men, and were by Wood subdued into more polite formulae, though even so they brought a libel action upon him. Cooper, too, when making up the saleable article from his studies, subdued them diminuendo into the prim gold oval of the locket. In the finished versions of the Cromwell portrait (of which several exist), much of the freshness has inevitably vanished from the handling, while the sitter's shoulders are encased in the regulation armour. If a completed version of the Hobbes ever turns up, it is a fairly safe bet that his shoulders will be wrapped in the regulation loose black cloak.

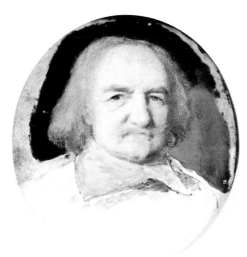

Plate 91
Thomas Hobbes (1588–1679) by Samuel Cooper, 1660
Vellum, 6.7 × 5.7 ($2\frac{5}{8} \times 2\frac{1}{4}$)
The Cleveland Museum of Art, Edward B. Greene Collection

Writing in 1641, Sir Kenelm Digby had compared life-size oil portraits with miniatures, saying that the former gave 'pictures so like as some people think them even the worse for it. The best faces are seldom satisfied with Van Dyck; whereas not the very worst even complained of Hoskins'. This is another tribute to Van Dyck's integrity in comparison with the prettifying performed by Hoskins (who was probably Cooper's first master) in his miniatures. By the time Cooper attained his maturity, the case was reversed; it is the miniaturist who now records every quirk and sally of the features, especially so in the case of his male sitters, but also to a remarkable pitch of honesty in the case of his women.

Cooper's rival in portraiture on a life-size scale was Peter Lely, whose career in England ran from about 1645 till his death in 1680; he was a most able painter, but his prime abilities lay in the composition of canvases sonorous in colour and rich in movement, and not in the recording and interpretation of his sitter's character.[57] The contrast between his and Cooper's portrait of Cromwell is a little unfair to him, if, as I have suggested, his is based on Cooper's, but it is instructive, showing how the individuality of his sitter's features is generalized by the broad movement of the painter's style.

There is also, clearly visible in this case, that lengthening of the head that is demonstrable in the Elizabethans as in Van Dyck and which is a common principle of most fashionable painters and illustrators, down to the fashion-illustrators of the

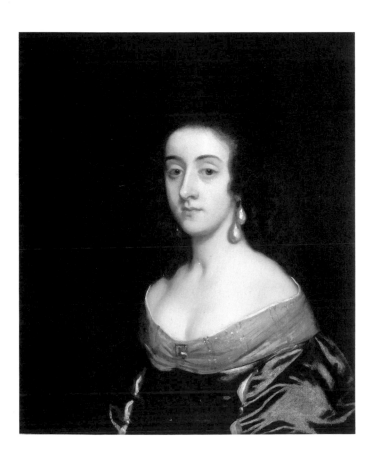

Plate 92
Dorothy Osborne, Lady Temple
(1627–1695) by Sir Peter
Lely, 1653
Oil on canvas,
76.5 × 63.2 (30⅛ × 24⅞)
Lady Pamela Hicks

glossy magazines of today. Lely had taken Van Dyck's place as the leading portrait-painter in England by the late forties, and in common with most practising portrait-painters, his style depended very heavily on Van Dyck. In his more modest head-and-shoulders portraits before the Restoration, however, he has very much his own style, which lies somewhere between that of Van Dyck and Cornelius Johnson, harsher, more blatant than Johnson, with a sometimes posed elegance that is nearer Van Dyck, but often honest and forthright enough. He did not have the social or political affiliations that confined Van Dyck to one circle of society, but was well content to paint Charles I, then Cromwell, and then Charles II, to design a frontispiece for Lovelace's *Lucasta*, or to paint the regicide Sir Harry Vane.

Dorothy Osborne, writing to her lover about her portraits, gives a good picture of the prevarications and hesitations that must have beset the making of most portraits then as now (Plate 92). In October 1653, she was

thinking of sending you my Picture till I could come my self, but a Picture is but dull company and that you need not, besyd's I cannot tell whither it bee very like mee or not, though tis the best I have ever had drawne for mee, and Mr Lilly will have it that hee never took more pain's to make a good one in his life, and that it was I think that spoiled it: he was condemned for makeing the first hee drew for mee a little worse than I, and in makeing this better hee has made it as unlike as tother. . . .

In June of the next year, 1654, she had apparently abandoned the Lelys as unsuitable, and was turning to Cooper:

I would have had [a picture] drawne since I cam, and consulted my glasse every morning when to begin, and to speak freely to you that are my friend, I could never find my face in a condition to admitt on't, & when I was not satisfied with it my selfe I had noe reason to hope that any body else should; but Ime afraid as you say that time will not mend it and therfore you shall have it as it is, as soone as Mr Cooper will vouchsafe to take the pain's to draw it for you. . . .[58]

Dorothy Osborne's comments make it clear that amongst the gentry of any standing it had become a normal part of living to have one's portrait taken, for one's friends or for one's family; the habit had not yet spread much wider, and amongst those who could afford some likeness of themselves, religious scruples would sometimes intervene. Henry Newcome, a modest and soul-searching minister, for long refused the request of his family that he should be painted; he consented at length for his children's sake, but was disturbed when the portrait arrived:

I was but too much taken with my own shadow when it came home; but then I thought, a man should study both to be blameless and eminently active, that presumes to leave a picture behind him. If it put in mind of evil or of no good done by him, it is to little or bad purpose.[59]

The extreme Puritan would have rejected the idea of a portrait out of hand as a mortal vanity.

V

Restoration Baroque

THE POPULAR impression of the transition from the Interregnum to the Restoration is perhaps much of an iron austerity yielding almost overnight to a gay ebullience, that might approach licence, but if so was still not unattractively human. In fact, in spite of Puritan restriction of such frivolities as the public performance of plays, the outward show of living had been brightening since about 1650. In May 1654, Evelyn wrote that 'the Women beegan to paint themselves, formerly a most ignominious thing, and used onely by prostitutes',[60] but Izaak Walton had commented on the use of 'Artificial Paint or Patches in which [women] so much pride themselves in this age', over a year before.

Such evidence is very difficult to interpret; patches never appear in portraits and the amount of paint probably depended on the social status of the painter. John Evelyn probably referred to the gentry; Samuel Pepys (rising middle-class) saw his wife wear black patches on 30 August 1660, and it was as late as 1667 that he wrote, not certainly of his wife: 'I find her painted which makes me loath her.' It is, however, fairly clear that a desire for a more vivid self-presentation was making itself apparent through the fifties; clothes were silkily voluminous in the skirt and loose in the sleeve; the dressing of the hair becomes steadily more elaborate.

For the men, the establishment in 1660 of a court interested in clothes did have an immediate and startling effect; the long hair was waved into curls and flowed more thickly over the shoulders; the simple turn-down collar broke into a flat foam of lace covering half the shoulders and chest, while the sober black and white colour-scheme of suit and shirt exploded in an exuberance of white linen, many-coloured suits, ribbons and lace (Plate 94). Both the exuberance and the cut of fashion were stimulated by Louis XIV's court in France, a dependency that some Englishmen felt to be regrettable; a positive revolt, Charles II's attempt to rationalize men's clothing in a relatively severe black and white scheme once again, fell flat when Louis XIV put the lackeys in his court into identical uniform.

The tone in women's dress was no longer set by the Queen, as it had been in the society of Charles I; it was set by the King's mistresses. No coherent record of the rapidly changing detail in everyday dress survives; that provided by the portrait painters is of dishabille, the sweet disorder that so attracted Herrick. The shoulders are bare and in the case of the King's mistresses sometimes to the waist; but the dishabille, which is of the late supper table if not of the boudoir, is set in other contexts, Olympian or Arcadian landscapes, and the sitter provided with a shepherdess's spud or Minerva's helmet. The attribute of Nell Gwyn is not an orange, but a lamb (Plate 95). Barbara Palmer, later Duchess of Cleveland, appears

Plate 93 (*facing page*)
Eleanor Needham, Lady Byron (1627–1663?)
by Sir Peter Lely,
*c.*1663–1664
Oil on canvas,
156.8 × 132.7
($62\frac{3}{4}$ × $52\frac{1}{4}$)
Royal Collection (by gracious permission of Her Majesty The Queen)

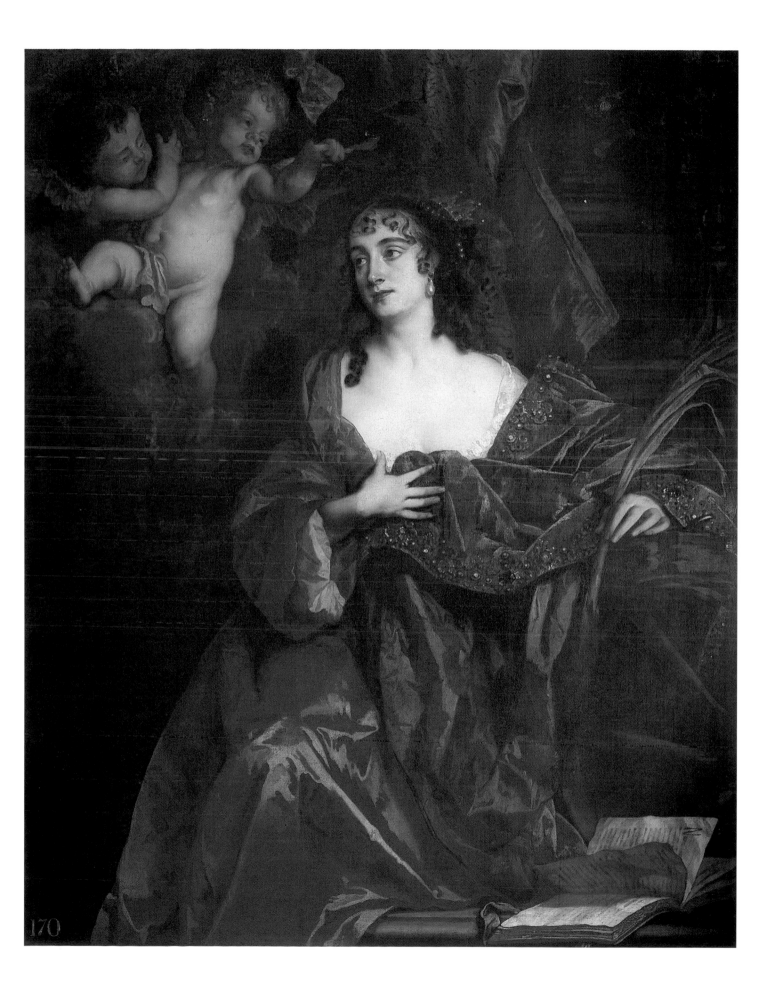

as an erotic and unconvincingly repentant Magdalene in a wilderness (Plate 114), as St Catherine or as her namesake St Barbara, as well as Minerva. Her most outrageous posture, together with one of her bastards by Charles II, was sent by her later on, according to a story put about by Horace Walpole, to another of her children who was in a convent in France. It was there placed gratefully over an altar, until the nuns discovered that it was not, in fact, a representation of the Madonna and Child (Plate 96).[61]

The tone of portrait-painting was set by the mistresses, thus disguised as goddesses or shepherdesses; following them, more reputable ladies were disguised as royal mistresses, only slightly more buttoned-up, and so on down the social scale, the designs set by the most fashionable painters, especially Lely, being repeated verbatim except for the head; so, on 15 February 1666, John Hayls began to paint Mrs Pepys 'in the posture we saw one of my Lady Peters, like a St Catharine'.[62]

The high priest of this transformation scene was Sir Peter Lely, of whom John Dryden wrote: 'he drew many graceful pictures, but few of them were like and this happen'd to him because he always studied himself more than those who sat to him.'[63] Pepys, when he saw the newly-painted Beauties which are now at Hampton

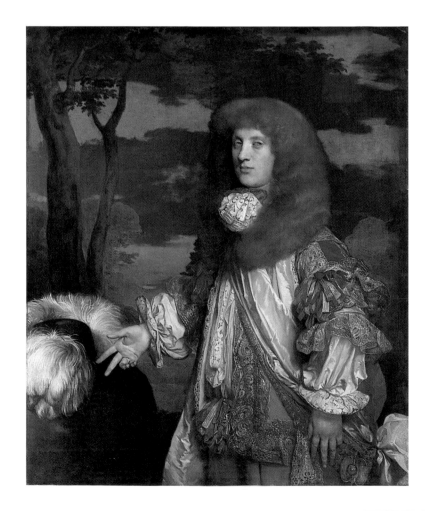

Plate 94
John Hay, 2nd Marquess of Tweeddale (1645–1713) by Gerard Soest, *c.*1665–1670
Oil on canvas, 126.4 × 106 (49¾ × 41¾)
Glasgow Museums and Art Galleries

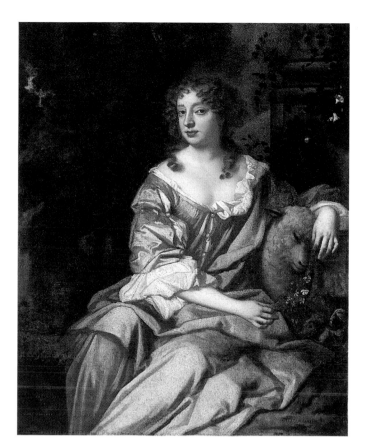

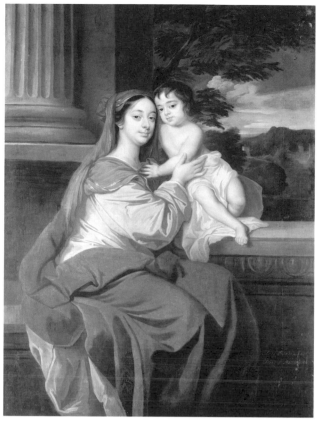

Plate 95 *(above left)*
Nell Gwyn
(1650–1687) from the
studio of Sir Peter
Lely, *c.*1675
Oil on canvas,
127 × 101.6 (50 × 40)
National Portrait
Gallery, London

Plate 96 *(above right)*
Barbara Villiers,
Duchess of Cleveland
(1641–1709) after Sir
Peter Lely,
*c.*1665–1675
Oil on canvas,
175.2 × 114.3
(69 × 45)
National Portrait
Gallery, London

Court, put it another way: 'very good, but not like'[64] (Plate 93). Lely indeed rarely makes a profound statement upon the individual character of his sitters, but he betrays himself profoundly in every picture he painted, and, because he was so happily in tune with the visual display of the court he was called upon to portray, he tells us much in general about that limited circle of society. He was an opulent man, and his pictures reflect a tactile and baroque opulence of paint, of stuffs – gorgeous undulations of fine lawn, of silks and satins, whether the vestments of a bishop, the robes of a Knight of the Garter or the undress of a woman – and of flesh, a rich, plump, drowsy flesh, well-filled as upholstery.

His style, that early on could catch something of a morning mystery, as in his Dorothy Osborne, is, after the Restoration, of the blatant and sonorous afternoon, immensely able, often openly vulgar. The vulgarity, in the works which are by him rather than by his assistants, is redeemed by the pleasure of the paint. It is often so Dutch in temper that some of his pictures of this period can even by trained eyes be confused with those of the Dutchmen Nicholas Maes or Jan Mytens. During his reign, which lasted from 1660 to 1680, almost the whole of Charles II's, there were of course other painters, but beside the miniaturist Cooper, only Michael Wright, and, very briefly, John Greenhill, preserved much individuality. The others aped Lely, but Wright in his dry way sometimes conveys, through a modest, slightly

99

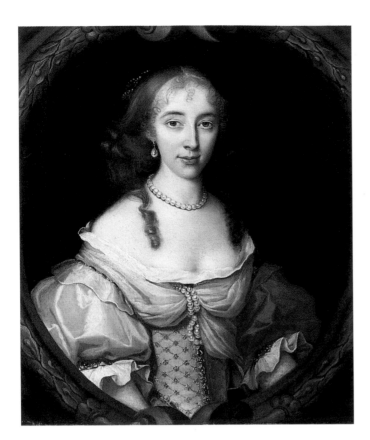

Plate 97
Magdalen Aston, Lady Burdett by
John Michael Wright, *c.*1665
Oil on canvas, 72 × 60
(29 × 24)
Nottingham Castle Museum
and Art Gallery

questioning reticence that recalls the characterizations of Cornelius Johnson, a person (Plate 97).

The fashionable face, examples of which can be found in the late work of Lely and his followers, especially of William Wissing, between about 1670 and 1685, is a horizontal one, a wide face. The tendency is visible in Lely's portraits of the sixties, but not so much in the faces, which still (even in the much-maligned Beauties at Hampton Court) have a fresh clarity. In his three-quarter lengths of women, generally seated, the horizontal or shallowly diagonal stresses are very marked, in the movement of the arms, the slow swathe of silks; in the seventies this pictorial rhythm captures the faces too, now treated much more broadly, often more coarsely, indistinguishable one from the other. The eyes bulge from long slots in the flesh, the hair is built out at each side of the head, first with a wire support for dangling ringlets, and later consolidated into a cluster of curls; mouths too are largely wide, full, with ripe and pouting underlip; the horizontal of the eyebrows is heavily marked, and the exaggerated top-lighting casts a shadow swagged about the chin, suggesting a second chin even when there is not one. Clearly, flesh is in fashion; the Elizabethan painters seem sometimes to be searching for 'the skull beneath the skin' – for Lely, the skin sufficed.

Men's faces, too, yielded to a fat Baroque curvature, and in their case to a Baroque not only of a painter's style; they capitulated to the wig. The wig is a factor for which a modern observer can hardly make too great an allowance; it first caught hold generally on English male heads in the early 1660s, and it survived until over a century and half later. It was not of course an unknown phenomenon; wigs were fashionable in Assyria and in Egypt; later, the German tribes ran a profitable business exporting blonde hair to Rome, and the early Church Fathers denounced periodically the wearing of false hair. Throughout history women seem to have toyed with false hair (already in 1615, Barnaby Rich was denouncing the 'lowsy commodity of periwigs' and 'monstrous mop-poles of hair').

But the masculine fashion for wigs at this particular period is generally said to have its roots in France, in the 1620s, at the court of Louis XIII. Generally, it is fashionable for at least some hair to be worn; not to wear hair at all is to flout convention, which replies woundingly by ridicule; and when a profusion of hair is accounted a virtue, it is splendid to have more hair than anyone else. It happened, at Louis XIII's court, that long hair was fashionable for those of high rank, but unfortunately the highest-ranking of them all, the king, began to lose his hair prematurely. To begin with, he probably only supplemented what remained to him, but gradually the complete wig was adopted, and the court, by courtesy, followed suit; the extraordinary fashion was launched upon its long career, and for more than a century Europeans cropped their hair in order to wear someone else's. They seem to have been known in England during the fifties, and even earlier the Cavalier lovelock perhaps often had to be artificially produced; in 1655 the fifteen-year-old Francis Throckmorton was buying curling-tongs for his wig in Cambridge, but it was not until after the Restoration of 1660 that Charles II set the royal seal of approval on the fashion by going into a wig himself. He was turning grey.

The gradual yielding to the fashion is chronicled by Pepys. In 1662 his wife, short of ringlets, had taken to 'a pair of perruques of hair, as the fashion now is',[65] in May 1663, he himself was toying at his barber's with two or three 'borders' and periwigs – 'yet I have no stomach for it, but that the pains of keeping my hair clean is so great'. It took him six months to succumb, until on 30 October he bought a wig, but still hesitated before appearing publicly in it. On 2 November he was encouraged by the Duke of York saying that he was going to wear one; on the third he took the decisive step, and had all his hair cut off – though, he admits, it went to his heart to part with it. On the fourth, apprehensively, he showed himself in public, wigged. To his relief there was no great comment, and even the severe scrutiny of the congregation at church next Sunday was not outraged.[66] In 1665, he had second thoughts, grew his hair, but then cut it all off again because he found 'the convenience of periwigs is so great'. The fashion was in.

Opposition seems to have been very slight; the Anglican Church adopted it, after a little pamphleteering (the Archbishop of Canterbury, Sumner, still put on his wig to marry the Princess Royal in 1858, sixty years after it was generally abandoned); the left wing of the Church, the puritanically-minded and the Quakers resisted longer. John Mulliner, Quaker, in a pamphlet of 1677, *Against Peri-wigs and Peri-wig*

Making and Playing on Instruments of Music among Christians, describes how he 'was troubled and took a wig and burned it', but by 1717 even the Quakers, while deploring 'extravagant' wigs, admitted those that could be described as 'modest, decent, or necessary'.

The chief arguments in favour of the wig were probably, as indicated by Pepys, those of cleanliness and, curiously, convenience. To wear short hair was unthinkable, as it immediately reduced a man visually to the rank of apprentice; facilities for washing were primitive, and the time expended on keeping long hair clean and groomed, before the wig, must have been considerable.

A man of any standing would have at least two wigs, so that one would always be ready. Other arguments put forward in its history on its behalf seem tendentious – the claim, for example, that a wig protected its wearer from colds: what happened in fact was that, on arriving home and removing the wig, one had to compensate for it by a turban-like cap or one did catch cold. To the eye it had considerable virtues; it lent maturity to the callow, and youth to the old, and it cancelled out baldness. Hogarth delighted to ridicule its excesses, but even he remarked that 'the full-bottomed wig, like the lion's mane, hath something noble in it and adds not only dignity but sagacity to the countenance'.[67]

Visually, it is of course just as much a manifestation of the Baroque style as is Lely's swirling paint, its sinuous and curling fall more satisfactorily linking an often obstinately rugged head to a posed and drapery-wreathed body than a mere neck. But for a full realization of its stylistic possibilities one generally has to seek out the work of foreign artists, as in the Frenchman, Honoré Pellé's bust of Charles II (Plate 98). It is curious how precisely, with its massive emphasis on the head, the career of the wig coincides with the age generally known as that of Reason: all the great men of reason wore it: Locke, Newton, Addison and Pope; Lord Burlington, even Hume, even Dr Johnson – and yet it is essentially such an unreasonable fashion, cutting off one's own hair in order to wear someone else's.

There were various sources for the hair of a wig; one could, like Pepys, have one's own hair shorn and made into a wig; some certainly had their wife's hair made into a wig for themselves (and she, presumably, got someone else's); there was the hair of the dead, only not in times of plague; there were the fertile heads of the children of the poor, and probably, as in ancient Rome, some importing of Teutonic blonde hair. (In France there was a minor economic crisis when Colbert discovered how much gold was leaving the country to pay for golden hair coming in from Germany.) One could appear fair in the morning, and dark in the evening, to taste, but red hair was not used, for red is the colour of Judas.

The reign of the wig in its classic – that is, full-bottomed – form lasted some seventy years, from the 1660s into the 1730s. The wig as first worn by Charles II was tightly-curled, flat on top, falling below the shoulders; thence it developed (with variations) in fullness, the curls loosening, in length, and in height, growing above the head for some inches, sometimes into twin horns; it attained its maximum about

Plate 98 (*right*)
Charles II
(1630–1685) by
Honoré Pellé, 1684
(detail)
Marble, over life-size
Victoria & Albert
Museum, London

Plate 99 (*far right*)
Charles II
(1630–1685) from the
studio of John
Michael Wright,
*c.*1660–1665
Oil on canvas,
126.4 × 101
(49¾ × 39¾)
National Portrait
Gallery, London

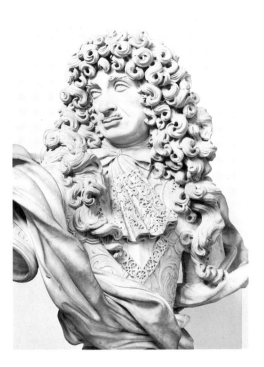
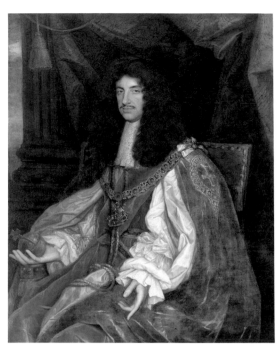

1700 and held it until about 1720 (Plate 99). Lavater, the great apostle of the lore of physiognomy, was later to admit to some indecision about hair: 'if it is not admitted to rank with the members of the human body, it is at least a part adherent to it.' In the heyday of the full-bottomed wig, hair, though adjacent rather than strictly adherent, is of such splendour that the human face that it is intended to frame becomes, if not impossible to see, nevertheless impossible to assess in wig-less terms. Some have complained that Kneller's portraits of the members of the Kit-cat Club, all painted when the wig was at its zenith, represent a lot of wigs with Whigs inside them; there is an element of justice in the accusation, and the modern eye often has considerable difficulty to make out what is going on inside.

The demand for portraits had increased at a remarkable rate during the second half of the seventeenth century, quite naturally as a result of a rising population and prosperity of the gentry. Building boomed, and a new standard of domestic display came in. In most houses of any standing, portraits were becoming usual furniture. A helpful work, *Polygraphice*, first published in 1675 but subsequently often re-issued, is in part a guide to social etiquette, and devotes a chapter to the Disposing of Pictures and Paintings: in the Dining Room the pictures of the King and Queen, or their Coat-of-Arms

forbearing to put any other Pictures of the life, as not being worthy to be their Companions, unless, at the lower end, two or three of the chief nobility, as attendants of their Royal Persons;

in the inward or withdrawing chambers, other portraits 'of persons of Honour, intimate or special friends, and acquaintances, of Artists only'. But the purely family portraits are for the bedchambers –

your own, your wives and childrens pictures, as only becoming the most private Room, and your Modesty; lest (if your wife be a beauty) some wanton and libidinous guest should gaze too long on them and commend the work for her sake.

Such a discretion was certainly not generally observed, though it is curious to find Evelyn hanging the portrait of his extra-marital love Margaret Blagge – even though his most platonic and spiritual love – in his own and his wife's bedchamber. It aroused some comment from one of Mrs Evelyn's friends and seems to have been moved fairly swiftly to the parlour.[68]

Modesty indeed is antithetical to the main-spring of portraiture, which is vanity. All these people, increasing every year, who had themselves painted did not do so for reasons of self-effacement. They wished to put themselves on record in the light most becoming, not only to their physical charm but also to their social station. Hence Mrs Pepys was painted in the pose and costume favoured by a lady of title. The progress of her husband's portraits is also interesting. In 1666 (when the Diary was in full spate) a middle-class urban civil servant with an unusual taste for the

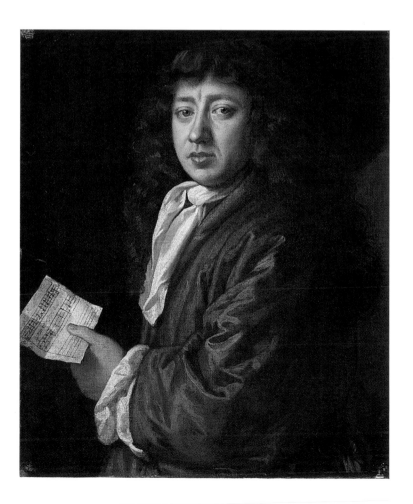

Plate 100
Samuel Pepys
(1633–1703) by
John Hayls, 1666
Oil on canvas,
75.6 × 62.9 (29¾ × 24¾)
National Portrait
Gallery, London

Plate 101 (*right*)
John Maitland, 1st
Duke of Lauderdale
(1616–1682) by Sir
Peter Lely, *c*.1665
Oil on canvas,
124.5 × 101.6
(49 × 40)
Scottish National
Portrait Gallery

Plate 102 (*far right*)
John Maitland, 1st
Duke of Lauderdale
(1616–1682) by
Benedetto Gennari,
c.1674
Oil on canvas,
127 × 101.6 (50 × 40)
The Lord
Tollemache,
Helmingham Hall

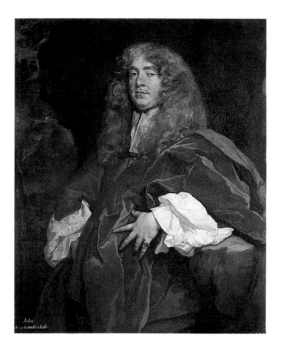

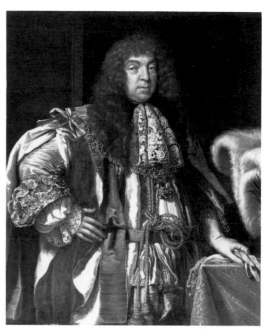

refinements of living (for that, rather than for the arts, as such), he sat to John Hayls (Plate 100). The latter was an imitator of the most fashionable painter, Lely, but also of course much cheaper than Lely. Pepys did not conform to the extent that his wife did. He bought a loose drapery, a rich 'Indian gown', specially for the occasion in order that he might be conventionally draped, but otherwise the portrait is unusual, and he gave Hayls a great deal of trouble.

Hayls painted a landscape background, and Pepys, after some hesitation, had it painted out; he holds a sheet of music on which is written a tune of his own composing. There was trouble before that was clearly legible, a trouble recorded in the Diary and also in an X-ray photograph of the painting, where further trouble is also disclosed with Pepys' right arm which does not show in the finished picture, but was originally held forward. The exaggerated turn of his neck was perhaps of his own choosing, too, though he complains that it gave him a violent crick in the neck.

Sorbière, the French traveller in England in the early 1660s, commented on the intolerable pride and haughtiness of the English nobility, and a reflection of this pride pervades the portraits of even gentlemen of the period. Yet it is curious to see how variously different painters may interpret the expression even of a proud aristocrat. The Duke of Lauderdale (Plates 101–3) offers in his person an exceptional example:

haughty beyond expression, abject to those he saw he must stoop to, but imperious to all others [with] a violence of passion that carried him often to fits like madness.

He was in Scotland an able and extremely brutal administrator; at Charles II's court, though one of the five great, the leaders of the Cabal, 'He made a very ill appearance: He was very big: His hair red, hanging oddly about him: His tongue was too big for his mouth, which made him bedew all that he talked to: And his whole manner was rough and boisterous, and very unfit for a court.' Another witness repeats the charge:

his head was towards that of a Saracen fiery face, and his tongue was too big for his mouth, and his pronunciation high Scotch, no highlander like him. . . . This lord although not invited, ever intruded himself.

And yet all agree also on his extraordinary learning, 'not only in Latin, in which he was a master, but in Greek and Hebrew', in divinity and in history.[69] He was often painted; the three reproduced here show him in his late forties to mid-sixties; the first, by Lely, about 1665, contrives to impart an almost groomed, though slightly Dutch, chic; the second, of a few years later, is by the Italian Benedetto Gennari, nephew of Guercino, who produces in his hard, metallic light the full horror of the face – the bully, the thug, capable of a most sinister joviality. The third, of about 1680, is by the English painter, John Riley, in whose work critics discern a specifically English temper, a melancholic, atmospheric feeling for his sitter's character; and here indeed is a face of an elderly clubman, irritable, with gout perhaps in some extremity, and intolerant, but with some subtlety; the face of a man whose learning in Greek and in divinity one might accept without surprise, and a face that consorts oddly with the faces of the same man shown by Lely and Gennari.

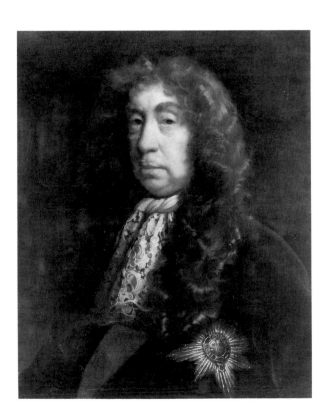

Plate 103
John Maitland, 1st Duke of Lauderdale
(1616–1682) by John Riley, *c*.1680
Oil on canvas, 76.2 × 63.5 (30 × 25)
The Duke of Northumberland

VI

The Polite Mask of the Augustan Age

LELY DIED in 1680; his close follower (also Dutch), Wissing, in 1687. A year later came the Glorious Revolution, and with it a less ostentatious fashion in portraiture. To Lely succeeded Kneller. Sir Godfrey Kneller, German-born, trained in Holland and Italy, acknowledging in his style both Bol and Maratti, arrived in 1674. He saw at once what was wanted, and, to begin with, painted portraits that are sometimes so close to Lely's that they have been mistaken for them; but essentially his is a swifter and a leaner style than Lely's, vertical compared with what had hitherto been predominantly horizontal.[70]

The seated women now sit up instead of reclining, and the men emerge in close-fitting velvet coats, as the billowing tide of draperies recedes. Faces stay plump (indeed a double chin now seems an essential of masculine and feminine beauty), but they lengthen, and noses are worn lofty and long; the narrowed elongated eyes remain and become even more of a formula. The mouth remains full, but now succinct, in the case of the woman, as a standard impression from a rubber-stamp charged with lipstick. Feminine hair goes up, right up, leaving the face sometimes cruelly naked; a severe and forbidding style very often, and, particularly when elaborated by that strange towering structure of lace known as the *fontange*, no longer an allurement, but a defence mechanism (Plate 105). A long, well-fleshed face, framed in the voluminous but ordered foliage of the wig served men for some forty years between 1690 and 1730; with women the ideal seems to have been an unblemished long oval, set at an angle on the long smooth neck, reminiscent of the feminine beauty celebrated by Mannerist painters like Parmigianino.

It is generally a very summary portraiture; the niceties of character, and very often all character, escape it. Kneller himself, at his best a most subtle artist, could at his best catch the individuality beneath the wig, and better still when the wig was off, but almost all his women are insipid, and, now that the evanescent chic of fashion has long since evaporated, plain. Kneller was not of course the only painter, but he was during his long reign, right up almost to his death in 1723, the most fashionable one, and facially his rivals, Dahl, d'Agar, Richardson, Murray, Closterman, repeat the theme which is known as his. He was the chosen painter of the Whigs, and has left a splendid record of them in the portraits of the members of the Kit-cat Club, but he also painted indiscriminately the rival party, including Harley and Bolingbroke; nor could anyone claim that those particularly under Harley's patronage, notably Dahl and Richardson, produced portraits in any way illuminating a specifically Tory *Lebensanschauung*. Kneller was also the most prolific painter of them all; teutonically industrious, he was also a master of business

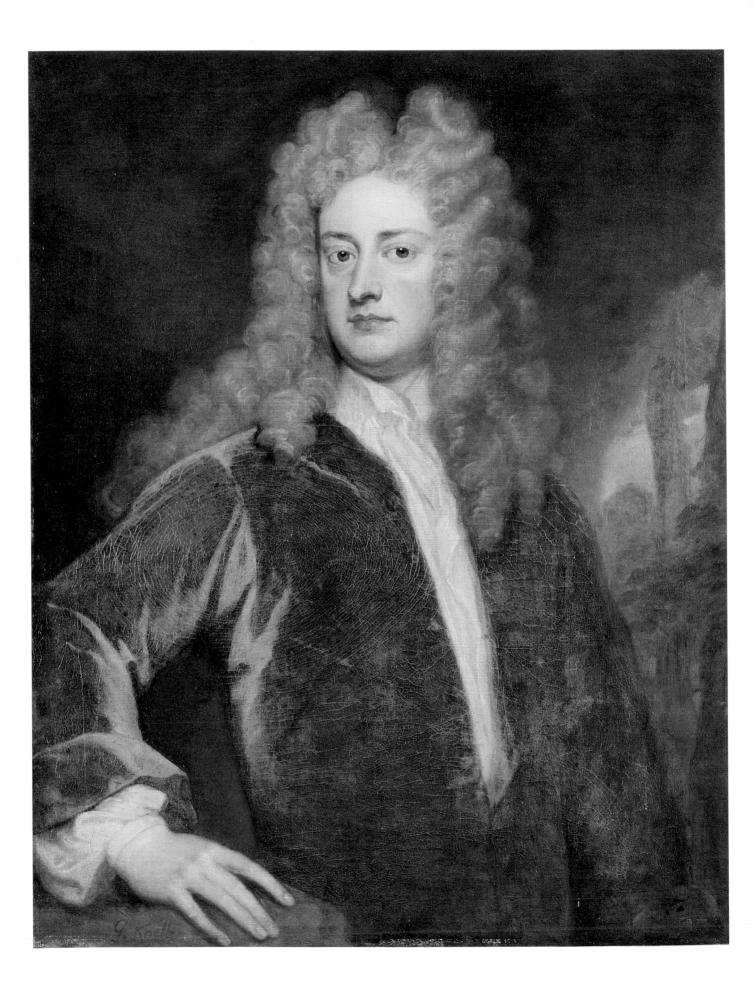

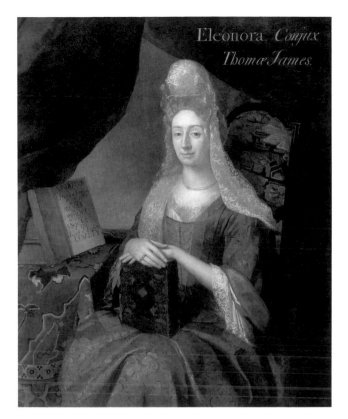 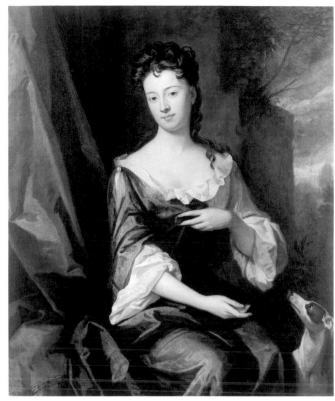

organization, and his studio came far nearer to a factory than Van Dyck's or even Lely's: virtual mass-production explains a great deal of the standardization of his products.

Yet part of this standardization, this generalization, is due to the temper of the age. Kneller formulated the Augustan face, a polite and urbane mask. His average presentation of his sitters (though not in the fully formal and official whole-lengths) is a 'model of the middle style; on grave subjects not formal, on light occasions not grovelling, pure without scrupulosity, and exact without apparent elaboration; always equable, always easy. . .'.[71] That, of course, was not written of Kneller, but is from Johnson's famous assessment of Addison's prose style. It applies equally, however, to Kneller's best middle style, as in the Kit-cat portraits, as in his portrait of Addison himself – equable, easy; his shirt loose at his throat, he inhabits his wig as inevitably as his sense his prose (Plate 104). But he is not familiar; sociable, but not intimate; he might smile agreeably, but already (in 1694) one of Congreve's characters, anticipating Lord Chesterfield, had laid it down that 'there is nothing more unbecoming to a man of quality than to laugh'. (How true to life this formally informal impression of Addison may be is another matter; it was Chesterfield himself who described him as 'the most timid and awkward man in good company he ever saw'.) The topography of his face is broadly treated, and rounded; the minute exploration of the terrain that Kneller's French contemporary, Rigaud, would have undertaken is not even attempted, while his clothes sit easy on him instead of crepitating with a Gallic, lacy vigour of their own.

In the painting of the face of Kneller's Anne Sotheby, of 1692, this generalization is even more marked, as is usual in his portraits of women (Plate 106), the face becomes almost an abstract design (see the drawing of the eyebrow in one curve into the nose, the simplified eyes, the perfect rounding down cheek into chin and up again); she is fashionable youth. Yet, when stirred, Kneller could rise to heights far above even the pure middle style of the Addison; in his portrait of Sir Isaac Newton, for example, as rare an interpretation as any genius could hope for (Plate 107). Seen from a distance it is a stock head-and-shoulders portrait, a wigged man draped in the conventional meaningless drapery, set in the conventional painted oval within the rectangular canvas. Move closer, and the thing becomes alive with urgency. It is painted fast with the muscular vigour that may sometimes remind one that Kneller worked for a time under Bernini. It is also almost, in the modern sense, expressionistic, and uses distortion deliberately – the loaded iris of his right eye too great for the lids to contain it, and the wig not stuffy about his head, but lambent as an aura.

Kneller's average world, and that of all the society-portrait painters of his time, is of the middle style, its inhabitants detached, each one scrutinized in his or her role as gentleman or gentlewoman. They never do anything extraneously in their pictures;

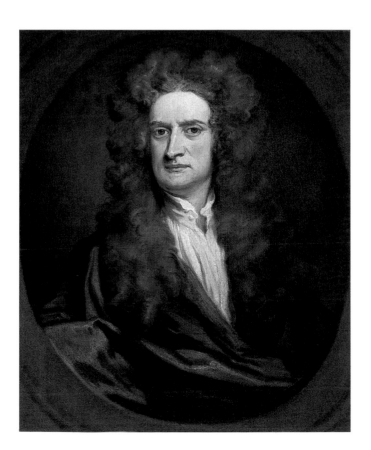

Plate 107
Sir Isaac Newton (1642–1727)
by Sir Godfrey Kneller, 1702
Oil on canvas, 75.6 × 62.2
$(29\frac{3}{4} \times 24\frac{1}{2})$
National Portrait Gallery,
London

Plate 108
Jacob Tonson I (1656?–1736)
by Sir Godfrey Kneller, 1717
Oil on canvas, 91.4 × 71.1
(36 × 28)
National Portrait Gallery,
London

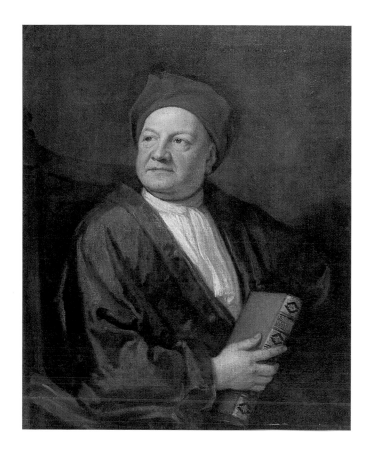

to pose is full occupation. Towards the end of Kneller's long reign he painted Alexander Pope in the classic attitude of melancholy, visibly thinking, and before that painters like Jervas and Richardson had painted writers (Swift and Prior) actually with pen poised over paper. But that was the sign of a thaw in formal portraiture that was not to become general until the middle of the eighteenth century. Jacob Tonson, a late Kneller of 1717, is shown in an informal turban-cap instead of a wig (others in the Kit-cat portraits are shown thus, but Tonson, surrounded by peers, knights and esquires, is the only one designated on his frame as 'Mr.'), clutching *Paradise Lost*, from which he made copious money; his expression however is not that of a contented tradesman, a publisher, but awful, as though in communion with the spirit of Milton (Plate 108).

During the latter part of the seventeenth century the portrait-painters found their clients in a rapidly widening field. English country-houses, great and small, are full of ancestors of this period, of most callings, and mostly painted in the manner of Lely and then in the manner of Kneller; to be painted, they usually stripped themselves of any vestiges of their profession, and clad themselves in the uniform wig and loose cloak of the gentleman. Those, like Thomas Tompion with his clock, who admit to a mechanical skill, are rare, though those concerned with the liberal and humane arts and sciences may admit a book or an astrolabe; Kneller recorded himself with his grand new country house in the background.

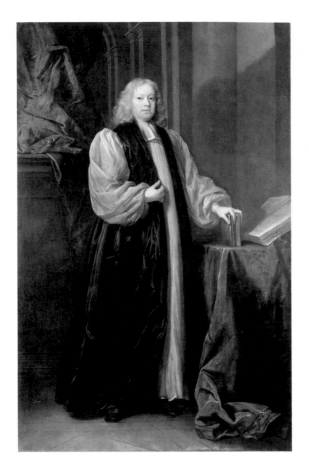

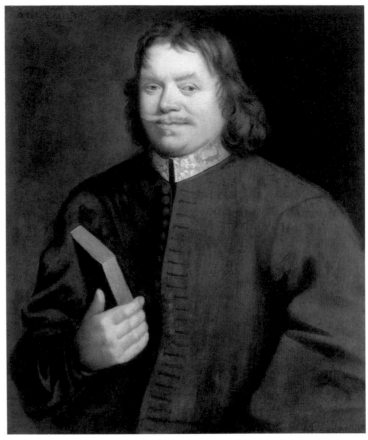

Soldiers and sea-captains appear; Lely in his fine series of admirals gave them a rugged if somewhat Dutch individuality, but when Kneller and Dahl continued the series at the turn of the century, little smack of the sea was left clinging to them. Marlborough looks a little ill-at-ease in his breastplate, and the thunder of Blenheim did not shake the fabric of Kneller's canvases. At this time, too, the clergy, particularly bishops, began to sit with that unflagging assiduity in which they have persevered ever since; they are distinguished by their black gowns and plain bands, and, for the bishops, their splendid sweltering rochets of white lawn; but they, too, while differentiated by their costume, are gentlemen (Plate 109). The Anglican Church went into the wig with perhaps less questioning than did the Catholic, where there was even at one time a question of tonsured wigs. In expression they are benign, and on the whole, I think it is fair to say, plumper than the laity: Béat-Louis de Muralt, in 1695, was surprised to see in England 'most of the clergy looking so healthy and prosperous and it is a pleasure to look at all these fat and rosy chaplains'. The more radical wing of the religious movement, that of the Puritans and the Quakers, is of course very scantily recorded in portraiture, with the exception of Bunyan, whose blunt, brawny yet visionary enthusiasm still informs and transcends the mediocre painting of him by Thomas Sadler (Plate 110).

Plate 109 (*above left*)
Thomas Sprat
(1635–1713) by
John Riley and
John Closterman,
*c.*1690
Oil on canvas,
241 × 147 (94$\frac{7}{8}$ × 57$\frac{7}{8}$)
Walker Art Gallery,
Liverpool

Plate 110 (*above right*)
John Bunyan
(1628–1688) by
Thomas Sadler,
1684–1685
Oil on canvas,
74.9 × 63.5 (19$\frac{1}{2}$ × 25)
National Portrait
Gallery, London

The painted portrait was not the only way of preserving the face. The spark of genius seems to have deserted the miniaturists after Cooper's death in 1672, and did not kindle again for almost a century; a summary statement of character does not suit the scale, but this was what taste demanded, and so miniatures degenerated into little Knellers, Jervases and Hudsons, insipid and characterless. Between the 1660s and 1700 there was, however, a short fashion for miniature portrait-drawings in plumbago, or blacklead. The chief exponents of this art were David Loggan, born in Danzig and trained in Amsterdam, but of Scottish family; his pupil, Robert White, and Thomas Forster.[72] Loggan, both in his topographical work and his portraiture, was much influenced by Hollar, and he has a scrupulous eye for minute detail; his portraits offer a refreshing contrast with the schematized features of contemporary life-size portraits. He worked in Oxford and in London; he was not expensive though very popular, and the backbone of his clientele seems to have been the professional middle-classes, people of some book-learning, modest in their living, sometimes suspect of an agreeable, mild eccentricity, unspectacular but unflinching in their appearance – dons, doctors, clergymen, all ingenious men (including John Aubrey, a drawing now, alas, lost), and almost for the first time in British portraiture, wives: not disguised as women of fashion, or as saints or goddesses, but fine and wonderful wives.

Loggan's approach was informal; he could even take his likenesses in a coffee-house. To represent his unpretentious but veracious work, the portrait of a certain Mrs Harrison (Plate 111) drawn in 1681, must serve – a homely wife, her face unshaped by fashion; posing of course, and frankly pleased to be

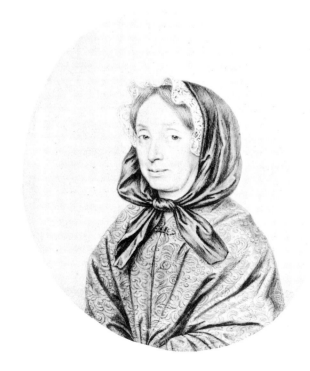

Plate 111
Mrs Harrison by David Loggan, 1681
(detail)
Plumbago, 14×11.5 ($5\frac{1}{2} \times 4\frac{1}{2}$)
Private Collection, location unknown

doing so, but timeless: you could easily meet her in the porch after the Sunday morning service today. Robert White was less incisive in his modelling, but has preserved some remarkable people, not least amongst them Sir Thomas Browne and Titus Oates.

A similar veracity is hardly to be expected of the sculptural portraits. In John Bushnell[73] England had a baroque, Bernini-like sculptor of some talent, but his works are mostly sepulchral (Plate 112); straightforward portrait-busts for domestic purposes are very rare during the second half of the seventeenth century, and until about 1720.

The busts, made up from life-masks, which came into some sort of fashion in the 1650s, are known only by account (both Pepys and Huyghens sat for them and describe the process); with their glass eyes, they must have been very distressingly life-like, but they were made of plaster, and not one certain one of the period is now known. By the end of the century, too, the wax-work show had arrived in London, and has continued, probably with hardly a break, until today; about 1700, Ned Ward was much astonished at the liveliness of the figures at Bartholomew Fair, 'art's nicest imitation of human nature', but the wax figures of course were even more perishable than the plaster busts (Plate 113).

Very important, as a disseminator of the fashionable face, was the popularization of engraving. Portrait engravings were published towards the end of the sixteenth

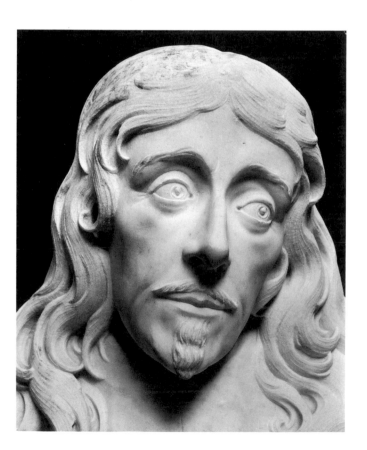

Plate 112
Thomas Bruce, 1st Earl of Elgin
(1599–1663) by John Bushnell,
after 1663 (detail)
Marble, life-size
Maulden Church, Bedford

Plate 113
William Turner by an unknown
artist, *c.*1690 (detail)
Wax effigy, life-size
Kirkleatham Church, Cleveland

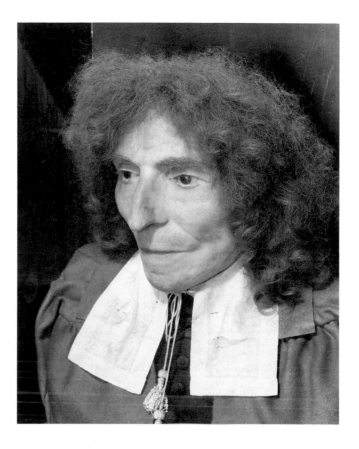

century, but they remained for long small in scale and woodenly inferior in quality
to the painted portraits. With the beginnings of Wenceslaus Hollar, a Czech, in
England, they took a livelier turn, and his small etchings from his own drawings
from the life anticipate Loggan already in the 1640s. But line-engraving, at the
pitch of excellence to which it was brought by 1660 by William Faithorne (who had
learned much from Nanteuil in France), and then mezzotint-engraving, sponsored
in England by Prince Rupert and John Evelyn in the sixties, with its almost magical
illusion of the sensuous depth and chiaroscuro of oils – these brought the portraits of
those in high fashion out from the private palaces into the public print-shops of St
Paul's Churchyard.

The popular illustrated magazine is almost in sight, and it is to Pepys, of course,
that one turns again for the first account of that enduring phenomenon, the pin-up
girl. The first one was not an actress; Nell Gwyn is now firmly established, I suppose,
as the archetype, as it were, of the average Englishman's bawdy – 'pretty, witty
Nell' as Pepys described her, and she is recreated by each age in its own fashion; but
she was not the first. The honour fell to Charles II's first mistress of consequence,
Barbara Villiers, Lady Castlemaine, later Duchess of Cleveland. In 1662 Pepys saw
at Lely's studio 'the so much desired by me picture of my Lady Castlemaine, which
is a most blessed picture; and one that I must have a copy of'. This may well have
been the whole-length of her, head on hand, melancholily arranged as a Repentant

Magdalene in a wilderness (Plate 114) (one version of this belonged to Pepys' master, Montagu) but thereafter, although Pepys' exclamations of wonder at the original lady are frequent, the portrait is lost sight of until suddenly, on 7 November 1666, he found Faithorne with the Castlemaine picture 'done by him from Lilly's, in red chalk and other colours, by which he hath cut it in copper to be printed . . . the finest thing I ever saw in my life' (Plate 115).[74]

Faithorne, however, would not part with the drawing as he had not finished the engraving; he promised that Pepys should have it as soon as the engraving was done, but he seems to have failed to keep it (it is probably the drawing now in the Victoria & Albert Museum, London) and the last sight we have of the portrait is of Pepys calling at Faithorne's again on 1 December, publication-day of the engraving, and buying three prints of it. This was an entirely respectable engraving, superficially at least; others that were to come, particularly of Nell Gwyn, were less so, *décolletée* to the waist, or even nude, lightly disguised as cupid with a pair of wings. Charles II had a painting by Lely, a whole-length nude; it was kept behind a sliding panel on which one Danckerts had painted a landscape, a device that was used again in Victorian days to camouflage more than one of William Etty's nudes. What may well be this very painting is here reproduced (Plate 116); it has one of the least mannered and most charming of Lely's heads, and, if it really be Nell Gwyn, explains her persistent charm better than any other portrait.

It is now impossible to gauge the demand for all these pictures of beautiful

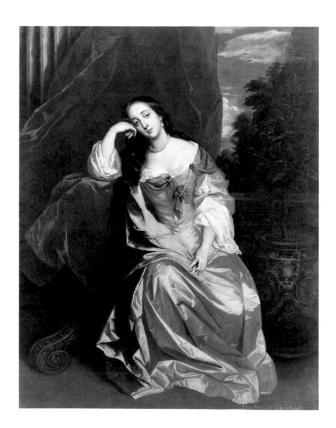

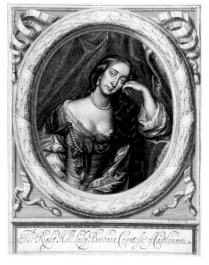

Plate 114 (*far left*) *Barbara Villiers, Duchess of Cleveland* (1641–1709) by Sir Peter Lely Oil on canvas, 177.8 × 142.2 (70 × 56) Lady Henrietta St George

Plate 115 (*left*) *Barbara Villiers, Duchess of Cleveland* (1641–1709) by William Faithorne, 1666 Engraving, 35.3 × 27.5 ($13\frac{7}{8} \times 10\frac{3}{4}$) British Museum, London (Department of Prints and Drawings)

Plate 116
*Nell Gwyn and her son,
the Duke of St Albans,
as Venus and Cupid* by
Sir Peter Lely, *c*.1665
Oil on canvas,
123.2 × 157.5
(48½ × 62)
The Trustees of the
Denys Eyre Bower
Bequest,
Chiddingstone Castle,
Kent

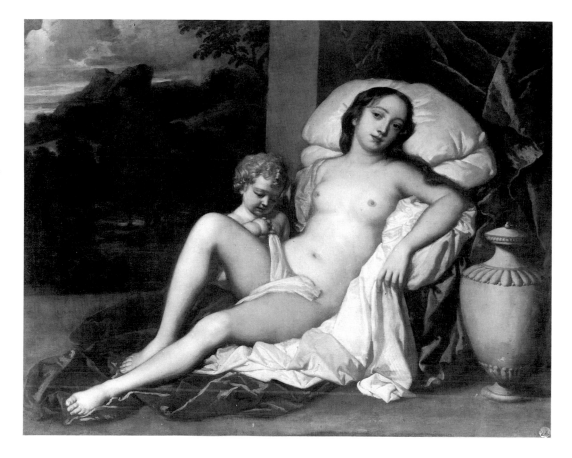

women, but it must have been considerable, apart from the engravings; Lely's
stock, when sold in 1682 after his death, included no less than twelve paintings of
Lady Castlemaine. From the 1670s onwards the output of engraved portraits was
relatively very large, and their scope very wide. The Royal faces, as ever, were
probably the most popular, but most people who achieved some public fame or
notoriety were now recorded by their visual journalism; not only the actresses and
the politicians, but the major criminals from Titus Oates downwards (though these
tended to be very crude woodcuts incorporated in broadsides, often showing only
an unrecognizable body dangling from the gallows). Really resonant *causes célèbres*
would produce a host of prints, mostly pirated; Sir Edmundbury Godfrey's face was
everywhere on the prints after his murder on Primrose Hill, as were those of the
Seven Bishops whom James II consigned to the Tower. And a little later, in Ralph
Thoresby's Diary, we find ingenious men of learning exchanging engravings of
themselves somewhat like visiting cards.

But there are hardly any serious portraits yet of the less than well-to-do. Servants,
odd pages, even negro boys, occur in formal portraits occasionally, but as
decoration, as trappings; there are few isolated studies, like Riley's well-known
painting of the scullion at Christ Church, Oxford (Plate 117), but they are exceptional. Only one odd glimpse would I preserve here, from Peter Angelis' record of a

ceremonial occasion with 'Queen Anne and the Knights of the Garter', in all the billowing baroque of their great blue and white robes and their powdered wigs; amongst them, solid and expressionless, a Beefeater, already a century out of date in costume and in face yet almost precisely, except for the lack of a ruff, as you can see him at the Tower of London today (Plate 118). There are not even any crowd scenes; one or two Dutch or Flemish artists of genre painting, Heemskirk, Tilborg, were working over here at the close of the seventeenth century, but their crowd characters seem indistinguishable from the Dutch low-life they were accustomed to paint. Some writers already perceived a lively, swarming and lusty picturesque in English everyday life, like Ned Ward in the Royal Exchange distinguishing French from Spaniards ('lank-haired formalists . . . walking with as much state and gravity as a snail o'er a leaf of a cabbage'), 'the Lord's vagabonds, the Jews', and then

a kind of lean, carrionly creatures, with reddish hair and freckly faces, very much given to scratching and shrugging, as if they held lousiness no shame and the itch no scandal; stooping a little in the shoulders, as if their backs had been us'd to a pedlar's pack. . . . These, I found, were a compound of Scotch and Irish. . . .[75]

The painters had yet to turn their eyes to this kind of subject-matter; when the *London Spy* began to appear, in November 1698, Hogarth was but one year old.

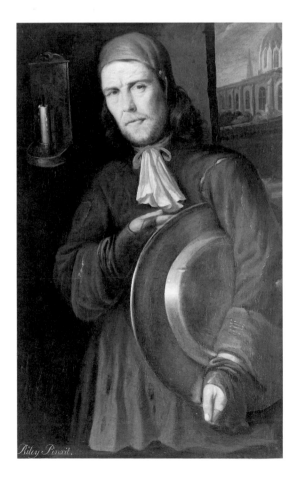

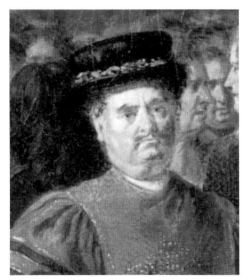

Plate 118 (*above*)
A Beefeater (detail from *Queen Anne and the Knights of The Garter*) by Peter Angelis, *c.*1713
Oil on canvas, 62.2 × 74.9 (24½ × 29½)
National Portrait Gallery, London

Plate 117 (*left*)
William Forde (?), a scullion of Christ Church by John Riley
Oil on canvas, 96.5 × 58.4 (38 × 23)
The Governing Body, Christ Church, Oxford

Character Not Caricature

AT THE BEGINNING of the eighteenth century, a long-nourished resentment against the low standing generally allotted to painting among the other arts began to find public expression. Painting was in fact not widely admitted as a genteel occupation; the painters' concern, though not openly avowed, when formulating its claims as a liberal art, was as much with their own social position as with the honour of their art. It was generally acknowledged that painting in classical times had been a liberal art, for the unimpeachable evidence of great Greek and Latin authorities was a record to that effect, but it was held that in modern times the art had declined from grace into a mechanical trade.

Sir Thomas Elyot, in the widely-read and influential book *The Governour*, 1531, had already as good as stated this; Stow in 1615 said so specifically:

sure I am, it [the art of Painting] is now accounted base and mechanicall, and a mere mestier of an artificer and handy craftsman. Insomuch as fewe or no Gentleman or generous & liberal person, will adventure by practising this art.[76]

Hilliard's passionate apology for the art of limning as a gentleman's art may well have been provoked by this, but Hilliard's manuscript remained unpublished until the twentieth century. There were of course distinguished amateurs, practitioners of the art distinct from connoisseurs, men like Sir Nathaniel Bacon and General Lambert, but they did not practise professionally. Sir Anthony van Dyck was knighted by Charles I, and so was Lely, while Kneller was the first to achieve, in 1715, a baronetcy; but these were exceptions (besides being all foreigners) and the truth was that painters had not the social recognition that was readily accorded to men of letters.

Poets indeed were soon to have almost a fan following, and in the late twenties, Voltaire observed that the 'picture of the Prime Minister hangs over the chimney of his own closet, but I have seen that of Mr. Pope in twenty noblemen's houses'. Addison, Congreve, Steele, Garth, Vanbrugh, all hang on a level with men of the noblest blood in the informal precincts of the Kit-cat Club, but no painter is represented; Kneller's portrait belonged to Tonson, but not as part of the series, almost as it were on sufferance – and on almost a miniature scale. It was well over a century after Sidney wrote his *Apologie for Poetry* in about 1581, that Jonathan Richardson, painter, attempted an apology for painting in various publications dating from the first quarter of the eighteenth century.

Richardson maintained that a great painter had to be endowed with a learning equal to that of great scholars, plus an intimate knowledge of anatomy, osteology, geometry, perspective, architecture; he had also to be a poet, a man of imaginative genius. In addition to all this, he had also to be a

Curious Artificer, whereby he becomes Superior to one who equally possesses the other Talents, but wants That. A *Rafaëlle* therefore is not only Equal, but Superior to a *Virgil*, or a *Livy*, a *Thucydides* or a *Homer*.[77]

The justification for such a contention would naturally be found in that branch of painting which gives the widest scope to all these qualities, and that was not portrait-painting, but 'history-painting', the imaginative representation of scenes from history and mythology:

It has been said of Painting [wrote the English connoisseur John Elsum in 1703] that it is like Musick, best in Concert. History-Painting is that Concert, comprizing all the other Parts of Painting, and the principal end of it is to move the Passions.[78]

Richardson, connoisseur though he was, and man of letters, panegyrist of Milton, was also by profession a portrait-painter, and so had to stress the liberal side of that branch of the art as well as of history-painting.

His argument much resembles that of the Italian theorists of the Renaissance (particularly Lomazzo); against the charge that portraiture is a mechanical copy of nature, he stresses its imaginative and its interpretative aspects. Likeness is not enough.

Thus to raise the Character: To divest an Unbred Person of his Rusticity, and give him something at least of a Gentleman. To make one of a moderate Share of good Sense appear to have a Competency, a Wise Man to be more Wise, and a Brave Man to be more so, a Modest, Discreet Woman to have an Air something Angelical, and so of the rest; and then to add that Joy, or Peace of Mind at least, and in such a manner as is suitable to the several Characters, is absolutely necessary to a good Face-Painter. . . .[79]

It is still a good text for portrait-painters who would have a fashionable prosperity, though some would resume it more tersely: flatter.

Portraiture, indeed, cannot but fit awkwardly into any intellectual theory of painting as a liberal manifestation of the imagination; it is tied too closely to imitation. A greater intellect than Richardson, the third Earl of Shaftesbury, writing (1712) at much the same time with a similar preoccupation, was more logically drastic: he deleted face-painting from the canon of true art altogether. 'Tis an abuse of real art which should (aye and will) be reserved for better purpose.' The only exception he makes is 'for small portraiture of heads only (for bodies would be mere puppets and ridiculous as everyone presently sees) which convenience and use renders agreeable and friendship amicable'. But any further claims for the face-painter he dismisses as ridiculous; it is not a liberal art nor to be so esteemed;

as requiring no liberal knowledge, genius, education, converse, manners, moral-science, mathematics, optics, but merely practical and vulgar. Therefore not deserving honour, gentility, knighthood conferred (Glance at Sir Kneller).[80]

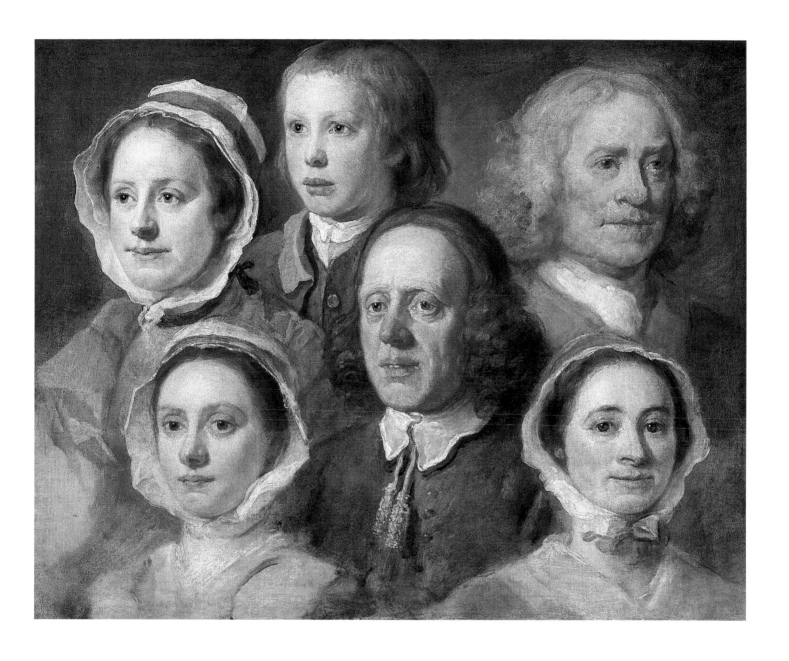

Plate 119 *Heads of Six of Hogarth's Servants* by William Hogarth, *c.*1750–1755. Oil on canvas, 62.2 × 75 (24½ × 29½). Tate Gallery, London

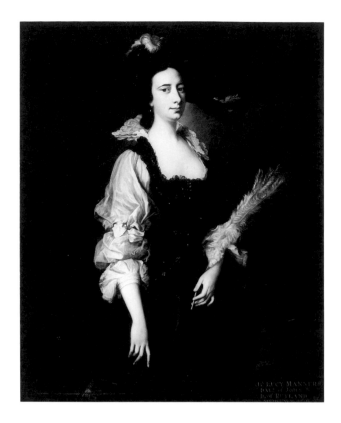

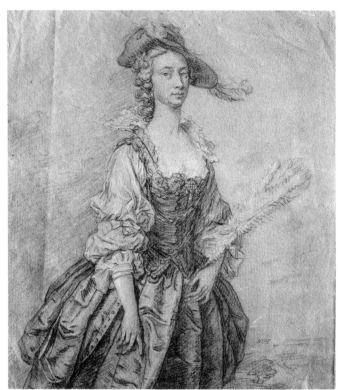

These notes, from Shaftesbury's uncompleted work on plastic art, were not published, and he was in advance of his time. But the unease they reflect was to spread widely until all British painters yearned to be history-painters. It was not that form of art, however, that was to prove the characteristic mould for the great eighteenth-century school of British painting. It was rather the despised art of portraiture, enlarged to the scale of history-painting, to concert-pitch, by Reynolds. His reading of Richardson's book is said to have played a large part in his decision to become a painter.

But Reynolds is still a long way off; and before his establishment in the 1750s thousands of faces had to be painted. The front on which he was to unleash his attack meanwhile was in some sectors softening up; in another, that of formal society portraiture, it set almost into a rigor. Richardson's own painting scarcely bore out his theories. In his larger, formal portraits he was not a remarkable innovator, though able enough, and it is his smaller, informal head-and-shoulder portraits that now have most appeal, for in them he seems to rely on an honest, fresh and literal transcription of his sitter's head, in exact opposite to his theory. In his treatment of the face he is notably more detailed and more particular than Kneller. Richardson had a heavy, accurate, rather leathery technique in painting the flesh which he passed on to his pupil, Hudson, who became one of England's leading society painters (Plate 120). In Hudson's work, and in that of his rivals, Hoare, Ramsay (with some reservations), Pond, and others, from the 1730s through the

Plate 120 (*above left*) *Lady Lucy Manners, Duchess of Montrose* (died 1788) by Thomas Hudson, *c.*1742–1745 Oil on canvas, 127 × 101.6 (50 × 40) The Marquis of Graham

Plate 121 (*above right*) *Lady Lucy Manners, Duchess of Montrose* (died 1788) by Joseph van Aken, *c.*1742–1745 Black and white chalk, 33 × 27.7 (13 × 10⅞) National Galleries of Scotland, Edinburgh

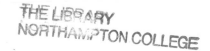

forties, and lingering on even into the sixties, society portraiture at last found a solution that seems logical to that dichotomy that oppresses all its practitioners – the cleavage between the necessary representation of the brute facts about a given face and the claims of the picture as a work of art.

We have seen Van Dyck's age, and Lely's, and Kneller's; the 1730s and forties are neither Hudson's, nor Hoare's, nor Vanderbank's – in society painting they belong to Joseph van Aken. He came to England before 1720 and died in 1749, and towards the end of his life was painting much of Hudson's, Ramsay's, Highmore's and others' portraits. They did the face, the brute facts, and the canvas was sent over to Van Aken who painted the body, fashionably attired and fashionably clothed (Plate 121). Hamlet Winstanley, a pupil of Kneller's with a large practice in

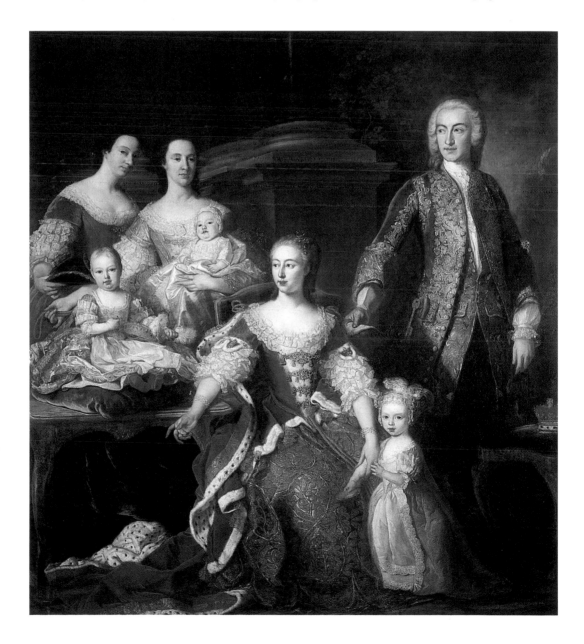

Plate 122
Augusta, Princess of Wales with members of her Family and Household by Jean Baptiste van Loo, 1739
Oil on canvas, 220.3 × 200.7 $(87\frac{3}{4} \times 79)$
Royal Collection (by gracious permission of Her Majesty The Queen)

the north, was perhaps his most extreme employer: he 'travelled about and drew pictures from the life in oil colours – often on small pieces of cloth, only the face; pasted them when sent to London on larger clothes', and sent them off to Van Aken in London, who did the rest with that 'excellent, free, genteel, and florid manner of pencilling, silks, satins, velvets, gold lace, etc.' which gave the finished product that essential, as it were Savile Row, cachet.

These compositions, gradually pitched higher and sharper in colour and light, are generally still within that tradition in which Kneller had worked; but the poses become more forced, and affected, and a certain sartorial precision is apparent, a crisp laundering of linen with a sometimes pleasantly Rococo life of its own; in the male portraits the swirling drapery is abandoned, although the fashion for Van Dyckian fancy-dress was in evidence during the middle of the eighteenth century. There was in general a shift of sympathy towards the French tradition of portraiture as described not entirely unjustly by Addison some time earlier (in 1711) – the faces

very remarkable for their smiles and a certain smirking Air . . . bestowed indifferently on every Age and Degree of either Sex. The *Toujours Gai* appeared even in Judges, Bishops and Privy-Counsellors . . . every part of the Dress was in a Flutter, and endeavoured to distinguish itself above the rest.

When Jean Baptiste van Loo arrived in London from Paris in 1737, he had a rush to his studio of the most fashionable sitters (Plate 122); he had a waxier *chic*, and a more minute technique in the rendering of the features than any British painter then working. The progression of this part of the art seemed to be indeed towards the ideal of presenting a two-dimensional illusion of a wax tailor's dummy.

At the end of the thirties, the Abbé le Blanc commented that in London the portrait painters were more numerous and more unskilful than ever they were before.

At a distance one would take a dozen of their portraits for twelve copies of the same original. . . . Excepting the single countenance or likeness they have all the same neck, the same arms, the same colouring and the same attitude. In short these pretended portraits are as void of life and action as of design in the painter.[81]

The faces, more detailed though they are, are still of the Augustan expression; polite and unimpassionable masks – the face of Lord Chesterfield, the urbane and cynical author of the *Letters to His Son*: the face of the well-entrenched Whig, at one (in expression, at least) with Sir Robert Walpole for stability and prosperity at home, and peace abroad.

There may be in some faces, outside the Royal Household, a certain thickening, a Hanoverian heaviness, but overall the ideally fashionable features have not changed much. They are still burdened with wigs, but always powdered from the 1720s onwards, and beginning to freak in decadence. The wig generally used for polite occasions shrinks up from the full-bottom in the 1720s and thirties; by 1753 the only members of the House of Commons wearing a full-bottomed wig were the

Speaker and the Attorney-General.[82] For their two offices the already obsolete fashion had fossilized, and the Speaker and Judges still wear full-bottomed wigs today. By that date, the variety of wigs was sporting in full profusion; there were the pigeon's wing, the comet, the cauliflower, the royal bird, the staircase, the wild boar's back, the she-dragon, the rose, the negligent, the cut bob, the long bob, the drop wig, the snail back, the spinage seed. . . . But even amongst this medley, Lady Mary Wortley Montagu's son caused a certain furore when he arrived back from Paris, in 1751, with an iron wig, spun out of the finest wire.[83]

Certain professions appropriated their own peculiar shape of wig: soldiers, the clergy (a very thick bob wig), coachmen and others. But a wig of some kind was essential for social occasions; virtuosi and even the nobility might be painted wigless, in a velvet turban-cap, but not for a more formal portrait.

A curious illustration of the effect of the wig on the appearance is offered by three portraits of Daniel, Earl of Nottingham and Winchilsea; a triple head by Kneller (reminiscent of Van Dyck's Charles I) in which he is seen bald from three angles; a formal portrait in peer's robes by Richardson, much bewigged; and a senatorial bust by Rysbrack, with his head sprouting a crisp crop of little curls (Plates 123–5). All three in their different ways are also examples of rejuvenation – the sitter is near or in his seventics.

Arthur Pond, in the late thirties, issued a rather scratchy etching of the celebrated Dr Mead, a connoisseur and physician with a European reputation, without a wig on (Plate 126); the doctor 'passionately desired Mr Pond to suppress it', probably because, as a contemporary wrote, it appeared 'like an old mumper, as Rhimebrandt's heads usually do: such works give pleasure to virtuosi but not the publick eye . . . and debase the idea of a polite person'.[84] (It was Lord Chesterfield who wrote, in 1751: 'I love la belle Nature; Rembrandt paints caricatures.' Soon after, Richardson issued a wigged version of the doctor, conceivably as counter-blast (Plate 127).

The formal portraiture of the women continued on the same lines as that of the men. In the twenties and thirties, with painters as different as Charles Jervas and John Vanderbank, the vertical line of Kneller is drawn still further out; slender women, 'who seem rather intended to hang up in the hall of an anatomist than for any other purpose' (as Henry Fielding's Fanny in *Joseph Andrews* was not); the necks stretch from the narrow, almost naked shoulders, scarcely expanding into the narrow but alert faces that sprout on top with hair. Spry, monotonous, plain faces; there were no doubt characters as visually expressive as the Kielmansegge, later Countess of Darlington, beloved of George I and described by Walpole as with

large fierce black eyes rolling beneath lofty arched eyebrows, two acres of cheeks spread with crimson, an ocean of neck that overflowed and was not distinguishable from the lower part of her body, and no portion of which was restrained by stays.[85]

But the Anglicized portrait-painters subdued them into a variant of the common mould. Sometimes they were enlivened by fancy dress; the pastoral conventions

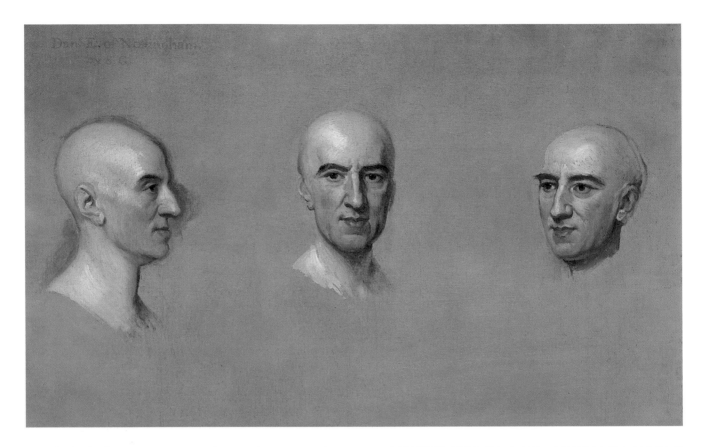

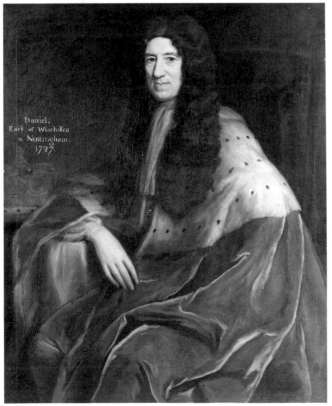

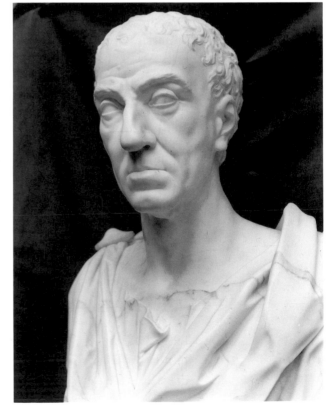

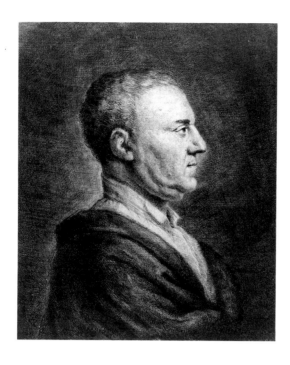

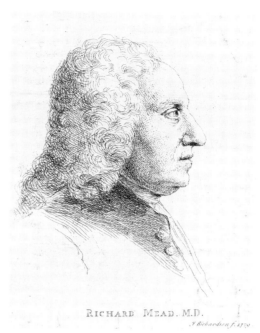

RICHARD MEAD. M.D.

died hard, and society shepherdesses were not uncommon, while the Duchess of Queensberry anticipated Marie Antoinette as a milk-maid. In the twenties there was a sudden vogue for being painted in Persian dress, with a fancy turban, and in the thirties, forties and fifties, a prudent rather gauche version of Rubens costume, with large-feathered hat, occurs again and again, often no doubt supplied by the expert modiste, Van Aken, to the works of Hudson, Ramsay, Knapton, Bardwell and others.

The faces are so uniform that a suspicion that they were modulated to the fashionable ideal, not only by the artist's paint but by their own, seems legitimate; some paint was probably used by women of fashion throughout the reigns of the four Georges, and certainly towards the end of the eighteenth century, but the evidence, as always with cosmetics, is very uncertain. The toilet preparations best described by Pope in the *Rape of the Lock* were probably not over-exaggerated, and satirical comment is vociferous through the century. Madame du Bocage, in London in 1750, may have been guilty of a Gallic condescension when she described the women 'who use no paint and are always laced (as was the custom formerly in *France*) . . . in their court-dresses they resemble the pictures of our great grandmothers'[86]; other witnesses are emphatic to the contrary, as Horace Walpole, calling for Lady Caroline Petersham and friend, in the June after Madame du Bocage was in town, found them 'having just finished their last layer of red, and looked as handsome as crimson could make them . . . gloriously jolly and handsome'.[87] Yet they probably were, by Parisian standards, archaic almost in dress, and English female portraits of the time show little or nothing of the paint and powder, glazed to a porcelain finish, of the faces of their French contemporaries.

The conservative school of society-painters, their doyen Thomas Hudson,[88] worked on into the 1760s; Hudson, who died in 1779, encompassed in his lifetime the careers not only of the sculptor Louis François Roubiliac (died 1762) and of William Hogarth (died 1764) but a great deal of his improbable pupil, Joshua Reynolds, who broke the Hudsonian tradition into fragments. But the sculptured faces that the first part of the eighteenth century has left us should first be considered; they are the first in time of the new movement. Sculptural portraiture remained, of course, firmly rooted in its funereal functions; the projects that brought in the big money for the sculptors were the great tombs of the great dead. Curiously, some of the liveliest, most animated, most baroque portraits of the late seventeenth century are to be found on tombs, where the effigies had long since risen from the old horizontal tradition into a fluid movement, sometimes approaching ecstatic aspiration. But in the third decade of the eighteenth century the three-dimensional likeness, in the shape of what were known as bustoes, began to win its place as a more domestic furnishing until, by about 1740, the bust-makers were so fashionable that they were said to be threatening the prosperity of the painters.

These busts tended to answer not to the Baroque, but to that precocious neo-classic taste, the Palladian, of which the third Earl of Burlington was the great protagonist. It was Burlington who imported the Italian sculptor, Guelfi, to England, and Burlington who employed Rysbrack to sculpture the statues of Inigo Jones and of Andrea Palladio that flank the stairs at Chiswick House. Rysbrack[89]

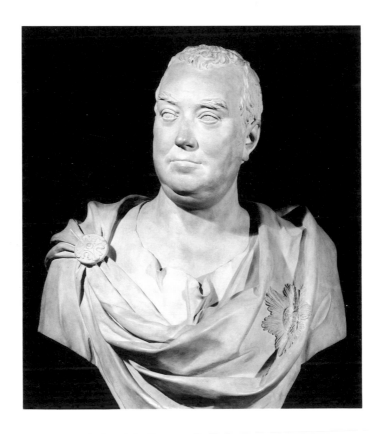

Plate 128
Robert Walpole, 1st Earl of Orford (1676–1745)
by J. M. Rysbrack, 1738
Terracotta, height 66 (26)
National Portrait Gallery,
London

made busts of those two pillars of the Burlington gospel, William Kent in the arts, Pope in literature; and he worked on busts for the Temple of Fame at Stowe in Buckinghamshire and for Queen Caroline's Grotto at Kew. His busts of the living are generalized polished statements, tending often to the senatorial, with a hint of toga; they seem to have been good likenesses, and for some characters are admirable – for Sir Robert Walpole (Plate 128), endowed with gloss, but a burly, genially cynical, well-fed, well-wined, most British Roman, the man who would say to young aspirants with their honest hearts yet untainted '*Well, are you to be an old Roman? A patriot? You'll soon come off of that and grow wiser*'. It was said to be very like him.

It may be noted that in the classical bust, though a formal object, wigs were not considered essential for the conveying of the idea of a polite person; the same Dr Mead, who objected to the bald etching made of him by Pond, was celebrated posthumously by a bust by Roubiliac, commissioned by Anthony Askew especially 'from a laudable veneration for the memory and public character of so great a patron of learning etc.' In most busts in the more classical manner, there were overtones of a similar celebration; it was by busts that the Ancients had immortalized their great men; it was by similar busts that the modern patrons of classical learning, and the artists who were rivalling the great classical artists, could be glorified. Non-funereal busts of women, and of purely society figures, are relatively rare; it was men like Pope and Handel, Bolingbroke and the Duke of Argyll and Walpole, who were suitable subjects and attuned patrons. A more informal note was introduced by Roubiliac in some of his best busts. Rysbrack was a Fleming, Roubiliac[90] a Frenchman, with that same deft feeling for the characteristic niceties, the quirks of an individual face, as had for example Van Loo, but with a far greater vitality, conveyed through an astonishing technique.

Roubiliac worked in England from the early 1730s until his death in 1764; he could compose in terms of a classic dignity, and so he created in 1745 even the diminutive Chesterfield with a naked deep-barrelled chest, eliciting from him the compliment that 'Roubiliac only was a statuary, the rest stone-cutters'; so, too, he preserved Pope in 1741, a head of quick intellectual beauty, and also, according to George Vertue, the most like portrait of the poet, while to Hogarth he gave a truculence more lucidly purposeful than Hogarth ever found in his own countenance, though this again was said to be very like (Plate 129).

The subjects which gave Roubiliac's remarkable realism its full scope were the old, particularly those whose features had been fired into extraordinary shapes by stubborn eccentricity – Martin Folkes of 1747, a bust acclaimed by Vertue as 'equal to any of present or former ages; his features strong and musculous with a natural and just air of likeness as much as any work of this kind ever seen'.[91] Perhaps most extraordinary of all, beside the marmoreal beauty of Pope, Pope's chief victim of the revised *Dunciad*, the aged actor Colley Cibber 'coloured from the life and extremely like', as Horace Walpole said (Plate 130).[92] Though recent critics have doubted the

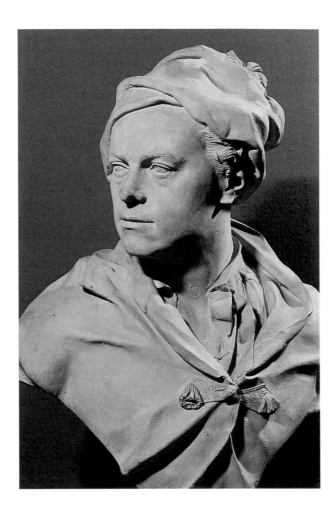

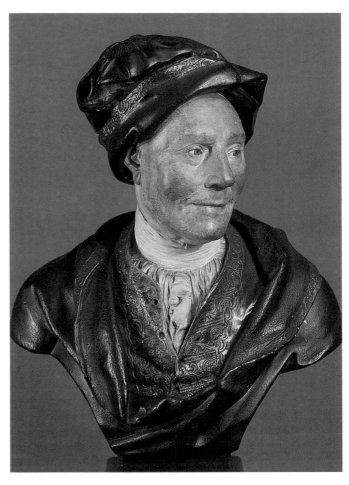

attribution to Roubiliac, it remains clever as a wax-work – with the glass-eyes and the turban-cap that lifts off to reveal the blue-veined bald pate – it avoids by a hair's-breadth that dead life-likeness of wax, and survives, inexplicably and disturbingly, in our midst, an old man with genial eyes, dreaming backwards perhaps in time but not unhappily, the mouth smiling on its toothless gums.

In fluid paint, the Baroque tradition tended to smooth out the minute particularity of such realism, even though it was by now generally breaking from its large sweep into the surface splash and ripple of the Rococo. The interest was nevertheless there, from 1730 onwards, betraying itself even in those engaged also in the most formal kind of portraiture, like Highmore. Highmore could and did produce state-portraits, more shimmering in texture, but as broadly grand as any of Kneller's and in Kneller's tradition. When dealing with his humbler clients, he produced portraits of an unassuming familiarity and relaxation that broke new ground, until, in the early fifties, he was capable of the astonishing *Mr Oldham and His Guests* in the Tate Gallery, London, a portrait of friends of the middle-class, including himself, having a drink together, and unsurpassed in its naturalness, its directness, its affection, by any conversation-piece painted in England (Plate 131).

Plate 129 (*above left*)
William Hogarth
(1697–1764) by Louis François Roubiliac,
*c.*1741
Terracotta,
height 71.1 (28)
National Portrait Gallery, London

Plate 130 (*above right*)
Colley Cibber
(1671–1757),
attributed to Louis François Roubiliac,
*c.*1740
Painted plaster,
height 67.3 (26½)
National Portrait Gallery, London

It is perhaps the most relaxed portrait painted in the eighteenth century. Before then, of course, portrait-painting had begun to explore levels which, though considered by the contemporary fashion to be beneath that of the society state-painters, are now considered high above them.

The vogue for the sort of 'conversation-piece' that is now recognized by that name, small-scale groups of figures, caught on in England a little earlier than 1730. Part of their importance is that they set their subjects in a social context; we see them *engagés*, performing the actions of everyday life. This type of group-portrait, that merges into the genre painting of Vermeer and de Hooch, had had a considerable success in Holland in the previous century in the hands of masters like Terborch; there it had flourished in a bourgeois society, in which dignity was not to be conveyed by the regalia of nobility nor by the sartorial conceits of courtiers, but by the air of solid decent prosperity with which the sitters occupy their compartments in time and space; the sitters are shown for what they are (though dressed, naturally, in their best) and with what they are, which includes, by a sort of empathy, even their furniture, the capital sunk in their plate, their harpsichords, their pictures and carpets. There are odd isolated examples in England before the eighteenth century; the Elizabethan group (though life-size, this) of card players at Knowsley; the Dutch painter H.G. Pot, visitor to England in 1632, was responsible

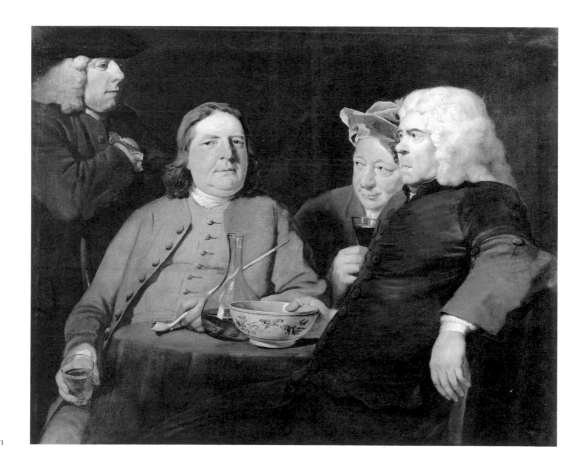

Plate 131
Mr Oldham and His Guests by Joseph Highmore *c.*1750
Oil on canvas,
105.4 × 129.5
(41½ × 51)
Tate Gallery, London

for a conversation-piece of Charles I and Henrietta Maria, but he was before his time and had no following. About 1700, on three occasions, the admiral Edward Russell, Earl of Orford, had himself painted with different groups of friends; other Stuart conversation-pieces, though larger in scale than those of the eighteenth century, are known.

The first sustained vogue took a rather different but characteristically English form – horse pictures; from the hunting scenes that Jan Wyck painted in the 1690s grew the paddock-scenes, groom or owner and favourite horse, that his pupil John Wootton, and Peter Tillemans, were painting from early in the 1720s onward, if not earlier. By 1735 several painters, including the Frenchman Philippe Mercier, Charles Philips, Gavin Hamilton, and Hogarth, with whose name the conversation-piece is for ever linked, were busily employed painting people in their homes, engaged in their ordinary occupations – taking tea was a favourite subject – at some specific moment in time (Plate 132). These pictures, like the Dutch ones, are not merely portraits of people, but include their furniture, their dogs and horses, houses, and familiar landscapes. The fashion was by no means confined to the middle-classes, as is sometimes suggested; it went as high as George II and his family, but it might show even almost the grandest busy with pursuits common to all classes with money enough to order a picture – not only could everyone drink tea, but everyone did.

Some of them have the air as of a number of single portraits rather awkwardly brought together, but in the best of them we have a kind of portraiture in which, at

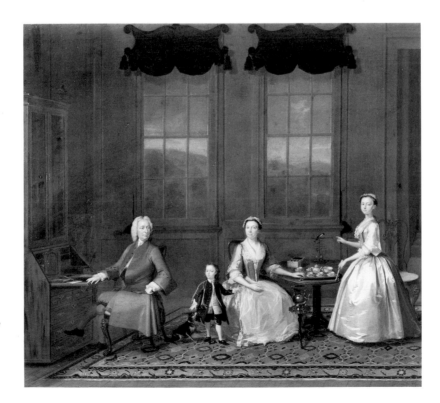

Plate 132
The Gough Family
by William Verelst,
1741
Oil on canvas,
76.2 × 85.8
(30 × 33¾)
Private Collection

last, the effigy has vanished from the scene. The faces are animated, the thoughts set not on the eternal, not entirely on the duty of looking one's best for posterity, but also on the here-and-now. This immediacy is predominantly the characteristic of Hogarth's essays in the new manner, though not confined entirely to his work. And in such essays the intention is no longer the impossible one that all portrait-painters sigh after, to capture a man's whole character, to paint his spiritual and physical biography in the composed confines of a face, but to catch the character in action, reacting to a specific impulse, the features in movement before passion, like water in a wind.

Thus the art widens in scope from that of portraiture into dramatic painting. For Hogarth all the world was a stage – 'my Picture was my Stage and men and women my actors who were by Mean of certain Actions and expressions to Exhibit a dumb show'.[93] In the course of time, it has even become uncertain whether some of his pictures are portrait conversation-pieces, or whether they are, more broadly, scenes from domestic life – such as Lord Northbrook's *The Broken Fan* – and, which ever they are, they are all so closely based on the life that through paint and through the engraver's burin come at last, teeming, the faces of the English crowd. In the truly dramatic pictures the faces are, of course, to some extent generalized, but Hogarth himself insisted, notably in a well-known engraving, on the fundamental difference between his art, which he called that of character, and that of caricature, as practised by the Italians from Leonardo da Vinci to Ghezzi.

In the engraving he refers the 'reader' to the preface of Fielding's *Joseph Andrews* for further enlightenment; there Fielding had written that

He who should call the ingenious Hogarth a burlesque [or caricature] painter, would, in my opinion, do him very little honour; for sure it is much easier, much less the subject of admiration, to paint a man with a nose, or any other feature, of a preposterous size, or to expose him in some absurd or monstrous attitude, than *to express the affections of men on canvas*.

Hazlitt's claim that Hogarth took his faces to the verge of caricature, but never went beyond it, is exaggerated. (The Earl of Iveagh's *Taste à la Mode* is surely caricature, and in many pictures individual heads overstrain the bounds of possibility.) But generally speaking his appraisal is luminously just: Hogarth's faces

carry all the conviction of reality with them, as if we had seen the actual faces for the first time, from the precision, consistency, and good sense with which the whole and every part is made out. They exhibit the most uncommon features, with the most uncommon expressions, but which yet are as familiar and intelligible as possible, because with all the boldness, they have all the truth of nature . . . *memorable* faces, in their memorable moments.

As has been well said, 'he supplied his public not only with the strip-picture and the caption, but also, and above all, with the close-up'.[94]

It was part of Hogarth's genius to catch in paint the human face at that pitch of contortion in which it becomes as it were a caricature of itself; while still individual and essentially human, the face becomes also a symbol of some quality (Plate 133).

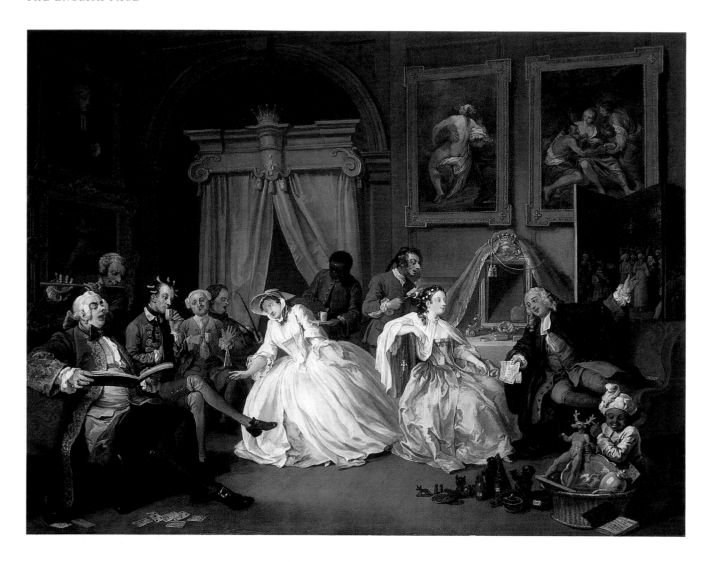

Plate 133
*Marriage à la Mode V:
The Countess's Levée*
by William Hogarth,
1743
Oil on canvas,
68.6 × 89 (27 × 35)
National Gallery,
London

That these qualities are usually of a low if not vicious order is due, first, to Hogarth's satirical purpose; second, to the fact that a vast number of faces are, at their most memorable moments, almost exactly as he depicts them; third, to an inherent shortcoming in nature. This Hogarth has described in *The Analysis of Beauty*: 'it is strange that nature hath afforded us so many lines and shapes to indicate the deficiencies and blemishes of the mind, while there are none at all that point out the perfections of it beyond the appearance of common sense and placidity'.[95] It is the perpetual struggle of the formal portrait-painter to prevent the unequal combat with the pictorial representation of common-sense and placidity resolving itself in the tedious, plain, and insipid clichés of society portraiture. Later commentators have again and again observed how true to the English face Hogarth's interpretation remains. It can be most strikingly demonstrated to the Englishman himself when, abroad, he suddenly sees perhaps a bus-load of compatriots unloaded in a remote French village, or spilled from a *vaporetto* on to the Piazza of San Marco.

How closely the characters in the series like the 'Progresses' were related to living contemporaries remains a matter for argument. Contemporary evidence on the engravings of 'Industry and Idleness' suggests that many were immediately and unmistakably recognizable (though Hogarth himself denied that it was meant to be so), just as were his topographical settings. He certainly exploited that universal human curiosity so well defined by Robert Browning – 'we're made so that we love/ First when we see them painted, things we have passed/Perhaps a hundred times nor cared to see'. Not only did the public turn to Hogarth with delight to discover themselves ('Bob —, Beadle of St — Parish . . . see his Nose, his Chin, and the damn'd sour Look so natural to poor Bob'), but Fielding,[96] father of the English novel, refers back to him for description of his own characters – for the immortal Mrs Bridget Allworthy, in *Tom Jones*: 'I would attempt to draw her picture, but that is done already by a more able master, Mr Hogarth himself – the woman walking to church in Hogarth's *Morning*' (Plate 134).

In some cases, his aim was more specifically journalistic; faces, as the engravers in the late seventeenth century had already found, might be news. Thus celebrated criminals were portrayed in broadsides, but the quality, at least of the artistic execution, was very low. In 1724 Hogarth's father-in-law, Sir James Thornhill, whose rare portraits are the most truly Baroque essays at portraiture by an English

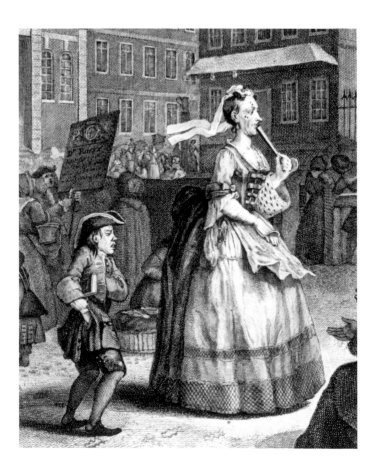

Plate 134
Morning by William Hogarth, 1738 (detail)
Engraving, 48.5 × 39.5
(19 × 15½)
British Museum, London
(Department of Prints and Drawings)

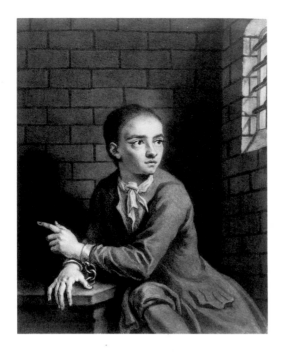

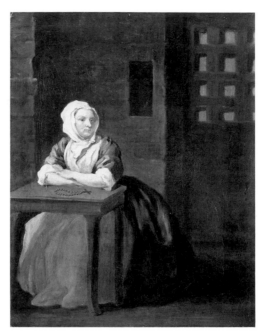

Plate 135 (*far left*)
John (Jack) Sheppard
(1702–1724) by
G. White after James
Thornhill,
5 November 1724
Mezzotint,
31.8 × 25.4 (12½ × 10)
British Museum,
London (Department
of Prints and
Drawings)

Plate 136 (*left*)
Sarah Malcolm
(1710?–1733) by
William Hogarth,
1733
Oil on canvas,
48.8 × 38.7
(19¼ × 15¼)
National Galleries of
Scotland, Edinburgh

painter, turned his hand to the portrayal, for a print, of the great highwayman, Jack Sheppard, as he awaited execution in Paris (Plate 135). It is curious to see Jack Sheppard, in spite of his cropped bullet-head, assume exactly the *contrapposto*, the desirable Baroque twist of body on head, with which Thornhill endowed his intellectual portraits of Newton and Bentley. Early in March 1733, Thornhill seems to have accompanied Hogarth to Newgate, where the sensational murderess Sarah Malcolm was awaiting execution (Plate 136). Hogarth's view of Sarah Malcolm (although he is said to have claimed to see in her features 'that she is capable of wickedness') is as remarkable for its lack of sensationalism as for its direct honesty: she is painted on the same scale as the conversation-pieces Hogarth was then producing. She is distinguished from his sitters of higher class not only by her clothes, but by her attitude, which is entirely unforced and wonderfully observed, the muscular bare forearms resting on the table as on a kitchen-table. The face is not prepossessing, but calm. Later, in 1746, when he drew the Jacobite rebel, Lord Lovat, he had a sensational subject with a sensational appearance. He did not waste the opportunity, but the result is said also to have been very like. The engraving had a huge success, and Hogarth for some weeks made the then fabulous sum of £12 a day out of it (Plate 137).

In his life-size, more formal portraits, Hogarth still conveys a liveliness, even here emphasizing expression in the face of his sitter (Plate 138). This is much more marked than in the portraits of his contemporaries, such as Highmore and Mercier, who were tending towards a greater degree of informality, which was, of course, at variance with the composed expressions that characterized the portraits of the old school. His women sometimes almost beam with cheerfulness, and his men appear busy, or about to be busy; it is a business that can even smack of fussiness, or seem a little affected, as though, in some cases, the single portraits were details snatched out of a conversation-piece, and left conversing with no-one. Here, the necessary formal isolation deprived him of occasion for his most characteristic talent, for drama. His portraits are nevertheless a most refreshing break in the tradition of portrait-painting, and most of them are indeed of members of an unpretentious middle-class, particularly of his friends, like the Hoadleys, or his relations; as a society-painter he never achieved a great success, and his output of life-size portraits was small, and, outside the years 1735–1742, sporadic.

He himself attributed his failure to catch on to a deliberate and malicious campaign against him by his rivals, alleging that the 'whole nest of Phizmongers' ran down his portraits of women as 'harlots' and his men as 'charicatures'. His artistic theories, as based on the famous Line of Beauty and elaborated in that confused and confusing book, his *Analysis of Beauty*, need not concern us greatly in this context. The line of beauty, the serpentine line, which might apply also to the structural undulation of the Baroque, is in Hogarth's practice the broken serpentine of the Rococo, descriptive or ornamental, rather than structural. His faces, in comparison with the ideally pure Knellerian oval, tend to accumulate more roundly in an interplay of plump convexities, cheek, and chin, and chin again, and popping eye; his mouths are full and fleshy, yet vigorous with a wiry flick of humour in the corners, and in a somewhat schematized drawing of a mouth one can see, for once, precisely how, in the shading of the upper lip, the S-line of beauty may apply; in the second sketch of a mouth, immediately below, a typical Hogarthian dramatic

Plate 137 (*right*)
Simon Fraser,
12th Baron Lovat
(1667?–1747) by
William Hogarth,
1746
Etching, 36.2 × 23.4
(14¼ × 9¼)
British Museum,
London (Department
of Prints and
Drawings)

Plate 138 (*far right*)
William Jones
(1675–1749) by
William Hogarth,
1740
Oil on canvas,
126.5 × 101.5
(49⅞ × 40)
National Portrait
Gallery, London

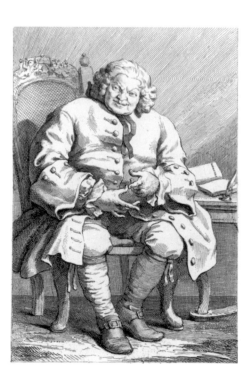

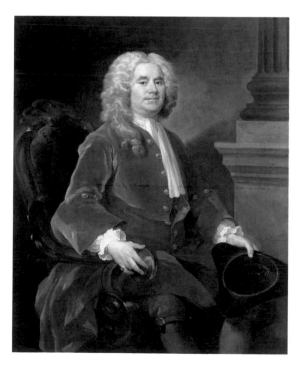

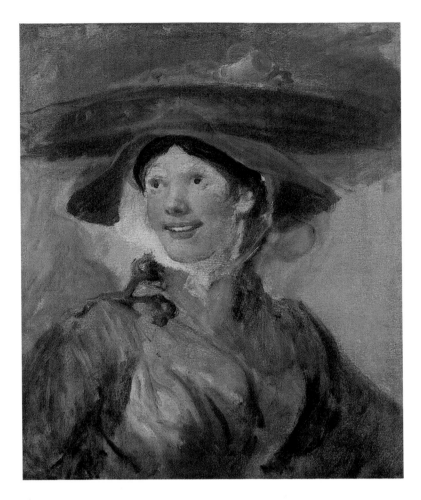

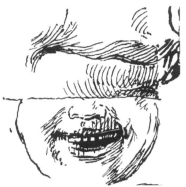

mouth in full expression, the theory of the S-line is detonated into fragments in the toothful grin of a spherical face (Plate 139).

His attitude to the interpretation of the human face, while by no means entirely sceptical of a causal relationship of character on feature – or rather, as always with him, on the expression of the features – was sensibly empirical: 'it is reasonable to believe that aspect to be a true and legible representation of the mind, which gives everyone the same idea at first sight; *and is afterwards confirmed in fact*.' A foolish or a wicked mind may lie behind a handsome face; it is likely to betray itself in expression when excited by passion, but even so the 'character of a hypocrite is entirely out of the power of the pencil' without some non-facial circumstance to help the characterization 'as smiling and stabbing at the same time'.[97] Yet how far Hogarth could go, in catching living comedy on the canvas in an isolated character, is for ever shown in the phenomenal *Shrimp Girl* vibrating still with the silent echo of her cry (Plate 140); on the other hand, some may find a more profound, more rounded, achievement in that wonderful canvas on which, in all sobriety and humility, he set down one by one the faces of his servants; no king could hope for such sympathy combined with such veracity from his portrait-painter (Plate 119).

Plate 139 *(left)*
Detail of drawing
from the manuscript
of *The Analysis of
Beauty* by William
Hogarth, 1753
British Museum,
London (Department
of Prints and
Drawings)

Plate 140 *(far left)*
The Shrimp Girl by
William Hogarth,
after 1740
Oil on canvas,
63.5 × 52.7 (25 × 20¾)
National Gallery,
London

Hogarth had no true following. Highmore, in his *Mr Oldham and His Guests*, comes near to the breath-taking simplicity of Hogarth's servants, but in no other work yet known. His illustrations to Richardson's *Pamela* are strictly illustrations, genteel, charming and, compared with Hogarth's comedies, inexpressive. For Richardson's more robust readers, Mercier produced a painting which was engraved that is pure pin-up; Pamela rising from bed, with a plump and lavish display of breast and thigh (Plate 141). But after Hogarth we generally see the lower classes either through patronizing or hygienic eyes (as in Wheatley's unusual *Mr Howard offering Relief to Prisoners*, 1787), or in the picturesquely bucolic character given them by Hayman (as in his Vauxhall decorations) and Gainsborough; or reduced to caricature ridiculousness by Rowlandson. Only Stubbs, and perhaps Ben Marshall – rather than George Morland – will survey them with a clear but sympathetic eye. But by 1764, when Hogarth died, the greatest movement in British portraiture was in full flower; Reynolds was firmly established in London, and Gainsborough in Bath; Romney had just arrived in London from Westmorland, Stubbs from Lincolnshire and Zoffany from the Continent; miniatures, in the hands of Meyer, Richard Crosse, Smart and Cosway, all already busy in London, were achieving a new stature and shaking off their temporary servility to the life-size portrait; and two years later, in 1766, the author of *Tristram Shandy* sat to Nollekens in Rome (Plate 153). The golden age of the British society portrait has begun.

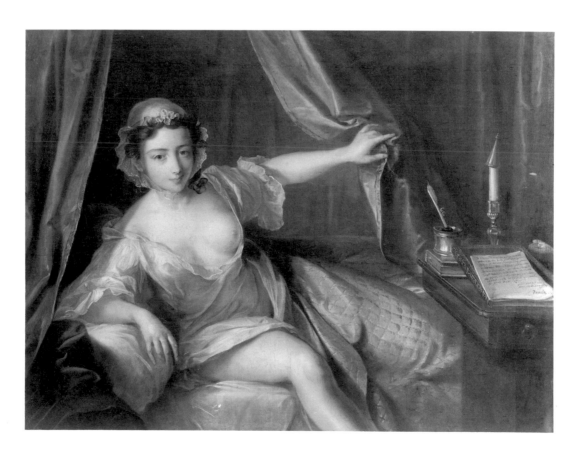

Plate 141
Pamela by Philippe
Mercier, 1743–1745
Oil on canvas,
99 × 125 (39 × 49¼)
Private Collection,
location unknown

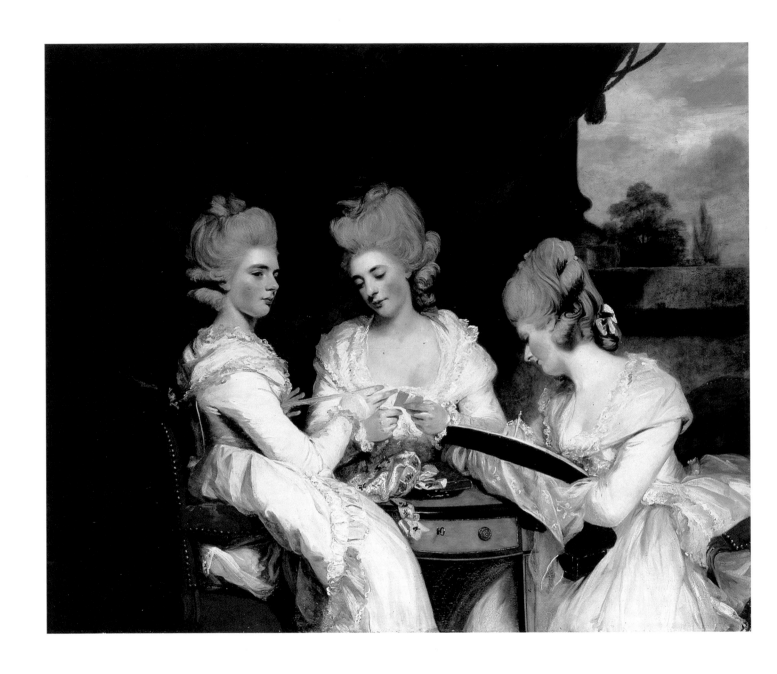

Plate 142 *The Ladies Waldegrave* by Sir Joshua Reynolds, 1780–1781. Oil on canvas, 143.5 × 168 (56½ × 66). National Galleries of Scotland, Edinburgh

VIII

The Golden Age of the Society Portrait

THE SHAPE of the feminine head in the eighteenth century moved from the tall Knellerian oval of about 1700, gradually plumping out in the twenties, until, particularly when supplemented by the popular mob-cap, it blossomed into the Hogarthian sphere of about 1740. Then the hair was closer curled, softening the outline and echoed by the deckle edge of the mob-cap. But hardly had this fashion established itself than the head began to lengthen once more; in the fifties the hair again tends to be drawn tight and smooth, back from brow and cheek; in the sixties it begins to mount above the forehead, a rise accelerating to the fantastic peaks reached in the decade between 1770 and 1780, those top-heavy artifices of wire, grease, powder, with many artificial flowers and feathers, and some natural hair, an unrepeatable and eagerly-grasped opportunity for the furious delight of the caricaturists.

Soon after 1780 the tall cumuli began to shrink (Plate 142), and by 1785 had melted almost away into a broadening crowd of curls at the sides of the head again, although height was still often lent by fountains of feathers erupting from the crowns of vast-brimmed 'picture' hats (Plate 143); in the last five years of the century the face again narrows towards the oval, the curls, thinning in quantity, moving from the sides of the head forward to the brow, sometimes almost into a fringe, but brushed or twisted forward in carefully calculated disorder: Sir Thomas Lawrence's romanticized version of the austere Empire style.

From at least 1740 onwards the dependence of the fashionable woman on artificial aids to smartness, if not beauty, seems to have been considerable. As early as 1737, approximately, Mrs Delany described Lady Baltimore at a royal birthday party as 'like a *frightened owl*, her locks strutted out and most furiously greased, or rather *gummed* and powdered . . .'[98] (Mrs Delany was probably prejudiced, as she was describing the wife of one of her own former suitors). But the fortunes of the cosmeticians and coiffeurs must have reached their height simultaneously with that of the tall style of hair, in the seventies. In 1770 a Bill was at least tabled for the consideration of Parliament:

that all women of whatever rank, profession or degree, whether virgins, maids or widows, that shall from and after such Act, impose upon, seduce and betray into matrimony, any of his Majesty's subjects by the scents, paints, cosmetic washes; artificial teeth, false hair, Spanish wool [a form of rouge pad], iron stays, hoops, high-heeled shoes and bolstered hips, shall incur the penalty of the law now in force against witchcraft and like misdemeanours, and that the marriage upon conviction shall be null and void.

An appearance as artificial as that which prevailed in the seventies was obviously a matter of some concern for the painters of portraits. Gainsborough, as was his nature, recorded it tolerably faithfully; in 1771 he was engaged in a portrait of Lady Dartmouth, which had not been found satisfactory; it appears to have been dressed in some kind of compromise, against the painter's wishes, and he writes to ask permission to

dress it in the modern way . . . I am vastly out in my notion if the face does not immediately look like; but I must know if Lady Dartmouth powders [probably meaning her hair] or not in common.[99]

As for the complexion, Gainsborough was criticized more than once for exaggerating; in 1772 it was for 'too glowing' colours, coupled with an admonition to 'borrow a little of the modest colouring of Sir Joshua Reynolds'.

As always, the fashion of face-painting was most prevalent and most remarkable amongst the courtesans – though it was not only Kitty Fisher but also the Countess of Coventry who was said to have died from the abuse of cosmetics – and the portrait practice of Gainsborough was further extended in that direction than was that of Reynolds. 'A favourite among the demi-reps' the *Morning Chronicle* called

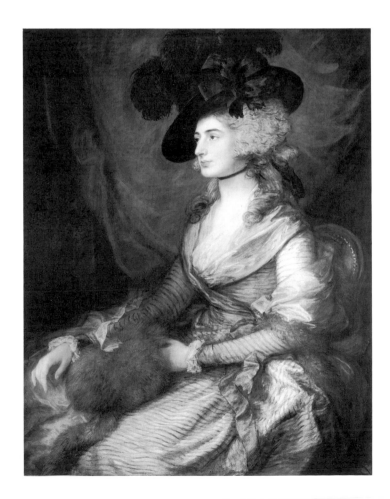

Plate 143
Mrs Sarah Siddons
(1755–1831) by Thomas
Gainsborough, 1785
Oil on canvas,
126.3 × 99.7 (49¾ × 39¼)
National Gallery, London

Gainsborough apropos of the Royal Academy Exhibition of 1778, where were hung three portraits of women of that kind:

very fit subjects for Mr. Gainsborough's pencil, since he is rather apt to put that sort of complexion upon the countenance of his female portraits which is laughingly described in the School for Scandal as 'coming in the morning and going away at night', than to blend what is, properly speaking, Nature's own red and white.[100]

The colour scheme for the fashionable face seems indeed to have been a vivid red mouth, and cheeks sometimes almost amounting to purple, on powder-white; the hair heavily powdered. Reynolds' testimony is often more modest indeed than Gainsborough's, in the seventies and eighties, but its value is difficult to assess as his flesh colours have faded, sometimes to an almost monochrome pinkish sallowness. In portraits, of course, the sitters are generally fully dressed as for formal social occasions, and undoubtedly display more furs and more paint and powder than they would normally in their homes. For the men, the same period saw the very gradual emancipation of the face from the wig. In 1700, the full-bottomed wig was in perfect bloom, and worn by all men of society for formal dress; by 1725 it could still be found frequently in undiminished luxuriance, though now grey-blonde with powder; by 1740 it was already obsolescent, and by 1753, as we have seen, the full-bottomed wig was already dead, surviving only in fossilized condition as an attribute of certain offices and professions.

Medicine was one profession that retained it beyond its natural term; in 1747 Dr Mead was shown in a wig in his state-portrait painted for the Foundling Hospital, London, but by 1778 Boswell diagnosed, gloomily, 'a general levity in the age. We have physicians now in bag-wigs'. The real shrink and freaking of the wig took place between 1720 and 1740, when it dropped almost flat on top of the head, and reduced its length till it was often clear of the shoulders: the sides might be a frizz of hair, or a simple or elaborate arrangement of curls; at the back the long tail might be plaited into one or more pigtails, but an enduringly popular mode was the bag wig (Plate 144). As the powder grew thicker on the wig, the thicker it shed upon the shoulders and back, so that it was found convenient to shave or crop one's own hair in order to wear a wig; to powder the wig heavily, and then to encase its back extremities in a bag so that the powder did not snow upon the clothes; and then, often (to prevent the disturbing flip-flap of the bag upon the back), to harness the bag about the throat by a black ribbon, tied at the front in a bow; this was called the *solitaire*, and has been claimed as the direct ancestor of the modern 'black tie'.

A hairdresser, writing in 1782, looked back with some regret to the mid-century when you could tell a man by his wig:

the tradesman by the snug bob, or natty scratch: the country gentleman by the natural fly and hunting peruke. All conditions of men were distinguished by the cut of the wig, and none more so than the coachman, who wore his, as some do to this day, in imitation of the curled hair of the water-dog.[101]

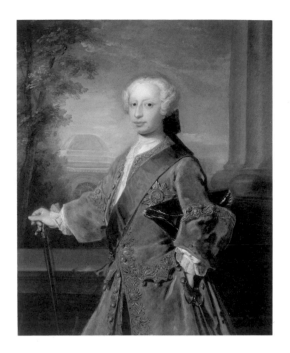

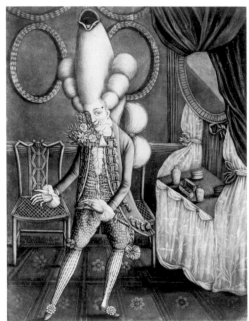

Plate 144 (*far left*)
*Frederick, Prince of
Wales* (1707–1751) by
Philippe Mercier,
*c.*1736 (?)
Oil on canvas,
123.8 × 100.3
(48¾ × 39½)
National Portrait
Gallery, London

Plate 145 (*left*)
The Pantheon Macaroni
by P. Dawe, *c.*1772
Engraving, 14 × 11.4
(5½ × 4½)
British Museum,
London (Department
of Prints and
Drawings)

The varieties, the refinements, were endless; the expense very great. The variety was not, however, a sign of health, and certainly by 1760 many men were wearing their own hair, although they acknowledged, by the use of grease and tongs and powder, the supremacy of the wig, disguising their own hair to look like one.

By 1765 the wig seemed to be no longer dynamic, for in that year the master peruke-makers, in a petition to George III, set forth their distress 'from the almost universal decline of the trade, occasioned by the present mode of men in all stations wearing their own hair'. A company of Body-Carpenters was thereupon promptly invented, exhorting his majesty to wear a wooden leg, and to enjoin all his subjects to appear in the royal presence with the same badge of honour.[102] In fact, the wig was far from done for, and within five years had sprouted again into its most extraordinary form yet: the wigs of the Macaroni (Plate 145).

These rivalled the simultaneous elevation of women's hair; at first the hair was brushed stiffly up from the forehead, and suddenly it soared, out of control, while the *queue* behind was bound into a greased club: powder, pomade and even plaster-of-paris were the ingredients, besides hair, but especially powder, greyish, pink, blue, violet, laced with scent. It is extremely difficult to get an exact idea of the heights to which these toupees grew: the evidence of the caricaturists, particularly Darley, is profuse but obviously exaggerated, and even the Macaroni seem to have hesitated to perpetuate themselves at the full height of fashion in formal commissioned portraits. There is a disparity literally of feet between the head-dressings shown even in the most modish portraits of Reynolds and Gainsborough in the seventies, and those shown by the cartoonists.

To judge by the more formal portraits, a fairly modest form of wig, or dressing of the hair in imitation of the wig, seems to have consolidated itself, rather than given way to the natural hair, between 1770 and about 1789. The French Revolution probably had something to do with the death of the wig, sweeping it in France from such heads as it spared; there was Rousseau's taunt at the rich depriving the poor of bread by using all the flour for their own heads; but a movement towards a greater relaxation in dress generally, headed by characters of the eminence of the Duchess of Devonshire (Plate 146) and Charles James Fox (Plate 147), seems to have been under way in England through the eighties. Soon young men at the Universities were cropping their hair, wearing it unashamed in its natural colour, unwaxed, braving the fury of the proctors and the nickname of 'Apollos'. The abandonment of the wig and of powder was however still gradual; about 1799 a bishop (Dr Randolph of Oxford) ventured to lay his aside, but he was severely rebuked. Powder was taxed by Pitt, after a bad wheat harvest; in 1795 a group of eminent Whigs, in order to deprive him of some revenue, ceremonially washed their hair at Woburn Abbey, and forbore to powder. The practice continued unabated in the army, with such devotion that, when during a flour-famine in July 1800, the consumption of flour for pastry was forbidden in the Royal Household (rice being used instead), the 250,000 members of the armed forces were still reckoned to be using a pound of flour per head per week.[103]

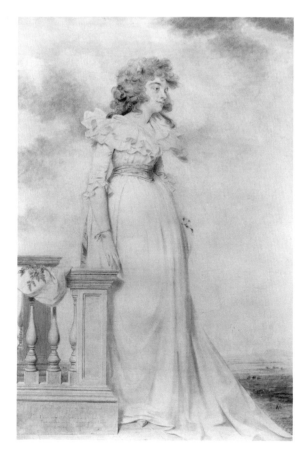

Plate 146
Lady Georgiana Spencer,
Duchess of Devonshire
(1757–1806) by John
Downman, 1787
Watercolour,
78.2 × 65.1
(30¾ × 25⅝)
The Trustees of the
Chatsworth
Settlement

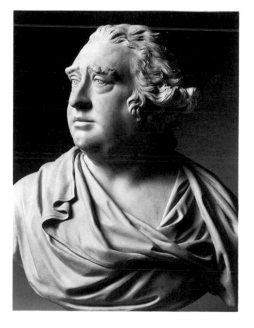

Plate 147 (*above*)
Hon. Charles James Fox (1749–1806)
by Joseph Nollekens, c.1791
Terracotta, height 52.7 (20¾)
National Portrait Gallery, London

From 1740 onwards, in spite of its vagaries, the general tendency of the wig is to recede from the face, leaving it more visible. Yet the face of the period is almost impossible to define; one can see the fashion-plate ideal perhaps behind the work of some of the more mannered, minor portrait-takers, especially in such as Downman, and to an extent even in Romney. The women approximate to a sharper-featured, less rounded type; one of the most celebrated of them all, Georgiana, Duchess of Devonshire, could indicate her own shortcomings thus: 'a moderate drawing might surely comprize A snub nose, a wide mouth and a pair of grey eyes' – and be described (by a writer in the *St James Chronicle* in 1783) as

in our opinion by no means an elegant woman. There is a hoydening affability about her, sanctified by her rank and fortune, which has rendered her popular. Mr. Gainsborough has given her as she might have been if retouched and educated by the Graces.[104]

Downman gives her almost as if sophisticated by nature.

The men too are less plump, often fleshy but no longer swagged with fat, and the young men tend towards a clean-cut face, that sometimes conveys an almost hygienic impression, like an advertisement for after-shaving lotion, and has an assured, sharply defined jaw-line. From Romney's portraits one could at last take faces, again and again, that might be submitted with confidence for star-leads in modern films. But anyone who knows the latter part of the eighteenth century well will not be deceived by such generalizations, for our deeper knowledge of its people is conditioned visually neither by Downman nor by Romney, but by Gainsborough, and, above all, by Sir Joshua Reynolds (Plate 148).[105]

Joshua Reynolds returned from his journey to Italy in 1752, aged 29; early in 1753 he set up in London, and there, for forty years until his death in 1792, he remained the dominant figure in British art. His triumph was one of application rather than of formal exploration and discovery; he applied the discoveries of the Old Masters to the British portrait. He is said to have been fixed in his determination to be a painter by the reading, when he was a boy, of Richardson's theoretical works, and in theory, like Richardson, he suffered from intellectual pretensions. He wished to be a history-painter, to paint subjects of a more general, spiritual and intellectual order than portraits: a realm of the pure imagination.

Fortunately – for he was not at his best there – the British public was not ready for such art, and so not prepared to support it in terms of hard cash; Reynolds therefore was doomed to remain primarily a painter of portraits. But to his portraits he brought his wide learning, of technique and of theory, of the Old Masters, and he treated his sitters honourably as material not merely for portrait-effigies but for imaginative compositions. A portrait must also be a picture, composed in terms of colour, of light and shade, of a pictorial architecture; and to the requirements of a picture the sitter must in a sense yield; at least he must admit some compromise.

Behind almost all society portraiture before Reynolds there is a basic, and dead, symmetry; on the surface of the picture is disposed the sitter, dead-centre;

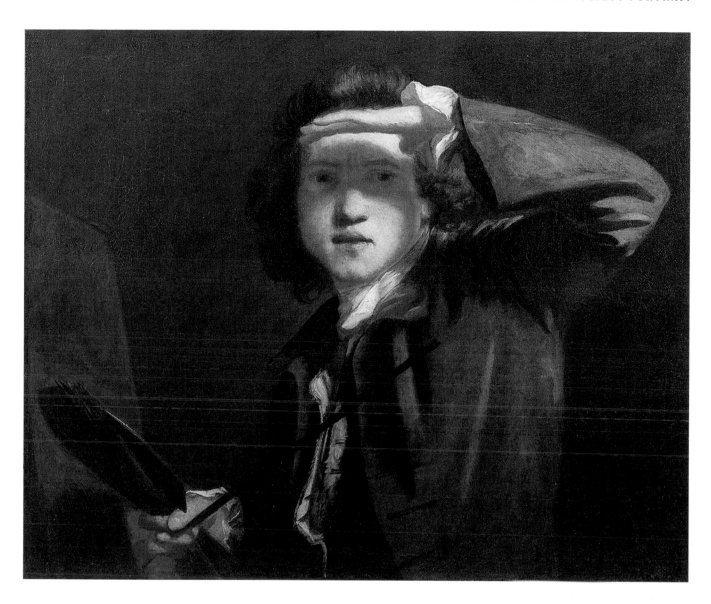

Plate 148
Sir Joshua Reynolds
(1723–1792), self-
portrait, *c.*1747
Oil on canvas,
63.5 × 74.3 (25 × 29¼)
National Portrait
Gallery, London

behind him, like a drop-set, or series of drop-sets receding in depth, is the back-ground. By no means is it always as simple as this, but such a description applies to almost all the portrait-maker's work immediately preceding Reynolds, that of Hudson and Hoare, and even, in the forties, of Ramsay and of Hogarth. Symmetry again is observed in the painting of the face; every sitter (except when seen in profile) has two eyes, two eyebrows, two nostrils and two modulated segments of the bow of the mouth; every face, though each departs in its individu-ality from the norm of the oval, acknowledges nevertheless that it is an oval. Very often, in a portrait by Reynolds, we find that his sitter is not in the middle of the canvas; his body being perhaps chopped off at a most unorthodox place and angle by the picture's edge. Often, too, the play of light and shade, deployed in much stronger contrast than by any previous British painter, seems to be active even between the spectator and the person in the picture; the sitter is involved in a shifting weather.

Further, the sitter's face, no longer composed into the symmetrical oval mask, may be involved with, or even corroded by, the shifting weather of life. Hogarth of course had shown faces similarly involved in action, but faces shattered from a basic symmetry occur only in his comic history pieces, not in his portraits, and the shattering is achieved by a faithful recording of the features when violently distorted by passion. Naturally, Reynolds' sitters, including the politest of polite society, did not distort their faces violently with passion when confronted by his urbane, if calculating, stare; their involvement with life is more subtle, less definable, but no less positive; they may be obviously doing nothing except pose for their picture, but Reynolds' recording transmits his own agreeable and sometimes faintly ironic acknowledgement of the fact (this applies particularly to his portraits of women).

In his best portraits there is much more than that. When asked to produce a written character of Johnson, Reynolds wrote that he doubted if he had the ability:

the habits of my profession unluckily extend to the consideration of so much only of character as is on the surface, as is express'd in the lineaments of the countenance.

He goes on nevertheless to attempt his best, asking that his presumption to 'investigate the peculiar colouring of [Johnson's] mind as distinguished from all other minds' be excused.[106] He has, in fact, in his portraits, abandoned the classic attempt to present a summary but rounded definition, for eternity, of a character; he deals with 'so much only of character as is on the surface', but he deals with it in action, involved with the moment. Titian and Van Dyck, said Northcote, painted hours; Sir Joshua moments. For him each portrait presented a fresh problem, not merely that of recording an individual facial likeness, but of *producing* – with all the theatrical implications of that word – a convincing, coherent character in action. Whereas Hogarth's conversation-pieces sometimes show a group in action, Reynolds at his best stages men and women in soliloquy; he may have abandoned the attempt to paint the mind (his panegyrists, of course, claimed that he did, as had been claimed for every portrait-painter from Holbein onwards), but few painters can rival him in the almost palpable rendering of the cast of thought.

Technically, he had grave shortcomings. He could not draw (as is perhaps too often stressed, for he could paint) and he was sometimes glaringly slip-shod; he experimented – with an irresponsibility to posterity curious in his character – dangerously, almost haphazardly, with tricks of technique. Even before his death, many of his portraits, painted with perishable media, had faded badly. Sometimes, as in some of his grandiose semi-allegorical portraits painted for exhibition at the Royal Academy in the seventies, he lost his sense of judgement to the point of painting actually ridiculous pictures; many times – inevitably, considering his huge output – he fell back on stock solutions. Yet, in his overall range and general variety, he stands unsurpassed amongst all great portrait-painters, and the inexhaustible marvel of his genius was recognized by his rival, Gainsborough, in his famous ejaculation of envy – 'Damn him! how various he is!' To the faces of his sitters he brought every time a fresh eye and that extraordinary sensitivity to the atmospherics of character-producing.

With all his formal preoccupations and his borrowings from the Old Masters, he produced nevertheless a new naturalism. Commissioned though he was to take a likeness, his eye leant impartially upon each face and he painted it as he saw it, not as a concept. Thus in his portrait of the aged Admiral Rodney (Plate 149) the light falls on each accident of the face, on the sunken eye, the craggy nose, the shrunk grim mouth that disdains false teeth; on the shadowy side of the face, he records, not – as Lely or Hudson would have done – the symmetrical anatomy of eye and cheek, but their submergence and dissolution into shadow. No longer is there a set formula of outline and of colour for each feature; Reynolds, painting a face, with an extraordinary, though by no means infallible, feeling for tonal modulation, paints the surface of an object as it is revealed in colour and shadow, and in depth, by light.

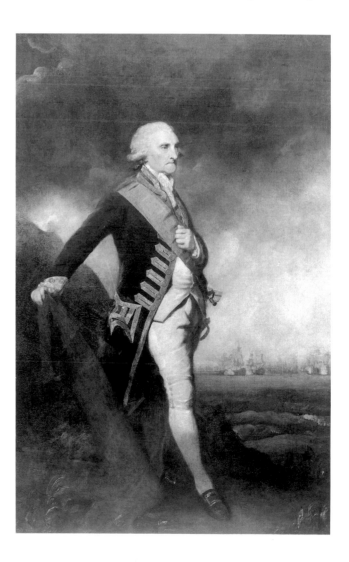

Plate 149
George Brydges, 1st Baron Rodney
(1719–1792) by Sir Joshua
Reynolds, 1789
Oil on canvas, 239.7 × 147.6
(94⅜ × 58⅛)
Royal Collection (by gracious
permission of Her Majesty The
Queen)

There is no standard 'Reynolds mouth' as there is a standard 'Kneller mouth'. The portrait of Rodney is a very late work (exhibited at the Academy in 1789), but Reynolds indicated his range in works painted in his first years in London, in paintings such as those of Lord and Lady Cathcart, and the first portrait of Admiral Keppel (Plate 150).

The latter is a key-piece, for it has not only the broad treatment of the face, lit by the stormy sea-light, a face painted – not drawn in terms of line – massively and freely, the far side sunk in shadow with but the glint of an eye, but it is based in pose on the *Apollo Belvedere* probably in direct emulation of Ramsay's similarly posed *Chief of Macleod* (Plate 151) painted about five years before. Ramsay had done much to soften up the conventions of society portraiture in the forties; yet his Macleod is a lay figure, symmetrically disposed on the surface of the picture, whereas Reynolds' Keppel walks and breathes in the broken light of the cloudy sea-shore. It was with works such as these, right at the beginning of his career, that Reynolds transformed the whole conception of British portraiture; and it was within the new freedom that he gave it that not only he but the other masters of the late eighteenth century were to deploy their forces.

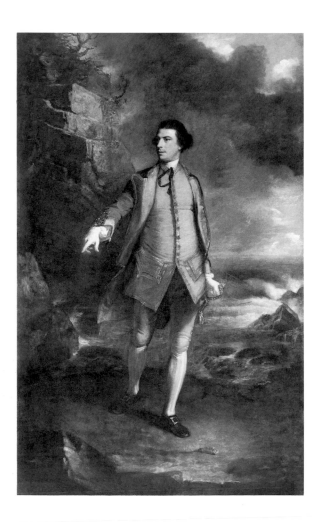

Plate 150
Augustus, 1st Viscount Keppel when Commodore Keppel (1725–1786) by Sir Joshua Reynolds, *c.*1753–1754
Oil on canvas, 238.8 × 147 (94 × 58)
National Maritime Museum, Greenwich

It may come as a surprise to those who are not specialists in English painting to know that Reynolds was notoriously unreliable in his ability to satisfy clients with a likeness; Hoppner once said that he was surprised that Reynolds dared send home some of his portraits, so little did they resemble the originals. Part of the reason for this doubtless lay in the fact that he painted moments, not hours; that he could produce almost snap-shot effects, sometimes perhaps fixing his sitters in expressions unusual to them. If you take a series of instantaneous photographs of anybody, a proportion of them will inevitably be judged, not only by the sitter, to be 'not like', or not 'characteristic'. However that may be, and though the accusation should not be forgotten, it is nevertheless now almost entirely academic, for it is precisely by the coherence and conviction of his characterizations that Reynolds now impresses most people – and by their range.

Largely aloof from politics, yet urbane and sociable, widely-read, a man of letters, a man of substance, Reynolds was sought out by an astonishing proportion of the cream of his time; he painted the aristocracy of blood and of intellect, of sensibility and even of professional sex. He painted the soldiers and the great admirals; he painted Rockingham, Bute, Burke, Charles James Fox (but the Pitts

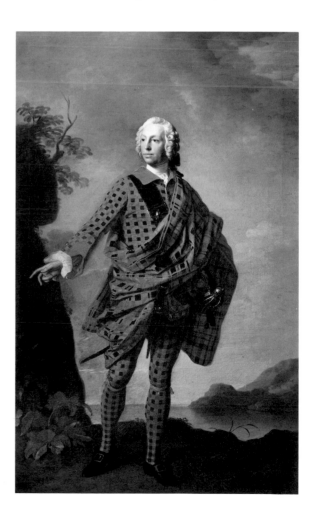

Plate 151
Norman, 22nd Chief of Macleod by Allan Ramsay, 1747–1748
Oil on canvas, 223.5 × 137.2 (88 × 54)
The Collection of Macleod of Macleod, Dunvegan Castle, Skye

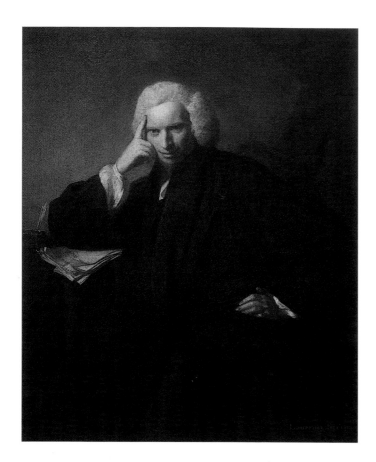

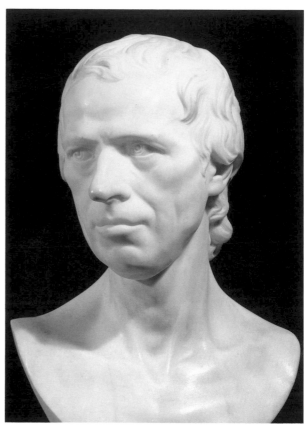

eluded him), he painted royalty and dukes, he painted bishops and Beckford, he painted high fashion, Georgiana, Duchess of Devonshire, or Kitty Fisher; he painted lawyers, virtuosi, actors (or *the* actor, Garrick), surgeons and country gentlemen; he painted Horace Walpole and he painted Dr Johnson.

It is perhaps in his portraits of the Johnson circle, of which he was himself an intimate, that his finest achievement, at least in male portraiture, lies. Laurence Sterne, practical joker, was not a member of the circle, and is earlier (1760) than most of the literary portraits but is the most disturbing and hypnotic face (Plates 152 and 153); of the circle proper Reynolds has left us Goldsmith, Dr Burney, Boswell and others, but above all Dr Johnson himself (Plate 154). Reynolds' views of Johnson, from the first sprawling three-quarter length of 1756 in the National Portrait Gallery to the last fantastic imaginary reconstruction of Johnson as a naked infant (1783) will add another dimension even to Boswell's account, and, in conjunction with it, bring anyone as close to that magic hulk as they will ever get. Reynolds' images of him, together, admit the validity of all the astonished reactions of Johnson's contemporaries.

Dr Campbell on first meeting him, was revolted:

the aspect of an idiot, without the faintest ray of sense gleaming from any one feature; with the most awkward garb and unpowdered grey wig on one side of his head, he is forever

Plate 152 (*above left*)
Laurence Sterne
(1713–1768) by Sir
Joshua Reynolds,
1760
Oil on canvas,
127.3 × 100.3
(50⅛ × 39½)
National Portrait
Gallery, London

Plate 153 (*above right*)
Laurence Sterne
(1713–1768)
by Joseph Nollekens,
*c.*1766
Marble, height 39.4
(15½)
National Portrait
Gallery, London

dancing the Devil's jig, and sometimes he makes the most driveling effort to whistle some thought in his absent paroxisms.

'His person was large, robust, I may say approaching to the gigantic, and grown unwieldy from corpulency', wrote Boswell lucidly but affectionately: 'His countenance was naturally of the cast of an ancient statue, but somewhat disfigured by the scars of that *evil* which it was formerly imagined the *royal touch* could cure'.[107] The 'ancient statue' is, of course, special pleading; there can be no more doubt that Johnson was physically appalling than that his fascination was all but irresistible. Here is Mrs Piozzi:

. . . his Sight was near, and otherwise imperfect, yet his Eyes though of a light blue Colour were so wild, so piercing, and at Times so fierce; that Fear was I believe the first Emotion in the hearts of all his Beholders.[108]

Later in the same description, though in a figurative passage, she almost succeeds in conveying the physical impact of his presence: 'Suffice it at once that he was great on all Occasions, and like a Cube in Architecture you beheld him on each Side, as his Size still appeared undiminished'.[109]

But words lap vainly at the contours of his physique as at some invincible continent; it is only Reynolds who was able to map the compatibility of that vast

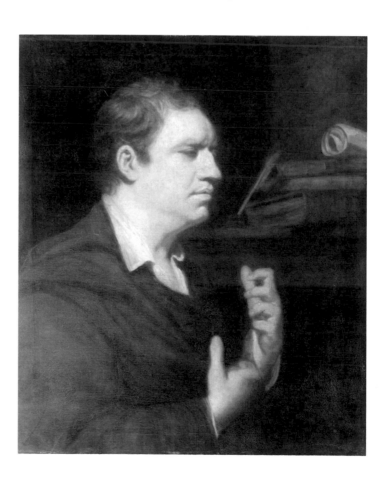

Plate 154
Dr Samuel Johnson
(1709–1784) by Sir Joshua
Reynolds, *c.*1769
Oil on canvas, 76.2 × 63.8
(30 × 25.1)
Tate Gallery, London

intellect with that vast mis-shape, and in the portrait reproduced here we have Johnson wrenching, half physically, thought into words.

With women, Reynolds was liable to be less successful than with men. He was profoundly a bachelor ('Married!' exclaimed Sir Joshua to an aspiring young painter: 'then you are ruined as an artist'.)[110]; as he grew older he tended to become distressingly avuncular in his attitude to the opposite sex, and to children; he often painted, not women, but the Ladies, who are only too prone to express themselves with a coyly roguish smirk; most of his children (and with them I would include even pieces such as the famous Master Crewe as Henry VIII) may fill the heart of a modern parent with a sickened rage of frustrated iconoclasm. But against his lapses there is always to be set a superb range of successes, from the grave, intimate candour of his portraits of the fifties and early sixties, when his approach to women was still direct and unaffected, to the justly famous Duchess of Devonshire and daughter (Plate 155), of the eighties, and the extraordinarily revealing head and shoulders of the Duchess's rival and successor, Lady Betty Foster.

Reynolds painted the moment, but he defined it with a massive finality. It was the special genius of his rival and contemporary, Thomas Gainsborough,[111] to catch the moment in transience; Reynolds gives us the 'still', Gainsborough seems to catch the face actually in motion. His career ran, in time, almost parallel with Reynolds';

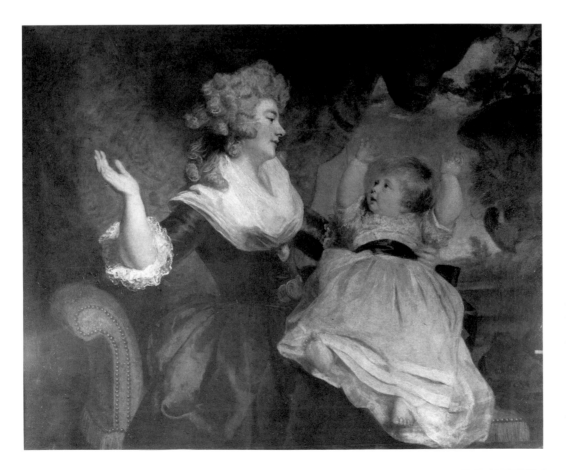

Plate 155
Lady Georgiana Spencer, Duchess of Devonshire (1757–1806) *with her daughter Lady Georgiana Cavendish* by Sir Joshua Reynolds, 1786
Oil on canvas, 113 × 140 (44½ × 55⅛)
The Trustees of the Chatsworth Settlement

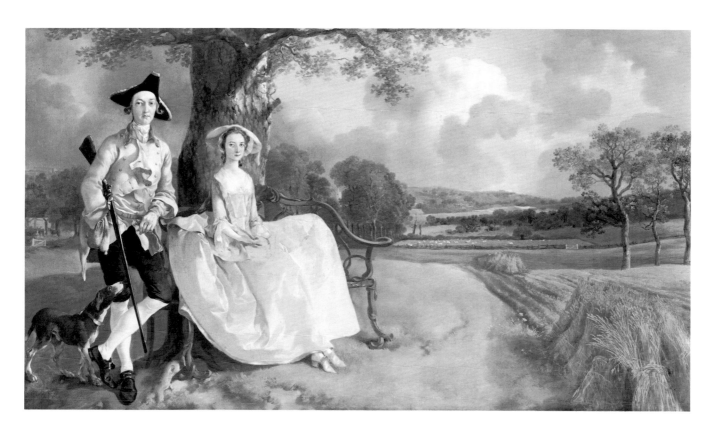

Plate 156
*Mr and Mrs Robert
Andrews* by Thomas
Gainsborough,
*c.*1748–1749
Oil on canvas,
69.8 × 119.4
(27½ × 47)
National Gallery,
London

in his first period, in Suffolk and in London, he was painting those direct little masterpieces, of which the greatest is the famous *Mr and Mrs Robert Andrews* besides a cornfield (Plate 156). His sitters are involved in no psychological drama; instead we have a direct and vivid record of country gentry at their ease in their countryside, their faces open and ingenuous and unconstrained by fashion. But in 1759 Gainsborough moved from Suffolk to Bath, and in that fashionable resort he had to come to terms with fashion; gradually he did so, without ever entirely losing that informality that at first seems to have shocked, not entirely disagreeably, the mannered visitors to Bath; thus Mrs Delany reacted in October 1760 to his whole-length of Anne Ford with a guitar (Plate 157) – 'a most extraordinary figure, handsome and bold; but I should be very sorry to have anyone I loved set forth in such a manner'.[112] 'Splendid impositions', she called his portraits. Thence he learned to ally his informality with a necessary social dignity, and all the time his style was opening out into that feathery flickering touch that renders his later paintings, after his establishment in London in 1774, almost airborne (Plate 158).

It was during his Bath period, however, that he produced perhaps his most sensitive appreciations of individual faces, modelled with a minute delicacy of touch that is only equalled by Van Dyck, on whom he was at the time deliberately remodelling himself. Later, in his looser manner, he seems still to have retained his power of catching a likeness, for which, unlike Reynolds, he was famous. Personally, in contrast again to Reynolds, he conducted his business of painting almost as a tradesman, without intellectual or social overtones ('many a real genius is lost in the fictitious character of a gentleman'). His avowed intention was to satisfy the client by the delivery of a likeness, which he described as 'the principal beauty and intention of a portrait'.[113] To achieve this, he liked to begin his portrait in a reduced light, even by candlelight; by this method, according to his colleague Ozias Humphrey,

with incessant study and exertion, he acquired the power of giving the masses and general forms of his models with the utmost exactness. Having thus settled the groundwork of his portraits he let in (of necessity) more light for the finishing of them . . .[114]

Of the finished product, no more acute or revealing account has ever been given than that included by Reynolds in his Fourteenth Discourse, after Gainsborough's death in 1788; it is a passage that every painter of portraits should know.

The likeness of a portrait . . . consists more in preserving the general effect of the countenance, than in the most minute finishing of the features, or any of the particular parts. Now Gainsborough's portraits were often little more, in regard to finishing, or determining the form of the features, than what generally attends a dead colour; but as he was always attentive to the general effect, or whole together, I have often imagined that the unfinished manner contributed even to that striking resemblance for which his portraits are so remarkable. Though this opinion may be considered as fanciful, yet I think a plausible

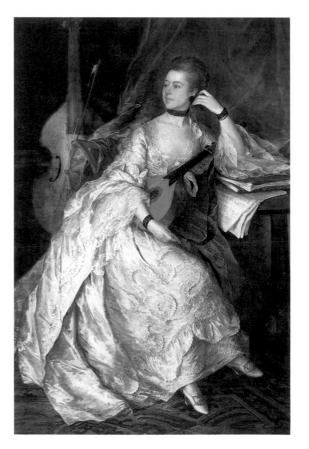

Plate 157
Anne Ford, later Mrs Philip Thicknesse
(1737–1824) by Thomas Gainsborough, 1760
Oil on canvas, 196.9 × 134.6 (77½ × 53)
Cincinnati Art Museum, Cincinnati, Ohio
(Bequest of Mary M. Emery)

Plate 158 (*facing page*)
Mr and Mrs William Hallett (The Morning Walk) by Thomas Gainsborough, 1785
Oil on canvas, 236 × 179 (93 × 70½)
National Gallery, London

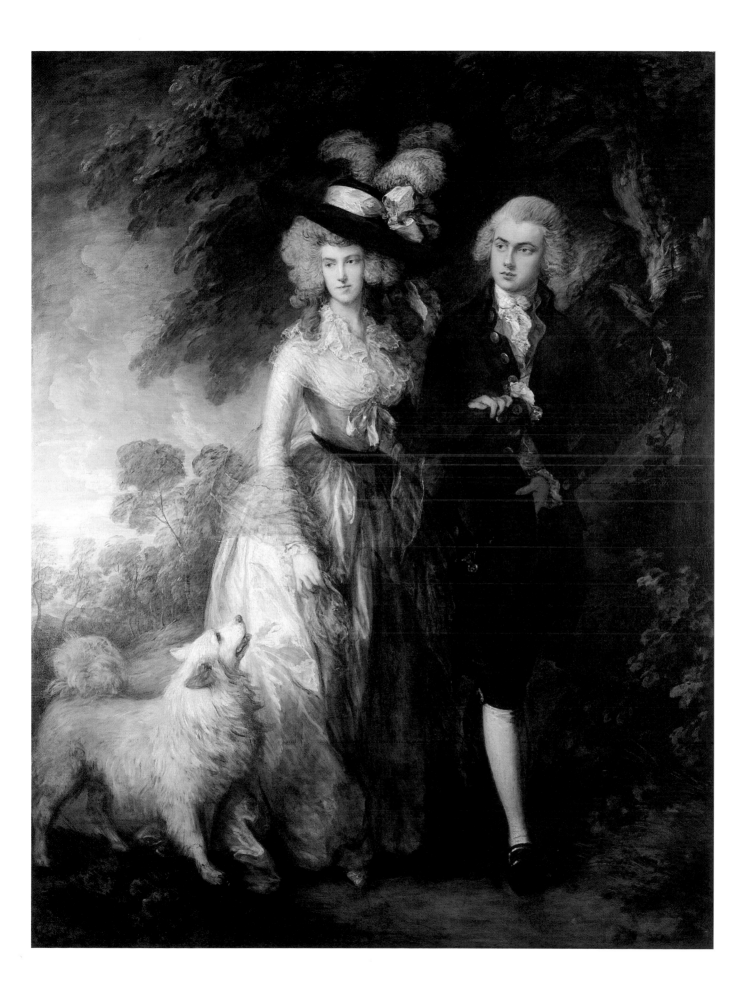

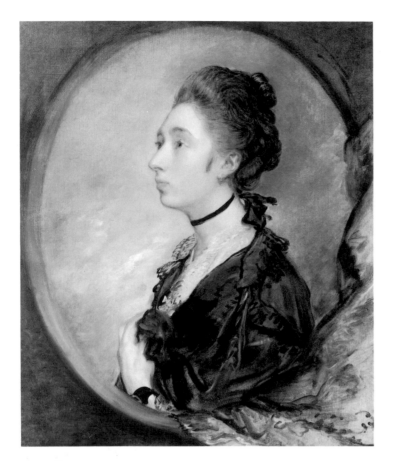 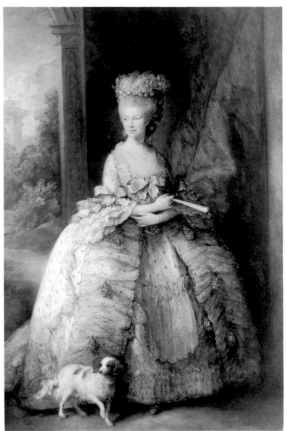

reason may be given why such a mode of painting should have such an effect. It is presupposed, that in this undetermined manner there is the general effect; enough to remind the spectator of the original; the imagination supplies the rest, and perhaps more satisfactorily to himself, if not more exactly, than the artist, with all his care, could have done. At the same time it must be acknowledged there is one evil attending this mode; that if the portrait were seen, previous to any knowledge of the original, different persons would form different ideas, and be disappointed at not finding the original correspond with their own conceptions; under the greater latitude which indistinctness gives to the imagination what character of form it pleases.[115]

Reynolds' own characterizations can be remarkable for the intensity of their definition; in Gainsborough's later portraits he uses in his characterization (but not in his colour) a kind of impressionism (Plate 159); the light but incomparably deft brush indicates, but does not define, a contour, or suggests, with three or four slight strokes, the upper eyelid and the tremulous mobility of the eyelashes. He gives the onlooker scope to move and to imagine, to adjust the sitter's expression according to his own fancy; the key-points of the features, those that control the expression, especially the eyes and the corners of the mouth, remain ambivalent, hovering amongst possibilities.

He was, however, concerned, as indicated by a letter already quoted, to paint his

Plate 159 (*above left*)
Margaret Gainsborough
(1752–1820) by
Thomas
Gainsborough, *c*.1772
Oil on canvas,
75.6 × 62.9
(29¾ × 24¾)
Tate Gallery, London

Plate 160 (*above right*)
Queen Charlotte
(1744–1818) by
Thomas
Gainsborough, 1781
Oil on canvas,
240.7 × 99.7
(94¾ × 39¼)
Royal Collection (by
gracious permission of
Her Majesty The
Queen)

sitters as they were, even to paint, powder and all the ephemeral vagaries of fashion. Reynolds, in practice and in theory, in his Seventh Discourse, was strongly against such practice, suggesting as compromise that the painter dresses 'his figure something with the general air of the antique for the sake of dignity and preserves something of the modern for the sake of likeness'.[116] The result, as Reynolds had to admit in Gainsborough's case, was to contemporaries usually a striking likeness, yet the strange thing is that, now that the originals have gone down into dust, and that the question of 'like or not like' is academic, it is Reynolds' portraits, unlike though they may have been, that carry in most cases the more vivid and positive impressions of living individuals.

Gainsborough's people, in his later portraits, are so loosely defined that they tend to merge one into the other, the stuff that dreams are made of, under the veil of his brilliant most personal paint; and it is in sheer paint that Gainsborough's enduring magic resides. One can catch a glance of the spell being woven through Northcote's eyes, when he describes Gainsborough and his nephew Dupont sitting up all night by candlelight working on the whole-length of Queen Charlotte (Plate 160): ''Tis

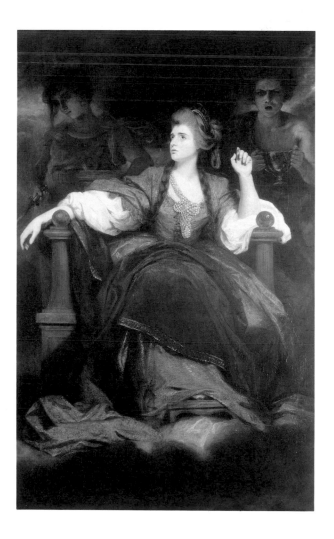

Plate 161
Mrs Sarah Siddons (1755–1831) *as the Tragic Muse* by Sir Joshua Reynolds, 1784
Oil on canvas, 236 × 142 (93 × 56)
Henry E. Huntington Art Gallery and Library, San Marino, California

Plate 162
*Margaret Lindsay, Mrs Allan
Ramsay* (died 1782) by
Allan Ramsay, *c.*1759–1760
Oil on canvas, 76.2 × 63.5
(30 × 25)
National Galleries of
Scotland, Edinburgh

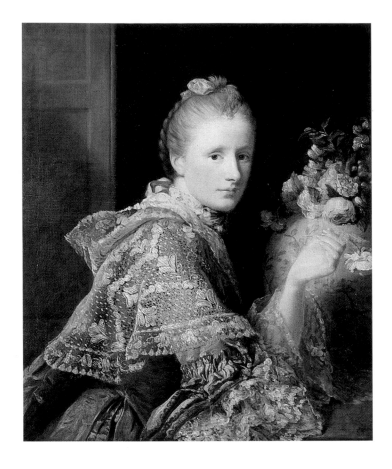

actual motion, and done with such a light airy facility. Oh! it delighted me . . .'[117] a rhythmic modulation of line and colour that, like music, can catch into incredulous sharp pleasure the hearts of those who are in love with it.

Reynolds was a dramatic painter; it is Gainsborough who endowed our history with lyric faces. His clientele was much narrower than Reynolds', and largely confined to Suffolk and Bath of course for the first twenty-five years of his painting career. Portraits of an intellectual weight, such as were Reynolds' forte, were not for him, and his finest portraits tend to be those of his family and his intimates, who were not members of the Johnson circle, but included musicians, eccentrics and demi-reps. When Reynolds painted Mrs Siddons (Plate 161), he turned to Michelangelo for inspiration, and painted her, on stage, in draperies – as 'The Tragic Muse'; when Gainsborough painted her (Plate 143), he painted her as she sat in his studio, a smart woman of fashion, with a sharp, spry and eloquent nose, and a great deal of powder, ready for the Mall.

Reynolds and Gainsborough are the two supreme portrait-painters in the later eighteenth century, and, in the forty years between 1750 and 1790, they covered a great deal of ground, producing well over 2,000 portraits between them, no inconsiderable proportion of the top strata of society from which almost all their sitters came.

They held of course no monopoly. The later careers of some of the best of the conventional painters of the preceding era overlapped even the early maturity of Reynolds and Gainsborough. Ramsay, who, in his constant search for fresh designs, had prepared the way in the forties for Reynolds, lived on until 1784, but painted very little after 1770. Although contemporaries had noted in his earlier portraits a novel complexion (achieved by an underpainting of the flesh in bright red) and a 'licked' brushwork that was reminiscent of French painting, the expression and character of most of the portraits of the period is little different from those of Hoare and Hudson (who died respectively only in 1792 and 1779), the pillars of the old school. In Ramsay's later work there is a certain debt to the new freedom bestowed upon portraiture by Reynolds, but also a subtlety and reticence, particularly in portraits of women, that was outside Reynolds' own range; he could be a painter of perfect tact and courtesy, without blandishment (Plate 162).

Hudson and Hoare both soldiered on with few concessions to the new freedom of

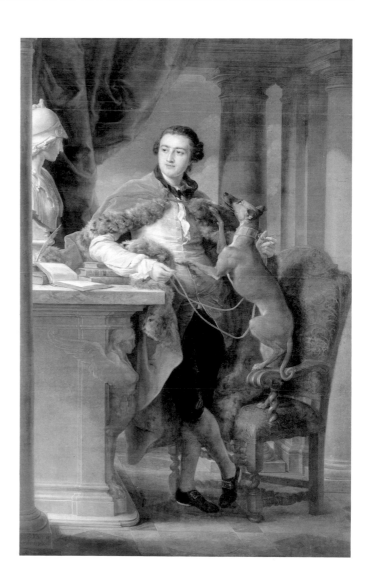

Plate 163
Charles Compton, 7th Earl of Northampton (1737–1763) by Pompeo Batoni, 1758
Oil on canvas, 237.7 × 149.2 (93$\frac{1}{2}$ × 58$\frac{3}{4}$)
Fitzwilliam Museum, Cambridge

manner; in this they seem curiously like provincial adherents of the conventional portraiture of the Continent, from which Reynolds, with all his debts to the great Mediterranean masters, stood clearly apart. In 1778, Northcote wrote from Rome that artists there delighted in running Sir Joshua down. In Rome, the twin deities in portraiture were the German-born Anton Raphael Mengs, and Pompeo Batoni, both – but especially the latter – much patronized by Englishmen in Italy on the grand tour. Batoni's whole-lengths of young, gravely holiday Englishmen, shown steeped in the antique, in a world of statuary, drawings, urns and elegant ruins and excellent clothes, still hang in many English houses (Plate 163). It was perhaps from Batoni that George Romney, on his Italian journey in 1773–1775, learned that air of amiable but nobly aloof nonchalance that distinguishes perhaps too many of his portraits. For many of his contemporaries Romney's star was as bright as those of Reynolds and Gainsborough; though it is dimmer now, he was at one time seriously encroaching on Reynolds' clientele. He is, *par excellence*, a painter of handsome men

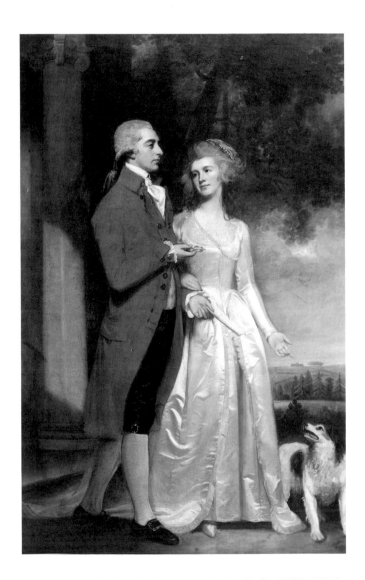

Plate 164
Sir Christopher (1749–1801) *and Lady Sykes* (1748–1803) by George Romney, *c.*1786 (?)
Oil on canvas, 218.5 × 155 (86 × 61)
Sir Tatton Sykes, Sledmere House, Yorkshire

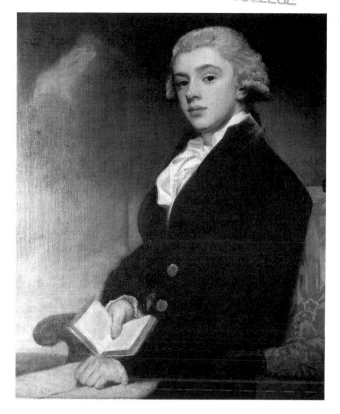

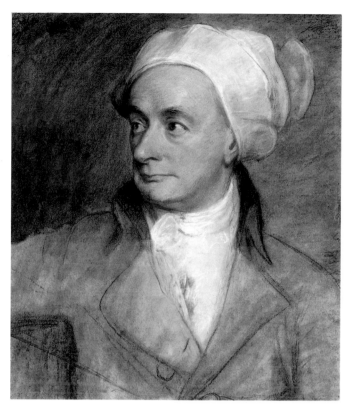

Plate 165 (*above left*)
Charles, 2nd Earl Grey
(1764–1845) by
George Romney,
1784
Oil on canvas,
86.4 × 68.6 (34 × 27)
The Provost and
Fellows of
Eton College

Plate 166 (*above right*)
William Cowper
(1731–1800) by
George Romney,
1792
Pastel, 57.2 × 47
(22½ × 18½)
National Portrait
Gallery, London

and women, and the interpreter of a certain high-bred, aquiline sensibility of repression (Plate 164).

By the quick or tardy movement of the fibres around the lips, he was accustomed to estimate the degrees of sensibility in his sitters; and of himself, in this particular, it might have been said with truth,

His own example strengthens all his laws:
He is himself, THE SENSITIVE he draws.[118]

So wrote his panegyrist, Hayley; in fact he was at his best, not with women and men, whom he over-clarified often into a banal fashion-tailored line of brow and nose and chin, but with adolescents. He can be seen at his best in the Provost's Lodge at Eton, for which he painted several of the fine series of 'leaving portraits' (Plate 165). In these, awkwardness hesitates into elegance, shy yet splendidly-mannered, and Romney's clarity is here vernally delicate, avoiding slickness by a hair's breadth. And elsewhere, at his very best, he could pull effects out of the bag that no one else had in their power – as in the pastel head of that archetypal poet of sensibility, William Cowper (Plate 166), Romney himself considered this the 'nearest approach that he had ever made to a perfect representation of life and character', an attempt to catch 'the poet's eye in a fine frenzy rolling'. Cowper himself rose to the occasion in a sonnet to Romney, praising the painter, once again, for tracing 'The mind's impression too on every face'.[119]

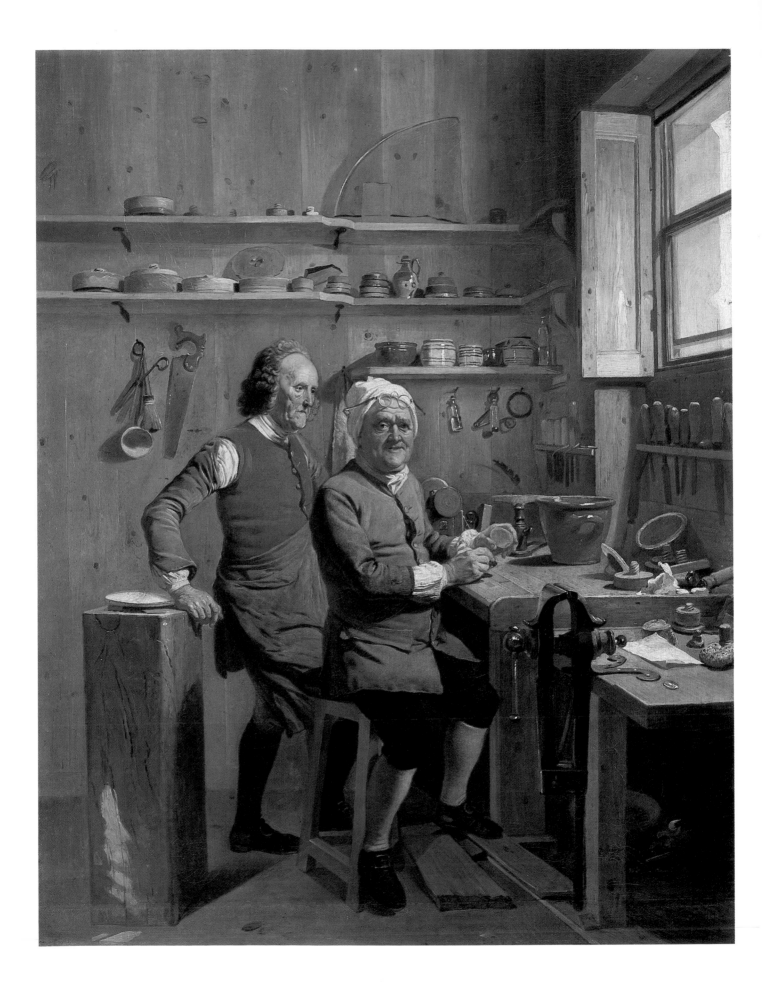

IX

The Face in Miniature

THE TAKING of portraits, the presentation of likenesses, was practised in the late eighteenth century as never before in all media. One extreme was the literal naturalism of the London dentist Van Burtchell, who in 1775 kept his embalmed wife in a glass case in the drawing-room ('and though she has been dead three months she looks as well as when alive')[120]; another novelty was the art of the 'shade' or silhouette, which, in its basic form, is not a portrait at all, but one's shadow fixed on paper.

In particular, the art of miniature-painting, lost for a century in the servile imitation in small of the type of image purveyed by the oil-painters, found itself again; where the miniaturists were influenced by the life-size painters – as Ozias Humphrey generally was by Reynolds, and Jeremiah Meyer sometimes apparently by Cotes and by Gainsborough – the effect was not disastrous, as the life-size painters themselves were now so concerned with the transcription of the particularities of their sitters' faces. The most naturalistic of the miniature-painters was John Smart, who aimed above all at exactness of likeness, had no truck with the frills and graces, yet achieved a sparkling prettiness (Plates 168 and 169). In sculpture, fashion rejected scornfully the rococo animation of Roubiliac, and settled

Plate 167
(*facing page*)
John Cuff and an Assistant by Johan Zoffany, 1772
Oil on canvas, 89.5 × 69.2 (35¼ × 27½)
Royal Collection (by gracious permission of Her Majesty The Queen)

Plate 168 (*right*)
Colonel Robert Frith by John Smart, 1791
Miniature on ivory, 6.4 × 4.6 (2½ × 1⅞)
Private Collection

Plate 169 (*far right*)
Mrs Robert Frith by John Smart, 1791
Miniature on ivory, 6.4 × 4.6 (2½ × 1⅞)
Private Collection

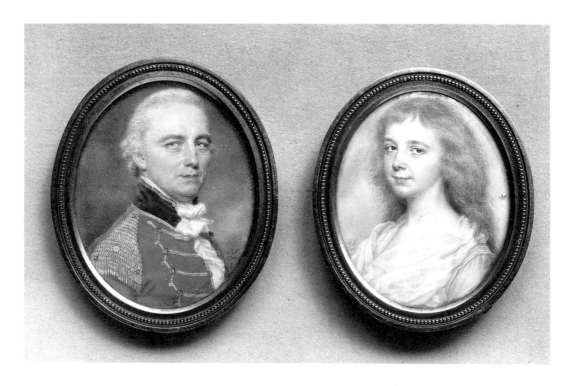

severely into antique taste. In their portraiture men like Wilton, Bacon, Nollekens and then Flaxman, only too often carved into boring practice the theory laid down by Reynolds, but happily only rarely acknowledged by him in the painting of his faces: that

the whole beauty and grandeur of art consists, in my opinion, in being able to get above all singular forms, local customs, particularities, and details of every kind.[121]

A sentimental taste for the antique lay behind the success of profile portraits in the second half of the eighteenth century. Life-size representations of the head in profile are difficult to manage, the centre of the picture being a plateau or tundra of cheek, and the pose, turned decisively away from the onlooker, cold and unfriendly. But reduced to miniature size, the profile can assume a fragile exquisiteness and a flattering classic simplicity. Such portraits were made in wax by Isaac Gosset, for example (Plate 170); in ivory; and, by the prolific Tassies, in a hard paste in imitation of intaglio; and above all they were made by the silhouettists, from 1780 onwards.

As I have already indicated, the silhouette is not really a portrait at all: in its basic form it is made by tracing the shadow – it is not merely a portrait of one's shadow, it is virtually the actual shadow, stilled and fixed on paper. However, even if it be not a true portrait – and the relationship of the person to his shadow is doubtless open to philosophical argument – it is absurd not to admit that at the time it was (barring

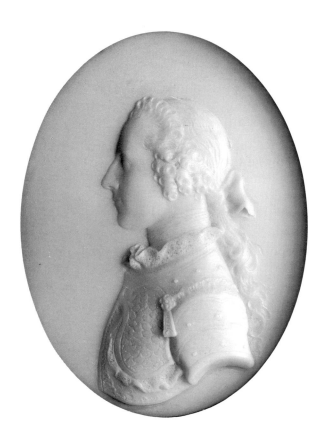

Plate 170
Henry Seymour Conway (1721–1795) by
Isaac Gosset, 1760
Wax medallion, 10.2 × 7.6 (4 × 3)
National Portrait Gallery, London

masks taken from the face) the most exact method of recording the outline of anybody's profile. It was for that reason that Lavater, the Swiss apostle of the science of physiognomy, largely used silhouettes to illustrate his treatises. They had an extraordinarily wide vogue throughout Europe, not merely with cranks but with men of the calibre of Goethe downwards, from 1780 until well into the nineteenth century.

The prestige given by Lavater to the silhouette must in turn have augmented considerably its appeal. Burke, in line with his friend Reynolds, had written that 'a portrait is the ideal of an individual, not of men in general', but Lavater's comment on this definition was that

a perfect portrait is neither more nor less than the circular form of a man reduced to a flat surface, and which shall have the exact appearance of the person for whom it was painted, seen in a camera obscura.[122]

Failing that, the best experimental material for one who hoped to demonstrate precisely the character of the man from his features was, apart from the man himself, the facsimile of his profile offered by the silhouette. For ornamental purposes, however, a life-size silhouette is unwieldy and even incoherent; reduced to miniature scale, they can be decorative trifles. They are, moreover, both extremely quick and cheap to make, whether cut out of paper, or drawn or painted; hence, partly, their popularity – they have been called 'the poor man's miniature'. Artistically, the best are those that were taken freehand without the help of any mechanical appliance; such was the early work of John Miers, in Leeds and London, in the 1780s – head-and-shoulder profiles, painted in jet-black on a white

Plate 171 (*far right*)
A woman of the Fairholme Family by John Miers
Silhouette painted on gesso, 9 × 7 ($3\frac{1}{2} × 2\frac{3}{4}$)
Private Collection

Plate 172 (*right*)
A man of the Fairholme Family by John Miers
Silhouette painted on gesso, 9 × 7 ($3\frac{1}{2} × 2\frac{3}{4}$)
Private Collection

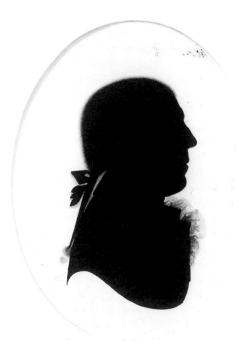

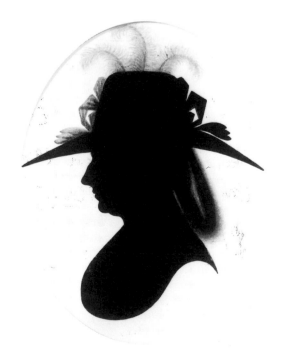

plaster ground, with a very sensitive outline that softens with feathery delicacy in the hair (Plates 171 and 172). Few however were of this order, and the cutting of silhouettes was also a tremendous parlour-game for amateurs.

The professionals who, to begin with, often made a virtue out of the severe limitations of their art, soon, in a hunt for novelty, went whoring after other dimensions. They hatched their black with gold or bronze, touching their black faces with pink lips, and even setting black, flat faces in portraits that were otherwise normal miniatures in full colour. A large display of silhouettes is as repulsive as smallpox, but taken singly the best examples of this very minor art do support contemplation, and distil, from their remote and final simplicity, a disturbing poignancy; it is as though, instead of Peter Schlemihl losing his shadow, the shadow had lost Peter.

Technically, the silhouette is of considerable interest as it heralds and in some ways anticipates the portrait photograph. Many professionals used mechanical contrivances to ensure the accuracy of their likenesses: such were the Ediograph, the Prosopographus and the Physionotrace; such was Charles Schmalkalder's Delineator, Copier and Proportionometer, registered at the Patent Office in 1806, which, at one end, passed a steel rod delicately over the sitter's features, while, at the other end, it simultaneously drew, or cut out, a miniature silhouette of them.

Other devices worked very like a camera – such was a box with an opening towards the sitter. Inside the box was a mirror so angled that it threw the image of the sitter on to a piece of frosted glass let in at the top of the box. Like the photographer, the silhouettist could offer his subject a sitting of only a minute or two; he could also repeat his portraits if wanted. John Miers charged, to start with, half a crown (including frame), and always kept a copy himself, as a photographer keeps his negative, so that he could provide further 'prints' (two shillings each) if wanted. Those who cut out their silhouettes could make a 'negative' without trouble by cutting the original out of a folded sheet of paper.[123]

The list of media in which portraits were taken towards the end of the eighteenth century is far from exhausted; the interest in them was reaching its peak, and so, inevitably, freaking a good deal. Thus the Society of Artists in the seventies, a serious body, admitted portraits such as that of a *Nobleman Worked With a Needle in His Own Hair*, submitted by one or other of the Misses Lane, who specialized in that line. A mock advertisement in a paper on behalf of a 'Mynheer —, just come over from Germany', who had invented a method of taking a likeness by the sitter looking into a mirror and having the glass heated so as to bake the impression, is said to have produced a queue of would-be clients next day at an innocent perfumer's shop in Bond Street.[124]

Portraiture, both of the present and the past, seems to have fascinated people. It was the age of Granger, one of the first serious students of historical portraiture, whose *Biographical History of England* (1769) sparked off the fashion to which he gave his name – Grangerizing, the extra-illustration by engravings of standard historical works such as Clarendon and Burnet, and Granger's own *History*. Meanwhile, in the hands of the contemporary practitioners, British engraving had reached its highest pitch of quality as a method of reproduction. Earlier in the century, portrait painters had been well served for publicity by excellent mezzotint engravers like John Smith and Jean Simon, and later by John Faber the younger; when there were no public galleries, and pictures were only to be seen in the houses of the well-to-do or at auctions, the mezzotinters and line-engravers were invaluable. They were broadcast by the print-shops, the windows of which fulfilled to some extent the functions of the illustrated dailies and weeklies of today. We have already seen Thornhill and Hogarth practising this sort of visual journalism; in 1761 Goldsmith, disguised as a Chinaman, approached a print-shop somewhat optimistically:

Here, thought I, the painter only reflects the public voice. . . . But, guess my surprise when I came to examine the depository of noted faces! All distinctions were levelled here, as in the grave, and I could not but regard it as a catacomb of real merit. The brickdust man took up as much room as the trunchconed hero, and the judge was elbowed by the thief-taker; quacks, pimps and buffoons increased the group, and noted stallions only made room for more noted strumpets.[125]

The subjects were not all 'straight' portraits of course. Indeed, the chief revenue of the print-shops was probably derived from the sale of satirical, grotesque and caricature prints – but with those I shall deal briefly in the next chapter. Respectable, pretty genre pieces, featuring pretty girls in domestic occupations, were engraved by James McArdell after Mercier in the fifties – *Girl with Cat, Girl*

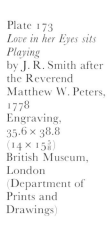

Plate 173
Love in her Eyes sits Playing
by J. R. Smith after the Reverend Matthew W. Peters, 1778
Engraving, 35.6 × 38.8 (14 × 15⅝)
British Museum, London (Department of Prints and Drawings)

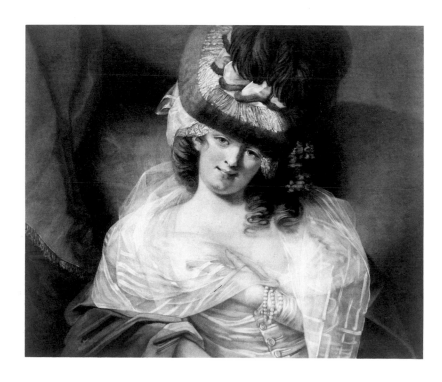

Plate 174 (*below*)
Catherine Moore, Lady Chambers (died 1797) by James
McArdell after Sir Joshua Reynolds, 1756
Mezzotint, 32.4 × 22.5 (12¾ × 8⅞)
British Museum, London (Department of Prints and
Drawings)

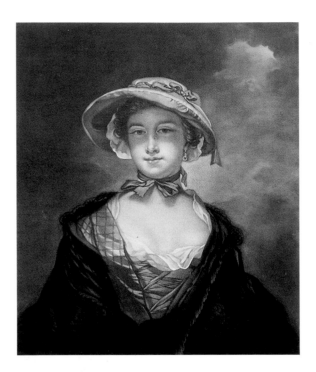

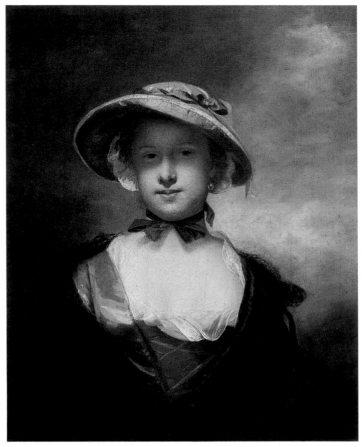

taking Tea; similar works by Hubert Gravelot and Arthur Pond were popularized, and later those by Henry Morland and others. In the seventies a more saccharine sweetness of sentimental attitude was dispensed, notably by the engravings of J. R. Smith after the works of the Reverend Peters – *Hebe, Love in Her Eyes Sits Playing* (Plate 173) – in a distressing style based on Reynolds, isolating his latent arch roguery and spreading it with an unction for which the word has only comparatively recently been invented: cheesecake.

But Smith, in his subject-matter, was fairly comprehensive; he engraved, for more delicate sensibilities, topical matters such as the *Lady coming from the Circulating Library*, after Singleton, of 1781, to the very genteel anglicized *Sturm und Drang* of the *First Interview of Werther and Charlotte*, of 1782. There is, in such works, no more profound study of the face than a mannered rendering of the fashionable expression, which was – in the case of Peters – refined vulgarity. But the masters of serious portraiture had no cause to complain of their engravers; after a falling away in quality in the forties and early fifties (apart from Hogarth, who was served by himself), engraving revived, particularly in the hands of the mezzotinters. James McArdell, who died before he was forty, in 1765, led in the great school of British mezzotint engraving. Reynolds once expressed the opinion (not foreseeing the

Plate 175 (*above*)
Catherine Moore, Lady Chambers (died 1797)
by Sir Joshua Reynolds
Oil on canvas, 69.8 × 57.1 (27½ × 22½)
Iveagh Bequest, Kenwood House (English Heritage)

public gallery and the photograph) that it was through McArdell's reproductions of his paintings that he, Reynolds, would be immortalized (Plates 174 and 175), and when McArdell died he was succeeded by engravers of almost equal ability like Valentine Green (Plate 176); and their works dispensed the new aesthetic throughout the country.

The vast majority of the clients of the masters came of course as always from the top levels of society, although the clients were now far more variously rendered than before. More and more people were being painted, but the tendency of the portrait was still to level them desirably up, fashionably and socially. Population had increased enormously; the industrial revolution was changing the face of the countryside and the life of the people; Rousseau was busy in men's imaginations like yeast in the dough; France was about to explode in political and social revolution. There is little sign of any reflection of such portents in the faces of the time as they survive for us. Romney returning from 'the Sussex Peasants, with faces round with health, and expressions of contentment everywhere' might remark on the approach to London of the 'sharpness of countenance' of the Londoners, 'with passions so strongly marked . . . deep design, disappointed ambition, envy, hatred, melancholy, disease and poverty'[126] – but Romney did not paint these faces. Hogarth (aided, admittedly, by a natural squint in his sitter's eye and some malice in his own) had shown how to draw a radical agitator in the face of Wilkes; Romney did draw Tom

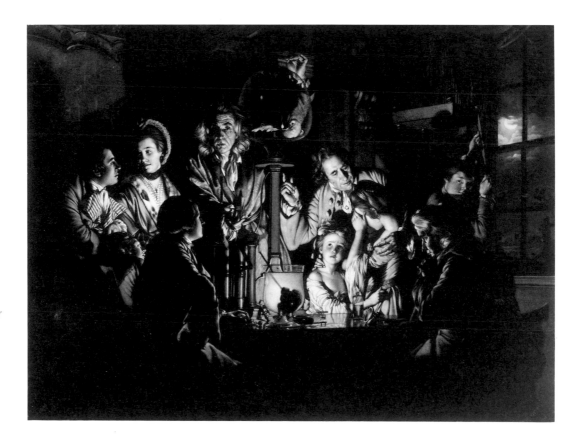

Plate 176
A Philosopher shewing an Experiment on the Air Pump by Valentine Green after Joseph Wright of Derby, 1769
Mezzotint,
44.5 × 58.5 ($17\frac{1}{2}$ × 23)
Victoria & Albert Museum, London

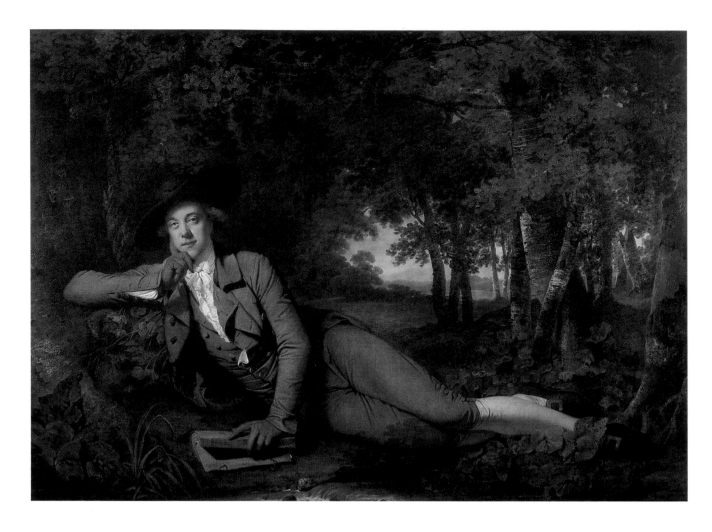

Plate 177
Sir Brooke Boothby Bt
(1743–1824) by
Joseph Wright of
Derby, 1781
Oil on canvas,
148.6 × 207.6
($58\frac{1}{2} \times 81\frac{3}{4}$)
Tate Gallery, London

Paine, but he drew him as a gentleman and little more. The Russian visitor, Karamzin, coming from France ('where beauty is so rare a phenomenon') found England 'the land of female beauty,' but ranged the male physiognomies in three classes:

surly, good-natured or brutish. I can safely swear that in no other country have I seen so many brutish faces as here, and I am now convinced that William Hogarth drew from nature.'[127]

Hogarth, however, had no true successors of any ability. Though Wright of Derby painted Sir Brooke Boothby (Plate 177) prone in a landscape with a volume of Rousseau in his hand, nature is still a park and Sir Brooke's face emotionless, painted firmly and composedly in a style that reminds one that Wright was Hudson's pupil. There are no industrial faces, as such, but occasionally one does get a glimpse of a face that is bluntly tough, with an atmosphere that has not been caught before. Such perhaps is Wilkinson's face, by Abbott in the National Portrait Gallery (Plate 206), and Arkwright's, by Wright of Derby; faces that sit well and

Plate 178
Thomas Daniell
(born 1715) and Captain
Morcom by John Opie,
1786
Oil on canvas, 99 × 124.5
(39 × 49)
The Royal Cornwall
Museum

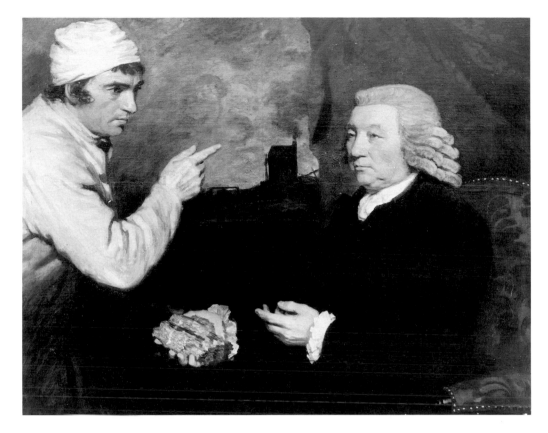

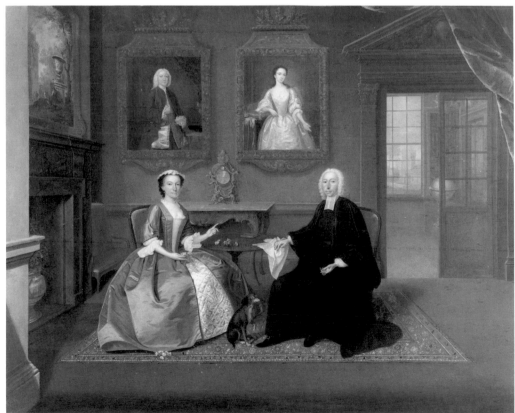

Plate 179
The Reverend Streynsham
Master and his Wife by
Arthur Devis, 1742–1744
Oil on canvas,
82.5 × 100.3 (32½ × 39½)
Private Collection

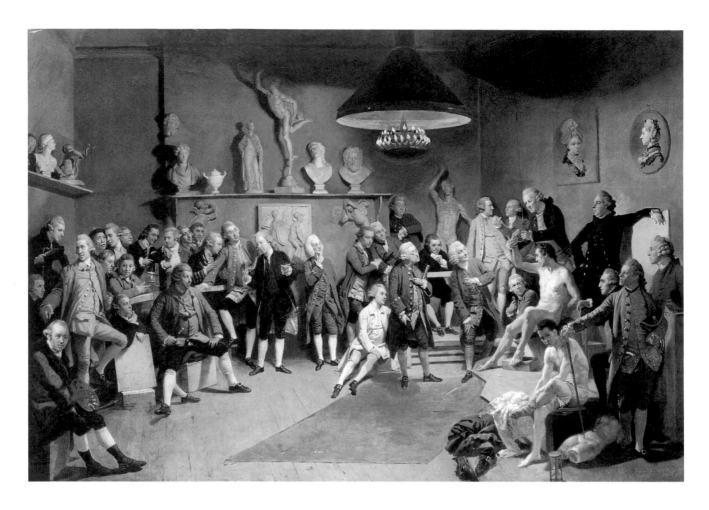

aptly on an iron-master (who ultimately had himself buried in an iron coffin) and on the inventor of the spinning-jenny. Opie, in his still brilliant youth, could strike with a vivid and almost unsentimental naturalism the faces of village children at a school, and once, in his painting of a Cornish mine-owner and his manager of 1786, he achieved a most unusual and contemporary characterization, coarse, powerful and vital (Plate 178).

The practitioners of the conversation-pieces are, for faces, disappointing; here, in the painting of faces involved with and uninhibited by action, Hogarth again had little following. Devis's charm rests in his colour and in his doll's-house *naïveté*; if you isolate the faces of his men and women they are almost always as blank as dolls, painfully stupid (Plate 179); Zoffany, more sophisticated, may be but little more illuminating, painting group-portraits more often than conversation-pieces – but he produced some remarkable exceptions to that generalization: for example, in his extraordinary *tour de force* of the *Academicians of the Royal Academy* (Plate 180), you see artists as they are, void of glamour, sharp with their intent precise vision, in all the idiosyncrasies of their flesh: a close-up not unworthy of Hogarth. And in his painting of the optician Cuff and his assistant in his workshop (Plate 167), there is a

Plate 180
The Academicians of the Royal Academy by Johan Zoffany, 1772
Oil on canvas,
100.7 × 147.3
($39\frac{3}{4}$ × 58)
Royal Collection (by gracious permission of her Majesty The Queen)

Plate 181
*Antinous, a horse
belonging to His Grace
the Duke of Grafton* by
George Stubbs, 1764
Oil on canvas,
101.3 × 127.6
(39⅞ × 50¼)
The Duke of Grafton

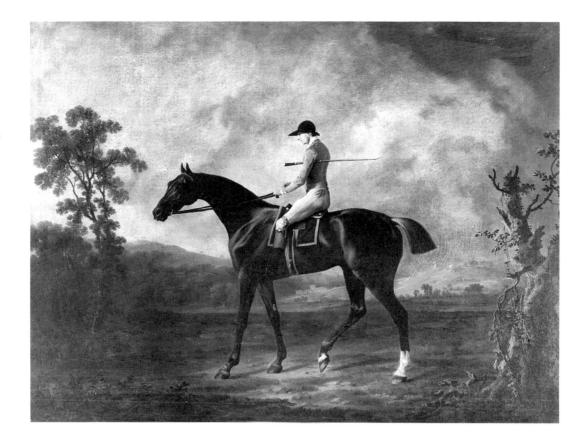

fascinating literal reflection of the artisan craftsman; but this was not a picture that appealed to the arbiters of taste and the patrons. 'Extremely natural', Horace Walpole commented on it at the Academy in 1772, 'but the characters too common nature and the chiaroscuro destroyed by his servility in imitating the reflexions of the glasses'.[128] Zoffany did not repeat the experiment: academic art could not yet stomach 'characters too common nature', but they are to be found outside the Academy. The young Gainsborough, before he sought the patronage of society, had painted country gentlemen in their ordinary life, and Stubbs, despised as an 'animal painter', painted grooms and coachmen, country gentry and even soldiers, with the same veracious dispassionate sympathy as he painted horses; his jockey, with that fine thrusting profile, ages not (Plate 181). These are truly rural faces, as distinct from the picturesque rustic or bucolic faces that even Morland generally paints. The unusual atmosphere in Wright of Derby's candle-lit pieces, though striking and sympathetic, is achieved by a by no means new technical trick of illumination rather than by a new approach to character.[129]

X

The Age of Lawrence

THE LEADERS of late Georgian society expressed, by their patronage, their confidence in Thomas Lawrence's flair and ability to paint them at their best. Lawrence[130] first showed his full powers in the paintings that he sent to the Royal Academy in 1790, when he was twenty-one years old. They included two female whole-lengths that still rank among his masterpieces: the portrait of the actress, Elizabeth Farren (Plate 182), and that of Queen Charlotte in the National Gallery, London. His early style was based on the late style of Reynolds, and Reynolds, at the private view in the Academy of 1790, is said to have indicated that it was on Lawrence that his mantle should fall: 'In you, Sir, the world will expect to see accomplished what I have failed to achieve'.[131] The world's expectation was to be deceived, if Reynolds thought that Lawrence would prove at last to be the world's awaited history-painter.

Lawrence in practice confined his interest to portraiture – despite his theatrical ventures, like the *Satan* and the *Cato* – far more exclusively and far more happily than did Reynolds. Even there he was a more limited artist than Reynolds himself. In the nineties he heightened portraiture with a more flowing elegance, a greater clarity and splash of colour, and a more brilliant expression. His faces are pointed and heightened by often exaggerated lights, that sit palpably as tears in the eyes or as salve on the lips; the great end of painting, he had written when but eighteen, is 'the expressing with truth the human heart in the traits of the countenance',[132] a sentiment which Reynolds would surely never have expressed: the human mind or the human soul perhaps, but not the heart.

Lawrence's characterizations tend in fact to have a double aim: to portray the public, superficial creature of fashion and society in poise and dress, and, primarily in the face, to indicate the more private sensibilities of the heart, in the parted lips, the dilated brilliant eyes, the sable curls in profusion on the forehead high and pale. In tonality indeed he often anticipates a Byronic beauty; his sitters mostly wear their own hair, and it seems generally to be dark against a pale skin – but they lack the physical vigour and conviction of a Corsair or a Don Juan. They may be at once stagey and curiously asexual.

Lawrence never painted Byron himself, but late in his career he set down a verbal portrait that shows a close sympathy:

Lavater's system never asserted its truth more forcibly than in Byron's countenance, in which you see all the character: its keen and rapid genius, its pale intelligence, its profligacy, and its bitterness; its original symmetry distorted by the passions, his laugh of mingled merriment and scorn; the forehead clear and open, the brow boldly prominent, the eyes

Plate 182
(*facing page*)
Elizabeth Farren, later Countess of Derby
(1759?–1829) by Sir Thomas Lawrence, 1790
Oil on canvas, 238.8 × 146.1 (94 × 57½)
Metropolitan Museum of Art, New York, Bequest of Edward S. Harkness)

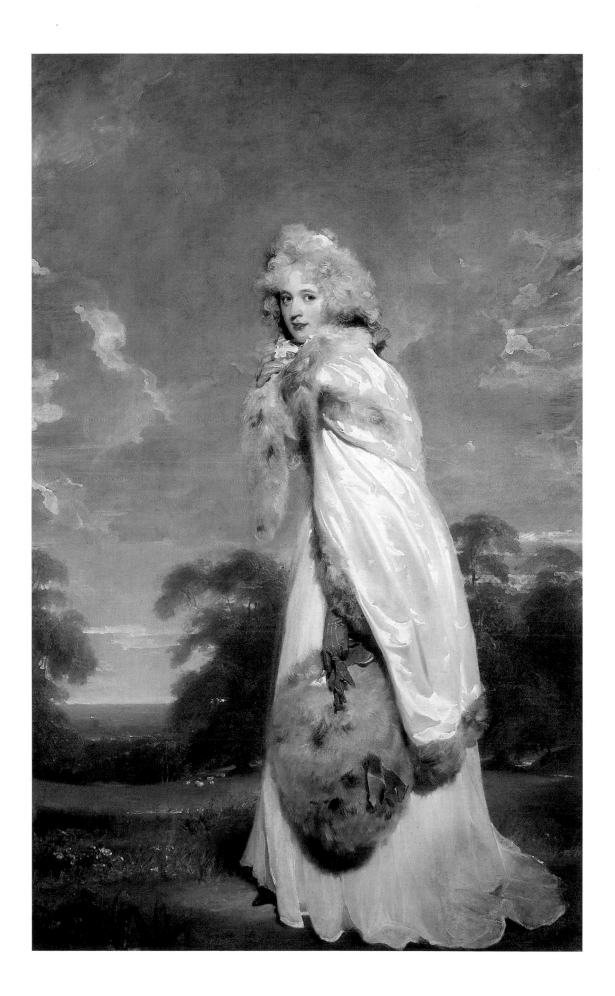

bright and dissimilar, the nose finely cut, and the nostril acutely formed; the mouth well-made, but wide and contemptuous even in its smile, falling singularly at the corners, and its vindictive and disdainful expression heightened by the massive firmness of the chin, which springs at once from the centre of the full underlip; the hair dark and curling, but irregular in its growth. . . .[133]

Sanders' portrait of the poet (Plate 183), though not approved ('It does not *flatter* me, I think, but the subject is a bad one . . .'), offers at least a windswept cloudiness, in strong contrast to the neo-classic clarity of Thorwaldsen's bust of him (Plate 184). Looking back, in 1858, Trelawney described Byron's appearance as the realization of that ideal standard with which imagination adorns genius. Although hints of it are visible already in the characters of some of the Gothick novels, notably those of Ann Radcliffe, it may be that Byron not merely realized but formulated that standard.

Many of Lawrence's male portraits point towards it, keen and rapid, with brilliant eyes, dark and irregular hair, flaring nostril and curling upper lip. Bitterness and vindictiveness however escape Lawrence, and disdain, though ineradicable from certain mouths, is always softened by the expression of the eyes. If Lawrence had drawn Byron, he would probably have caught more of the 'succinctness and gentlemanliness' of his appearance, as noted by Leigh Hunt, than of that inimitable cohabitation of sharp irony and romantic imagination; it is, of course, Delacroix who should have painted the poet.

Lawrence was after all a society-painter, and his work as a whole is a retraction from the wider horizons established by Reynolds to those of the drawing-room. If

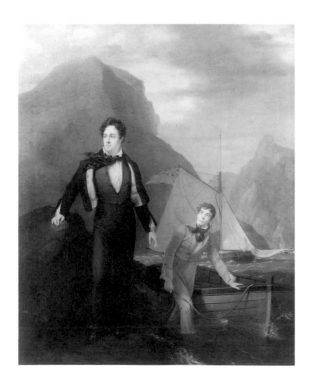

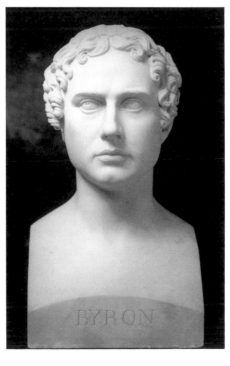

Plate 183 (*far left*)
George Gordon, 6th Baron Byron
(1788–1824)
by George Sanders, *c.*1809
Oil on canvas,
63.5 × 53 (25 × 21)
Royal Collection (by gracious permission of Her Majesty The Queen)

Plate 184 (*left*)
George Gordon, 6th Baron Byron
(1788–1824)
by Bertel Thorwaldsen, 1817
Marble, life-size
Private Collection

Plate 185 (*right*)
Arthur Wellesley, 1st Duke of Wellington (1769–1852) by Sir Thomas Lawrence, *c.*1815–1816
Oil on canvas, 91.4 × 71.1 (36 × 28)
Wellington Museum, Apsley House, London

Plate 186 (*far right*)
Arthur Wellesley, 1st Duke of Wellington (1769–1852) by Francisco de Goya, 1812
Oil on panel, 64.3 × 52.4 (25¼ × 20½)
National Gallery, London

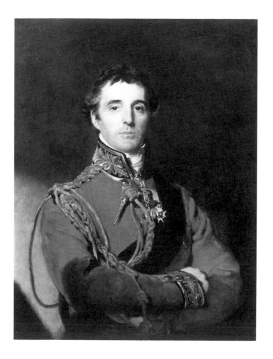

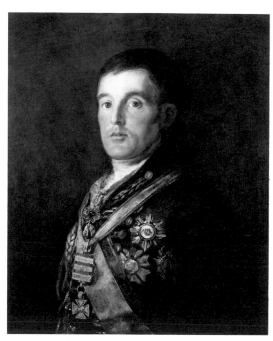

he escapes the drawing-room, it is most often for the parade-ground or the stage, and his characters are bathed in a soft limelight. Northcote called him 'a sort of man-milliner painter – a meteor of fashion'; Northcote was biased and extremely jealous, but his criticism is not entirely unjust. Magnificently successful as are, within their convention, Lawrence's series of whole-length masterpieces of the victorious allied statesmen and generals in the Waterloo Chamber at Windsor, the convention is that of the stage, theatrical rather than essentially dramatic, of martial glamour rather than of true martial grandeur as demonstrated, for example, by Reynolds in his *Lord Heathfield*.

Lawrence's face of Wellington (Plate 185), well-drawn as it is, well-fitting as a glove, is perhaps too conscious of the work of the barber, too defined in the eyes, those perfect steady irises, lit each by one perfectly-placed and formulated highlight. Compare the tough, almost hostile sensitivity of Goya's handling of the same face, in Madrid in 1812 (Plate 186); it is that of an explorer, rather than of a tailor. Lawrence paints the lion of Waterloo in his social context as an English aristocrat, fresh from a bath after exercise on the playing fields, perhaps, of Eton; Goya, who knew nothing of the playing fields of Eton, saw a conqueror, a bleak, high-blooded man with the strained and fanatic stare of war.

But for a surface recording of Regency society, Lawrence's brilliance and *chic* were exactly right, as right as Lely's for the Restoration Court, except that Lawrence omits the visible evidence of profligacy that was certainly there. He is one of the most valuable witnesses for the Crown against the overwhelming condemnation of history. In 1815 he exhibited a portrait of the Prince Regent aged fifty-two (Plate 187); it was noticed by Hazlitt:

Sir Thomas Lawrence has with the magic of his pencil recreated the Prince Regent as a well-fleshed Adonis of thirty-three . . . we could not, as we stood before this very admirable picture, but derive a high degree of good-natured pleasure from imagining to ourselves the transports with which His Royal Highness must have welcomed this improved version of himself. It goes far beyond all that wigs, powders and pomatums have been able to effect for the last twenty years.[134]

Lawrence generally painted his sitters within a tight social context; one can scarcely blame him for failing with the irreducible egg-head of Sir Walter Scott – it baffled all the many artists who attempted it. Even the portrait by Raeburn (here, one might have thought, on his home-ground [Plate 188]) was dismissed by the *Repository of Arts* in 1810:

This last of the minstrels shows how lamentably the race is degenerate, for never was a more unpoetical physiognomy delineated on canvas; we might take him for an auctioneer, a travelling dealer or chapman; in short for any character but a bard.

Scott's face appears to have been incompatible with the authorship of *Marmion* and the Waverley novels.

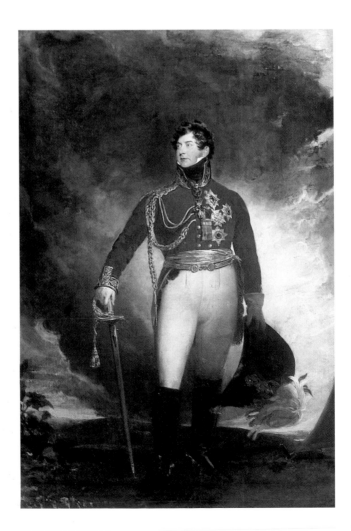

Plate 187
George IV when Prince of Wales
(1762–1830) by Sir Thomas
Lawrence, 1814
Oil on canvas, 271 × 171.5
($106\frac{3}{4} \times 67\frac{1}{2}$)
By permission of Sotheby's

But Lawrence badly misplaces other characters, especially upstarts on the wave of industrial and scientific progress. Humphrey Davy is an exception, for that poor Cornish boy was born not only a brilliant chemist but meat for Lawrence, outwardly a natural aristocrat. But in the case of James Watt, father of steam-power, Lawrence has reduced a face of Scots granite to glossy alabaster. It was Lawrence's later style, gradually tightening towards both a greater solidity and a more uniform polish in the painting of the flesh, that beat the retreat to the drawing-room. And in the drawing-room it could be entirely adequate and successful, as is his *Countess of Blessington* (Plate 204), which would be perfect illustration to a perhaps more metropolitan version of *Sense and Sensibility*.

The society portraiture of the years between 1790 and 1840 was almost entirely conditioned by the achievements of Reynolds and Lawrence. Most of the painters worked somewhere between their two styles, although in the thirties some painters, influenced by their Italian visits, like John Partridge and Sir George Hayter, were moving back towards the continental academic tradition, in a more precise and tight style. Hoppner, notorious for his swing from one to the other, died in 1810, four years after Opie; and in the last twenty years of his life, between 1810 and 1830, Lawrence had no near rival. There were numerous other painters of ability, but none with that personal genius that stamps the face of an epoch with its own

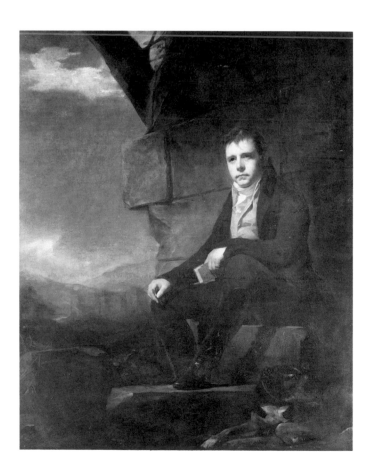

Plate 188
Sir Walter Scott Bt (1771–1832)
by Sir Henry Raeburn, 1808
Oil on canvas, 182.8 × 127
(70 × 57)
The Duke of Buccleuch and
Queensberry KT

imprint: William Owen, Sir William Beechey, James Northcote and John Jackson, then the rising stars of Martin Archer Shee and Thomas Phillips, and the close followers of Lawrence like the short-lived George Harlow, Richard Evans and Samuel Lane.

In Scotland, however, a more individual course was taken by Raeburn, painting steadily away in Edinburgh from his return from Italy in 1787 until his death in 1823. By using forced lighting Raeburn revealed the faces before him, often almost brutally; he is the master of a new realism, painting his sitter 'in his habit as he lived', from the Edinburgh urban blacks and greys to the Tartan picturesque clamour of the plaid and the kilt. His use of chiaroscuro had of course distinguished antecedents; as R.L. Stevenson remarked, his Mr Wardrop (now in Melbourne) might be palmed off on a layman as a Rembrandt, but Raeburn had in fact a far less subtle attack than either Rembrandt or Reynolds, and the concentration of light tends too often to lead not to greater penetration, but to a Hollywood production of the obvious (Plate 189). Already in 1801, Farington wrote of Raeburn's work that 'that which strikes the eye is a kind of Camera Obscura effect'[135], the effect, in fact, of an over-illuminated photograph. His portraits tell wonderfully when reduced in size in the half-tone block or the photogravure. Confronted in the paint, they are often very vulgar – particularly his portraits of children and of young men and women of fashion. In older faces it was Raeburn's forte, with that direct, forthright certainty, the famous 'square touch' of the brush, to discover an enduring structure of character and experience. He is the first truly Scottish portrait-painter of more than minor stature; George Jamieson, in the early seventeenth century, is like a lesser Cornelius Johnson; later the Scougalls have a recognizable but dull style; Sir John Baptist Medina was a contemporary of Kneller and his work is often confused with that of Kneller; William Aikman, and later Allan Ramsay, that impressive painter, both moved to set up practice in London. Raeburn, though he made unsuccessful forays to London to see if it would support him, practised and throve in his home town, the northern capital rather than a city of the provinces, with a vigorous, enlightened and very independent society.

From Raeburn depends a whole native Scottish School of portrait-painters, from Watson-Gordon to Fiddes Watt, but more interesting was the work of William Dyce in Scotland in the thirties, earning scanty bread by portraiture which included some fascinating excursions in the manner of Titian, and that of the *émigré* Scotsman, David Wilkie in London. After his continental travels, and particularly after Lawrence's death in 1830, Wilkie largely abandoned the small-scale genre-painting that had brought him fame and prosperity, and began working in a much broader manner that some alleged to be Spanish, but which was, as Haydon observed, 'something like Lawrence and Raeburn, and not like himself; and yet fine, but not original'. They have indeed (those that have not been eaten away by bitumen) still something of the glamour and bravura of Lawrence.

There were also some odd little pockets of achievement, never followed up, by

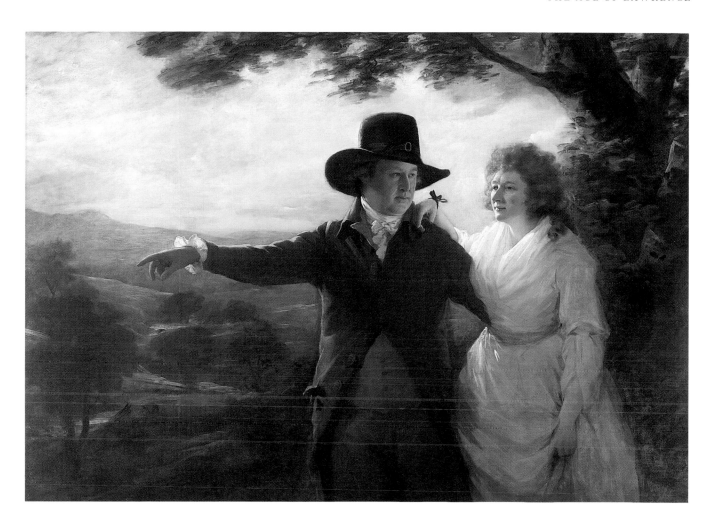

Plate 189
*Sir John and Lady
Clerk of Penicuik* by Sir
Henry Raeburn, 1792
Oil on canvas,
145 × 206 (57 × 81)
National Gallery of
Ireland

painters who were later to turn away from portraiture. Such was a remarkable group of paintings by William Etty in his early twenties, of members of his family, recorded unconventionally with a deeply felt intimacy and an entire lack of conventional inhibition. Such, too, were the portraits by Constable, painted with a searching, almost heavy, veracity, between 1810 and 1820. And later there was Haydon, forced into loathed common portraiture by poverty. His real pot-boilers are drearily bad, while of the ninety-seven portraits included in his large painting of the *Reform Banquet*, Lord Jeffrey found he was unable to recognize a single one. Yet, in those few heroic portraits that he took on deliberately (pursuing the Duke of Wellington with letter upon letter until he sat), there is more than a hint that here, given only a greater technical ability, might have been a worthy successor to Reynolds. Haydon, in his Wordsworth brooding on Helvellyn (Plate 190), achieves a characterization of a mind in action that is no mean performance. It is far more truly a heroic portrait than any of Lawrence's, despite its clumsy and sluggish paint. (When Wordsworth sat, the delighted Haydon 'found him, to my wonder, eight heads high, or 5 feet $9\frac{7}{8}$ inches, and of very fine heroic proportions'.[136])

In all other media the spate of portraiture continued. Between about 1780 and 1805 Richard Cosway (Plate 191) was painting his finest miniatures, often as large as 3 inches high, in thin colour brilliant over the white ivory. Himself a sartorial fop of prowess, a notable eccentric, claiming to have had several sittings from the Virgin Mary for her picture, and a personal friend of George, Prince of Wales (Plate 192), he was even better fitted than Lawrence to present sympathetically the *bel idéal* in Regency faces. His characters are winsome with enormous melting eyes, a little hectic in the cheek and with a calculated negligence in the hair; sometimes their heads are almost as wide as their shoulders; but they are presented with such three-dimensional skill that they convince. A curious, brief but intense freak of the miniature-art that now came into fashion was the eye miniature, which aimed to capture the most intimate glance of 'the windows of the soul' (Plate 193); more often, it captured a repulsively detailed, almost anatomical, account of the mere surface of the eye and the contiguous flesh, and the human eye, hardly more than that of a fish, is not an object that profits from detachment from its context. They are not common now, but may sometimes be found jostled together in a cardboard box in an auction-room, viz.:

Lot 18. An Eye Miniature inset in the bezel of a ring which is inscribed 'Genl. Arabins Right Eye 1798'; another in paste frame and mounted as a brooch; another inset in the lid of a Vinaigrette, 1¼ in., contained in leather case; and five other Eye Miniatures all mounted as brooches.

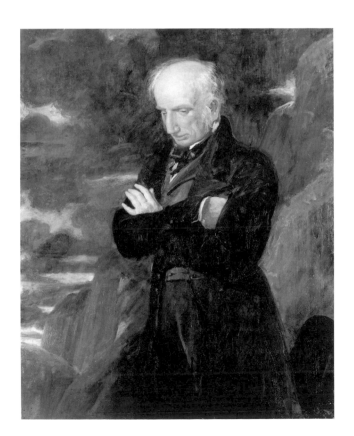

Plate 190
William Wordsworth (1770–1850)
by Benjamin Robert Haydon,
1842
Oil on canvas, 124.5 × 99.1
(49 × 39)
National Portrait Gallery, London

Plate 191 *(right)*
Richard Cosway
(1740–1821),
self-portrait
Pencil and wash,
10.5×7.9 $(4\frac{1}{8} \times 3\frac{1}{8})$
National Portrait
Gallery, London

Plate 192 *(far right)*
George IV when Prince
of Wales (1762–1830)
by Richard Cosway,
*c.*1792
Watercolour on ivory,
9.8×7.3 $(3\frac{7}{8} \times 2\frac{7}{8})$
National Portrait
Gallery, London

Plate 193 *(below*
centre)
Eye miniature by an
unknown artist
Watercolour, *c.*1.8 × 2
$(\frac{5}{8} \times \frac{3}{4})$
Victoria & Albert
Museum, London

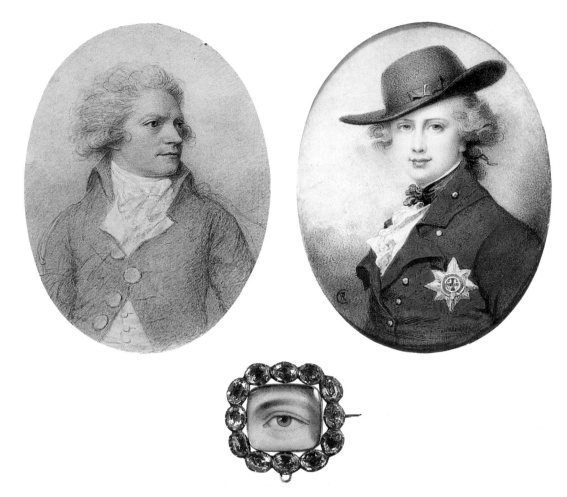

From the bottom of the cardboard box, the General's eye stares up, the veins of the white a little blood-shot as is only proper in a General, the iris a steady military grey; on one of the other eyes – its original owner long lost and unidentified – there glistens, almost wet, a *trompe-l'œil* tear.

Like miniatures, the small-scale portrait drawing also throve. Cosway practised them; Henry Edridge (Plate 194) and Thomas Heaphy, amongst others, had a thriving practice in them. They are able enough. Forerunners of the cabinet photograph, they seem destined to stand upon a piano, but they offer no novel facial characterization, and are, when confronted by one of the many drawings in the same format that Ingres made of British visitors to Rome after the peace of 1815, suddenly naïve and gauche. On a life-size scale, and smaller, the pastellists also flourished. The Swiss artist Jean Etienne Liotard, active in England in the 1750s, had set a standard of almost libellous verisimilitude; as Sir Ellis Waterhouse pointed out, it is from Liotard's portraits that we can tell which of the children of Frederick, Prince of Wales, had adenoids. From this standard the pastellists gradually withdrew; Francis Cotes, in his pastels, achieved a liveliness rare in his oils, but his successor was John Russell, a Methodist of stern principles but with a saccharine sweetness and affectation in his portraits (Plate 195). Broader, indeed sloshy, effects were needed by an emulator of Reynolds, Daniel Gardner, and to achieve them he mixed his pastels in a heady concoction that included brandy.

The bust-makers continued to fashion, by no means always for funereal purposes. Nollekens, whose exhibiting career at the Academy lasted from 1771 to 1814, had an enormous practice, dependent upon his ability to convey a lively likeness within a limited senatorial formula. Although he rarely achieved the vividness of his early busts, such as that of Sterne (Plate 153), the best works of his later period, from his Dr Johnson to his second bust of Fox (1802) and as late as his Wellington (1813), are strong characterizations – in the case of Fox, formidably Roman. In the work of Nollekens' successor as the most fashionable sculptor, Sir Francis Chantrey, the vigour is visibly abating in the cold zone of the ever-spreading neo-classic taste as formulated by Winckelmann in the 1760s. A major tenet was that 'expression detracts from beauty', a theory upheld by Reynolds in his Fifth Discourse of 1772 though often forgotten in his portraits, but put into interminable practice by the

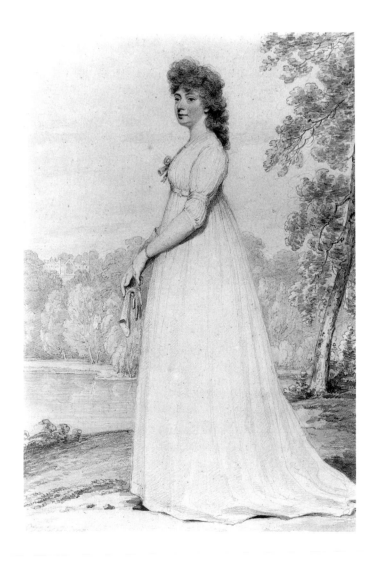

Plate 194
Anne North, Countess of Sheffield
(1764–1832) by Henry
Edridge, 1798
Pencil and wash, 26.7 × 18.4
$(10\frac{1}{2} \times 7\frac{1}{4})$
National Portrait Gallery,
London

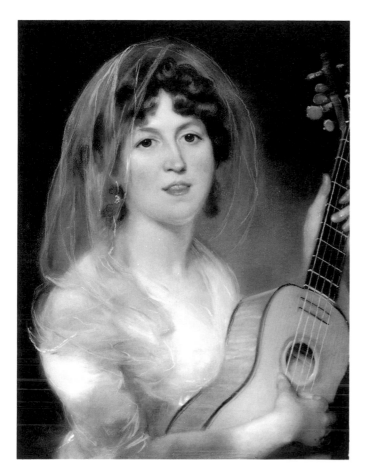

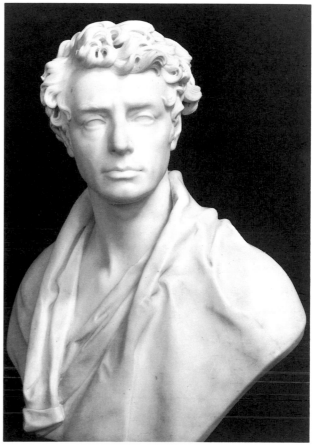

Plate 195 (*above left*)
Elizabeth Bannister
(1752–1844) by John
Russell, 1799
Pastel, 61.6 × 46.4
(24¼ × 18¼)
National Portrait
Gallery, London

Plate 196 (*above right*)
Robert Southey
(1774–1843) by Sir
Francis Chantrey,
1832
Marble, height 76.2
(30)
National Portrait
Gallery, London

most famous sculptor in Europe, Canova. Chantrey, in his best work, like the bust of Robert Southey (Plate 196), escapes its limitations, but the large bulk of his work abides inexpressively within them, whereas the busts of some sculptors such as Richard Westmacott are no longer portraits but variations on a classic head.

Some of the less mannered portraits in the round may now be found more interesting: the wax mask of Nelson's face from his effigy in Westminster Abbey, modelled by Catherine Andras (Plate 197) and said to be very like, or the vivid life-mask of Keats, taken by B.R. Haydon in December 1816 (Plate 198).

The popularity of busts was remarkable, and it was felt natural to enshrine the great popular figures, the party leaders, in marble as household tutelaries; Nollekens is said to have sold 100 busts of Fox, and 150 of Pitt. The ensuing prosperity of the sculptors may be judged by the fortunes they made. Nollekens, though admittedly of a notorious miserliness and very long-lived, accumulated well over £200,000; Chantrey, who died aged only sixty-one in 1842, is said to have been worth £150,000.

In sharp contrast to the extremes of neo-classicism represented in their differing ways by Westmacott and the tenderly severe Flaxman, but parallel with a boom in popularity of the Dutch seventeenth-century masters of low-life painting, came the

British School of painters of contemporary low-life. It was headed, of course, by David Wilkie,[137] who arrived in London from Edinburgh in 1805, aged twenty, and who, by the time he was twenty-five, had scored a resonant success that was not only popular, but was supported by the approval and active patronage of the great connoisseurs headed by Sir George Beaumont.

Wilkie's was not, like Hogarth's, satirical or moral painting; no incubus of responsibility was placed upon the spectator. He was endowed with a shrewd, accurate and, above all, an enjoying eye, and he painted in many of his best pictures a society, that of the Scottish village, that was in its relaxation sprightlier and less inhibited than its English counterpart. He had a remarkable memory for facial expressions and quirks of character and his work teems with portraits, from that of his father (who, as a strict minister, was furious when he found out) in his early *Pitlessie Fair* of 1804, to the veterans in the *Chelsea Pensioners reading the Gazette of the Battle of Waterloo* (Plate 199), suggested to Wilkie by the Duke of Wellington in 1816.

After 1830, generally speaking, he fell victim to a blight of artistic theory. His patrons and his public found him to be the British Teniers, though he rarely shows Teniers' interest in the grotesque; compared with Hogarth he shows as very much a *petit maître*, choreographer of a pretty, vivid and small world as if seen through the wrong end of a telescope. But part of his success undoubtedly came from the fact that he appealed to a growing public taste for the laughable and the quaint, and for sentimental anecdote, although he himself painted almost always without condescension and without sentimentality. The same is true of his much-neglected

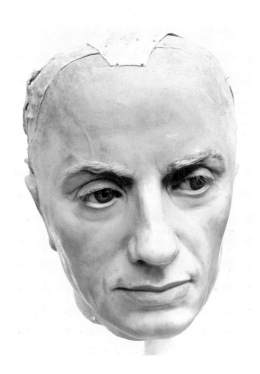

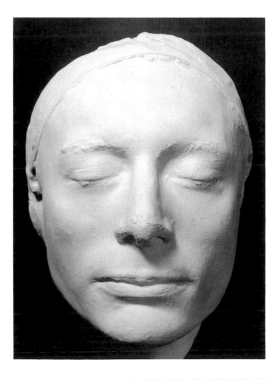

Plate 197 (*far left*)
Horatio, 1st Viscount Nelson (1758–1805) by Catherine Andras, *c*.1805 (detail)
Wax and wood effigy, life-size
Westminster Abbey, London

Plate 198 (*left*)
John Keats (1795–1821) by Benjamin Robert Haydon, 1816
Plaster cast of life-mask, height 23.5 (9¼)
National Portrait Gallery, London

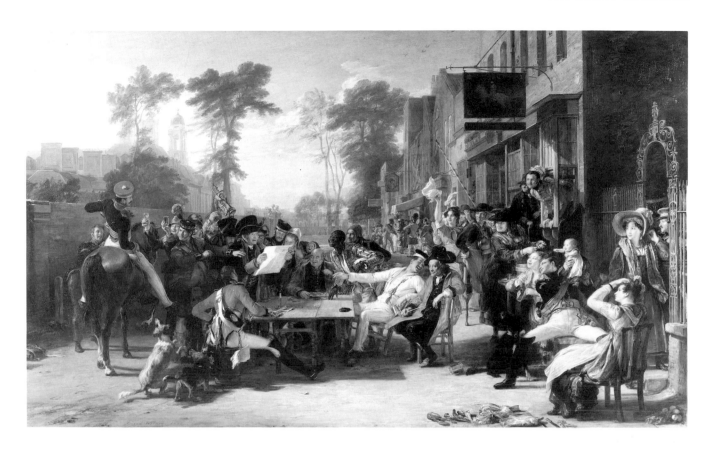

English contemporary, William Mulready,[138] a painter with a sometimes most admirable grasp of sheer pictorial values, but beloved by the public for his subject-matter, especially for his small boys, generally fighting. In the generation following Wilkie and Mulready, the sentimental approach of the public to the contemporary scene would swiftly corrupt the painters.

Other facets of society, already seen, continued to be portrayed. Ben Marshall, with an entirely different technique, preserved something of Stubbs' sturdy transcriptions of jockeys and grooms, and painted some remarkable portraits of prize-fighters. John Ferneley specialized in the painting of the English sportsman astride, austerely but intimately involved in a wintry inexpressive bliss amongst the hounds; and Francis Grant, in his early sporting pictures of the thirties, caught for ever the essence of the dandaisical ennui of the sporting gentleman, best perhaps in the cold dawn limbo of his famous *Melton Breakfast*.

The propagation of portraits by the engravers also continued prosperously, in the hands of practitioners as skilful as Charles Turner, who in his long life-time (1774–1857) reduplicated over 600 portraits; the demand for public heroes, the Nelsons and Wellingtons, was insatiable, and we find also 'personalities', in the modern sense, commissioning Turner to engrave their portraits and publishing themselves in aid of their own publicity campaigns; thus the prize-fighter Belcher published his own portrait in 1810, as had the famous fat man, Daniel Lambert, in

1806. But print-sellers, besides disseminating in reproduction many 'straight' portraits, were also sponsors of one of the most remarkable efflorescences in British art: the satiric caricature.[139] A host of artists, working in this medium, sprang up between 1770 and 1830, representing all facets of middle-class opinions suddenly and brutally involved in politics.

The genius of the personal caricature was Gillray; Rowlandson, though capable, as in his portrait of George Morland, of vivid even naturalistic likenesses, was in his satire more generally social than political or individual. Caricatures are sometimes – and to me, it seems, wrongly – disallowed as portraits. They were presented along a range between the manner of Hogarth, the comic history-painter, and that of Ghezzi, of the traditional Italian caricature. But however far they go in distortion – and Gillray in extremes developed a fantastic romantic expressionism – the best of them remain of, and well rooted in, the person on whom they are based. By emphasizing the physical eccentricities of their subject, they focus a shocked astonishment in ridicule upon them.

These faces are often much more than ridiculous; they may particularize some specific energy. Often Gillray seems to be illustrating the man-in-the-street's distrust and incomprehension of – and helplessness before, those forces now often referred to as 'They': arbitrary forces that move mysteriously and out of sight, dispensing, unaccountable and unappeasable as the weather, now war, now peace; now famine, now plenty; but all the time a rain of laws, ordinances, decrees, regulations. In the political cartoons, these forces become incarnate in faces recognizable as those of the Royal Family, of Napoleon, of Pitt and of Fox: faces still just human but also the figurehead, now of a self-indulgent gluttony of a court or party indifferent to the misery of country, now of invading war toppling not only the established kingdoms of Europe but the established overseas markets of England, and so on. It is heroic portraiture turned inside out; whereas the society-portrait ennobles the particular towards an agreed ideal of beauty, without losing sight of its subject, satirists like Gillray distort the particular as far as possible away from the same agreed ideal of beauty, to the extent that this is consonant with retaining the human identity of his sitter. Just as the portrait-painter enhances his subject with attributes (as Reynolds' *Lord Heathfield* with his wonderful key), with official robes, or even turns them into gods or goddesses, so Gillray in reverse.

Gillray ridicules excess in terms of excess, but his ridicule is fired by a profound distrust, and by fear that sometimes seems to try to control a hostile, superhuman force by giving it a known human face. His hero, often John Bull in one form or another, is usually being imposed upon: a sucker. At other times, his caricatures seem to be statements of pure revulsion against the mendacious uplift of fashionable high art. Romney had glamorized Lady Hamilton endlessly in terms of a flawless, almost synthetic beauty (Plate 200); to Gillray, she was stouter than she ought to be and also a strumpet, and so he drew her as 'Dido in Despair' (Plate 201), in 1801,

Plate 200 (*right*)
*Emma Hart, Lady
Hamilton* (1761?–1815)
by George Romney,
c.1785
Oil on canvas,
62.2 × 54.6 (24½ × 21½)
National Portrait
Gallery, London

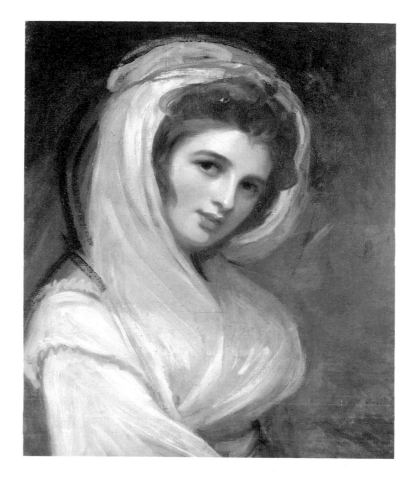

Plate 201 (*below*)
*Emma Hart, Lady
Hamilton* (1761? 1815) in
Dido in Despair by James
Gillray, 1801
Etching, 25.5 × 36.2
(10 × 14¼)
National Portrait
Gallery, London

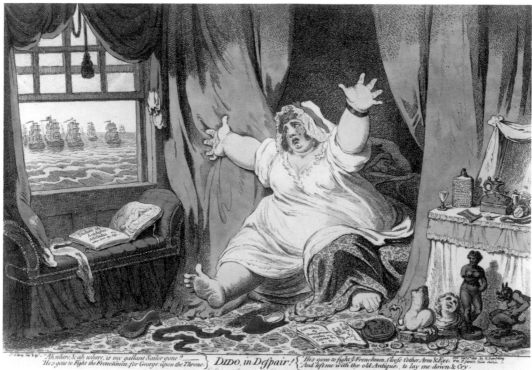

but elephantine – cataracting from her bed (in a gesture borrowed from the most heroic of all Reynolds' paintings, his *Death of Dido*), while outside the window the topsails of her sailor lover vanish beyond the horizon, towards the triumph of the Nile. But Gillray's range was remarkably large; he did not always need to exaggerate, and one may reasonably suspect that his *Voluptuary under the Horrors of Indigestion* comes nearer to the life than any other portrait of the Prince of Wales, later George IV, now left to us.

The raw material that served all these diverse takers of portraits was conditioned, as ever, by shifting sartorial fashion and by the fashionable facial expressions of the moment. With women, the neo-classic – or now, more strictly what was conceived to be neo-Hellenic – taste, had pushed the waist high, and with it, inevitably, the breasts. The hair was worn, if not necessarily cut short, with a short appearance, gathered in a bun high at the back, with a rich profusion of curls at brow and temples.

In about 1798 we find Lawrence compounding this fashion with his own vision of ideal feminine beauty, which he seems to have found personified in the women of the Kemble family, especially Mrs Siddons and her two daughters Sally and Maria, with all three of whom he was more or less, from time to time, in love. A profile drawing of Sally, about 1800, has the classic Greek outline, the nose continuing the forehead in almost a straight line, the chin large and firmly shaped; in paint, as in his *Mrs Siddons* of 1798 (Plate 202), the classic regularity is softened by the clustering curl and a dark, liquid melancholy in the eyes. (Byron records that his own 'first

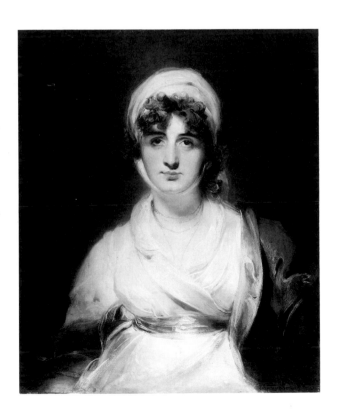

Plate 202
Mrs Sarah Siddons (1755–1831)
by Sir Thomas Lawrence, 1798
Oil on canvas, 76.2 × 63.5 (30 × 25)
Tate Gallery, London

dash into poetry' – at the age of twelve, in 1800 – was an ebullition of passion for his cousin Margaret Parker: 'Her dark eyes! her long eye-lashes! her completely Greek cast of face and figure!'[140]). And classicism, for Lawrence, was diluted, if not contradicted, by the influence of the curious view of it expounded in England by the German-Swiss Henry Fuseli, whom Lawrence acknowledged gratefully as 'the noblest poetically inventive genius that perhaps our modern ages have produced'.

It was to Fuseli that a new Mannerism was primarily indebted, for its attenuation of form and that 'tip-toe' effect in whole-lengths derided by Haydon. (Lawrence's debt is most obvious, of course, in his *Satan*, but it is also there in the transfiguration of the Waterloo Chamber.) It was also Fuseli who, with his dark and violent atmospherics, illustrated best that sensibility for the 'horrid' that found its expression elsewhere in the *Sturm und Drang* of the young Goethe, in the Gothick novels, at Fonthill, and also still in Coleridge's *Christabel* and in one part of Byron.

Lawrence reflects these atmospherics perhaps sometimes in the eyes and in the forced twist of the neck on the head, but most palpably in the lowering backgrounds against which the spot-lit figures of his more heroic portraits are set. For the face, in a society-portrait, they were obviously unsuitable, and it is only very rarely that one finds a characterization entirely in their terms; such a one is perhaps Lawrence's unfinished portrait of Maria Siddons (Plate 203). The daemonic appearance of this, so far removed from the clarity of Lawrence's drawing of her, has led to the suggestion that he painted it after her death – in hatred and fear, almost in an attempt at exorcism. Lawrence, it will be remembered, had first been in love with

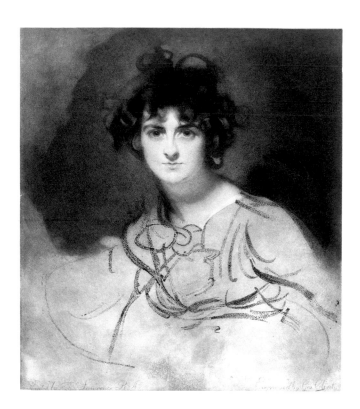

Plate 203
Maria Siddons (1779–1798)
by George Clint after
Sir Thomas Lawrence,
c.1797
Mezzotint, 28.2 × 23 (11⅛ × 9⅜)
British Museum, London
(Department of Prints and
Drawings)

her sister Sally, had transferred his affections, in a temporary infatuation, to Maria; when that was over, he had reverted to Sally. Maria's vengeance was the promise that she, on her deathbed, extracted from Sally, that Sally should never marry Lawrence.[141]

Almost all Lawrence's female portraits concentrate rather on the brilliant reflection of youth, of prettiness if not beauty, and of elegance. The curls gradually vanish from the brow, and in his *Countess of Blessington* (Plate 204) of about 1821, and still more in his drawing of his last Kemble love, Fanny, about 1828, the smooth hair, symmetrically parted in the middle and drawn back, anticipates the propriety of the prevailing mode of the early Victorians. The brooding, that has the faintest threat of violence in Mrs Siddons, has become purely wistful. Such of the heart as is visible in the face would not seem to register other than domestic longings.

For men, the period saw a complete revolution in dress. By 1800, not only had the wig vanished, but so had colour from clothes, and gradually the male splendour subsided into the drab which has only recently been relieved; the sartorial glamour of the Regency was built, not on colour, but on cut and outline. Byron, the outlaw from society, may have worn (though he certainly did not usually do so) the open collar the better to display the noble column of his throat, but the significant figure for the future appearance of nineteenth-century man was neither he nor the over-

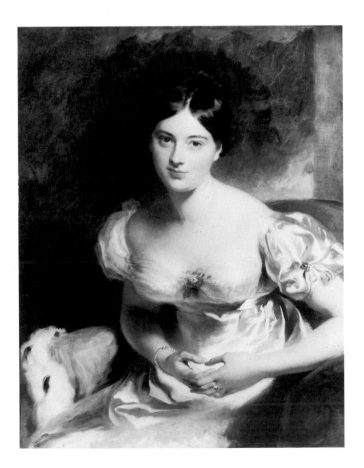

Plate 204
Marguerite Power, Countess of Blessington (1789–1849) by Sir Thomas Lawrence, *c.*1821
Oil on canvas, 91.5 × 67.9
(36 × 26¾)
The Wallace Collection

lavish, flamboyant Prince Regent himself, but Beau Brummell. The codification of manners and dress begins with Beau Nash at Bath; Mrs Thrale observed that Johnson had been forestalled, by some twenty years, in the famous phrase he applied to Addison – 'an Arbiter Elegantiarum, a judge of propriety, was yet wanting' – by the author of the epitaph on Nash's memorial at Bath. Nash, however, had to cope with such elementary crudities as squires who wished to attend functions at the Pump Room in hunting boots; he but prepared the ground for Brummell.

Byron described Brummell as having nothing remarkable in his dress, only 'a certain exquisite propriety'. Any undue emphasis or flamboyance would be profoundly distasteful to him, including that of the wig, of powder, of scent. No man of fashion should use perfumes, he said, but should instead send his linen to be washed and dried on Hampstead Heath. According to legend, he employed three hairdressers who worked in unison upon his hair, but the desired result was no more and no less than the concealed but self-sufficient perfection of art. One of the worst things that could happen to a gentleman was to attract attention to his outward appearance. Brummell relied on cleanliness, disciplined elegance and the best tailors. The face, it may be, was for him a mortification. There it was, necessarily exposed, and there was little that could be done about it, beyond keeping it trim and clean – and his own face, indeed, almost escapes us. All that is known (apart from a betrayal beyond his control, when his mother – presumably – had Reynolds paint him still in the fluffy skirts of a four-year-old) is an engraving from a lost miniature; it seems distressingly pert.

The metaphysics of Brummell, and of Dandyism, did not concern Englishmen very much until Oscar Wilde. (Partly distilled from Brummell's legend, and partly invented, in a sort of satanism, by writers like Barbey d'Aurevilly and Baudelaire, it had earlier a great *succès d'estime* in France.) But the practice of Brummell, the insistence on cut, on sobriety, and above all upon not standing out from one's fellow men, which became, in the hands of ordinary mortals, mere conformity – these were to develop, persist and fossilize, not in Dandyism, but in the dark urban uniform we still acknowledge today. By about 1810, trousers were established instead of breeches, the white cravat was about to yield to the black, and the head, stripped of the wig, accepted the burden of the top-hat. The face itself, after more than a century of clean-shaving, was threatened by the first out-flanking movement of hair, advancing in side-board whiskers down the cheeks.

For the vanguard of fashion, Brummell's discipline was too severe an imposition. Chateaubriand, writing in the forties, remembered the English so-called dandy of the twenties as presenting, by duty,

an unhappy and ailing figure; he was expected to have something neglected about his person: long nails; beard worn neither full nor shaved, but seeming to have sprouted at a given moment by surprise, through forgetfulness, amid the pre-occupations of despair; a waving lock of hair; a profound, sublime, wandering and fatal glance; lips contracted in

Plate 205
Alfred, Count d'Orsay
(1801–1852) by Sir George
Hayter, 1839
Oil on canvas, 127.3 × 101.6
(50 $\frac{1}{8}$ × 40)
National Portrait Gallery,
London

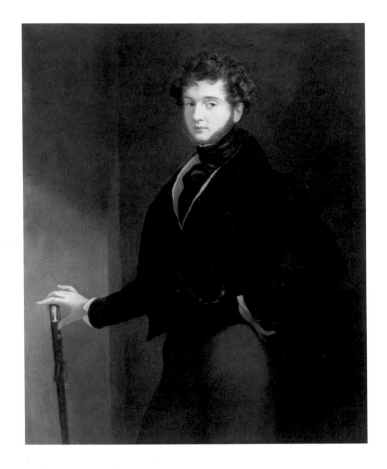

scorn of the human race; a heart bored, Byronian, drowned in the disgust and mystery of existence.[142]

(Romantic beauty was often ailing; Lawrence found it in the consumptive Misses Siddons; it is sharp and eager in the face of Keats, and in Byron it was enhanced by a club-foot.) This, one suspects, may have been a fashion mainly cultivated in *avant-garde* literary circles, rather than in high society.

In the thirties, d'Orsay (Plate 205), radiant with health and scent, led a more bluff and colourful assault on uniformity in dress, with a neat close-curled beard now fully encircling his face; he had known Byron, and he mingled a dash of the Byronic with the precision of Brummell, restraining but not stifling a true French loudness. He had no wide influence; the presentation of body and face was henceforward to be, perhaps not controlled by, but anchored in, the urban middle-classes. It was of the middle-classes that Fielding had written already in 1751:

Nothing has wrought such an alteration in this order of people, as the introduction of trade. This hath indeed given a new face to the whole nation, hath in great measure subverted the former state of affairs, and hath almost totally changed the manners, customs, and habits of the people, more especially of the lower sort. The narrowness of their future is changed into wealth; their frugality into luxury, their humility into pride, and their subjection into equality.[143]

The ranks of the traders were soon to be swollen by the industrial pioneers and magnates. But in the uniform now worn by society for the ordinary formal business in life, it is trade – and specifically the trade in magic money – that still prevails now: the uniform of the City. Even the Brigade of Guards climbs quickly out of its gorgeous uniform, as soon as off-parade, into that of the City gent; its badge should be reversible, and one side would show crossed umbrellas over a bowler hat.

In the latter part of the eighteenth century and in the first half of the nineteenth century, men of talent, determination and accomplishment could rise with little embarrassment, as James Watt did from the family of a bankrupt small merchant, as Stephenson did from far humbler origins, and as did countless others. The portrait painters to whom they sat in due course, as one of the normal consequences of their success, incorporated them without effort into the top ranks of society, of those who had had their portraits painted. Some painters, like Wright of Derby, had a natural plainness of vision that might preserve something of the unaffected in sitters like Arkwright, and the unknown painter of Macadam seems to have caught the tough, hard-wearing surface of the roads in their maker. But normally the painter tidied up the sitters into the polite format, disguising them, as it were, in Academy dress.

Very occasionally the industrialists themselves sponsored curious novelties. Such were the money tokens issued by Wilkinson, the iron-master (Plate 206), to his

Plate 206 (*far right*)
John Wilkinson
(1728–1808)
by Lemuel Francis
Abbott
Oil on canvas,
73.7 × 61.6 (29 × 24¼)
National Portrait
Gallery, London

Plate 207 (*above right*)
Money token by an
unknown artist
showing John
Wilkinson
(1728–1808)
Copper,
diameter 2.9 (1)
British Museum,
London (Department
of Coins and Medals)

Plate 208
Obverse of Plate 207,
showing a tilt-forge

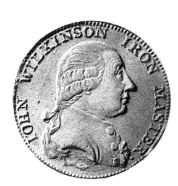

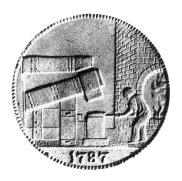

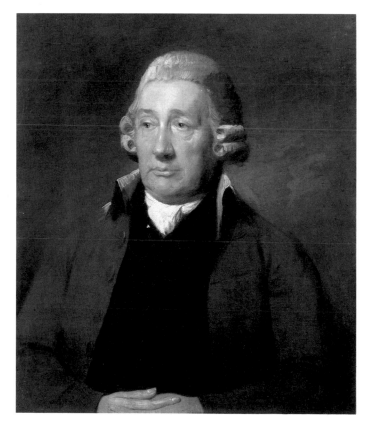

workmen in the shape of coins (Plates 207 and 208): on one of them, where normally would be the royal head, and Britannia or another emblem, the symbols of the power behind the money, he has set his own head and his massive tilt-forge; the whole thing as potent an emblem of *auctoritas* as ever was. But of that other nation that was beginning to form up, at first in the seventies in hysterical mobs of machine workers, and then gradually coalescing over the next seventy-five years into Unions, the working-classes, the *proletariat*, their faces are scarcely glimpsed at all. The genre painting of the period, from Gainsborough, Wheatley and Morland through Wilkie and Mulready to the beginnings of the true Victorian anecdotal painters like Webster and Frith, is confined to rural (if not bucolic) and metropolitan subjects. By the time Victoria ascended the throne, revolution had threatened, as in the 'Massacre of Peterloo' in Manchester in 1819, more than once, and the division of society, between masters and men, was acknowledged. Men, from the masters' point of view, were not a picturesque subject, and radical journalists like William Cobbett did not yet tour England with an artist to record what they saw.[144]

But also, by the time of Victoria's accession in 1837, the heroic period of portraiture in England was over. With the exception of Lawrence, the opinion of the best artists had been hardening steadily against the slavery of the portrait. Fuseli, of course, and Barry, abominated it; even Opie told the students at the Academy that his very soul was sick with hearing crowd after crowd revolving round the exhibitions with only two questions: 'Who is that?' and 'Is it like?' Fuseli and Opie and then Haydon still believed that the alternative was the *ignis fatuus* of history-painting, but, as Opie spoke, the three real geniuses active in English painting were already forging their own realms of imagination: Blake (to whom the name of Reynolds was anathema) in the visionary; Turner and Constable in landscape. There was no comparable genius in portraiture, and the society-portrait between 1790 and 1840 shows a steady regression, all in all, from the dramatic, involved painting of Reynolds to the depiction of effigies once more.

XI

Pre-Raphaelite Longing

IN 1837 Queen Victoria succeeded to the throne of England; also in 1837, in France, Louis Daguerre became the first man to fix permanently the image of the camera obscura, and established the first practicable process of photography.[145] In 1841 Richard Beard opened in London the first public photographic portrait studio in Britain; by the end of the next year London had two more, by 1851 about a dozen; by 1861 over 200, of which 35 were in Regent Street. In those twenty years photography arrived.

The reaction amongst artists was varied; Paul Delaroche, on first seeing a daguerreotype, was appalled and announced that painting was dead, while even Turner was moved to see in it the end of Art: 'Thank God I have had my day.'[146] Their fears of course were exaggerated, but there were casualties – not only the crude forerunner of the photographic shadow-picture, the silhouette – but miniature-painting itself as a living craft. On his death-bed the last of the important miniaturists, Sir William Ross, lamented that 'it was all up with future miniature-painting'; that was about 1860, and his announcement was correct, but belated.

For the first ten years of portrait photography, two methods in the main were used. The first was that patented and baptised by Daguerre, and when Beard patented in England the refinement of tinted daguerreotypes, photography offered a completely satisfactory substitute for the miniature-painting, plus various advantages – that of novelty, to begin with; of speed – a single exposure sometimes of much less than a minute (depending on the weather), compared with several sittings each perhaps of an hour or more; and, of course, of veracity. Veracity, however, was a double-edged quality in portraiture, and it was precisely on this that the painter Chalon's confidence rested when he made his famous rejoinder to the Queen's doubts that the camera would ruin the miniature: 'Ah non, Madame, photographie can't flattère'.[147] Photographers soon found that the photograph was open to titivation, and any query could be turned by the truism that the camera cannot lie.

But seen backwards in historical perspective, the miniature looks as though it had been straining upon self-immolation in the photograph since about 1800. In 1801 Andrew Robertson arrived in London from Edinburgh, where he had been much encouraged by Raeburn; Robertson's aim was to give to the miniature the substantiality of oil-painting, and he claimed to have been amongst the first 'to explode the pink cheek and lips, and blue beards of the old style, and to introduce truth, warmth and harmony'. He acknowledged that what had recommended him to the public was his 'careful drawing and correct form'.

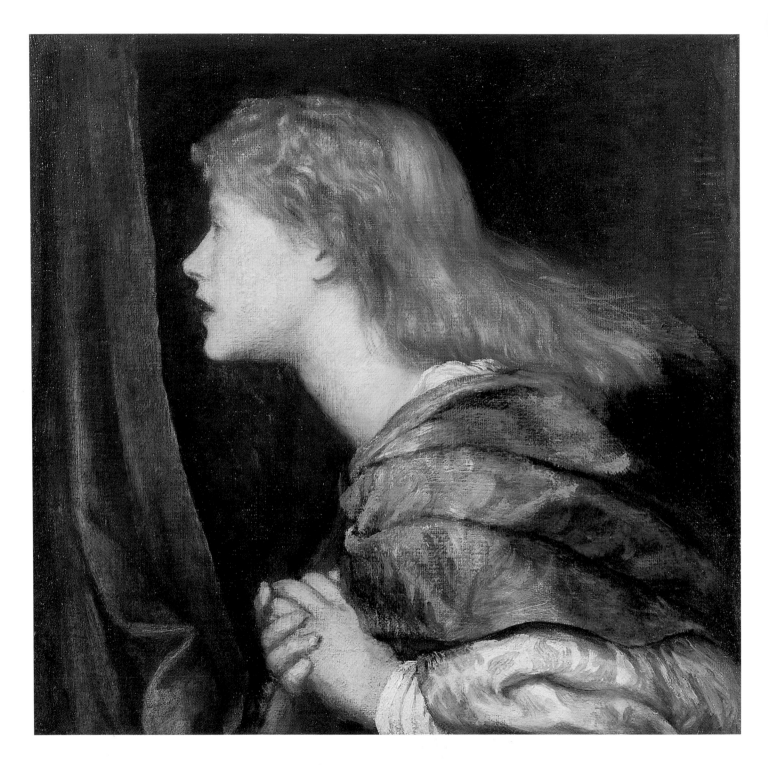

Plate 209 *(Alice) Ellen Terry* (1847–1928) by George Frederic Watts, *c.*1864–1865. Oil on canvas, 59.7 × 59.7 ($23\frac{1}{2}$ × $23\frac{1}{2}$).
National Portrait Gallery, London

In place of the artefact, the heightened conceits of Cosway, miniaturists began to attempt to supply their clients with a facsimile in miniature. Their paintings grew steadily larger, until one of the most popular formulas was a three-quarter length seated, with one hand resting on a table by the chair, set in a mount with a slightly arched top (Plate 210): it was a life-size formula in small, but even more was it the precise formula that was to make the fortunes of Beard and of Claudet, when applied to the daguerreotype (Plate 211); several miniaturists moved from the practice of painting their sitters to that of photographing them with little effort of adjustment. Henry Collen was one of them, and his miniature of Lord Langdale might almost be a coloured photograph – but it was painted in 1829.

One of the qualities that endeared the daguerreotype to the early Victorian public was its brilliant rendering of minute detail, and it was the daguerreotype that monopolized the attention of the professional studio photographers all through the forties (Plate 212). The rival method, the first to use the now standard negative/positive process, known as the calotype, is associated with the name of that brilliant but unattractively jealous pioneer, Fox Talbot. It produced a broader effect that found less favour with the contemporary public, but it did help those two great Scottish photographers, David Octavius Hill and Robert Adamson, to make masterpieces which in artistic quality have still to be surpassed (Plate 213).

In 1851, another technical advance – the wet collodion process, invented by Frederick Scott Archer – combined the advantages of the daguerreotype – its fine detail – with those of the calotype: a larger size and the negative/positive system by which it could be reduplicated (daguerreotypes were generally less than four inches high, and each was unique); twenty years later, dry-plate photography began to be developed, and thence it was only a short matter of time before the hand-camera

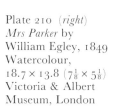

Plate 210 (*right*)
Mrs Parker by
William Egley, 1849
Watercolour,
18.7 × 13.8 (7⅛ × 5⅛)
Victoria & Albert
Museum, London

Plate 211 (*far right*)
Charles Babbage
(1792–1871) by
Antoine Claudet,
*c.*1847–1851
Daguerreotype, 7 × 6
(2¾ × 2⅜)
National Portrait
Gallery, London

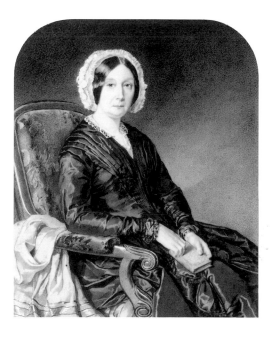
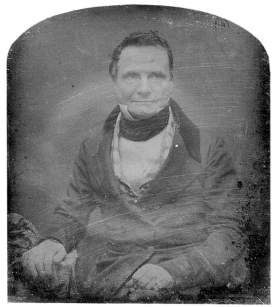

Plate 212
Sir Charles Wheatstone (1802–1875) *and his
Family* by Antoine Claudet, *c.*1851 (detail)
Stereoscopic daguerreotype (right plate
illustrated), 7.3 × 5.7 (2⅞ × 2¼)
National Portrait Gallery, London

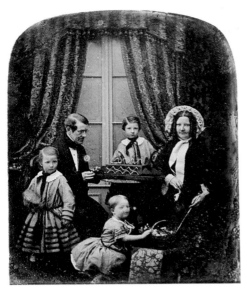

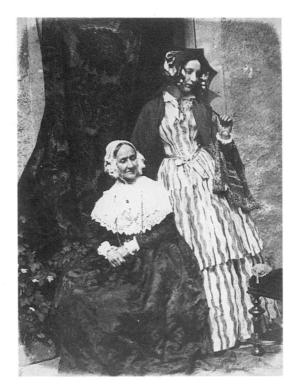

Plate 213
*Anne Palgrave, Mrs
Edward Rigby*
(1777–1872) *and her
daughter Elizabeth, later
Lady Eastlake*
(1809–1893) by
David Octavius Hill
and Robert
Adamson, *c.*1845
Calotype, 20.1 × 14.8
(8 × 5⅞)
National Portrait
Gallery, London

came in. The first Kodak was marketed in Britain in 1888, and man was finally exposed indefensibly before the myriad ruthless recording eyes of the snap-shooters and the press photographers.

The impact of photography upon life-scale portraiture – in paint or in sculpture – was initially probably very slight. It may well have endangered the livelihood of many second-rank painters, particularly in the provinces, but it could offer nothing that seriously disturbed the prestige of the life-scale portrait as an object of pomp and circumstance. As far as quality goes, the situation with the painters was not good; of the Academy Exhibition in 1838, the *Athenaeum* observed that the place of Sir Thomas Lawrence was as far from being filled as ever. While acknowledging the power of some of Wilkie's portraits, it disparaged the affectation and false colouring in others; and then –

Willing as we are to give all honour due to Phillips, and Pickersgill, and Shee, and Briggs, and Wood, and Say, and Eddis, and Laurence, each of whom exhibits works rather above than below his recognised standard of excellence, we are still compelled to confess that none of them rose above mediocrity.

Posterity has endorsed the verdict of the *Athenaeum*, and forgotten all the names of these painters, save that of Wilkie, and he is remembered not for his portraits but for his genre painting.

Nor was the situation, in the ranks of the orthodox Academy painters, to improve for a long time. The standard of technical ability remained very high, but of artistic exploration and discovery there was almost nothing. Now those painters named, and others like Margaret Carpenter, were followed by men such as Sir Francis Grant, J.P. Knight, J.C. Horsley in the forties, fifties and sixties; by Millais (Plate 214) and then Holl in the seventies and eighties. Through these long years, as the figures stand out more and more sharply against the backgrounds, more and more entries in the catalogues of the Academy exhibitions are followed by the note – 'Presentation Portrait'.

Simultaneously, that mute invasion of the squares and parks of British cities (and of the cities of the Empire) by whole-length statues gathers way; piety becomes public, and sites its monuments no longer only in the churches, but in the highway, and in the board-rooms and the council-chambers of public and semi-public institutions, that now become in part also shrines; town halls, water boards, charity commissions, schools, universities. In 1856 this mood created its focus in the National Portrait Gallery, the first of its kind in the world, and the kind apparently peculiar to the British taste, for it has hardly been adopted outside these islands; it may also not be irrelevant to remark that at the time of the founding of the Portrait Gallery, professional British portrait-painting was at one of the lowest ebbs in its history.

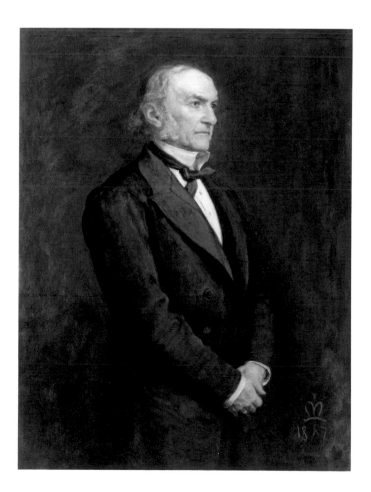

Plate 214
William Ewart Gladstone
(1809–1898) by Sir John Everett
Millais, 1879
Oil on canvas,
125.7 × 91.4 (49½ × 36)
National Portrait Gallery,
London

The Gallery's purpose was to be not artistic, but historic; decently sentimental, and not merely educational, but inspiring. 'There cannot', said Palmerston when moving the Vote for its financial support,

there cannot be a greater incentive to mental exertion, to noble actions, to good conduct on the part of the living, than for them to see before them the features of those who have done things which are worthy of our admiration and whose example we are more induced to imitate when they are brought before us in the visible and tangible shape of portraits.

The official school of portraiture was in full sympathy with such sentiments; the difficulty was to paint them in the features of their sitters. In their portraits of public men they could no longer indicate them by a heroic orchestration of rich colour; colour had gone out of dress, and power resided more in the frock-coated House of Commons than in the Lords, who anyway were becoming increasingly self-conscious about ermine. The formulas became more and more static, more and more those of the effigy. It may seem incongruous at first thought, but the artistic forebear to whom the painters perhaps most referred was no longer Lawrence, nor Reynolds, nor Van Dyck, but Velazquez. Sir Francis Grant acknowledged that he 'owed much of his success to Velazquez'.[148] Millais was much interested in him and was only deterred from studying him in the Prado by the well-known discomforts of travelling in Spain; Frank Holl was actually dubbed 'the English Velazquez'. None of them – not even Holl – recognized in Velazquez what we now recognize as his genius, the way he used paint in the building of pictures (as of course their near-contemporary Manet did in France); they were interested by the icon that he produced, a resolution in matchless dignity of the problem of painting a state-portrait of a man dressed in sombre, boring and difficult blacks and greys.

With women, the problem was different; colour abounded but the shape of clothes somewhat offset it. By about 1840 the hooped skirt was on its way in, and soon the crinoline was in full flower; the society-portrait painters hesitated before it, and seem to have preferred if possible to minimize its extravagance by showing its wearer seated. It was left to the painters especially patronized by the court to catch it in its wide prime; and amongst them, above all, to the famous international court-painter, Winterhalter. He – and to a lesser degree the English painters affected by continental academicism, like Hayter and Partridge (they all stood apart from the English Academy) – worked in what was in effect at once a more smoothly polished and more naturalistic style than did the painters in the English tradition.

But it seems odd that Winterhalter should have been rebuked by English critics for too earthy an approach, now that he is remembered as the most quaint and 'period' of Victorian portrait painters: 'The Queen and Prince [Consort]', said the *Athenaeum*, of the sentimentally delightful portrait-group by Winterhalter of the Queen and her family in 1847 (Plate 215), 'though likenesses, are yet sensual and fleshy versions of those distinguished persons.' The Queen's arms and hands, it was

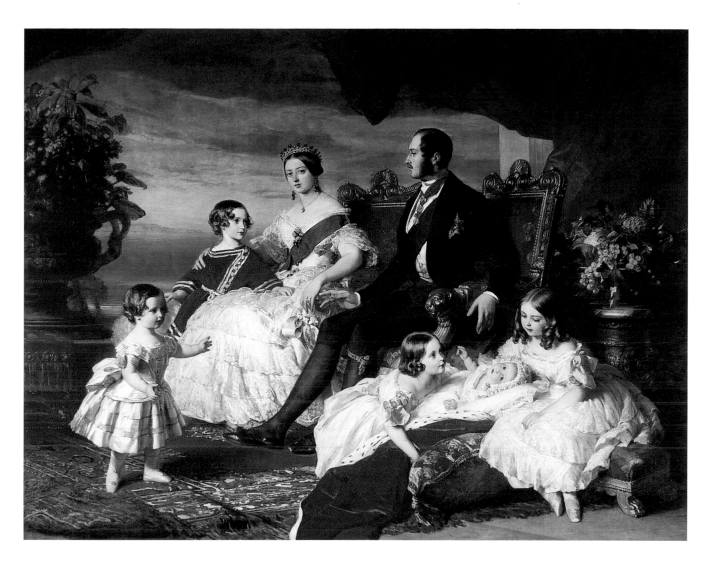

Plate 215
Queen Victoria
(1819–1901) *and her*
Family by Franz
Xaver Winterhalter,
1846
Oil on canvas,
249.5 × 316
(98⅛ × 124½)
Royal Collection (by
gracious permission of
Her Majesty The
Queen)

found, were 'expressed in contours that speak more of hard work in the kitchen than of the occupations of a palace,' and there was such 'a coarseness in the details – such an odour, we may say, of paint, and such a want of taste – as make us frankly rejoice that it is not from the hands of an Englishman'.[149]

The English painters, indeed, specialized in a more sweetly spiritual key, particularly when dealing with young women: here the paragon among artists was George Richmond, who admitted that a portrait should represent the truth – 'Ah! but the truth lovingly told'.[150] He was the most accomplished of a considerable number of portraitists who challenged the photographers with chalk drawings of heads – sometimes life-size. The head is tilted on the long neck, meek yet resilient as a narcissus bud that fills to flower; the expression may be over-sweet, but it is wrong to dismiss it as a simper; smooth though he was, and though one may doubt the claim that his portrait of Ruskin was 'more exact than any photograph', he was famous for his power of catching a likeness, and some truth surely remains behind the highlights of love.

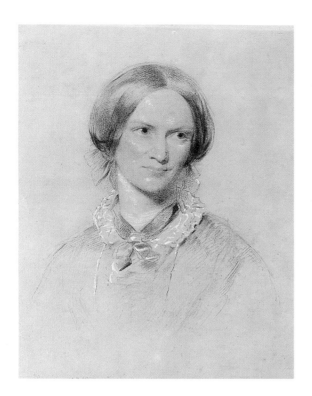

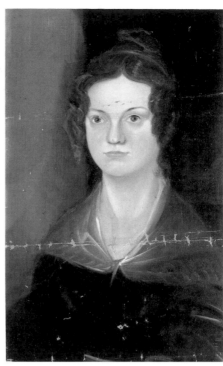

Plate 216 (*far left*)
Charlotte Brontë
(1816–1855) by
George Richmond,
1850
Chalk, 60 × 47.6
($23\frac{5}{8}$ × $18\frac{3}{4}$)
National Portrait
Gallery, London

Plate 217 (*left*)
Charlotte Brontë
(1816–1855) by
Patrick Branwell
Brontë, *c*.1834
(detail)
Oil on canvas,
90.2 × 74.6
($35\frac{1}{2}$ × $29\frac{3}{8}$)
National Portrait
Gallery, London

As an extreme example, one may take his portrait of Charlotte Brontë (Plate 216): some may reject out of hand this suave account of a successful society authoress, with the melting eyes, and turn rather to the primitive version of the authoress of *Jane Eyre*, only begetter of Mr Rochester, by her brother Branwell (Plate 217). Yet the truth probably ranges all the way between the two portraits. Richmond left a curious record of his conversation with her when she sat; she arrived on 13 June 1850, aged thirty-four, wearing a hat, and nervous: she took off her hat, showing a small square of merino resting on top of her head.

George Richmond: 'Miss Brontë, you have a little pad of brown merino on top of your head – I wonder if I might ask you to remove it.'

Miss Brontë: (bursts into tears).[151]

The Pre-Raphaelites, in their brief and vivid spring, in the fifties, scrutinized faces with eyes more piercing and (except in the case of Rossetti) more minutely loyal to accident. Portraiture, as art, did not interest them much, but with their insistence on faithfulness to nature, they filled their compositions with real faces drawn from the life, the faces of themselves, and of their friends and relations. So Elizabeth Siddal lay immersed in a large bath for Millais' *Ophelia*, and one of the results (according to W.M. Rossetti) was probably the best likeness ever taken of her; both the Rossettis, W.B. Scott, F.G. Stephens and Millais' father and his sister-in-law are said to appear in *Lorenzo and Isabella*; for the two depressed emigrants in *The Last of England* (Plate 218), Ford Madox Brown used himself and his wife, and 'to insure the peculiar look of *light all round* which objects have on a dull

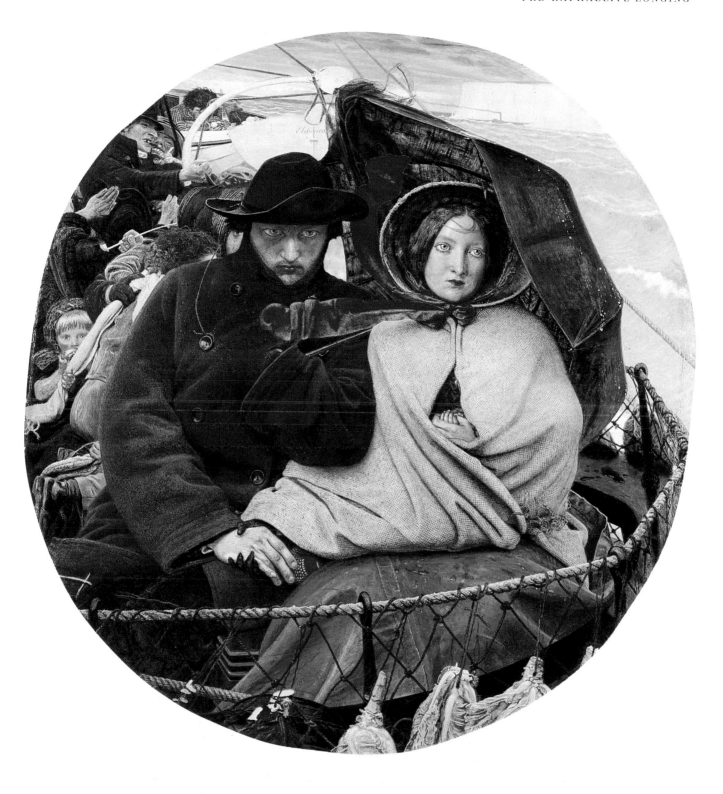

Plate 218 *The Last of England* by Ford Madox Brown, 1855. Oil on panel, 82.5 × 75 (32½ × 29½). Birmingham City Museums and Art Gallery

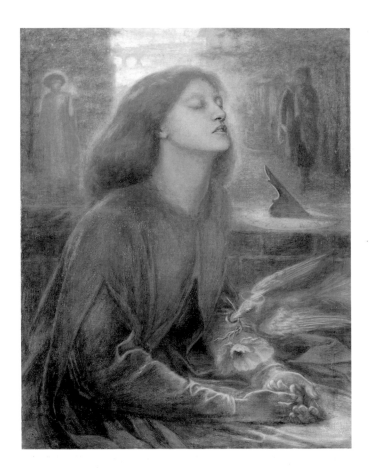

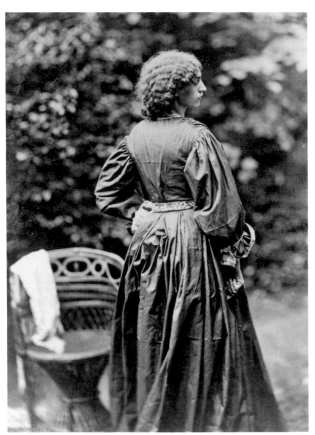

day at sea, it was painted for the most part in the open air on dull days, and, when the flesh was being painted, on cold days'.[152]

But the creation of a new type of face was the achievement of Rossetti; a face that is often wrongly called the typical Pre-Raphaelite[153] face, and (perhaps also partly wrongly) the face of Elizabeth Siddal, Rossetti's wife and lost dead love. It is a face hazed with a mystically sensuous contemplation, the mouth clearly defined for love, the eyes cast down, the golden hair about the shoulders.

> Look in my face; my name is Might-have-been;
> I am also called No-more, Too-late, Farewell.

And yet also:

> Above the long lithe throat
> The mouth's mould testifies of voice and kiss,
> The shadowed eyes remember and foresee.
> Her face is made her shrine . . .

It is the shrine of an ideal love rather than of the image of Elizabeth Siddal, known as Guggums. That so characteristic line of jaw is in some of the drawings almost masculine, and well it might be, for it is Dante's; in modern English women Rossetti found it more in Jane Borden, later Mrs Morris, than in his wife. His *Beata*

Plate 219 *(above left)*
Beata Beatrix
by Dante Gabriel
Rossetti, 1864–1870
Oil on canvas,
86.4 × 66 (34 × 26)
Tate Gallery, London

Plate 220 *(above)*
Jane Morris
by John Parsons,
1865
Bromide copy print
from the original
albumen print,
17.4 × 14.8 ($6\frac{3}{4} \times 5\frac{3}{4}$)
National Portrait
Gallery, London

Beatrix (Plate 219), begun in 1864 shortly after Lizzie Siddal died, is his haunted memory of his wife, but the face is already nearer to Jane Morris – the face that glows palely until the end of the century (Plate 220). That it is a typical mid-Victorian face is hardly true; it burns on, a personification of a certain state of exaltation that finally faints in the truly never-never mediaevalism of Burne-Jones. But the rich new patrons from the North who were amongst Rossetti's best clients would have been dismayed to find their wives as intense within such monastic draperies as are Rossetti's women; only in the mid-seventies, with the beginning of the 'aesthetic' movement in dress, did the figures from the Rossetti and then the Burne-Jones pictures move out from the canvases into the drawing-rooms and streets of London, into *In the Front Row of the Opera* (Plate 221). For a deliberate attempt to sum up the Victorian face for posterity, one has to turn to George Frederic Watts.[154]

Watts spans the Victorian age; he exhibited first at the Academy in the year of the Queen's accession to the throne; he survived her by three years. As painting, some of his early work, done partly in Italy, is the most satisfying; under the impact of the South and of the warm colour of the Venetians, the withdrawn and ascetic young man from London became almost resplendent. Upon his return to England, his capture by the Pattle sisters, and his settling into the establishment at Little Holland House in an atmosphere of high thinking and discreetly high

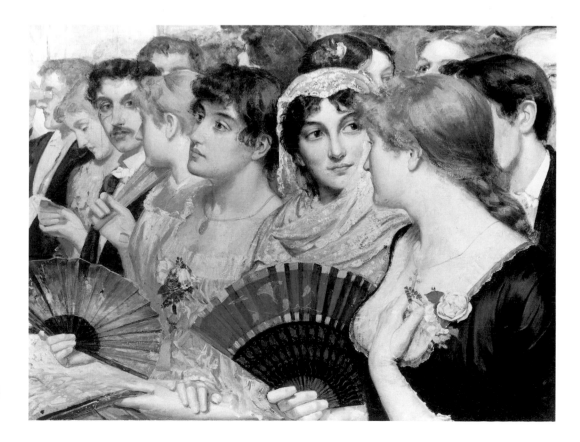

Plate 221
In the Front Row of the Opera by William Holyoake
Oil on canvas,
61.6 × 81.4 (24¼ × 32)
Glasgow Museums and Art Galleries

living, he settled to his vocation which was moral. Art was the means to an end, 'to affect the mind seriously by nobility of line and colour'. In his main attack, he failed, or so it seems at present. It was to present visually a new mythology, to illustrate the unwritten bible of agnosticism.

Fundamentally a religious painter, he had no religion – no basic plot, no coherent tradition of imagery with all its accumulation of associations, upon which to draw. He was not, unlike Blake, passionate enough in his vision to invent a new symbolism; he borrowed, and the result is pastiche; he tried to invent, and was restrained by good taste and propriety into flaccidity. It is not then his mythological and allegorical pictures that are now of most interest, underrated though many of them are, but his portraits. W.M. Rossetti indicated accurately the reason for this as early as 1862:

In portraiture Watts is still as ideal as the form of art allows him to be so; but this controls the tendency, and prevents it from passing into vagueness. Ideal tendency in ideal subject is always in danger of losing itself 'as Water does in Water'.[155]

Watts' imagination, impulsive but weak in architectural skill, needed a recalcitrant material, a stubborn irreducible fact, to work against, in order to bring out his best; the immutable skeleton of his sitter's head provided just that.

Already by about 1850 he had hit on the idea of a series of portraits of the worthies of his time, a sort of Victorian pantheon, which he would (and did) bequeath to the National Portrait Gallery. He painted most of them to a standard size about 25 by 20 inches or 63 by 50 centimetres, which just allows a life-sized head and some indication of the shoulders; the focus is on the face. The mood is monumental, and his portraits are variations on the theme: 'Let us now praise famous men'. When Tennyson sat to him in 1859 (for the portrait now at Eastnor Castle) the poet asked him what he wished to achieve in painting a portrait, and Watts' answer is said to be incorporated in the lines in *Lancelot and Elaine:*

> a painter poring on a face,
> Divinely thro' all hindrance finds the man
> Behind it, and so paints him that his face,
> The shape and colour of a mind and life,
> Lives for his children, ever at its best
> And fullest.

There is nothing new in such purpose, nor was it foreign to some of Watts' contemporaries – Holl spoke of his aim as 'to drag upon canvas the identity of the man himself'. What was new was the intensity and concentration with which Watts dwelt on the face as the arena in which the character is shown; allegorical allusion and rhetoric of pose and body play little part in his portraits, he is intent upon soul and mind and their achievement scored on the face. That he should fail was inevitable; the greater part of his portraits are probably dead for most people, and he has paid, as have most successful portrait painters, the penalty of painting too

Plate 222 (*right*)
Alfred, 1st Baron
Tennyson (1809–1892)
by George Frederic
Watts, *c.*1863–1864
Oil on canvas,
61.3 × 51.4
(24 1/8 × 20 1/4)
National Portrait
Gallery, London

Plate 223 (*far right*)
Alfred, 1st Baron
Tennyson (1809–1892)
by Julia Margaret
Cameron, *c.*1867
Albumen print,
32.4 × 25.3 (12 3/4 × 10)
National Museum of
Photography, Film
and Television,
Bradford

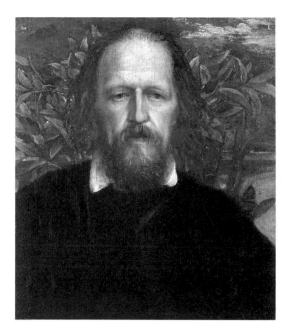
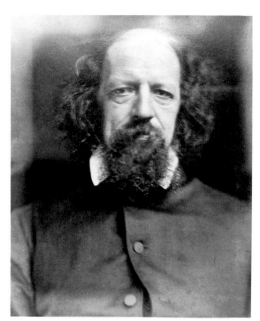

many portraits. Nevertheless, his best paintings will be found, I think – given a fair scrutiny – both evocative and commensurable with such mental grandeur as their subjects have bequeathed to posterity. These faces, many of them, can support their owners' genius, and to make them able to do so, Watts arrived, about 1860, at a technique that can almost foreshadow that of expressionism.

It is far removed from the hard naturalism of Millais' later style, or from that of any of Watts' British contemporaries. It is becoming visible, already in 1859, in his portrait of Gladstone, in his Lord Lawrence of 1862, and he never carried it further than in his Tennyson of about 1863 (Plate 222). Here is the poet, the bard, of *In Memoriam*; sombre, searching, and yet somehow rather sumptuous in doubt. Watts was not often to achieve portraits of this order again, but almost right up to his death in 1904 he did from time to time rival them, in, for example, the Swinburne, the Manning (Plate 224), the Walter Crane; and it is these and others that place him fairly in the ranks of the great English portrait painters, and as a heroic painter.

With women, he is generally less happy; although some of his whole-lengths, such as the Mrs Huth in Dublin, are gracious and noble ventures in the grand English manner, and his portraits of his brief, unsuitable wife Ellen Terry are enchanting and beautifully painted sentiments (Plate 209), he tends generally to over-sweeten his young women with Venetian memories, and to worry the life out of old women. He was almost certainly frightened of the sex, not only of George Eliot, which is comprehensible enough (he longed for her, but knew 'that the features belonged to a type he would have found most difficult, and afraid of not doing the great mind justice, he did not venture to make the attempt'), but any strange women, other than those who dominated him, those to whom he was used, and those who had built a chaste affection about him like a studio.

Plate 224
Henry Edward Manning
(1808–1892) by George
Frederic Watts, 1882
Oil on canvas, 90.2 × 69.9
$(35\frac{1}{2} \times 27\frac{1}{2})$
National Portrait Gallery,
London

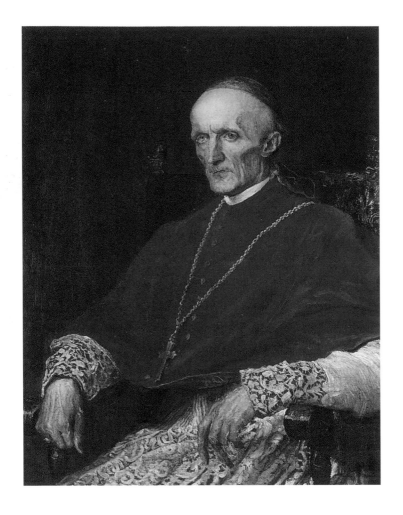

His approach to the great men of his time was not made in pure adulation; he chose them from the men whom he thought would hereafter be deemed to have made or marred their country, and he confessed to Cecil Rhodes, during a sitting: 'I'm not sure myself which you are doing'. There was also some bias in his selection; Gladstone, of course, but it is difficult to imagine him even considering the possibility of painting Disraeli. Nor did all his sitters approve of their images; Carlyle, to whom I shall return, was furious, Rossetti uncertain, and Morris's friends thought the portrait almost libellous; Watts was tough in his integrity to his conception, and it was a heroic conception. Sir Henry Taylor wished to be immortalized as a 'jovial modern'; Watts insisted on a 'modern Jove'.

The achievement of Watts links the evaporating glory of Lawrence's school in the forties with the kindling blaze of Sargent in the seventies. By 1870 the photograph had already taken a heavy toll in the ranks of the portrait painters; a comparison of figures at the Academy Exhibition is significant. A hundred years earlier, at the second exhibition of the newly-founded Academy, some 265 objects were shown; over a third were portraits, including six sculptured portraits. Sixty years later, in 1830, in the by now enormously swollen show, just over half the exhibits were

Plate 225
Adelina Patti (1843–1919)
by James Sant
Oil on canvas,
109.9 × 85.1 (43¼ × 33½)
National Portrait Gallery,
London

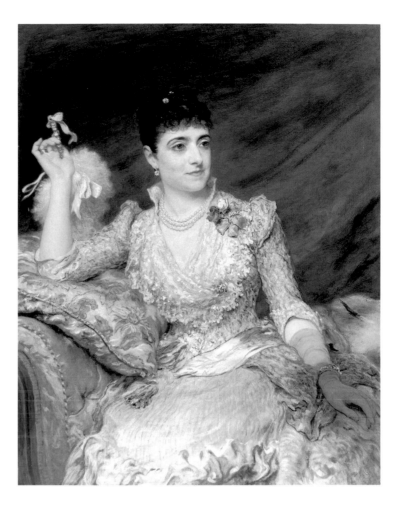

portraits, about 643 out of 1,278, of which about 300 were miniatures or small water-colours, and some 87 in sculpture. In the next forty years photography became a thriving business, and the figures at the 1870 Academy speak for themselves. Portraits account for a bare fifth of the exhibition, 247 out of 1,229. The miniatures have been decimated, 32 instead of 300, but three-dimensional portraits have actually increased to 117. They fulfilled a monumental function that photography could not, and a function in which the Victorians took a keen pleasure. (In the eighties and nineties there was even a revival, for the great Blougram-like prelates, of the false pride of the whole-length recumbent effigy.)

The life-scale painted portraits in the Academy echo the monumental theme: gentlemen upright in dark and heavy respectability, an uprightness emphasized by the narrower, more vertical shape that Millais used for his three-quarter lengths; the ladies as lavishly material and as congested with dress as their drawing-rooms, and often as vulgar. Millais and Sant (Plate 225) had the true Midas-touch when they laid their brush on women. They are almost all parade portraits; either the continuation of the line, equal in size and state to those of the ancestors in the ancestral home, or they represent the founding of a new line, or they are household gods for institutions. The portrait that one gave away for love or friendship – that would now, or soon, be in the form of a photograph.

In the sixties the photograph album became a craze; they housed the kind of photograph known as the carte-de-visite, and were virtually portable portrait galleries. At the beginning of the book came the royal family, in full, followed by contemporary celebrities, followed by the family and friends of the owners. About the same time various volumes of biographical notices of celebrities, together with their photographs, began to appear, and sold very well; the attitude of the sitters is not without interest. Between 1856 and 1860 a publication, the *National Gallery of Photographic Portraits*, was under way, and the preparatory correspondence has survived. A considerable proportion of the personalities involved were in no way averse, and fully content to be publicized, though there were exceptions. Matthew Arnold considered himself insufficiently celebrated; J.S. Mill wrote that he had no desire to figure in a collection and did not think that his personal appearance could be a matter of any interest to the general public; women of course were still in a minority, and their reactions varied sharply: Harriet Beecher Stowe was willing, Mrs Gaskell was splendidly Victorian: 'Other women may not object to having their portraits taken for the public, and sold indiscriminately, but I feel a strong insurmountable objection to it.' But the root of feminine reluctance to be photographed was indicated by Helena Faucit Martin: 'All the photographs of me have so signally failed that I have come to the conclusion never to undergo the ordeal again' (Plate 226). The difficulty of obtaining raw, or

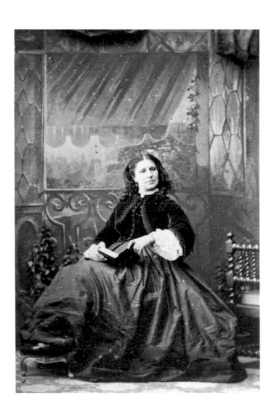

Plate 226
Helena Faucit Martin (1817–1898)
by Camille Silvy
Albumen carte-de-visite, 8.4 × 5.7 (3¼ × 2¼)
National Portrait Gallery, London

untouched-up, studio photographs of feminine celebrities for record purposes can still occur today.[156]

Pictorially, the professional photographers had still little to contribute. For their whole-lengths, they relied for the most part on the formulae sanctified by painters from Van Dyck to Lawrence, dropping a painted landscape backcloth behind their sitters, and furnishing them with the conventional poses and the conventional pillars and urns. The most remarkable work was being done by amateurs like Lewis Carroll, and most notably, by Julia Margaret Cameron.[157] The wife of a coffee-planter, she turned to photography as therapy for a fit of domestic depression in 1863. She was one of that energetic family, the Pattles, and one of her sisters was the dominant Mrs Prinsep who housed and ordered Watts at Little Holland House, and it was there that Mrs Cameron snared many of her most distinguished sitters. Watts himself she knew well, and he often advised her on questions of art.

Like Watts, she specialized in intellectual subjects, and concentrated on the seat of intellect, the head, often wrapping the shoulders in a loose dark drapery; her pietistic attitude to the great whom she photographed was again like that of Watts, though far less critical; when they were before her camera, she wrote,

My whole soul has endeavoured to do its duty towards them in recording faithfully the greatness of the inner as well as the features of the outer man. The photograph thus taken has been almost the embodiment of prayer.

The success of her portraits rested on the excellence of her eye, her insistence on a beautiful effect, and the deliberate 'imperfection' of her technique. She profited by accidents almost as much as some painters of the abstract expressionist school.

When focusing and coming to something which to my eye was very beautiful, I stopped there, instead of screwing on the lens to the more definite focus which all other photographers insist on.[158]

Her portraits are visually in fact out of focus, and to the qualities of definition that were amongst the greatest virtues of photography for the ordinary exponent she was indifferent. She used very large plates, and also an abnormally long exposure, from three to seven minutes, for which length of time it is almost physically impossible for average sitters to remain still. They moved, giving Mrs Cameron's portraits a still softer and broader modulation of form.

To compare the results achieved by Watts and Mrs Cameron, I reproduce the painter's Tennyson of about 1863 and the photographer's version three or four years later (Plates 222 and 223). The comparison is not quite fair on Mrs Cameron, as two of her other photographs of Tennyson are superior to this one, but it does indicate exactly what the two methods could achieve; Watts' simplification into general terms, his exaggeration of the length of the already long narrow face, his monumental quality. Mrs Cameron's portrait tells more of the incidentals, the quirks, of Tennyson's face, especially of how his beard grew, but in spite of the deliberate softening of detail, an entirely coherent general statement on the poet's face is not achieved. On occasions, she was better than this; the famous photograph of Sir John Herschel (Plate 227) is an astonishing example, where all hazards have joined propitiously.

But the immediate future of the portrait photograph did not lie in a development of Mrs Cameron's methods; they were too rarefied and not what the public wanted. The public wanted the crisp definition of the professional studio photographer, and it got it. Of greater interest is the development of a more journalistic tendency, and here the photograph could offer something that the portrait-painter hardly ever attempted: the man on the job. J.C. Horsley was an able painter, decorously of his time – known to Whistler as Clothes-Horsley, from his objection to drawing from the nude. His portrait of the engineer Isambard Kingdom Brunel (Plate 228) is an able and polished performance on traditional lines, the portrait of a successful engineering architect, sweetly dressed with his white plans in his office (very much so had Kneller painted Wren a hundred and fifty years earlier). But the extraordinary photograph of Brunel (Plate 229) standing in front of the chains of his most ambitious creation, the biggest ship in the world, the *Great Eastern*, is an incomparably more vivid document – the engineer on the site, in his wrinkled working clothes, a cheroot thrust in the corner of his mouth.

Such unflattering, though trenchant, faithfulness was not the ideal of the thousands who now wished, and were able to, perpetuate their own likenesses. In 1861 *The Photographic News* exclaimed that

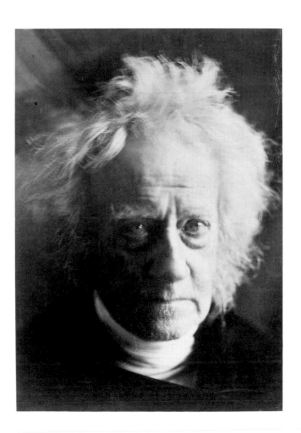

Plate 227
Sir John Herschel (1792–1871)
by Julia Margaret Cameron, 1867
Albumen print, 33.3 × 27.9 (13⅛ × 11)
National Portrait Gallery, London

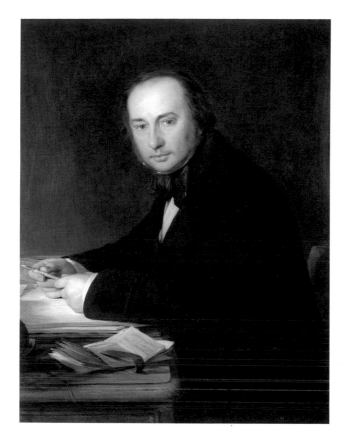

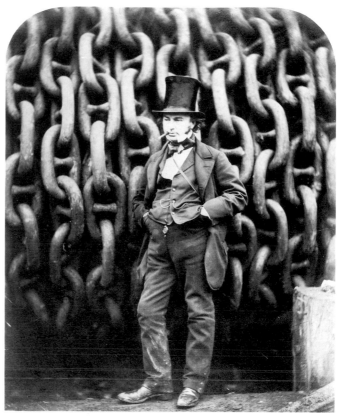

Plate 228 *(above)*
Isambard Kingdom
Brunel (1806–1859)
by John Callcott
Horsley, 1857
Oil on canvas,
91.4 × 70.5 (36 × 27¾)
National Portrait
Gallery, London

Plate 229 *(above right)*
Isambard Kingdom
Brunel (1806–1859)
by Robert Howlett,
1857
Albumen print,
38.6 × 22.5 (11¼ × 8⅞)
National Portrait
Gallery, London

photographic portraiture is the best feature of the fine arts for the million that the ingenuity of man has yet devised. It has in the sense swept away many of the illiberal distinctions of rank and wealth, so that the poor man who possesses but a few shillings can command as perfect a life-like portrait of his wife or child as Sir Thomas Lawrence painted for the most distinguished sovereigns of Europe.

The standard of comparison is still that of the glamorous Lawrence; no one would have dreamed of comparison with the standards of the realist painters already vigorous in France, like Courbet, who proclaimed himself as a painter

not only socialist, but also democrat and republican, in short partisan of the whole revolution and further entirely a realist, sincere friend of the true truth.

In France indeed, in the sixties and seventies, art was in the melting-pot, and that technical exploration that was in the end to challenge the central European tradition of painting as an imitation of nature, and particularly the art of portraiture, was already under way. In 1863, anti-academism received a semi-official, back-handed accolade in the establishment of the *Salon des Refusés*; in 1870 Monet and Renoir were in London (discovering, amongst other things, Turner). Although it was to be a long time before a similar spirit of investigation found its full scope amongst British artists, the *avant-garde* was busy in London from 1860 onwards, in the person of the American James McNeill Whistler.

217

XII

Carlyle – The Face of History

IT IS CURIOUS to inspect the same object as seen from the very different points of artistic view that were taken up in the mid-nineteenth century; the most convenient object (in this context) is the face of Thomas Carlyle. He was, and is, in spite of his failings, a creative historian of considerable eminence; he was a public figure and a mind or at least a character of great influence, and he had a heroic view, which may be called fascist but which nevertheless had grandeur; he is now, moreover, very unfashionable; but he is very much of his time. Also he was undeniably picturesque, in a thorny and unorthodox way. His own position in relation to the arts is still held by a large number of people. 'Ah well', he said to W.B. Scott,

I can make nothing of artists, nor of their work either. . . . Empty as other folk's kettles are, artists' kettles are emptier, and good for nothing but tying on the tails of mad dogs.[159]

In a picture, the only thing that interested him was the subject matter; although, when outraged by the subject, he might explode with a Munnings-like scorn (Holman Hunt's *The Light of the World* – 'a poor mis-shaped presentation . . . a mere papistical fantasy'), on the whole he was indifferent, with one exception: 'Painting is worthless, except portrait-painting'.[160] As a biographer, as a historian, portraits were for him serious, they were documents. Hence, with the added incentive of considerable vanity, his repeated long suffering as a sitter for the artists.

He was born in 1795, but we know little of his appearance until he was in his late thirties, when he was chosen by Daniel Maclise (Plate 231) for his series of what would now be called 'Profiles' of literary men in *Fraser's Magazine*. The drawing is a late development of the brief fashion, born in the 1790s, of small scale, cabinet, whole-length drawings, that had flourished in the hands of Cosway, Buck and especially Edridge; Maclise's drawings often border delicately upon caricature. Here is an unexpected Carlyle, neither the struggling, indignant and irritable writer and brilliant conversationalist of the early years in Scotland, nor the hard-hitting, opinionated, courageous and irritable grand old man and *vieux terrible* of London in his last years; Maclise shows him oddly dandaisical.

Carlyle thought Woolner's portrait medallion of 1851 (Plate 232) 'a rather clever thing' (it is surely a little rejuvenated: he is fifty-six years old); it is also interesting as the view of the only sculptor who was amongst the original Pre-Raphaelite Brethren. Though Woolner was doubtless, if only for a brief spell, in full accord with the moral and artistic tenets of the Brethren, it is as difficult to lay one's finger on the visible evidence of those tenets in his work as it is in the very disparate painting of the

Plate 230
(*facing page*)
Arrangement in Grey and Black, no. 2:
Thomas Carlyle
(1795–1881)
by James McNeill Whistler, 1872–1873
Oil on canvas,
170.2 × 142.2
(67 × 56)
Glasgow Museums and Art Galleries

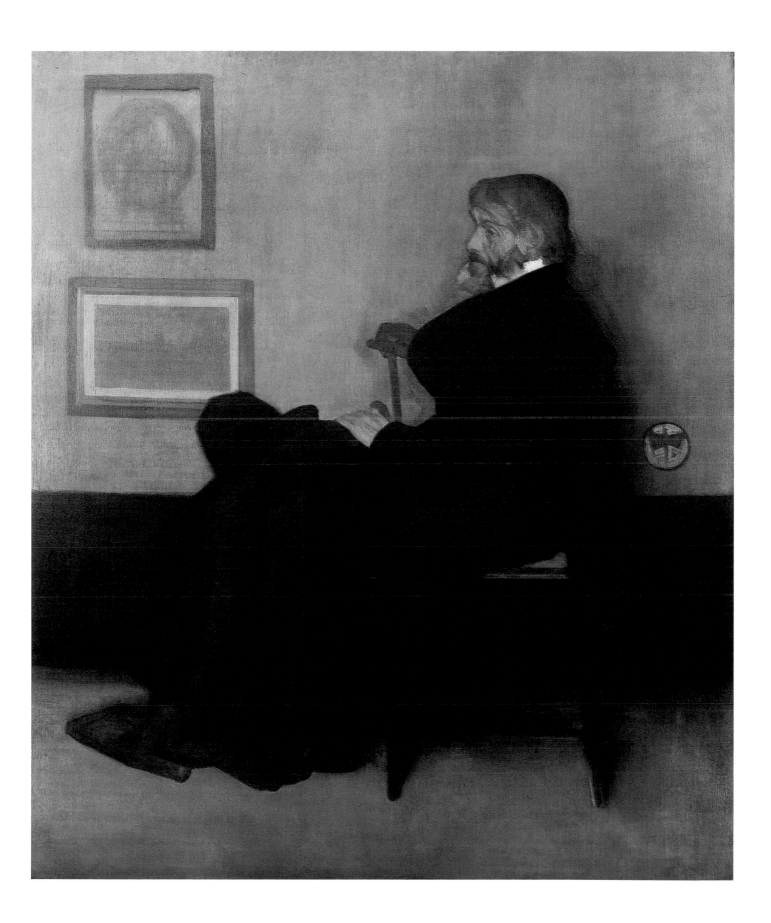

Plate 231
Thomas Carlyle (1795–1881)
by Daniel Maclise, 1832
Pencil, 26.7 × 16.5 (10 $\frac{1}{2}$ × 6 $\frac{1}{2}$)
British Museum, London
(Department of Prints and
Drawings)

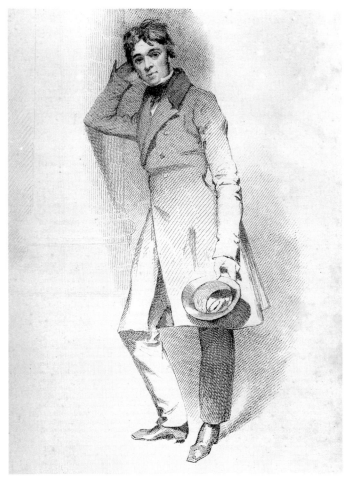

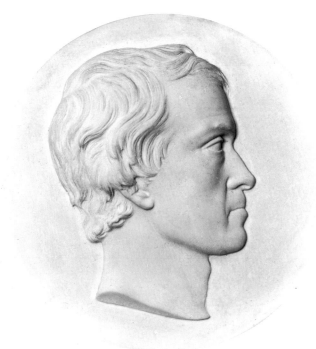

Plate 232
Thomas Carlyle (1795–1881)
by Thomas Woolner,
modelled 1851 and reworked
1855
Plaster medallion,
22.4 (8 $\frac{7}{8}$) diameter
Scottish National Portrait
Gallery

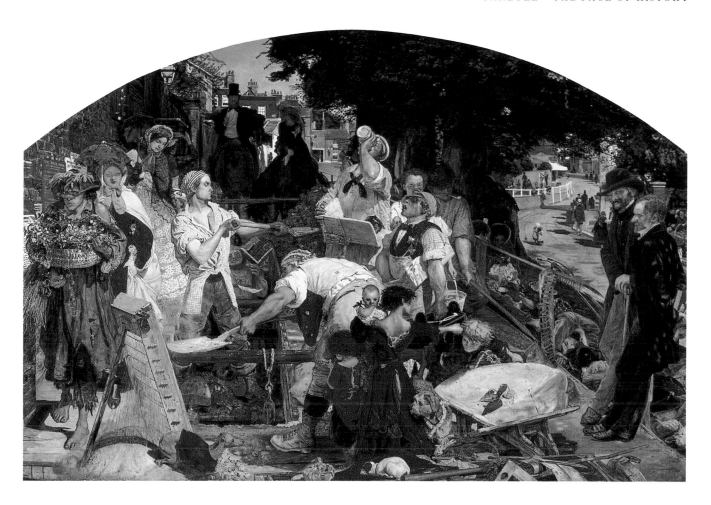

Plate 233
Work by Ford Madox
Brown, 1852–1865
Oil on canvas,
137 × 197·3
$(53\frac{15}{16} \times 77\frac{11}{16})$
Manchester City Art
Gallery
Thomas Carlyle is
shown second from
the right

young Millais, of Hunt and of Rossetti. It has, however, at this stage a clarity and a vigour that make most other Victorian sculpture of this period appear soft and sentimental in contrast. Later his style was less secure, often relapsing into a trite naturalism. Many of his busts only differed from others of the later Victorian period in his affectation of 'growing' them out of a plain rectangle of marble rather than shaping them to the traditional socle (a device used by the extreme neo-classicist, Thorwaldsen). In 1865 he produced a bust of Carlyle, with some difficulty, commenting that his sitter's likeness was as difficult to catch as a flash of lightning; to assist him, Carlyle underwent 'such a sitting to photographers as never was heard of', and the use of photographs may have been a factor in the deterioration of Woolner's style.[161]

Before this, in 1859, Carlyle had been sitting, also via a photographer, for Ford Madox Brown, who was already in his prolonged travail with the satirical and propaganda picture called *Work* (Plate 233). Rossetti said that it illustrated 'all kinds of Carlylianisms', and it is in part a demonstration of the dignity and the unjust material poverty of work in the shape of a group of road-menders, contrasted with the butterfly condition of certain rich passers-by; in it figure Carlyle and the

Plate 234
Thomas Carlyle (1795–1881)
by George Frederic Watts,
1868
Oil on canvas, 64.7 × 52
(25½ × 20½)
Victoria & Albert Museum,
London

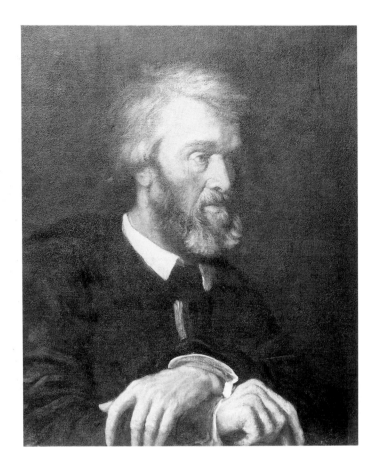

Christian Socialist parson, F.D. Maurice; in support of the physical labourers, they represent the brain-workers, who – in Brown's own words –

seeming to be idle, work, and are the cause of well-ordained work and happiness in others – sages, such as in ancient Greece published their opinions in the market square.[162]

But the likeness of Carlyle is expressed in terms far from a neo-Grecian ideal beauty; it was widely criticized as a caricature – by Holman Hunt amongst others. It seems, however (from independent evidence), to have been a faithful recording of a characteristic grimace of Carlyle; Brown's own expressed intention was 'to delineate types and not individuals', but he was not to be shifted from his view of Carlyle, for so the face had appeared to him in a moment of animation, and to typify did not involve a departure from the truth of an actual moment.[163]

Nine years later, in May 1868, Carlyle sat to a painter with ideas of truth far removed from the Pre-Raphaelite insistence on sheer physical actuality – to Watts (Plate 234). To Carlyle, Brown's Prophet of Work, was opposed the Prophet of High Art; the battle appears to have been brisk but inconclusive. Carlyle would away with the whole of the Elgin Marbles, away with them all into space, on the grounds that there was not a clever man amongst the Grecian riders; their jaws were not prominent enough. 'Neither God nor man can get on without a jaw.'[164] The

Plate 235
Thomas Carlyle (1795–1881) by Julia
Margaret Cameron, 1867
Albumen print, 33.3 × 24 (13⅛ × 9½)
National Portrait Gallery, London

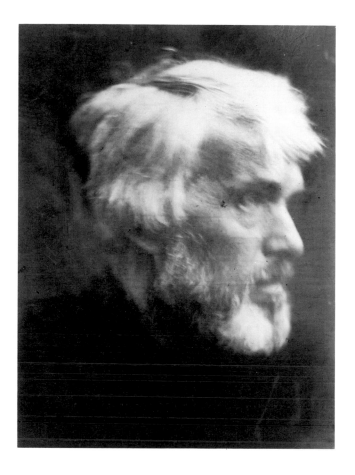

long upper lip was a sign of intellect; Watts countered with the examples of
Napoleon, Byron and Goethe. In the end, Carlyle found Watts 'a very wearisome,
"washed-out" dilettante man'.[165] Watts found Carlyle very difficult, and made
three fresh starts, maddening his sitter by refusing to let him see till the portrait was
finished. When Carlyle at last saw himself, he restrained himself to an unusual
degree: 'Man, I would have you know I am in the habit of wearing clean linen'.[166]
Later, in other company, he expressed his disgust at being turned into a

mad labourer . . . insufferable . . . a delirious looking mountebank full of violence,
awkwardness, atrocity and stupidity, without recognisable likeness.

Yet Meredith found in the same portrait the look of Lear encountering the storm on
the Kentish coast; and Chesterton caught in it

the strange combination of a score of sane and healthy visions and views, with something
that was not sane, which bloodshot and embittered them all, the great tragedy of the vision
of a strong countryside mind and body with a disease of the vitals and something like a
disease of the spirit. In fact, Watts painted Carlyle 'like a mad labourer' because Carlyle
was a mad labourer.[167]

In sharp contrast to the opinions of Watts on Carlyle, and Meredith's and
Chesterton's opinions, is Mrs Cameron's photograph (Plate 235) taken at about the

same time. Carlyle was not enthusiastic about it, but he was not impolite, and he was perhaps worried by it:

It is as if suddenly the picture began to speak, terrifically ugly and woebegone, but has something of a likeness – my candid opinion.[168]

As a picture it touched Roger Fry to the quick, and he wrote of it:

Neither Whistler nor Watts come near to this in the breadth of the conception, in the logic of the plastic evocations, and neither approach the poignancy of this revelation of character.[169]

The first two of these contentions seem to me indisputable (though the crisper side-whiskers, nearer the lens and so presumably in a sharper focus, may be judged out of logic), but the third implies an over-simple conception of portraiture. This is certainly a most moving and a most beautiful portrait, but that it conveys more of Carlyle than Watts' image of him is very open to argument; it is possible that the very breadth and logic praised by Fry have suppressed the extraordinary paradoxes of the man, those indicated by Chesterton – and that bristly crankiness that gleams in the Madox Brown, the stamina that could seem at times almost of Scots granite, and the harsh vigour of the Boehm.[170]

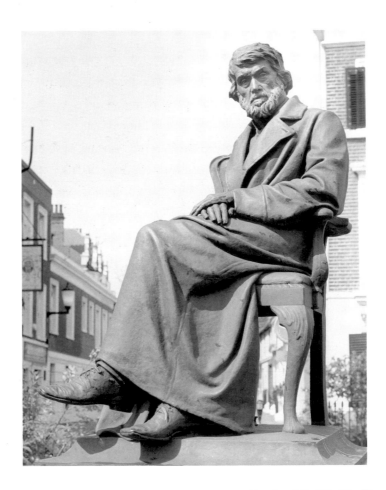

Plate 236
Thomas Carlyle (1795–1881)
by Sir Joseph Edgar Boehm,
1874
Bronze, life-size
Cheyne Walk, London

Boehm's statue (Plate 236) (a bronze of it presides over the gardens by Cheyne Walk) was made six years later, in 1874, and is perhaps the sculptor's masterpiece. Sir Joseph Boehm (an Austro-Hungarian from Vienna) settled in London in 1862 and immediately and permanently became immensely successful, everywhere from the court downwards, until his death in 1890. A sculptor of remarkable natural talent, with the help of a large studio team he produced far too much, capitalizing on his skill in producing a sort of three-dimensional photograph, unpretentious, swift and completely indifferent to the plastic evocations that Fry was to reveal in art to a later generation. His work epitomizes the movement of later Victorian sculptors away from the neo-classicism of sculptors like Edward Hodges Baily, and especially of those like John Macdonald and Gibson who worked in Rome, to a brisker but generally skin-deep naturalism.

Boehm seems to have got on very well with Carlyle (taking in good heart the writer's dishearteningly bluff opening gambit: 'I'll give you twenty-two minutes to make what you can of me').[171] There is a thrust and drive, almost a rhythm, in spite of the limp and vapid coat collar, that is rare in his work. This is most marked in the bust taken by a 'squeeze' from the original plaster done from the life (so much of late Victorian sculpture moves straight from the unpublished model from life to the monument in marble of certain death). The statue roused Ruskin to praise in his *Academy Notes* which ended with a just epitaph on much mid-Victorian sculpture:

It is generally a note of weakness in an Englishman when he thinks he can conceive like a Greek; so that the plurality of modern Hellenic Academy sculpture consists merely of imperfect anatomical models peeped at through bath-towels. . . . Let us go back to less dignified work.

But a collar and tie are difficult subjects for sculptors, and the naked chests and throats often persist, the fine classical torsos sprouting a late Victorian head, often as uncomfortable as an English garden in a tropical exile.[172]

In 1877 Carlyle sat to the by now chosen painter of prosperity, Millais, fully weaned from Pre-Raphaelitism (Plate 237). Before it was finished, Millais had a brush with a sharp lady from Glasgow, Mrs Anstruther, who described it as

in Millais' usual style, hard, clever, forcible painting. The outline, the features, all correctly given and with great power of brush. But merely the mask, no soul, no spirit behind. I said it looked modern, and in fact I did not like it. . . .[173]

Millais never finished it, though the face is complete; it rejuvenates the eighty-two-year-old considerably; it endows him with good health, a frank manly gaze (compare the Boehm and the Watts) and a certain slick and venerable romance in the hair. It is admirable evidence as to why Millais succeeded as a fashionable society-painter.[174]

To enumerate all the portraits of Carlyle would be wearisome; there are many more, but I will limit myself to the Whistler (Plate 230). The encounter seems improbable; it was arranged by Mme Venturi, a friend of both parties, in 1872. Both parties were baffled. Carlyle sat: 'Now fire away, man.' Seeing Whistler astounded, he added that if you were fighting battles or painting pictures, the only thing to do was to fire away. The sittings were innumerable; Carlyle complained that if he moved, Whistler would scream at him, but that at the same time the painter was far more concerned with the painting of the coat than of the face. When it was all over, he said: 'Well, man, you have given me a clean collar and that's more than Mr. Watts has done'.[175]

From Carlyle's constant sitting for portraits, and equally constant disappointment with the results, one may suspect that the apostle of the heroic creed hoped that one day he would find himself on canvas or in marble, perhaps warted, but also in heroic proportions, a blend of Cromwell and Frederick the Great, broadened with a dash of Goethe. Yet the portrait that in the end he said he liked the best was one of several by his friend, Helen Allingham, a water-colour painter best known for her rendering of rustic cottage gardens in full bloom; it is perhaps that by her now in the Scottish National Portrait Gallery (Plate 238). It shows Carlyle, reclining whole-length in a chair, reading in his slippers and dressing-gown, a curiously comfortable portrait of a dear if slightly musty old man.[176]

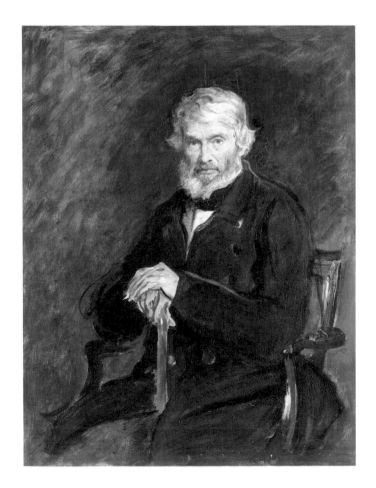

Plate 237
Thomas Carlyle (1795–1881)
by Sir John Everett Millais,
1877
Oil on canvas, 116.8 × 88.3
(46 × 34¾)
National Portrait Gallery,
London

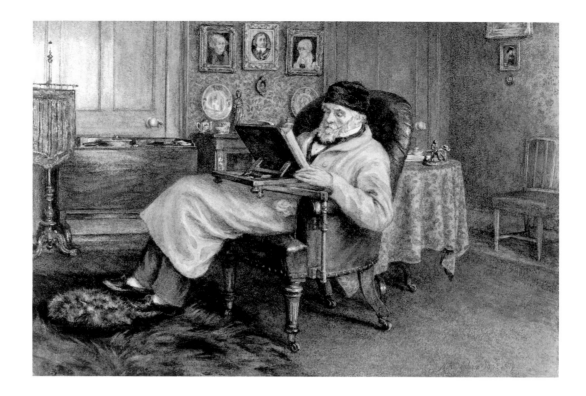

The Carlylean anecdote has perhaps been liberally used in the preceding pages. It has been exercised not only for its own sake, but to illustrate the sort of resistance that a portrait painter has to contend with. The result of the sittings to Whistler was one of the most enchanting British portraits to come out of the nineteenth century, even if not so successful a painting as a few others by Whistler. But Whistler was not a true portraitist, and the picture is significant of the direction in which the dominant interests in the best European painting were shifting. Carlyle's comment about Whistler's interest in his coat is not irrelevant, and Whistler called the picture, not 'Portrait of Carlyle', but *Arrangement in Grey and Black*. As he had said of an earlier picture with the same title –

now that is what it is. To me it is interesting as a picture of my mother, but what can or ought the public to care about the identity of the portrait?[177]

Contrast Watts' creed as he himself formulated it:

A portrait should have in it something of the monumental; it is a summary of the life of a person, not the record of accidental position or arrangement of light and shadows.

A true portrait painter must be not only interested in his sitter, but must yield to him. Soon painters will be organizing in space; what they organize will be of slight importance; the movement is basically opposed to portraiture.

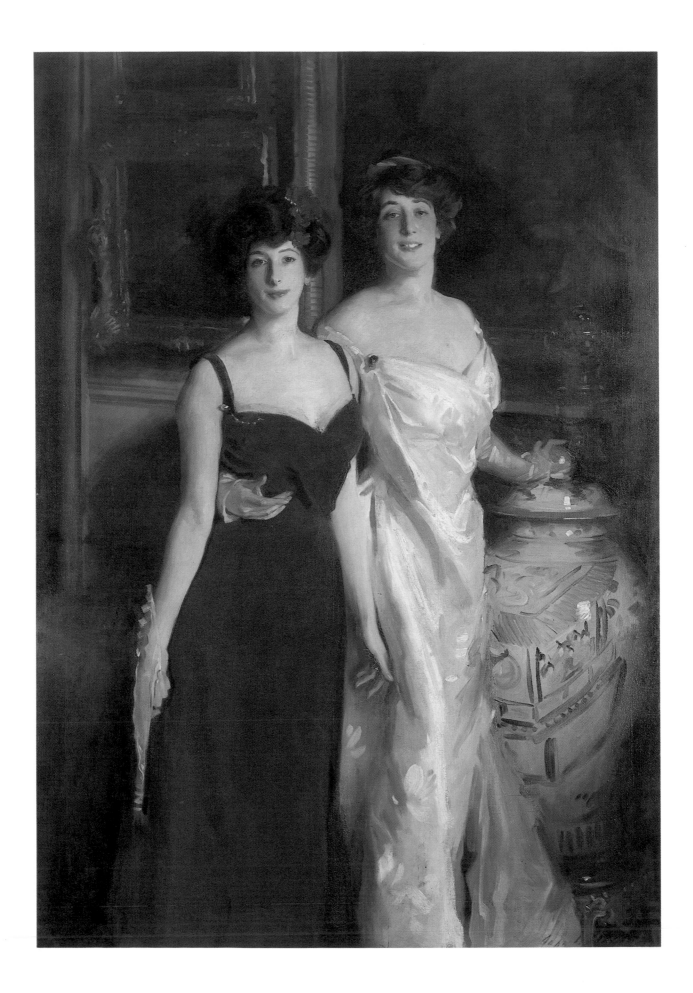

Victorian Effigy to Impressionist Portrait

IN SCULPTURE, naturally, the triumph of the Victorian effigy was even more marked than in painting. Headed by John Gibson, who worked almost all his life in Rome, the British version of the style approved by Winckelmann and practised by Canova and Thorwaldsen wore on. Huskisson wore a top-hat upon the occasion, in 1830, when he became the first man to be run over by a railway locomotive; in his memorial statue, by Gibson, he wears a toga (Plate 240). By the fifties, trousers were becoming generally admissible in statuary; Gibson would have none of them, and would have refused to undertake the Sir Robert Peel in Westminster Abbey if modern dress had been insisted upon:

The human figure concealed under a frock-coat and trousers is not a fit object for sculpture, and I would rather avoid contemplating such objects.[178]

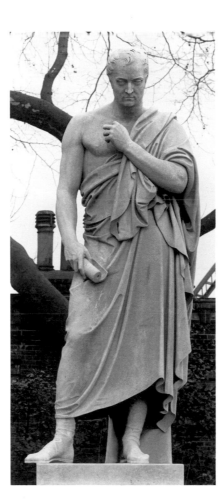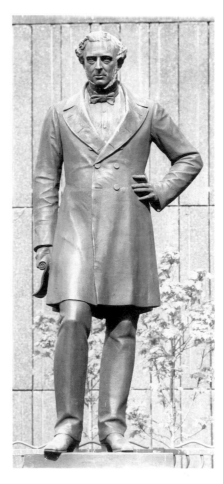

Plate 239 (*facing page*)
Ena and Betty Wertheimer by John Singer Sargent, 1901
Oil on canvas, 185.5 × 131 (73 × 51½)
Tate Gallery, London

Plate 240 (*right*)
William Huskisson (1770–1830)
by John Gibson, 1848
Marble, height 243.8 (96)
Pimlico Gardens, London

Plate 241 (*far right*)
Robert Stephenson (1803–1859)
by Baron Carlo Marochetti, 1871
Bronze, life-size
Euston Station, London

Gibson's stress in portraiture was upon the character of intellectual greatness:

It should give us an idea of [the subject's] soul, and this may be done by taste and judgement, without trespassing too much upon the individuality of the person.[179]

In practice, the trespass amounted almost to the obliteration of all individuality.

Although the neo-classic fascination held some sculptors in its grip throughout the century, by the time Gibson died in 1866 a brisker movement had been abroad for some years, in the hands of sculptors like Baron Marochetti, an Italian artist of vigour, acumen and some cynicism ('For those who worship Gibson anything is good enough.').[180] He celebrated Robert Stephenson at Euston Station in bronze trousers and frock-coat, with a suggestion of statesmanship added by the scroll in the right hand (Plate 241); to Brunel, he allowed a pair of compasses. In statuary, naturalism proliferated modern costume through the city squares and places of recreation of the British Isles, reaching peaks of one kind in Taubman's portrait of the merchant knight, Sir Sidney Waterlow, erected within his lifetime in 1900, in Waterlow Park, Highgate, London (in one hand he holds the bronze key to the park; in the other his bronze hat and bronze umbrella); and in the curious marble figure by Count Gleichen of Queen Alexandra wearing gown and marble mortar-board of a Master of Music in the Royal College of Music.

But royalty, statesmen, and, above all perhaps, generals and field-marshals, were the most popular subjects, not only out of doors, but, usually bust-size, also in the churches, clubs and halls. In 1835, Madame Tussaud's peripatetic show of wax-works had come to rest at the first permanent establishment in Baker Street in London, and through the years offered a more varied selection of up-to-the-minute effigies to the curious. They ranged from the really celebrated criminals, from the Mannings, Palmer the Poisoner and Charles Peace to sportsmen like Fred Archer, to the Queen. The Madame Tussaud of marble, though choosing his subjects within more select limits, was Boehm, but he had many competitors in his business of catching a deft likeness in stone. More important than any of them was one of his own assistants, who proved to be perhaps the finest British portraitist in sculpture of the nineteenth century: Alfred Gilbert. Gilbert demonstrated again, after a long lapse, that a portrait-bust could convey a lively impression of an individual without sacrificing a uniting, artistic rhythm (Plate 242). Although – in a sense, like Watts – his full capability was sapped by too great a dependence on the artistic heritage of the past, so that he was unable to achieve a creation so coherent and so compulsive as that of his elder contemporary, Rodin, Gilbert's was a brilliant talent with a sculptural feeling, particularly for bronze, that is lacking in all his British contemporaries and predecessors except Alfred Stevens.

In a few of Gilbert's busts of the eighties and nineties, there is a movement and expressiveness that recalls Hogarth perhaps rather than Roubiliac; it might be hoped that an expressiveness of the same order would be found in the paintings of contemporary life and also the caricature in which the Victorian period was so rich.

Plate 242
George Frederic Watts
(1817–1904) by Sir Alfred
Gilbert, 1888–1889
Bronze, height 58.4 (23)
Tate Gallery, London

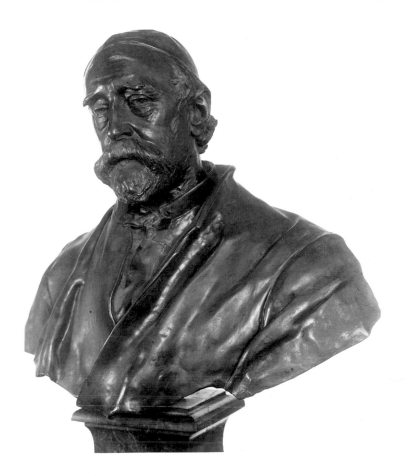

On the whole, this is far from so. The documentation of the aspect of the times is profuse; in the fifties the Pre-Raphaelites and their sympathisers opened up the contemporary scene in paintings like Brown's *Work* (Plate 233), in the early work of Millais and of W.B. Scott; in 1851 Frith too turned his attention from the depiction of literary and 'costume' incidents to contemporary life. There remained however an atmosphere of charade in his work; he did not disdain the use of photographs as preliminary studies for his paintings, yet the finished works remain contrivances, skilled as they are. On the sands at Margate the voluminous middle-classes disport themselves; on Derby Day the racecourse crowds picturesquely behave themselves; at the Railway Station a celebrated criminal is arrested by two celebrated detectives with the rhetorical gestures of the stage. Only perhaps in *A Private View at the Royal Academy in 1881* (Plate 243), does a note, if not of passion, at least of indignation appear, in the looks cast upon Oscar Wilde by those at a safe distance from him.

With Hogarth, comic emotion was as passionate as the tragic; for the Victorians, in paint the comic became the laughable, or the quaint, as in Webster's *Village Choir*, and the tragic became the pathetic. Often the pathetic degenerated into the lachrymose or the pietistic (as Frith's series, *The Road to Ruin*). But it could maintain a moving dignity of sentiment as in Egg's series of the faithless wife, and, later in the

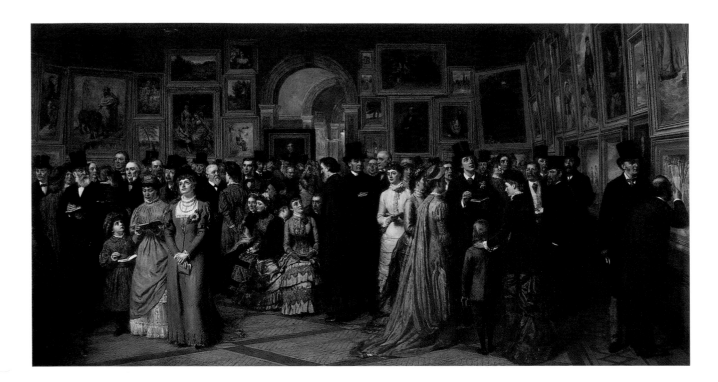

century, some of Fildes' and Holl's genre pieces (Plate 244). Of faces moved by passion, there is little trace; the unspeakable things must also be invisible; all is decency, and repentance is usually enough to indicate that there has been sin.

The world shown by the popular genre painters is one where poverty is neat and respectful, a world in which everyone knows his place. The scene abounds with courtesy, of the lover to the beloved, of the rich to the poor, of the painter to his subject; charity is graciously given and gratefully accepted. Such was the way of life, and few painters probed more deeply; Madox Brown, in his *Work*, was one, but none of them conveys an underlying tension hinted at by some visitors, like the American, Nathaniel Hawthorne, at Liverpool in 1855. Hawthorne saw the poor in all manner of dirt and rags, waiting for soup tickets

and waiting very patiently too, without outcry or disturbance or even sour looks – only patience and meekness in their faces . . . there does seem to be an insolence of riches and prosperity, which one day or another will have a downfall.[181]

Five years later Dostoevsky was in the Haymarket in London – the district where in certain streets at night prostitutes gathered in their thousands – and the Haymarket teemed in the gaslit dusk with his characters, like the consumptive prostitute, with a secret melancholy and a kind of thoughtful anxiousness: 'certainly superior to that crowd of miserable women, or what meaning has the human face? But she was drinking gin . . .'.[182] The misery and tragedy of urban and industrial England was not for the painters: why should it be? Dickens excelled in the portrayal of desolation and was the champion of the downtrodden; he was also a

Plate 243
A Private View at the Royal Academy in 1881
by William Powell Frith, 1883
Oil on canvas,
102.9 × 195.6
(40 ½ × 77)
A. Pope Family Trust

232

champion of Frith and the man who discovered in the freshness of Millais' *Carpenter's Shop*, which showed the Holy Family as a humble working family, 'the lowest depths of what is mean, odious, repulsive, and revolting'.[183] Even in the popular prints, satire died, after a dwindling rearguard action by Cruikshank and by C.J. Grant in the thirties.

The art criticism of Thackeray indicates the role that art must play – elevating, doing good, making decent people more decent and warm and happy; an art from the heart to the heart. It was an art too that spoke continually of comfort, of the comfort of the conventional unshakeably fortressed against the unconventional, of a middle-class consolidated in wealth, until the working-class appears to be composed of a number of stock characters with stock 'funny sayings' repeated endlessly in *Punch*, even below the drawings of the most brilliant and objective English draughtsman of the century, Charles Keene (Plate 245).

The socially-conscious group of illustrators who worked for the *Graphic* paper in the seventies were moved by a genuine interest and sympathy, but the school did not survive long, and the best-known of them – Holl, Herkomer and Fildes – all rapidly became leading society-portrait painters. John Thomson, the first photographer with an interest in social documentation, followed exactly the same course (Plate 246). After his remarkable *Street Life in London*, published in 1877, with its studies even of down-and-outs, he became a society-portrait photographer in Mayfair in the eighties. None of them, though Holl went to the lengths of borrowing real East End rags with which to drape his models, had the clear uncompromising

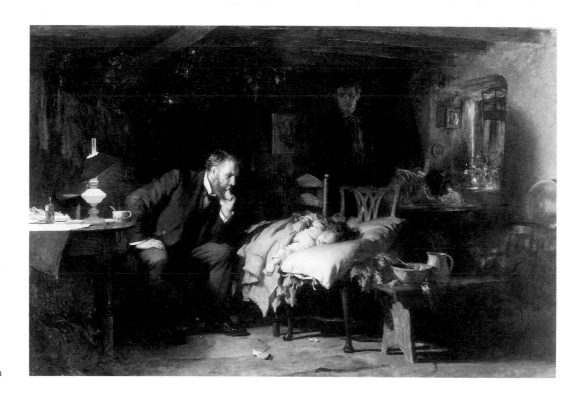

Plate 244
The Doctor by Sir
Luke Fildes, 1891
Oil on canvas,
166.4 × 241.9
$(65\frac{1}{2} \times 95\frac{1}{4})$
Tate Gallery, London

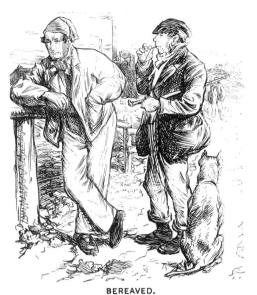

BEREAVED.

First Pitman. "THOU HESSENT BEEN AT THE TOUN LATELY, GEORDIE. HOO'S THAT, MAN?"
Second Pitman. "THOU KNAWS THE DOG'S DEED, AND AW KENNET GETTEN ANOTHER; AN' A CHAP LEUKS SA FOND WIVOUT A DOG!"

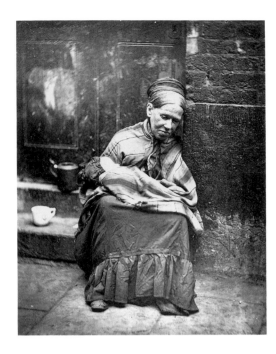

Plate 245 (*far left*)
'*Bereaved*' by Charles Keene, 3 December 1870
Pen and ink drawing
Reproduced by permission of *Punch*

Plate 246 (*left*)
The Crawlers by John Thomson, 1876–1877
Bromide print from wet collodion glass negative, 11.5 × 8.7 ($4\frac{1}{2} \times 3\frac{1}{2}$)
Museum of London

eye for the starkly melodramatic horror of London that the foreigner Gustave Doré brought to it.

It was not Doré, however, that Ruskin recommended to the public; in that famous letter (1877) in *Fors Clavigera* in which he accused Whistler of flinging a pot of paint in the public's face, he suggests also that Tissot[184] – if only he would obey 'his graver thoughts', instead of painting 'mere coloured photographs of vulgar society' – would better occupy the attention of the public than Doré. Yet Tissot was far more than a mere photographer – an artist of extraordinary manual dexterity and deftness in composition. His people relax in an endless, admirable leisure, while time and sunlight circulate amongst them like money easily and well spent, and their eyebrows lift out of ennui at the gleam of pleasure. Frederick Gustavus Burnaby (Plate 247) was one of the many and varied personifications of that impulsive, exploratory and often eccentric Victorian energy that took shape also in people like Florence Nightingale, Livingstone, the Napiers and Jameson; an energy for which the confines of this island were generally too small, an energy which perhaps only the portrait-painters were able to tame. Yet Tissot's painting of Burnaby catches perhaps something of the man's character, more than the mere military dandy with the cigarette and the waxed moustache; six foot four in height, he could carry a small pony under one arm and was a master-balloonist, yet was obliged to travel for his health, and did so in the obscurer parts of Africa and the Middle East. He was painted by Tissot in 1870; fifteen years later he died with a dervish's spear through his throat.

None of this is of course explicit in the portrait, but the painter had a power of evoking mystery out of the precision of everyday objects that is reminiscent of the

Plate 247
*Frederick Gustavus
Burnaby* (1842–1885)
by James Jacques
Tissot, 1870
Oil on panel,
49.5 × 59.7
(19½ × 23½)
National Portrait
Gallery, London

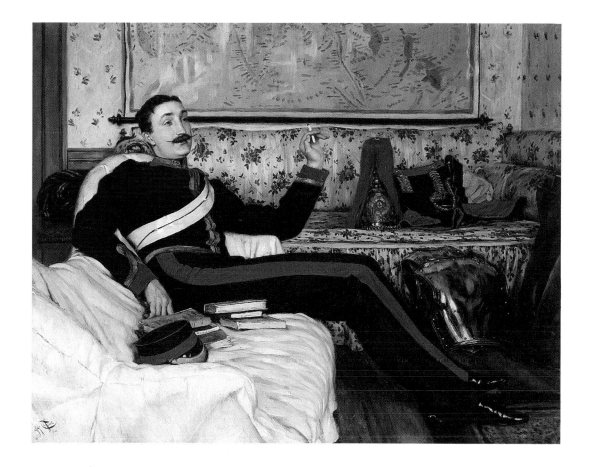

best seventeenth-century masters in Holland: a mystery more demonstrable of course in his harbour scenes, with their promises of voyages and discovery, but the promise is also there behind the enigmatic faces of his women. Tissot returned to France in 1882; and though a somewhat similar rendering of high-life was pursued by Sir William Orchardson among others in the eighties and nineties, with more anecdotery, Orchardson's was a talent of great ability, but without magic. (Tissot's 'vulgarity', *pace* Ruskin, was a true and honest vulgarity of pleasure in opulence, not to be confused with a taste for 'low-life' subjects.)

One of the most typical forms of late Victorian genre painting was the recording on large canvases of social scenes; Frith's *A Private View at the Royal Academy in 1881*, was one, and Jamyn Brooks and Henry Barraud specialized in them. In spite of the academic sophistication of the technique, they tend to have a curiously 'primitive' look, stuffed with people, for everybody or almost everybody has to be visible and recognizable. Private views, race meetings, Royal garden parties, the Royal Yacht Club at Cowes, Jubilee processions, they were all painted – and then engraved with the prospect of a reasonably certain subscription from at least the less celebrated participants in the scene. Simultaneously, the photographic portrait-groups, smaller in compass but even more diverse in range, begin to accumulate – the teams: the whiskered rugby players in three rows with tasselled caps, the cricketers and the Scottish shooting parties; the family groups, the fertile great-grandparents amidst their multiplication; the loyal employees, even the banded strikers with banners.

And what of the Victorian face amongst this medley? At the beginning of the reign, women's faces were meek, and respectable. In the forties, the hair was divided precisely and centrally by a parting; each cheek was veiled by a curtain of those long spaniel ringlets, forever associated with Elizabeth Barrett Browning, and then still further blinkered by the huge wings of the poke bonnet. In the fifties the curls vanished and the hair sat close and smooth as a cap hiding the ears. Romanticism, like the art of cosmetics, was out; Thackeray demanded

a fresh, dewy, healthy rose out of Somersetshire; not one of those superb, tawdry, unwholesome exotics, which are only good to make poems about. Lord Byron wrote more cant of this sort than any poet I know of. . . .

In the portraits, the freshness and dew are glazed into a porcelain finish, and the rose is almost always a bud, hardly ever full-blown – such are the maidens (Plate 248); when they flower, they do so without riot and in full control, lifting their heads calmly to their matronly status ('locks not wide-dispersed,/Madonna-wise on either side her head'), that of Tennyson's Isabel:

> The stately flower of female fortitude,
>   Of perfect wifehood and pure lowlihead.

The exotics of course still existed, women like the formidable Caroline Norton, with a face 'most dangerous, terrible, beautiful', hair 'violet black . . . eyes very large with dark lashes, and black as death . . .'; or the great Florence Nightingale – but the dangerous and the terrible escaped the portrait-makers.

In the sixties the hair, still smooth, grows out of the back into a chignon (necessitating often false hair), and the bonnet gives way to the hat, though the hat by some was considered immoral. The entire packaging of the body, achieved by the combination in day-dress of bonnet and crinoline (with the face only naked, as at the window of the convent, peeping but not looking), is alleviated; in the seventies the crinoline is pushed behind, becomes the bustle; the counterpoise bosom and head thrust forward like a ship's figurehead; stateliness is upon woman. The chignon remains, enlarged by still more false hair, but the hair also begins to go up on top of the head, and to fringe the forehead, and ears emerge boldly; in the shoulders an apparently anatomical metamorphosis takes place. Robert Surtees' heroines were shouldered like hock-bottles ('a fine girl – fine drooping shoulders'), but with the new thrust forward of the upper part of the body the shoulders quite suddenly, about 1880, become square, until in the great leg-of-mutton sleeves of the nineties they rise almost to the ear.

The Rossetti jaw emerges from the obscurity of an aesthetic coterie into high fashion, displacing the modest rounded early Victorian chin; the chignon draws up to a bun, the hair swells at the sides and the top; a masculine collar and a vast hat

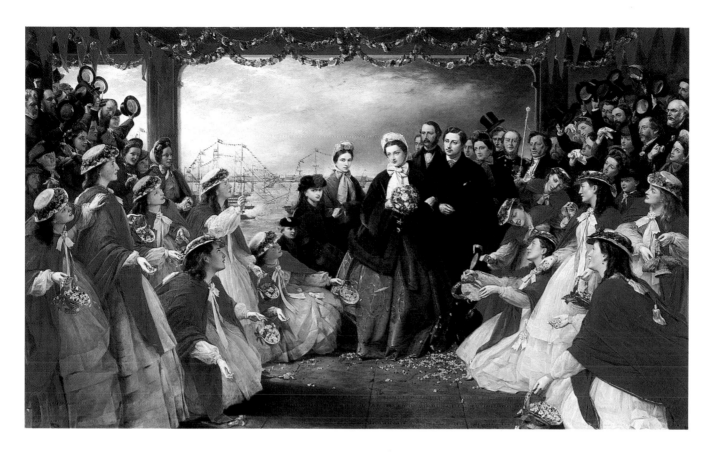

Plate 248
The Landing of Princess Alexandra, 7 March 1863
by Henry Nelson O'Neil, 1864
Oil on canvas,
132.1 × 213.4
(52 × 84)
National Portrait Gallery, London

burdened with fruit, feather and flower sail forward into the Edwardian era. The faces are bolder, the heads straighten from their pensive droop. A Frenchman in England in the late seventies noted the lack of affectation compared with that of French women, and their candour and openness, valuing health above gracefulness: a hearty eater and a woman who, 'though she may not make love to her husband, will not make it to any other man either';[185] the tennis girls, the bicycling girls, and amongst them already, the militant suffragettes. Yet the parade-portraits, as by Millais and even Sargent, often produce an effect of glitter that is almost of brass in the jewelled ballroom women; the day of Sir Francis Grant, whose success, according to a contemporary, lay in the fact that his gentlemen were always gentlemen and his ladies ladies, was over by 1870.

In the male face, the dominant characteristic, of course, was hair. The wig had put its emphasis on the seat of reason, while faces were shaved clean; the Victorians often turned this habit upside down, arching the glistening bald dome from a luxuriant wilderness of beard. The beard, after an abeyance of almost two hundred years, was threatening in the forties; the last restraint was broken by the Crimean War in 1854. In November of the following year the address by the gallant Duke of Cambridge at a meeting in honour of Florence Nightingale was reported by the *Manchester Guardian*:

The frank and joyous eye of the Duke was admired, but not much else of the Duke's face was visible – he was bearded 'like the pard' – lip, cheek and chin being alike innocent of the razor. In a camp shaving is pursued under considerable disadvantages; and the Duke is no doubt right; but our young men at home, who can ring for their shaving water as usual on getting up in the morning, are beginning to make his royal highness the 'glass of fashion and the mould of form', and are cultivating a beard in addition to a luxuriant moustache and whisker. Let Sheffield look to it, therefore, and pray for an early termination of the war.

Sheffield was to be disappointed; long after the war was over, the razors were still laid aside. The beard never became as ubiquitous, or *de rigueur*, as had been the wig, but was nevertheless formidable in its full flowering in the sixties, particularly in intellectual circles like that of Little Holland House. The seers of the age are almost to be recognized from differences in topiary work rather than in features. Although not the hall-mark of the Victorian innovation, the Grand Old Man (for the most famous of them, Gladstone himself, spurned it), the beard flourished on most of them, ranging in size from the Mephistophelian goat-tuft of Disraeli to the wiry entanglement of whisker and spectacle behind which Trollope's face was almost invisible under the bald crown.

Darwin's face, when melodramatically lit as in the well-known and regrettable portrait by Collier, the eyes glinting beneath overhanging eyebrows and over a

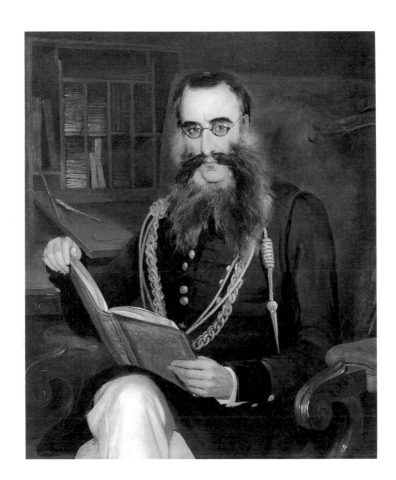

Plate 249
Sir Charles James Napier
(1782–1853) attributed to
?Smart
Oil on canvas, 35.3 × 28.9
($13\frac{7}{8} × 11\frac{3}{8}$)
National Portrait Gallery,
London

white profuse beard, echoes curiously that of the ape in whom he found human origin; Morris gives off a nimbus of red hair like palpable energy; Watts' beard derives from the early Church fathers as represented by the Venetians; Clerk Maxwell's is professorial, Burne-Jones' is limp as that of W. G. Grace is energetic and thirsty. But perhaps the most idiosyncratic beard of the nineteenth century is that of Charles James Napier (Plate 249), a beard that now, it may be feared, would be found almost mutinous by the War Office, but which, combined with the flash of naked spectacles under the topee as he rode into battle, no doubt facilitated in some degree the conquering of Sind.

Even those – as later did most of the younger men – who shaved their chins usually grew large side-whiskers, or a moustache, or both, and the variety of presentation was remarkable, including Dundreary, weeper and mutton-chop. In 1887, of the 700-odd Members of the Jubilee Year Parliament, just under a third had beards, but only about 30 were truly clean-shaven, the rest all having fringes of one kind or another. The bare-faced of the time included not only the *avant-garde* of intellectual and artistic fashion – the Wildes, Beardsleys and Beerbohms, but also coming politicians, notably Grey, Asquith and Chamberlain (Plate 250).

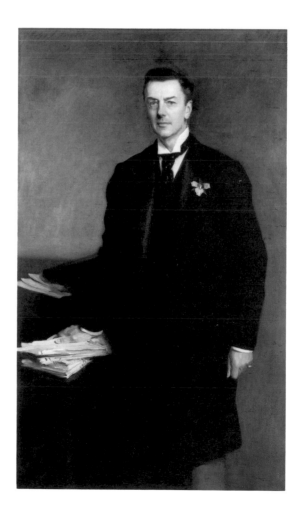

Plate 250
Joseph Chamberlain (1836–1914) by John Singer Sargent, 1896
Oil on canvas, 161.9 × 91.4 (63¾ × 36)
National Portrait Gallery, London

The reasons behind the cult of face-hair are difficult to demonstrate; it did not extend to the hair of the crown of the head, which was early macassared, and then became shorter and shorter, generally split by a white straight parting (though while Wilde shaved he let his top-hair grow). Fundamentally, it was probably but another outlet of the same male exuberance that had formerly expressed itself in coloured clothes. The Victorians were capable of splendid eccentricities of dress, particularly in check trousers and knickerbockers, but for business, daily wear, they subdued themselves steadily into the drab uniform of the City. The picturesque of Empire was paraded in the scarlet coats and feathered hats of the general officers who held the border marches in India and in Africa. The reflection of true imperial power is preserved in the paintings of the statesmen, in mood very close to that of the sixteenth-century portraits by Mor and the Elizabethan painters; but now the frock-coat is sufficient as armour and as symbol (Plate 214). Individual virility decently expressed itself mainly in the top-hat and in face-hair (and perhaps, as with Joseph Chamberlain, for example, in the size and expense of the flower in the buttonhole, and other accessories – the massive gold chain across the waist-coat, the minutely opulent cravat-pin or cane-top). A haze of hair also lent mystery, and a beard, worn always by God the Father, is venerable. Its erotic possibilities were never, as far as I know, publicly discussed by an Englishman – that was left to Guy de Maupassant.

Visually, the painters found Victorian sartorial fashions generally embarrassing and ugly; some, like Tissot, divined elegance in them, but none in England saw the black and grey drama, the possible heroic qualities in what Baudelaire, already in 1846, had called 'the necessary garb of our suffering age, which bears the symbol of a perpetual mourning even upon its thin black shoulders . . . a uniform livery of affliction'.[186] Manet and Guys each differently suggest this; in England, no one.

In formal portraiture, the Victorians sought for the dignity that becomes the public statue, a public composure of expression that while allowing no direct appeal to the admiring spectators, yet broods on their behalf. Broadly handled, as by Watts and also by the much-maligned Millais at his best, such portraits might have a sincere dignity, but more often they were wrecked by a contradictory insistence on petty detail. Millais, when he abandoned his meticulous Pre-Raphaelite manner for his later, broader style, was probably justified, as far as portraiture was concerned; the verdict of the *Art Journal* in 1864 on Pre-Raphaelite portraiture (one of Holman Hunt's) may still find some observers in agreement:

Whoever would wish to study the topography of the human countenance, in its declivities and concavities, in its mountain ridges or its ravines cut by the course of time, let him pause here and take his lesson. The result is marvellous. We can scarcely add, agreeable.

The attempt probably owes something to the indirect effect of photography upon the artists. That the camera had much effect on the composition of pictures before about 1880 is open to doubt (the so-called 'snap-shot' angles, for example, might

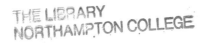

equally have been inspired by Japanese prints); that it had a profound effect on modes of perception is certain. In terms of light and shade the camera could record faithfully every strand of hair, every nook and cranny of the skin (even suggesting, as in some of Julia Margaret Cameron's photographs, a failure of the sitter to wash beforehand). It could seize relentlessly on every grace and every falter in the contour.

Therein lay its strength and its weakness; the public approved of the accuracy with which it rendered the graces and resented its cruelty to their weaknesses, and there too lay the terrible chance of the artists – to achieve a similar seeming-accuracy while actually ignoring the flaws. The dexterity of Ouless, of Cope, of Herkomer, in their various degrees achieved this, and Herkomer acknowledged his art master in the shape of a camera obscura: 'Nature is reflected and transcribed just as it ought to be painted.'

It is in such terms that the presentation-committees and the general public preferred to have perpetuated those whom they honoured, and their preference, in spite of some flirtation with Sargent and his followers, remains still generally consistent. It is perhaps curious that life-size coloured photographs have not yet caught on, as they might be thought to offer (allowing for re-touching) all the advantages, besides being far cheaper, and more accurate. In fact, colour photography cannot yet quite rival oil painting in illusionism (and in durability and sheer physical presence), though that no doubt will come, but there are other more enduring reasons against it. There is a deeply-entrenched and natural snobbery, for which the sheer glamour of oil-paint and gold frame, of the name of the famous artist (who has also, as is well known, painted royalty), is necessary food; so too is great expense, ostentatious consumption. According to Sir Max Beerbohm, Lord Northcliffe's answer to the painter, who asked for comment on a suggested pose for Lady Northcliffe, was: 'I don't care a damn, my good man, so long as you use the most expensive paints'. Not to expend a great deal of money (at least as much as the subscribers have offered) would be to depreciate the sitter. And the paintings may often prove high-class, hand-made pieces of craftsmanship, often wonderfully skilful, and satisfying to the immemorial human delight in sleight-of-hand.

In Britain the infiltration of those values most conveniently labelled impressionist was relatively slow. The demand for portraiture in full fig was, and is, inextinguishable. The Academicians soldiered on in high prosperity, fulfilling an undeniable demand with a very high and very highly paid professional dexterity. On the extreme ideal right wing was Watts, for whom the grammar and syntax of painting had been hammered out to a final adequacy by Phidias, Michelangelo and the Venetians, centuries before; on a more material plane, equally far to the right, were Millais, H. T. Wells, Sant and others, to be followed by Herkomer, Cope and Ouless (the 'pocket Millais'); right of centre was the extremely gifted and serious Holl. On the left was Whistler, with his sitters, or standers, dissolving more and more indivisibly into a luminous haze of paint and light and dark as his career advanced.

But in the eighties, the centre revealed itself in a blaze of colour, a daring of elegance and highlight not seen since Lawrence, and a neo-baroque movement of paint not seen since Lely; a grand talent, with his eye opened, at least, to the surprising colours of the rainbow by his friend, Monet; his eye made aware of the tonal transitions that Velazquez had demonstrated, through the teaching if not the practice of his master, Carolus Duran, whose order of the day was: 'Velazquez, Velazquez, Velazquez, étudiez sans relâche Velazquez!' – an exhortation which, as we have seen, Grant, Millais and Holl would have cordially seconded, but which was really put into action only by Manet. This talent was, like Whistler, an American: John Singer Sargent.[187]

Sargent's most profoundly influential mentor was, however, neither Velazquez, Duran nor any of his French contemporaries, but Frans Hals; he referred back again and again to Hals, generally in a technical sense; but more important than pure technique, for our subject, is Hals' approach to his sitters, particularly in his habit of catching those expressions which, while surely characteristic, are not those brave and arranged faces of a normal parade-portrait. Sargent's first appearances indeed were met with storms of disapproval; the famous *Madame Gautreau* was considered a caricature at the Salon in 1884; of the *Misses Vickers* (see p. 8), at the Academy in 1886, the *Pall Mall Gazette Academy Extra* observed that Mr Sargent was more eccentric than ever, and the paper's readers, in a referendum, voted it the bottom picture of the year. (In the nineteenth century the word 'eccentric' usually preludes an exciting departure; it was used, for example, of the Pre-Raphaelites.)

At this time Sargent himself was very conscious of the novelty of his art and of the opposition. But inside eight years he had become respectable, an A.R.A. paying his duty calls on his colleagues – 'those whose names I had hated for years and years' – he found, in 1894, often 'men of the world and altogether delightful – Sant, for instance, whom one considered the Anti-Christ'.[188] In but a few more years George Moore will be dubbing Sargent as but 'the apotheosis of modern fashionable painting, doing what Messrs. J. J. Shannon, Hacker and Solomon would like to do but what they cannot do'. By then the centre had, as is perhaps normal, swung almost to the extreme right.

Sargent himself was very much a man of the world, and the world – that part of it that one is a man of – was altogether delightful. His vision was confined to the facets of a certain society; beyond that, for portraits, his eye was not interested and his imagination undisturbed. Only in 1918 does he seem to have grasped that there was a war on; and to the consequences of that war, including even the minor one that the Edwardian way of life was over, he remained blind. Yet he had very much, as Vernon Lee noted, an eye for the exotic, and it was his great virtue, in his best portraits, to discover the bizarre and the exotic in the heavily rich and smartly-whorled cream of society that he painted. Entranced with surface effects, he painted a great deal to which the criticism of 'man-millinering', once applied to Lawrence, is only too apt. But on not a few occasions, his discernment in the choice of the surface effect – a discernment which is in its way that of genius – was allied to a pictorial working-out of the picture which was at least adequate. At best, he was perhaps a sketcher, rather than any other kind, of genius; a superb example is the head of Vernon Lee (Plate 251), toothy and bright, jewelled with spectacles; the portrait of a most sensitive intelligence, in which keenness and whimsy joined in style. Whimsy is now found almost obscene (like things that crawl out from under stones), and the style, the *belle-lettrisme*, in which it flourished, apart from the work of Henry James, thought as wearisome, washed-out, and as dilettante a thing as Carlyle thought Watts; that it produced remarkable achievements within its terms of reference is forgotten. So, too, is Sargent's achievement; Roger Fry's obituary comment still blankets it – Fry was sure that 'Sargent was no less distinguished and genuine a man than he was striking and undistinguished as an illustrator and non-existent as an artist'.[189]

Fry's view was almost puritanical in its specialization; his comment is an over-statement though partly true; it was so formulated partly no doubt to *épater le bourgeois*, specifically those – and they were legion and perhaps included Sargent

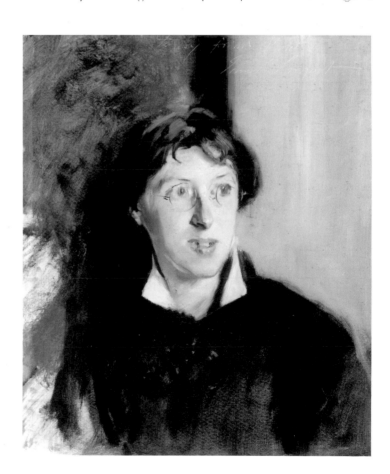

Plate 251
Vernon Lee (1856–1935) by
John Singer Sargent, 1881
Oil on canvas, 53.8 × 43.2
($21\frac{1}{8}$ × 17)
Tate Gallery, London

himself – who liked Sargent for the wrong reasons. But the criticism is really off-beam, almost as if a logician were criticizing a novel, or Mme Joachim Gasquet objecting that Cézanne's painting of her husband was not like him. Sargent was a taker and maker of characters.

He could also achieve a more purely pictorial splendour; although his broadness is too often vapid, he had a true feeling for the grand manner. He once indicated to a pupil: 'Don't concentrate so much on the features, they are only like spots on an apple. Paint the head. Never leave empty spaces, every stroke of the brush should have significance. . . . That's not a head, that's a collection of features'.

In comparison with his portraits, it is indeed only too clear that the other high Victorian artists collected features, that they all never left enough out and filled in too much.

With Sargent's more summary treatment he managed to retain the individuality of the sitters and, in his successes, to indicate in them types. The cultured, polished, and sometimes almost sinister, almost comic Jewish aristocracy, the Wertheimers (the powerful assurance of the elder generation, the affluent deprecation of the younger [Plate 239]), the Sassoons; the last of the English aristocracy, high-faced as when Van Dyck saw them, splendid in their final extravagances, Lord Ribblesdale as M.F.H., Sir George Sitwell and family; the intellectuals, a little wispy, like Patmore and Gosse; the slender, under-slept, aesthetic figure of the 'Nineties' in Graham Robertson (Plate 252). All of these have something of the bizarre; with the chocolate-box beauty he was not generally successful, often getting no further than the chocolate-box, and in his whole-lengths of grand women of the *grands salons*, would force eccentricity by some fling of pose that puts such works fairly into what Sickert called the Wriggle-and-Chiffon school of Boldini. Yet even in some of these there is the shock of a more genuine bizarre, from the contrast of the turbulent froth of clothes with the bony unbeautiful intransigence of the individual face of the woman amongst it all.

In 1886, the year that Sargent was found so eccentric at the Academy, eccentricity much influenced by France found a focus, when the New English Art Club was founded. Earlier than this, in Scotland, about 1880, French values had been rooted in the Glasgow School. Academic portraiture in Scotland had followed much the same course as in England, the broad manner of Raeburn hardening into the higher polish and detail of Watson-Gordon, and still further into that of the Scottish counterparts of Millais, like George Reid. The Glasgow School set up in deliberate opposition their scale of values learned in Paris; amongst the portrait-painters were the young James Guthrie and the young John Lavery. In the New English, early exhibitors included Sargent himself, Maurice Greiffenhagen, Arthur Hacker, J.J. Shannon and also Lavery – all of them later to become popular academicians; Walter Sickert was later to become a somewhat unruly member of the fold, as well as others like Henry Tonks and Philip Wilson Steer who never came to terms with the Academy.

Plate 252
W. Graham Robertson by John Singer
Sargent, 1894
Oil on canvas, 230.5 × 118.7
($90\frac{3}{4} × 46\frac{3}{4}$)
Tate Gallery, London

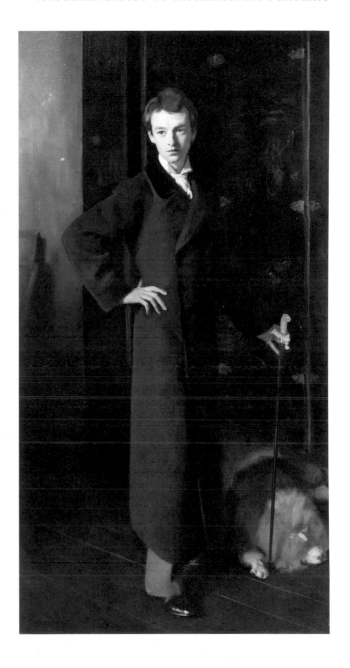

Steer, probably the finest painter amongst them, was very far from a professional portrait painter. Although he painted pictures of people from time to time – like the *Mrs Cyprian Williams and her daughters* of 1891 (Plate 253) – the people yield to a greater interest in pictorial values. So also do the people in Sickert's portraits, though to a lesser extent. His *George Moore* of 1890–1891 (Plate 254), a straightforward head-and-shoulders composition, nevertheless struck horror; at the Academy banquet it was described as the portrait of an intoxicated mummy. Moore's face was famously provocative anyway; many people spent much time thinking up epithets about it, and it was attempted in paint by Manet, Degas, Forain, Tonks, Orpen and many others (though perhaps most successfully by

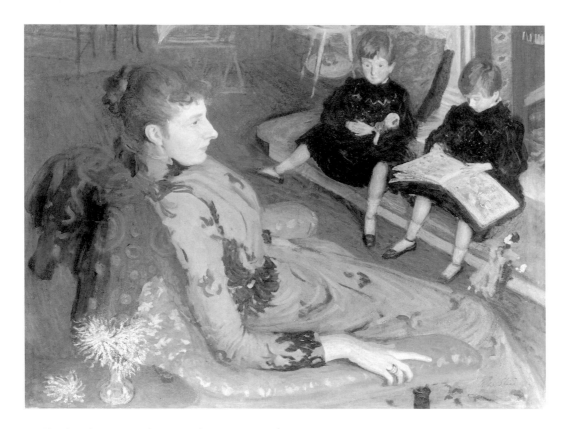

Plate 253
*Mrs Cyprian Williams and her
daughters* by Philip Wilson
Steer, 1891
Oil on canvas, 76.2 × 102.2
(30 × 40 ¼)
Tate Gallery, London

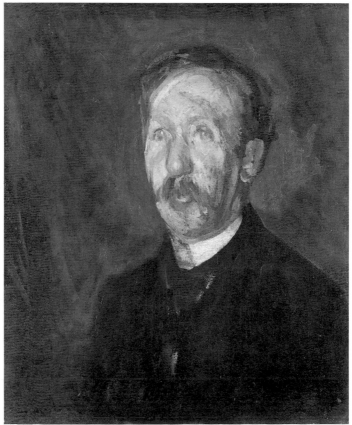

Plate 254
George Moore (1852–1933)
by W. R. Sickert, 1890–1891
Oil on canvas, 60.3 × 50.2
(23 ¾ × 19 ¾)
Tate Gallery, London

Beerbohm, and, in wax, by Dulac). But Sickert's real interest is not in the recording of Moore's face as such, but in the problem of organizing the series of planes that Moore set before him; shape recedes architecturally from the luminous nose in a most exact interlocking of arches. Later, in his second portrait of the novelist Hugh Walpole, he seems almost to portray, brilliantly, a yawn.

Thence the two trends continued and still continue, not in parallel course, but blending and breaking. The hard Academy polish was leavened by Sargent, and then loosened by his weakest works until the public eye became a pre-conditioned victim to the slash and slosh of de Laszlo, and the excesses of Lavery and Orpen in their later years. Yet all the time, into the twenties, William Ouless was painting away, and the painters of polished effigies, with their brilliant sleight-of-hand, still bewitch those who require portraits of public men and of women whose beauty is public news. Yet the grand manner persists and did not die with Sargent; in the late nineties a painter with comparable panache combined with a far more sardonic eye for the bizarre was emerging: Augustus John (Plate 255). The British have a greater difficulty than the French in throwing portraiture overboard; Victor Pasmore may abandon representational art for the abstract, but Graham Sutherland returned, in excursions, from the world of thorns to portraiture, braving the anger of those who will have their bishops and prime ministers jolly.

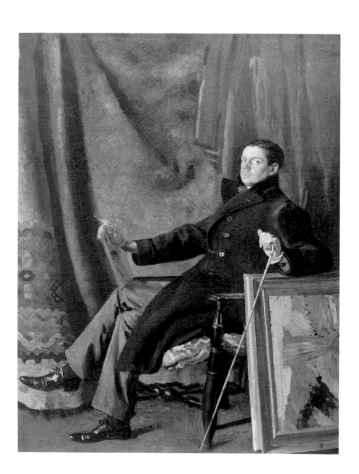

Plate 255
Sir William Nicholson (1872–1949)
by Augustus John, 1909
Oil on canvas, 190.2 × 143.8
($74\frac{7}{8} \times 56\frac{5}{8}$)
Fitzwilliam Museum, Cambridge

XIV

Not Beauty But Character

THIS BOOK was developed from a suggestion that an illustrated analysis of the Englishness of the English face was a subject worth the undertaking. I came to the conclusion that that aspect of the subject was outside my competence; it demands a trained ethnologist. It is in any event a theme, the illustration of which would be extremely difficult. Many people might have some vague visual conception of the appearance of the archetypal Englishman, Irishman, Welshman, or Scotsman, but if called upon to substantiate the images, the number of apt examples they could name amongst their acquaintances would be minute. And before one comes to assess a national face, one must have a clear realization of the distinction between national and racial faces. Any Britisher of allegedly Caucasian stock owes the shape of his head to an ancestry, the elements of which include most of the known branches of the white race; the British nations are all of vividly mongrel stock.

The ethnologist can demonstrate the facial and cranial characteristics of any given race convincingly enough; thus the darker Celtish faces are often found in Wales and Cornwall, whither the Celts, who had arrived on the island in the Iron Age, were ultimately pushed by the later Angles, Saxons and Jutes ('tall, heavy-boned, long-faced mesocephals'); black hair is relatively common in Cornwall and in Wales, but very rare on the east coast, where one may expect, and often does find, blonde men with clear light eyes, who would not be noticed in Denmark as foreigners. The variations through the country are great, and inconsistent, and the ethnologist, when asked what characterizes the British face, has, like all of us, to fall back on a largely subjective gleaning of broad experience.

Nevertheless, there is a sort of English face (one well known to Van Dyck) that can be recognized immediately abroad, even before one sights the GB plates on the car. But it is not a Scottish, nor a Welsh nor an Irish face – not even, say, a Midlands face. Nor is it the face of John Bull – thick-set, wide-faced and long-nosed.

But John Bull's history is relatively short; he was invented as a character by Arbuthnot early in the eighteenth century, but he did not settle into a fixed image until early in the nineteenth century (his image varies considerably in, for example, Gillray's cartoons [Plate 256]).[190] About 1855 he was well consolidated and could be recognized by an American, Hawthorne, as 'bulbous, long-bodied, short-legged, heavy-witted, material, and, in a word, too intensely English'; it is curious that he has less of the urban shopkeeper about him than of the tough roast-beef agriculturist. That he is an inadequate symbol for Englishness is evident to the English if not to some of their critics and enemies. But the attempt to sum up the English face is vain; in the 1920s three British scientists[191] produced experimentally

Plate 256
*John Bull Taking a
Luncheon* by James
Gillray, 1798
Etching, 24.4 × 35.6
($95\frac{5}{8}$ × 14)
British Museum,
London (Department
of Prints and
Drawings)

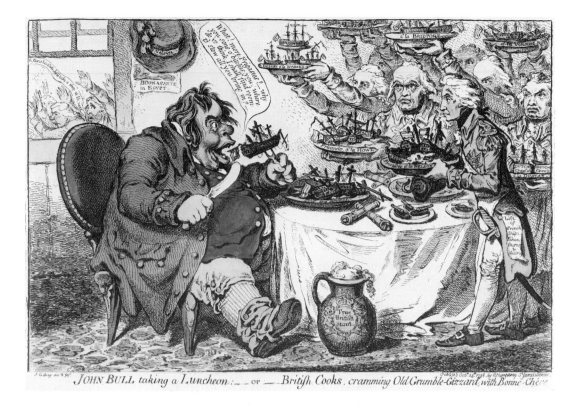

JOHN BULL taking a Luncheon: — or — British Cooks, cramming Old Grumble-Gizzard, with Bonne-Chère

a typical English face, both male and female. They superimposed a large number of silhouettes of different men and women; and arrived at a result which to the layman seems uninformative, except perhaps for use in support of Oscar Wilde's epigram on the English face — 'once seen, never remembered'.

My object, then, has rather been the more modest one of assembling a number of portraits from 1400 to 1900, from the beginnings, that is, of naturalistic portraiture in this country, and by my commentary to indicate how their relationship to the flesh and blood which they represent is controlled – by artistic and sartorial fashions, by the individualities of the sitter and the artist – and how through time this relationship alters. Every portrait is the result of a bargain between the sitter and the artist, and only in portraiture does the artist undertake a subject that can, and often does, answer back and argue; yet both are ineluctably of their time.

In a model, perhaps by Chinqua, a Chinese who was working in Madras about 1715, there is an unusual example of this compromise – a Chinese view of Western features (Plate 257). In Europe every national culture had its own view, constantly changing, of the ideal format of man and woman; thus in Lauderdale we saw an Anglo-Dutch, an Italian and an English view of a Scottish face (not that anyone would claim Lauderdale's as a typical Scottish face), each strikingly different. Not only did the artist compel his sitters into the rhythm of his style, but the sitter by dress, by constriction by corset, or by addition (at one time in the eighteenth

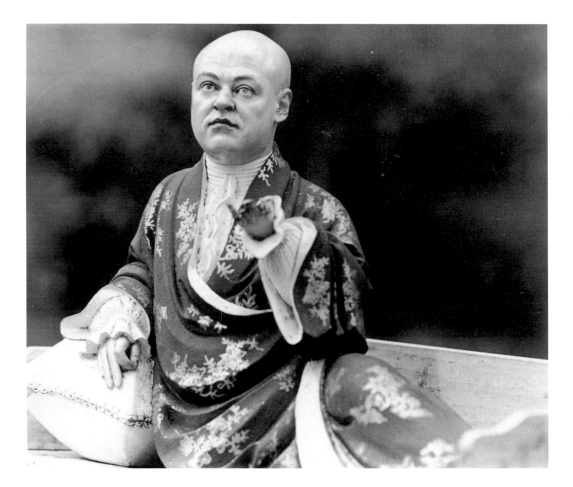

Plate 257
Edward Harrison
by ?Chinqua, *c*.1715
Coloured plaster
Private Collection

century false stomachs were not unknown), by manipulation of the hair and by face-paint, built him or herself into the fashionable mould. It was the business of the artist to catch the individual within this common mould: Hoppner, according to his own testimony,

used to make as beautiful a face as he could, then give it a likeness to the sitter, working down from this beautiful state until the bystanders should cry out: 'Oh, I see a likeness coming!' whereupon he stopped, and never ventured to make it more like.[192]

It is difficult to isolate any specifically English or British qualities that are constant through the ever-changing fashions of the beautiful in face and body. Stendhal, in 1817, located one with an attractive but doubtful precision: 'The characteristic of the English beauty . . . is to have a very long neck'[193] Stendhal had perhaps been looking at portraits by Lawrence, but of most periods this seems fairly true. Although it was almost entirely obliterated by the ruff in the sixteenth century, women have generally favoured 'the swan-straining, faire, rare stately neck' advocated by Herrick.[194] The painters were well aware of its importance; thus the society pastel-portraitist Russell, in 1777: 'As few necks are too long, it may be necessary to give some addition to the stem . . . nothing being more ungraceful than

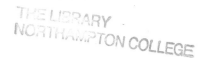

a short neck.'[195] In the case of men, the importance is less certain. 'Mr. Jorrocks was terribly thick about the throat – a sad sign of want of breeding', but many remarked admiringly of the colossal bulwark of Gladstone's neck. And anyway, neck, alone, is surely not enough. The ideal proportions of the face change continuously, but at any one time one may conform to the ideal standard and yet not be allowed beauty – and vice versa, as Hilliard already knew. When discussing the correct proportions, as laid down by Dürer, he pointed out that Christopher Hatton, famous for his beauty, was one of the goodliest personages of England, 'yet had he a very low forehead not answerable to the good proportion of a third part of his face'. Georgiana, Duchess of Devonshire, had a snub nose.

It is never beauty that is vital, but character, expressed visually in the various facets of *chic*, grooming, smartness, sex-appeal, all set off by the dizzy impermanence of youth. A few superficial traits are perhaps specifically English; the famous complexion of Englishwomen, one of the few consolations of our climate, is too subtle to be caught generally by the painters, though it is true that English portraits do not have as a rule that sharp, almost china, clarity of some of the French.

The general conclusion on the art of portraiture must be that it is very closely controlled by its conventions. The patterns of the conventions go hand in hand with those of biography, beginning with that most enduring form, the memorial, the monumental inscription, the obituary notice, with purposes commemorative, hagiographical, and didactic. Such portraits comprise, as it were, a resonant catalogue of their subjects' virtues, an indication of their earthly achievements, and none of their shortcomings; they are effigies. Their elements persist and may at all times be found here and there, but with the flowering of the Renaissance more individual traits, eccentricities of detail in a warmer humanity, begin to be emphasized, as those of Sir Thomas More in Roper's biography and in Holbein's portrait.

At this point Edmund Gosse's definition of biography, 'the faithful portrait of a soul in its adventures through life', begins to become valid. In the seventeenth century the majestic delineation of characters by Clarendon is answered in paint by Van Dyck and by Lely, and Clarendon accumulated, with deliberation and with advice from Evelyn, a large gallery of historical portraits, the ancestor of the National Portrait Gallery. A more detailed and at times very eccentric trend, the vivid verbal miniatures of Aubrey, were in their turn perfect captions to many of Cooper's portraits, and those of Loggan and White. The full concert blend, however, came at last with Boswell's Johnson, and simultaneously with Reynolds, and thence fades away, through Lockhart, to the standard three-volume biographies of the late nineteenth century (effigies again) until the sudden twist of satire in Froude's Carlyle.[196] In all the portraits of Carlyle that I have reproduced, this element does not enter in – he should have sat but once again, to the sardonic eye of Sargent.

To read portraiture, as to read biography, rightly, the conventions must be understood; it must not, even after the arrival of photography, be accepted as a literal method of transcription. The warning sounds platitudinous enough, but it still goes often unheeded; one still finds biographers, in particular, drawing conclusions entirely unwarranted by the facts, romancing upon faces, even on hands, which were but rarely those of the sitters (Reynolds usually drew hands from those of his servants).[197] I have said that a portrait is a bargain between two people, sitter and artist; but it needs a third, for it lies cold and dead till it quickens in the eye of the spectator; and every spectator sees it differently, in the light of his own eyes.[198]

I have already suggested that it was Holbein's image of Henry VIII that Sir Walter Raleigh had in mind when he said that the king was the pattern of all the merciless princes in the world. A later historian saw the same image differently – Carlyle:

I've always esteemed Henry VIII to be a much maligned man. When I look into that broad yeoman face and see those brave blue eyes of his, as they are seen in the Holbein portrait, I must conclude that an honest soul resided within his sturdy body.

Any interpretation of a portrait in terms of character is subjective, and as such valid

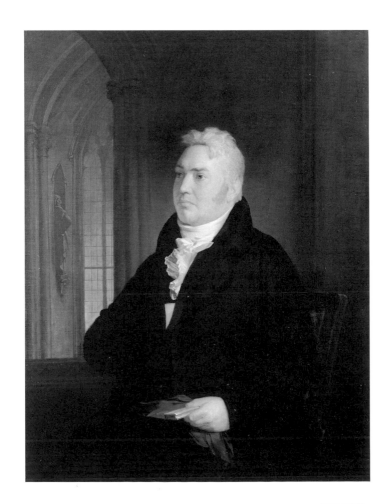

Plate 258
Samuel Taylor Coleridge
(1772–1834)
by Washington Allston,
1814
Oil on canvas, 114.3 × 87.6
(45 × 34½)
National Portrait Gallery,
London

(I have indulged perhaps in too many in this book), but it is not a statement of historical fact. And when dealing with portraits by great artists, the interpretation becomes even more ambivalent, for the great portrait-takers are really great portrait-makers, creators of characters whose unquestionable truth in the realm of imagination is not necessarily reconcilable with history: Charles I by Van Dyck exists in its own right just as Shakespeare's Richard III exists in its own right, and they are both images of such vitality that they have played a considerable part in the distortion, probably beyond hope of rectification, of the historical characters of Charles and Richard.

As in most historical quests, the search to reveal the man as he was from the wrappings supplied by his recording artists is beset with difficulties, and its end is uncertain. The great portrait-maker's genius enables him admittedly to create character, but we can never be sure how much of his creation is himself rather than his subject; for the average painter or sculptor of any conscience the problem must be maddening to despair. Here is Washington Allston, an average craftsman, recollecting in tranquillity his attempt to record Coleridge (Plate 258):

So far as I can judge of my own production the likeness is a true one. But it is Coleridge in repose, and though not unstirred by the perpetual groundswell of his ever-working intellect ... it is not Coleridge in his highest state – the poetic mood. When in that state no face I ever saw was like his, it seemed almost spirit made visible, without a shadow of the visible upon it. ... But it was beyond the reach of my art.[199]

Northcote, a better painter than Allston, once admitted resignedly that a portrait is only a little better memorial than the parings of the nails or a lock of hair (Plate 259); and Byron's cynicism – in his answer to the question, what is the end of fame – that it was

> To have, when the original is dust,
> A name, a wretched picture and worse bust[200]

was hardly to be entirely refuted by the quality of the recordings that artists were to leave of Byron. (The failure of great men to sit to the apposite painter is an endless source of regret.)

Yet even the most wretchedly executed portrait has generally some value, offering something that words cannot. Even the most incompetent or most mannered artist has had as starting-point a unique face; the body may be more often than not a symbol or a clothes-horse (and that is the reason why the emphasis in this book is on the face), but some attempt must have been made to catch the individuality of a face, each one unique. They hover dimly, the faces of the past, beneath the haze of time-darkened varnish, often shadowy as fish in neglected pools, in countless houses of Britain; thousands of them have lost their names, hundreds have acquired new and wrong names, yet each has its own mysterious identity. When the faces are of those well-known to history, they add a new dimension to history. Words cannot convey more than a vague impression, different

Plate 259
James Northcote
(1746–1831),
self-portrait, 1784
Oil on canvas,
73.7 × 61 (29 × 24)
National Portrait
Gallery, London

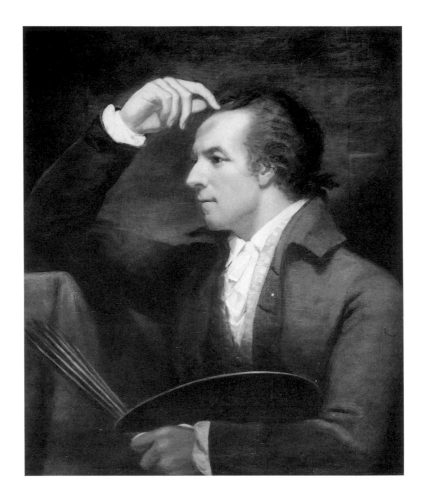

in every reader, of a character's physical displacement of time and space. It is the virtue of the portrait that it offers a definition, not a final one – and certainly not always a convenient one (it was, I think, Max Beerbohm who complained that so few people looked like themselves) – but nevertheless a positive and a measurable definition; it underlines its subject's humanity, the common heritage of perishable flesh. Through words the reader may become intimate with the whole range of an intellect, a character, a spirit, and in one sense the portrait may increase this intimacy, showing you the palpable shape of the man. In another sense, it may set up another and not unhealthy barrier between the reader and the man he seeks, for it places him in the long-dead trappings and the differences of his age; it walls him in apartness, the invulnerable isolation of everyman in the fortress of his own body, that no love can entirely overcome. These faces still fight vainly, but not without hope, against oblivion, whether it be oblivion by statistics or the grave. They are not resigned, and they remind the historian, and all other seekers, simply of individual men and women, in the inextricable circumstance of time and place, of flesh and blood.

Notes to the Text

Chapter I
Stone Effigy to Renaissance Portrait

1. See F. J. Mather, *The Portraits of Dante*, 1921.

2. British Museum Harl. MS 4866, f.88 (Illus. Plate 2).

3. See R. P. Howgrave-Graham in *Country Life*, CXI, 1952, p.82 ff.

4. For the early English royal funeral effigies, see W. H. St J. Hope in *Archaeologia*, 60, p.523 ff.

5. See L. Stone, *Sculpture in Britain: The Middle Ages*, 1955, p.193. A number of earlier sculptured portraits were probably also likenesses, but to what degree is problematic (see, e.g., J. Harvey, *The Plantagenets*, 1948).

6. See M. Davies, *The French School*, (catalogue, National Gallery, London), 1957 revised edn., pp.92–101; see also M. V. Clarke, 'The Wilton Diptych', *Burlington Magazine*, LVIII, 1931, pp.283–94; F. Wormald, 'The Wilton Diptych', in *Journal of the Warburg and Courtauld Institutes*, XVII, 1954, pp.191–203; J. H. Harvey, 'The Wilton Diptych – A Re-Examination', *Archaeologia*, 98, 1961, pp.1–24; S. Whittingham, 'The Date of The Wilton Diptych', *Gazette des Beaux Arts*, 1981, p.148 ff; eds. J. Alexander and P. Binksi, *The Age of Chivalry*, 1987 (exhibition catalogue, Royal Academy of Arts, London).

7. *Official Correspondence of Thomas Bekynton*, ed. Williams, Rolls Series, 1872, II, p.184.

8. F. H. Crossley, *English Church Monuments*, 1921, p.31.

9. See J. Pope-Hennessy, *Paolo Uccello*, 1950, p.142.

Chapter II
Holbein – Painter at Court

10. For portraits of Henry VII, see R. Strong, *Tudor and Jacobean Portraits*, 1969, pp.149–152.

11. *The Letters and Papers of Henry VIII*, ed. J. Gairdner, 1861–1863, II, p.396.

12. *Calendar of State Papers, Venetian*, ed. Rawdon Brown, 1864, II, p.1287.

13. A. F. Pollard, *Henry VIII*, 1951 edn., pp.31, 113.

14. W. Raleigh, *History of the World*, 1614, Introduction. For Holbein the most convenient source of illustrations is J. Rowlands, *Holbein: The Paintings of Hans Holbein the Younger*, 1985. For Holbein's drawings, see K. T. Parker, *Holbein's Drawings at Windsor Castle*, 1950. The Whitehall painting was destroyed by fire, but is known from Holbein's cartoon for the left-hand half (formerly at Chatsworth and now in the National Portrait Gallery) and by a small

copy by Remigius van Leemput at Hampton Court.

15. G. P. Lomazzo, *Trattato dell'arte della pittura, etc.*, 1584 (trans. R. Haydock, 1598); for the evolution of state portraiture see M. Jenkins, *The State Portrait* (The College Art Association of America), 1947; W. Bachstitz, *Studien zum Porträt des 16 Jahrhunderts*, Vienna, 1934; J. Pope-Hennessy, *The Portrait in the Renaissance*, 1966; L. Campbell, *Renaissance Portraits*, 1990.

16. L. Bradner in *Proceedings of the Modern Language Association of America*, September 1956.

17. A. F. Pollard, op.cit., p.153. The drawing, formerly at Weston Park, is now in the British Museum. I am not here referring to Anne's 'beauty', but rather to the human conviction of Holbein's drawing of her.

Chapter III
The Elizabethans – A Rock Against Time

18. For Scrots and Eworth, see R. Strong, *The English Icon: Elizabethan and Jacobean Portraiture*, 1969.

19. For Elizabeth's portraits, see R. Strong, *Portraits of Queen Elizabeth I*, 1963, with its valuable catalogue, not entirely superseded by his *Gloriana*, 1987.

20. N. Hilliard, *A Treatise concerning the Arte of Limning*, eds. R. K. R. Thornton and T. G. S. Cain, 1981, pp.85–86.

21. J. Pope-Hennessy, *A Lecture on N. Hilliard*, 1949.

22. J. Harington, *Nugae Antique*, 1779, II, pp.140–1.

23. H. Estienne, *L'Art de faire les Devises*, 1645 (trans. T. Blount, 1646); see R. Freeman, *English Emblem Books*, 1948.

24. De Maisse, *Journal, 1597*, trans. G. B. Harrison, 1931, p.25.

25. B. Jonson, *Works*, ed. C. H. Herford and P. Simpson, 1925, I, p.141.

26. W. Raleigh, *Selected Writings*, ed. G. Hammond, 1984, p.120.

27. For Elizabethan cosmetics and clothes see M. C. Linthicum, *Costume in the Drama of Shakespeare*, 1936; C. Camden, *The Elizabethan Woman*, 1952; C. W. and P. Cunnington, *Handbook of English Costume in the 16th Century*, 1954; A. Ribeiro and V. Cumming, *The Visual History of Costume*, 1989.

28. N. Hilliard, op.cit., p.76.

29. J. Aubrey, *Brief Lives*, ed. A. Clark, 1898, pp.182–4.

30. Acts of Court, 1560–1595 (MS in Mercers' Hall, London; reference supplied by Professor S. T. Bindoff).

31. R. Dallington, *A Survey of Tuscany, 1596*, 1605.

32. Annals of the Royal College of Physicians, 5 April 1596 (MS in the College).

33. R. Strong, *Tudor and Jacobean Portraiture*, 1969; D. Piper, *O Sweet Mr Shakespeare, I'll Have His Picture*, 1964, (exhibition catalogue, National Portrait Gallery, London); for John Taylor, see M. Edmond, 'The Chandos Portrait: a Suggested Painter', *Burlington Magazine*, CXXIV, 1982, pp.146–9.

34. Historical MSS Commission, Salisbury Papers, I, p.482.

35. Quoted by W. B. Rye, *England as Seen by Foreigners*, 1865, p.XLIV.

Chapter IV
Jacobean Melancholy

36. All the portraits mentioned (and others) are in the collection of his descendants at Powis Castle (National Trust).

37. I. Walton, *Lives*, 1675 edn. For doubts about the reliability of Walton's account, see P. Gardner in *Evidence in Literary Scholarship*, ed. R. Wellek and A. Ribeiro, 1979.

38. B. Jonson, *Works*, ed. C. H. Herford and P. Simpson, 1925, I, p.151.

39. Drummond's account, 1617, cited in B. Jonson, op.cit., I, p.138.

40. The most useful compilation on Van Dyck is that by G. Gluck, 1931; no appraisal and illustration of his English period has yet appeared, but an admirable summary is provided by O. Millar in *Van Dyck in England*, 1982, (exhibition catalogue, National Portrait Gallery, London); see also A. K. Wheelock Jr., S. J. Barnes and J. S. Held, *Anthony van Dyck*, 1991 (exhibition catalogue, National Gallery of Art, Washington).

41. R. Herrick, 'Upon his Julia' from *The Poems of Robert Herrick*, ed. L. C. Martin, 1965, p.138.

42. For a brief account of the iconography of Charles I, see D. Piper in *Charles I* (pamphlet published for the Historical Association), 1949; articles on the early portraits and on the bust, by M. R. Toynbee and by K. A. Esdaile, and E. K. Waterhouse on Bower's portraits, in *Burlington Magazine*, XCI, 1949, p.3 ff; Millar, op.cit; R. Strong, *Van Dyck: Charles I on Horseback*, 1972.

43. J. J. Keevil in *Journal of the History of Medicine and Allied Sciences*, 1954, IX, p.407 ff.

44. L. Johnson, 'By the Statue of King Charles at Charing Cross', from *The Complete Poems of Lionel Johnson*, ed. I. Fletcher, 1953, p.10.

45. F. P. Verney, *Memoirs of the Verney Family*, 1892, I, p.257 ff.

46. What was probably the original was sold from the Earl of Onslow's collection in 1828 but is reasonably identified with the portrait acquired by the National Portrait Gallery in 1961.

47. See M. Rogers, *William Dobson*, 1983, (exhibition catalogue, National Portrait Gallery, London).

48. For Cromwell see D. Piper, 'The Contemporary Portraits of Oliver Cromwell', *Walpole Society*, 1958, XXXI.

49. G. Vertue, 'Notebooks', *Walpole Society*, 1929–1930, XVIII, p.91.

50. P. Warwick, *Memoires of the Reigne of King Charles I*, 1701, p.247.

51. J. Evelyn, *Numismata*, 1697, p.339.

52. J. Evelyn, *Diary*, ed. E. S. de Beer, III, 1955, pp.309–10.

53. J. Aubrey, *Brief Lives*. The standard though bowdlerised edition is A. Clark, 1898; A. Powell, 1949, is easier to use, unbowdlerised, and will answer most purposes.

54. J. Aubrey, *Brief Lives*, ed. A. Clark, 1898, pp.347–9.

55. Ibid., p.105.

56. Ibid., p.91.

57. For Lely see O. Millar, *Sir Peter Lely*, 1978, (exhibition catalogue, National Portrait Gallery, London).

58. D. Osborne, *Letters*, ed. G. C. Moore Smith, 1928, pp.50, 58, 106, 166.

59. H. Newcome, *Autobiography*, ed. R. Parkinson (Chetham Society), 1852, p.97.

Chapter V
Restoration Baroque

60. J. Evelyn, op.cit, III, p.97.

61. H. Walpole, *Aedes Walpolianae*, 1742 edn., p.XVI.

62. S. Pepys, *Diary*, (15 February 1666), 1972, eds. R. C. Latham and W. Matthews, VII, p.44.

63. J. Dryden, *Of Dramatic Poesy and other critical essays*, ed. G. Watson, 1962, p.21.

64. S. Pepys, op.cit., (21 August 1668), 1976, IX, p.284.

65. S. Pepys, op.cit., (24 March 1662), 1972, III, p.51.

66. S. Pepys, op.cit., (9 May 1663), 1973, IV, pp.130, 357–364.

67. W. Hogarth, *The Analysis of Beauty*, ed. J. Burke, 1955, p.88ff.

68. W. G. Hiscock, *John Evelyn and His Family Circle*, 1955, p.48.

69. G. R. Burnet, *History of His Own Time*, 1723–1734, and T. Ailesbury, *Memoirs* (Roxburghe Club), 1890.

Chapter VI
The Polite Mask of the Augustan Age

70. For Kneller, see J. D. Stewart, *Sir Godfrey Kneller and the English Baroque Portrait*, 1983.

71. S. Johnson, *Life of Addison*, p.167.

72. C. F. Bell and R. Poole, 'English 17th Century Portrait Drawings', *Walpole Society*, 1925–1926, XIV, pp.43–80.

73. K. A. Esdaile, 'J. Bushnell, Sculptor', *Walpole Society*, 1926–1927, XV, pp.21–45.

74. S. Pepys, op.cit., (7 November 1666), 1972, VII, p.359.

75. N. Ward, *The London Spy*, ed. A. L. Hayward, 1927, pp.57, 59.

Chapter VII
Character Not Caricature

76. J. Stow, 'Of Graphice, or Art of Paynting, and of Pourtraiture, and of Stayning, and of Cosmetica', from *The Third Universitie of England or a Treatise*, 1615, p.986.

77. J. Richardson, 'Theory of Painting' in *Works*, 1773, p.17.

78. J. Elsum, *The Art of Painting*, 1703, p.66.

79. J. Richardson, *Essay on the Theory of Painting*, 1715, pp.35–6, 175.

80. A. Cooper, 3rd Earl of Shaftesbury, *Second Characters* ed. B. Rand, 1914, pp.134 ff.

81. J. B. le Blanc, *Letters on the English and French Nations*, 1747.

82. Historical MSS Commission, Trelawney Papers (1st Report), p.510.

83. Horace Walpole to Mann, 9 February, 1751.

84. G. Vertue, 'Notebooks', *Walpole Society*, 1933–1934, XXII, pp.125–6.

85. Quoted by G. E. C., *The Complete Peerage*, 1916, p.81, under Darlington.

86. Mme du Bocage, *Letters concerning England, Holland and Italy*, 1770.

87. Horace Walpole to Montagu, 23 June 1750.

88. For Hudson, see E. G. Miles and J. Simon, *Thomas Hudson, 1701–1779*, 1979 (exhibition catalogue, Iveagh Bequest, Kenwood House, London). See also E. Einberg, *Manners and Morals: Hogarth and British Painting 1700–1760*, 1987 (exhibition catalogue, Tate Gallery, London).

89. See M. I. Webb, *Michael Rysbrack, Sculptor*, 1954.

90. See K. A. Esdaile, *L. F. Roubiliac*, 1928.

91. G. Vertue, 'Notebooks', *Walpole Society*, 1933–1934, III, p.152.

92. H. Walpole, *Description of Strawberry Hill*, 1784, p.89.

93. W. Hogarth, op.cit., p.201.

94. A. P. Oppé, *The Drawings of William Hogarth*, 1948, p.22. A useful compendium on the paintings is R. B. Beckett, *Hogarth*, 1949; for the *Analysis of Beauty* (and the Autobiographical Notes) see J. Burke's edition, 1955. The subject however has been made almost his own by R. Paulson, especially in his *Hogarth's Graphic Works*, 1970; *Hogarth, His Life, Art and Times*, 1971; *The Art of Hogarth*, 1975. See also D. Bindman, *Hogarth*, 1981.

95. W. Hogarth, op.cit., p.141.

96. See R. E. Moore, *Hogarth's Literary Relationships*, 1948.

97. W. Hogarth, op.cit., pp.136–7.

Chapter VIII
The Golden Age of the Society Portrait

98. M. Delany, *Autobiography and Correspondence of Mary Delany*, ed. Lady Llanover, 1861, II, p.72.

99. M. Woodall, ed., *The Letters of Thomas Gainsborough*, 1963, p.51.

100. Quoted in W. T. Whitley, *Thomas Gainsborough*, 1915, p.154.

101. J. Stewart, *Plococosmos*, 1782, p.203.

102. *Gentleman's Magazine*, 1765, XXXV, p.95.

103. Captain Jesse, *Life of G. Brummel*, 1893 edn., p.33.

104. Quoted in W. T. Whitley, op.cit., pp.198–9.

105. For Reynolds, see E. K. Waterhouse, *Reynolds*, 1941; E. K. Waterhouse, *Reynolds*, 1973; E. Wind, *Vorträge der Bibliothek Warburg*, 1930–1931, IX, p.156ff; *Reynolds*, ed. N. Penny, 1986, (exhibition catalogue, Royal Academy of Arts, London); J. Reynolds, *Discourses on Art*, ed. R. R. Wark, 1975.

106. F. W. Hilles, *The Literary Career of Sir J. Reynolds*, 1936, p.161.

107. J. L. Clifford, ed., *Dr Campbell's Diary, 1775*, 1947, p.53.

108. R. Ingrams, ed., *Dr Johnson by Mrs Thrale: The Anecdotes of Mrs Piozzi in their Original Form*, 1984, p.68.

109. Ibid. See also J. Boswell, *Tour to the Hebrides with Samuel Johnson* (1786), 1936, eds. F. A. Pottle and C. H. Bennett; *Thraliana: the Diary of Mrs Hester Lynch Thrale (later Mrs Piozzi) 1776–1809*, ed. K. C. Balderston, 1942.

110. W. Hayley, *Life of Romney*, 1809, p.24.

111. For Gainsborough, see W. T. Whitley's biography, 1915; E. K. Waterhouse, *Gainsborough*, 1958, is very fully illustrated; see also M. Woodall ed., *The Letters of Thomas Gainsborough*, 1963; J. Hayes, *Gainsborough*, 1975; J. Hayes, *Thomas Gainsborough*, 1980, (exhibition catalogue, Tate Gallery, London).

112. W. T. Whitley, *Thomas Gainsborough*, 1915, p.36.

113. Ibid., pp.73 ff.

114. Ibid., p.392.

115. J. Reynolds, op.cit., 'Fourteenth Discourse', (10 December 1788), p.259.

116. J. Reynolds, op.cit., 'Seventh Discourse', (10 December 1766), p.140.

117. E. Fletcher ed., *Conversations of J. Northcote with J. Ward*, 1901, p.160.

118. Hayley, op.cit., p.300.

119. Ibid., pp.178, 182.

Chapter IX
The Face in Miniature

120. J. Harris, 1st Earl of Malmesbury, *Letters*, 1870, I, p.299.

121. J. Reynolds, op.cit., 'Third Discourse', (14 December 1770), p.44.

122. J. C. Lavater, *Essays on Physiognomy* (from the 17th English edition), p.315. For a critical study, see C. Steinbrucker, *Lavaters Physiognomische Fragmente im Vorhältnis zur Bildenden Kunst*, 1915.

123. E. N. Jackson, *Silhouette*, 1938, contains much information, though not always reliable (as a dictionary, it is superseded by S. McKechnie, *British Silhouette Artists and their work 1760–1860*, 1978; see also R. L. Megroz, *Profile Art*, 1948.

124. W. Hazlitt, *Conversations with Northcote*, ed. E. Gosse, 1894, p.89; the idea goes back at least as far as Fenélon's *Fables*.

125. O. Goldsmith, *Citizen of the World*, 1761, letter 109.

126. Hayley, op.cit., p.204.

127. N. Karamzin, *Travels from Moscow*, 1803, III, pp.203, 217.

128. Quoted in M. Webster, *Johan Zoffany*, 1976, p.72.

129. For Zoffany, see M. Webster, *Johan Zoffany*, 1976 (exhibition catalogue, National Portrait Gallery, London); for Stubbs, B. Taylor, *Stubbs*, 1971; J. Egerton, *George Stubbs 1726–1806*, 1984 (exhibition catalogue, Tate Gallery, London); for Wright of Derby, B. Nicolson, *Joseph Wright of Derby*, 2 vols, 1968; J. Egerton, *Wright of Derby*, 1990 (exhibition catalogue, Tate Gallery, London).

Chapter X
The Age of Lawrence

130. See K. Garlick, *Sir Thomas Lawrence*, 1989 (supersedes his earlier works on the artist); M. Levey, *Sir Thomas Lawrence*, 1979 (exhibition catalogue, National Portrait Gallery, London); for biographical details, D. Goldring, *Regency Portrait Painter: The Life of Sir Thomas Lawrence, P. R. A.*, 1951.

131. Goldring, op.cit., p.81.

132. Ibid., p.68.

133. Ibid., p.264.

134. Ibid., p.255.

135. J. Farington, *The Diary of Joseph Farington*, (23 September 1801), eds. K. Garlick and A. Macintyre, 1979, V, p.1631.

136. E. George, *Life and Death of B. R. Haydon*, 1948, p.209.

137. For Wilkie, see A. Cunningham, *The Life of Sir David Wilkie*, 3 vols, 1843; H. A. D. Miles and D. Blayney Brown, *Sir David Wilkie of Scotland (1785–1841)*, 1987 (exhibition catalogue, North Carolina Museum of Art).

138. For Mulready, see K. M. Heleniak, *William Mulready*, 1980; M. Pointon, *William Mulready 1786–1863*, 1986 (exhibition catalogue, Victoria & Albert Museum, London).

139. See *Catalogue of Political and Personal Satires*, British Museum, 1870–1954, with invaluable introductions; see also F. D. Klingender, *Hogarth and English Caricature*, 1944; M. D. George, *English Political Caricature*, 1959; D. Hill, *Mr. Gillray the Caricaturist*, 1962.

140. *Byron's Letters and Journals*, L. A. Marchand ed., 1979, IX, p.40.

141. Goldring, op.cit., p.163.

142. Vicomte de Chateaubriand, *Mémoires d'Outre-Tombe*, trans. de Metos, 1902, IV, p.72.

143. H. Fielding, *Enquiry into the Causes of the Late Increase of Robbers, etc.*, 1751, p.156.

144. For visual records of urban and industrial workers, see F. D. Klingender, *Art and the Industrial Revolution*, 1947.

Chapter XI
Pre-Raphaelite Longing

145. For photography, I am heavily indebted to H. and A. Gernsheim's standard *History of Photography*, 1955. See also M. Rogers, *Camera Portraits*, 1989 (exhibition catalogue, National Portrait Gallery, London and Washington).

146. A. M. W. Stirling, *The Richmond Papers*, 1926, p.123.

147. 'The Portraits of Queen Victoria', *Woman at Home*, 1897, VIII, p.812.

148. *Magazine of Art*, 1878, I, p.49.

149. See R. Ormond and C. Blackett-Ord, *Franz Xaver Winterhalter and the Courts of Europe 1830–1870*, 1987 (exhibition catalogue, National Portrait Gallery, London).

150. Stirling, op.cit., p.49.

151. Stirling, op.cit., p.60.

152. F. M. Hueffer, *Ford Madox Brown: A Record of his Life and Work*, 1896, p.100.

153. For the Pre-Raphaelites, see Holman Hunt, *Pre-Raphaelitism*, 1905; L. Parris ed., *The Pre-Raphaelites*, 1984 (exhibition catalogue, Tate Gallery, London); L. Parris ed., *The Pre-Raphaelite Papers*, 1984; for Rossetti, see V. Surtees, *The Paintings and Drawings of D. G. Rossetti*, 1973.

154. See R. Barrington, *G. F. Watts, Reminiscences*, 1905; M. S. Watts, *G. F. Watts*, 1912; R. Chapman, *The Laurel and the Thorn*, 1945; D. Loshak, *G. F. Watts*, 1955 (exhibition catalogue, Arts Council of Great Britain); *G. F. Watts: The Hall of Fame*, 1975 (exhibition catalogue, National Portrait Gallery, London).

155. W. M. Rossetti, 'The Royal Academy Exhibition', *Fraser's Magazine*, 1862, LXVI, p.77.

156. See Myers & Co., *Catalogue No. 373*, 1952, no. 366.

157. H. Gernsheim, *Julia Margaret Cameron: Her Life and Photographic Work*, 1975. See also J. Howard, *Whisper of the Muse: The World of Julia Margaret Cameron*, 1990 (exhibition catalogue, Colnaghi, London).

158. Gernsheim, op.cit., p.46.

Chapter XII
Carlyle – The Face of History

159. W. B. Scott, *Autobiographical Notes*, 1892, I, p.270.

160. W. Allingham, *Diary*, 1907, p.209; cf. Carlyle's often-quoted remark that 'the portrait was a small lighted candle by which the Biographies could for the first time be *read*, and some human interpretation made of them'. R. Ormond, *Early Victorian Portraits*, 1973, records over a hundred portraits of Carlyle.

161. A. Woolner, *Thomas Woolner, R. A.*, 1917.

162. Hueffer, op.cit., p.190.

163. Ibid., pp.165, 194.

164. D. A. Wilson and D. Wilson MacArthur, *Carlyle in Old Age (1856–1881)*, 1934, pp.130–1.

165. Ibid., p.168.

166. E. R. and J. Pennell, *Life of James McNeill Whistler*, 1908, I, p.170.

167. Wilson and Wilson MacArthur, op.cit., p.130; G. K. Chesterton, *G. F. Watts*, 1904, p.69.

168. T. Carlyle to J. M. Cameron, 9 June 1867, cited in Gernsheim, op.cit., p.189.

169. Gernsheim, op.cit., p. 189.

170. D. A. Wilson, *Carlyle to Threescore Years and Ten*, 1929, p.368.

171. C. Eaglestone, 'A Memoir of Sir Edgar Boehm', *Blackwood's Magazine*, 1891, CXLIX, p.348.

172. Wilson and Wilson MacArthur, op.cit., p.371 ff.

173. Ibid., p.405.

174. Wilson and Wilson MacArthur, op. cit., p.405. For Millais, see J. G. Millais, *The Life and Letters of Sir J. E. Millais*, 1899.

175. Wilson and Wilson MacArthur, op.cit., p.297 ff. For Whistler, see P. D. Maclean *et al.*, *The Paintings of James McNeill Whistler*, 1980.

176. Wilson and Wilson MacArthur, op.cit., p.435.

177. 'Mr James Whistler at Cheyne Walk', *The World*, 22 May 1878, p.4.

Chapter XIII
Victorian Effigy to Impressionist Portrait

178. T. Matthews, *Biography of John Gibson*, 1911, p.100.

179. Ibid., p.101. See B. Read, *Victorian Sculpture*, 1982, for the whole period.

180. I. McAllister, *Alfred Gilbert*, 1929, p.105. See also R. Dorment, *Alfred Gilbert: Sculptor and Goldsmith*, 1986 (exhibition catalogue, Royal Academy of Arts, London).

181. N. Hawthorne, *English Notebooks*, (19 February 1855), 1870.

182. Quoted by F. M. Wilson, *Strange Island*, 1955, p.224.

183. C. Dickens, *Household Words*, 15 June 1850, cited in L. Parris ed., op.cit., p.78.

184. For Tissot, see J. Laver, *Vulgar Society*, 1936. See also H. Zerner *et.al.*, *James Jacques Joseph Tissot: A Retrospective Exhibition*, 1968 (exhibition catalogue, Providence Museum of Art and Art Gallery of Toronto); K. Matyjaszkiewicz ed., *James Tissot*, 1984 (exhibition catalogue, Barbican Art Gallery, London).

185. Max O'Rell, *John Bull and His Island*, 1883.

186. Baudelaire, *The Mirror of Art* (trans. J. Mayne, 1955), p.127.

187. See E. Charteris, *John Sargent*, 1927; see also *Illustrations to the Sargent Exhibition*, 1926, (exhibition catalogue, Royal Academy of Arts, London); J. Lomax and R. Ormond, *John Singer Sargent and the Edwardian Age*, 1979, (exhibition catalogue, National Portrait Gallery, London).

188. Charteris, op.cit., p.141.

189. R. Fry, *Transformations: Critical and Speculative Essays on Art*, p.135.

Chapter XIV
Not Beauty But Character

190. See D. George's introductions to the *Catalogue of Satires*, British Museum, vols v–ix.

191. McLearn, G. M. Morant and K. Pearson, in *Biometrika*, 1928–1929, XXb.

192. Fletcher, op.cit., p.190.

193. Stendhal, *Journal*, 9 August 1817.

194. R. Herrick, 'The Description of a Woman', from ed. Martin, op.cit., pp.404–6.

195. J. Russell, *Elements of Painting with Crayons*, 1777, p.35.

196. I have followed Sir H. Nicholson's outline, *Development of English Biography*, 1928.

197. Cf. Northcote, *Life of Reynolds*, 1819, II, p.287. Lay-figures were also used, but the portrait of the body is normally a portrait of clothes; nude portraits are rare – they include Nell Gwyn's (see above, Plate 116) and the lost portrait of Beckford (of *Vathek*) naked, painted by Mengs.

198. For the 'character' and the mystique of the face, see J. Brophy, *The Human Face*, 1945; M. Picard, *The Human Face*, 1931; a remarkable passage on this subject is in W. de la Mare's introduction to his anthology *Love*, 1943, pp.LVLXII.

199. Quoted by W. T. Whitley, *Art in England 1801–1820*, 1928, p.236.

200. *Don Juan*, Canto I, p.CCXVIII.

Select Bibliography

During the writing of this book, the author was involved in his office hours in work on the catalogue of the seventeenth century portraits in the National Portrait Gallery, turning to more general scrutiny of the English face at home in the evenings. Both projects however were informed by long and close scrutiny of the formidable library of books, manuscript material, and photographs built up at the National Portrait Gallery by predecessors and colleagues on the Gallery staff, as well of course by the study of the portraits themselves, in the Gallery and elsewhere.

The publication of a full catalogue of the Gallery's permanent collection was conceived after the Second World War by the then Director, Sir Henry Hake, and so far five have been published:

Kerslake, J., *Early Georgian Portraits*, 1977.

Ormond, R., *Early Victorian Portraits*, 1973.

Piper, D., *Seventeenth Century Portraits in the National Portrait Gallery*, 1963.

Strong, R., *Tudor and Jacobean Portraits*, 1969.

Walker, R., *Regency Portraits*, 1985.

Pending completion (and updating in some way) of this series, the *National Portrait Gallery: Complete Illustrated Catalogue*, 1981, compiled by K.K. Yung, the first fully illustrated check-list of the primary collection, is especially valuable. The four volume *Dictionary of British Portraiture*, 1979–1981, edited by R. Ormond and M. Rogers is a check-list of known portraits of historical figures wherever they may be, and is a most useful starting point for any student interested in particular iconographies, but is not illustrated.

The books, exhibition catalogues and articles cited below constitute a short, select bibliography relating to portraiture which is not intended to be exhaustive.

Books and Articles

Adams, C. K., *Catalogue of Portraits in the Garrick Club*, 1936.

Adams, C. K. and W. S. Lewis, 'The Portraits of Horace Walpole', *Walpole Society*, XLII, 1968–1970.

Allen, B., *Francis Hayman*, 1987.

Archer, M., *India and British Portraiture*, 1979.

Blanchard, F., *Portraits of Wordsworth*, 1959.

Brilliant, R., *Portraiture*, 1991.

Brophy, J., *The Human Face*, 1945.

Byron, A., *London Statues*, 1981.

Campbell, L., *Renaissance Portraits*, 1990.

Clarke, G., ed., *The Portrait in Photography*, 1992.

Cunnington, C. W., *Handbook of English Costume in the Nineteenth Century*, 1937.

Cunnington, C. W. and P. Cunnington, *Handbook of English Costume in the Sixteenth Century*, 1954.

Cunnington, C. W. and P. Cunnington, *Handbook of English Costume in the Seventeenth Century*, 1955.

Cust, L., *Eton Portraits*, 1910.

Edwards, R. E., *Early Conversation Pictures*, 1954.

Farington, J., *The Farington Dairies*, 16 vols (I—VI ed. K. Garlick and A. McIntyre; VII—XVI ed. K. Cave), 1978–1985.

Farrer, E., *Portraits in Suffolk Houses (West)*, 1909.

Forrer, L., *Dictionary of British Medallists*, 8 vols, 1904–1930.

Foskett, D., *Dictionary of British Miniature Painters*, 1972.

Fox, C., *Londoners*, 1987.

Gent, L., and N. Llewellyn, *Renaissance Bodies: The Human Figure in English Culture c.1540–1660*, 1990.

George, M. D., *English Political Caricature*, 1959.

Gernsheim, H., *The History of Photography*, 1955 and later editions.

Gibson, R., *Portraits in the Collection of the Earl of Clarendon*, 1977.

Gombrich, E. H., *Art and Illusion*, 1956.

Gombrich, E. H., 'The Mask and the Face', in Gombrich, Hochberg and Black, *Art, Perception and Reality*, 1972.

Gombrich, E. H., 'The Experiment of Caricature' in *Art and Illusion*, 1956.

Gwynne-Jones, A., *Portrait Painters*, 1950.

Hake, H. M., *The English Historic Portrait, Document and Myth*, (Henrietta Herz Lecture, British Academy), 1943.

Hawkins, E., *Medallic Illustrations of the History of Great Britain and Ireland*, 2 vols, 1885.

Hayes, J., *Thomas Gainsborough*, 1975.

Henscher, F., *The Human Skull*, 1966.

Hilliard, N., *A Treatise concerning the Arte of Limning*, eds. R. K. R. Thornton and T. G. S. Cain, 1981.

Hind, A. M., *Engraving in England in the Sixteenth and Seventeenth Centuries*; I, *The Tudors*, 1952; II, *The Reign of James I*, 1955; III (by M. Corbett and M. Norton), 1964.

Hogarth, W., *The Analysis of Beauty [1753]*, *with the rejected passages from the Manuscript Drafts and autobiographical notes*, ed. J. Burke, 1955.

Ingamells, J., *The English Episcopal Portrait*, 1981.

Keynes, G., *The Portraiture of William Harvey*, 1949.

Keynes, G., *The Portraiture of William and Catherine Blake*, 1977.

Lambert, M., *Fashion in Photographs 1860–1880*, 1991.

Levitt, S., *Fashion in Photographs 1880–1900*, 1991.

Lloyd, C. and S. Thurley, *Henry VIII: Images of a Tudor King*, 1990.

Maas, J., *Victorian Painters*, 1969.

Macdonald, H., *Portraits in Prose*, 1946.

McConkey, K., *Edwardian Portraits*, 1987.

Martin, J. L., *The Portrait of Milton at Princeton*, 1961.

Millar, O., *Tudor, Stuart and Early Georgian Pictures in the Collection of H. M. The Queen*, 1963.

Millar, O., *Later Georgian Pictures in the Royal Collection*, 1969.

Millar, O., *Zoffany and His Tribuna*, 1966.

Miller, L., *Milton's Portraits* (special issue of the *Milton Quarterly*, Ohio), 1976.

Morison, J. and N. Barker, *The Likeness of Thomas More*, 1963.

Nicholson, B., *Joseph Wright of Derby*, 2 vols, 1968.

O'Donoghue, F. and H. M. Hake, *Catalogue of Engraved British Portraits in the British Museum*, 6 vols, 1908–1925.

Ormond, R., *The Face of Monarchy*, 1977.

Pepys, S., *Diary*, ed. R. Latham and W. Matthews, 11 vols, 1970–1983.

Piper, D., 'The Contemporary Portraits of Oliver Cromwell', *Walpole Society*, 1958, XLII.

Piper, D., *Kings and Queens of England and Scotland*, 1980.

Piper, D., *The Image of the Poet* (Clark Lectures), 1982.

Pointon, M., 'Portrait-painting as a Business Enterprise in London in the 1780s', *Art History*, VII, no.2, June 1984, pp.187–205.

Poole, R. L., *Catalogue of Oxford Portraits*, 3 vols, 1912–1925.

Pope-Hennessey, J., *The Portrait in the Renaissance*, 1966.

Praz, M., *Conversation Pieces*, 1971.

Read, B., *Victorian Sculpture*, 1982.

Reynolds, G., *British Portrait Miniatures*, 1952.

Reynolds, G., *Painters of the Victorian Scene*, 1953.

Reynolds, J., *Discourses on Art*, ed. R. R. Wark, 1975.

Ribeiro, A., *Dress and Morality*, 1986.

Ribeiro, A. and V. Cumming, *The Visual History of Costume*, 1989.

Robertson, J., *Practical Problems of the Portrait Painter*, 1962.

Rolley, K. and Aish, C., *Fashion in Photographs 1900–1920*, 1992.

Rowlands, J., *Holbein: the Paintings of Hans Holbein the Younger*, 1985.

Russell, F., *Portraits of Sir Walter Scott*, 1987.

Shawe-Taylor, D., *The Georgians: Eighteenth Century Portraiture and Society*, 1990.

Simon, R., *The Portrait in Britain and America*, 1987.

Singh, Prince Duleep, *Portraits in Norfolk Houses*, 2 vols, 1927.

Sitwell, S., *Conversation Pieces*, 1936.

Smart, A., *The Life and Art of Allan Ramsay*, 1952.

Steegman, J., *Survey of Portraits in Welsh Houses*, I, 1957; II, 1962.

Strong, R., *Portraits of Queen Elizabeth*, 1963.

Strong, R., *The English Icon: Elizabethan and Jacobean Portraiture*, 1969.

Strong, R., *The English Renaissance Miniature*, 1983.

Strong, R., *Henry, Prince of Wales and England's Lost Renaissance*, 1986.

Strong, R., *Gloriana*, 1987.

Strong, R., et al., *The British Portrait 1660–1960*, 1991.

Talley, M. K., *Portrait Painting in England; Studies in the Technical Literature before 1700*, 1981.

Turgenev, I., et al., *The Portrait Game*, trans. and ed. M. Mainwaring, 1973.

Vertue, G., *Notebooks*, (6 vols., *Walpole Society*, 1930–1954).

Waetzoldt, W., *Die Kunst des Porträts*, 1908.

Waterhouse, E. K., *Painting in Britain 1530–1790*, 1953, and subsequent editions.

Waterhouse, E. K., *Dictionary of British Eighteenth Century Painters*, 1981.

Waterhouse, E. K., *Dictionary of British Sixteenth and Seventeenth Century Painters*, 1988.

Wellesley, Lord G. and J. Steegman, *The Iconography of the First Duke of Wellington*, 1935.

Whinney, M. D., *Sculpture in Britain*, 2nd edn., 1988.

Wilson, F. M., *Strange Island*, 1955.

Wimsatt, W. K., *The Portraits of Alexander Pope*, 1965.

Wood, C., *Victorian Panorama*, 1976.

Exhibition Catalogues

Barber, R., *S. Pepys, Esq.*, 1970 (National Portrait Gallery, London).

Bayly, C., *The Raj: India and the British 1600–1947*, 1990 (National Portrait Gallery, London).

Crookshank, A. and the Knight of Glin, *Irish Portraits, 1660–1860*, 1969 (National Gallery of Ireland, Dublin, National Portrait Gallery, London and Ulster Museum, Belfast).

Egerton, J., *George Stubbs 1724–1806*, 1984 (Tate Gallery, London).

Egerton, J., *Wright of Derby*, 1990 (Tate Gallery, London).

Einberg, E., *Manners and Morals: Hogarth and British Painting 1700–1760*, 1987 (Tate Gallery, London).

Foskett, D., *Samuel Cooper and his Contemporaries*, 1974 (National Portrait Gallery, London).

Gibson, R., *The Masque of Beauty*, 1972 (National Portrait Gallery, London).

Hayes, J., *Thomas Gainsborough*, 1980 (Tate Gallery, London).

Hayes, J., *The Portrait in British Art*, 1991 (National Portrait Gallery, London).

Kerslake, J. F., *Mr Boswell*, 1967 (National Portrait Gallery, London).

Levey, M., *Sir Thomas Lawrence 1769–1830*, 1979 (National Portrait Gallery, London).

Lomax, J. and R. Ormond, *John Singer Sargent and the Edwardian Age*, 1979, (National Portrait Gallery, London).

Miles, E. G. and J. Simon, *Thomas Hudson 1701–1779: Portrait Painter and Collector*, 1979 (Iveagh Bequest, Kenwood House, London)

Millar, O., *Sir Peter Lely, 1619–80*, 1978 (National Portrait Gallery, London).

Millar, O., *Van Dyck in England*, 1982 (National Portrait Gallery, London).

Parris, L. ed., *The Pre-Raphaelites*, 1984 (Tate Gallery, London).

Penny, N., ed., *Reynolds*, 1986 (Royal Academy of Arts, London).

Piper, D., *O Sweet Mr Shakespeare I'll Have His Picture*, 1964 (National Portrait Gallery, London).

Rogers, M., *John Closterman. Master of the English Baroque 1660–1711*, 1981 (National Portrait Gallery, London).

Rogers, M., *William Dobson 1611–45*, 1983 (National Portrait Gallery, London).

Rogers, M., *Elizabeth II: Portraits of Sixty Years*, 1986 (National Portrait Gallery, London).

Rogers, M. *Camera Portraits: Photographs from the National Portrait Gallery 1839–1989*, 1989 (National Portrait Gallery, London and Washington)

Sartin, S., *Polite Society by Arthur Devis 1712–1787*, 1983 (Harris Museum and Art Gallery, Preston and National Portrait Gallery, London).

Shawe-Taylor, D., *Genial Company: the Theme of Genius in Eighteenth-Century British Portraiture*, 1987 (Nottingham University Art Gallery and Scottish National Portrait Gallery, Edinburgh).

Smart, A., *Allan Ramsay*, 1992 (Scottish National Portrait Gallery, Edinburgh and National Portrait Gallery, London).

Stevenson, S., *A Face for Every Occasion*, 1976 (Scottish National Portrait Gallery, Edinburgh).

Tomlinson, A., *The Medieval Face*, 1974 (National Portrait Gallery, London).

Webster, M., *Johan Zoffany*, 1977 (National Portrait Gallery, London).

Wheelock, A. K., Jr., Barnes, S. J., and Held, J. S., *Anthony van Dyck*, 1991. (National Gallery of Art, Washington).

Index